THE COMPLETE ILLUSTRATED GUIDE TO
NUTRITIONAL HEALING

THE COMPLETE
ILLUSTRATED
GUIDE TO
NUTRITIONAL
HEALING

The Use of Diet, Vitamins, Minerals, and Herbs for Optimum Health

DENISE MORTIMORE

ELEMENT

Shaftesbury, Dorset • Boston, Massachusetts • Melbourne, Victoria

First published in Great Britain in 1998 by
ELEMENT BOOKS LIMITED
Shaftesbury, Dorset, SP7 8BP

Published in the USA in 1998 by
ELEMENT BOOKS INC
160 North Washington Street, Boston, MA 02114

Published in Australia in 1998 by
ELEMENT BOOKS
and distributed by Penguin Australia Ltd
487 Maroondah Highway, Ringwood, Victoria 3134

NOTE FROM THE PUBLISHER

*Any information given in this book is
not intended to be taken as a replacement
for medical advice. Any person with a
condition requiring medical attention should
consult a qualified practitioner or therapist.*

Designed and created with
The Bridgewater Book Company Limited

ELEMENT BOOKS LIMITED
Creative Director *Ed Day*
Managing Editor *Miranda Spicer*
Senior Commissioning Editor *Caro Ness*
Project Editor *Katie Worrall*
Production Manager *Susan Sutterby*

THE BRIDGEWATER BOOK COMPANY
Art Director *Terry Jeavons*
Designers *Kevin Knight, Louise Howell, Paul Rollo*
Editorial Director *Sophie Collins*
Managing Editor *Anne Townley*
Project Editor *Caroline Earle*
Picture Research *Vanessa Fletcher*

Printed by Butler and Tanner, Frome, Somerset

British Library Cataloguing in Publication data available

ISBN 1–86204–175X

ACKNOWLEDGMENTS

*I would like to thank my partner, Mr. Philip
Cartwright, for helping me understand the idiosyn-
crasies of computers and word processing, for
proofreading, and all the other little peripheral jobs that
need to be done when writing a book.
I also want to thank my children, Lucy and Tom, for
being patient with me when meals were late, and for
doing my share of the housework when I was busy
writing. Thanks especially to Tom for drawing me the
New Pyramid, and to Lucy for keeping me laughing.
Thanks also to S.P.N.T. (the Society for Promotion of
Nutritional Therapy), and Lamberts Healthcare
Limited, for letting me use some of their information.*

With thanks to
*Mary Armstrong, Janine Bennett, Jacob Bevis, Patricia Blunt,
Philip Constable, Paul Golding, Alexandra Grant, Debbie Grant,
Sally Hardy, Sam Hollingdale, Louise Inch, Alastair Mackay, Derek Ockmore,
Helen Omand, Donna Paplett, Georgette Rae, Sharon Rashand, Abiola Roberts,
Ajebowale Roberts, Carolyn Jikiemi Roberts, Michelle Sawyer,
Andrew Stemp, Rebecca Vesti-Nielsen, Beth Webster, Louise Williams,
and also Solutions and Courts*
for help with photography

PREFACE

I T IS VERY TRUE *that until we are forced to examine the world in a different light, we go happily on our way with our conventional ideas of things. The importance of food to health was clearly shown to me when attempting to deal with the problems of a hyperactive child. Coming late to motherhood, it all came as a bit of a shock to find that not only had my own life to take a back seat for a while, but also that the daily struggles with a child who doesn't eat, sleep, or stay still is something akin to torture. Fortunately for me, at the time I was forced to give up my lecturing career, I found information on dietary treatment of children with hyperactivity, and started to apply the philosophy. Great changes occurred. This was the start of something big! Proof was given to me daily that what goes into our mouths not only has an effect on our general health, but also has a large part to play in what goes on in our minds and emotions.*

I embarked upon a course in nutritional healing, and haven't looked back. Time and time again in my private practice, it has been clearly demonstrated that anyone who is willing to undertake changes in eating habits and lifestyle, and stick to

The advantages of nutritional healing include an improvement in general health and a sense of well-being.

them, will reap many-fold the rewards of their work.

It is well known now that many of the thousands of people in hospital are there because of the side effects of drugs. More and more people are saying that they do not want to take drugs. Many have had "first hand" experience of healing through nutritional therapy and other alternative practices. Complementary medicine is becoming the natural choice of a larger and larger percentage of the population. There is absolutely nothing to lose and everything to gain. Give it a try!

Nutritional therapy is not just for adults, even young children can reap the benefits.

CONTENTS

PART ONE
THE BASIC PRINCIPLES
12–31

PART TWO
OPTIMUM NUTRITION
32–75

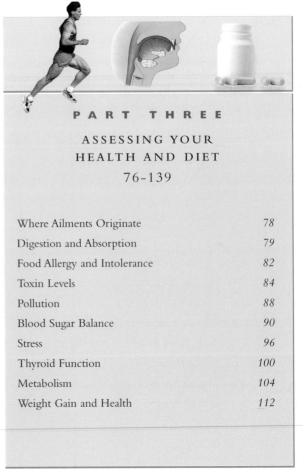

PART THREE
ASSESSING YOUR
HEALTH AND DIET
76–139

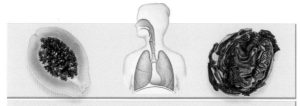

PART FOUR

NUTRITIONAL HEALING
FOR COMMON AILMENTS
140–181

PART FIVE

NUTRITION AND
FEMALE HEALTH
182–225

PART SIX

APPENDICES AND
USEFUL INFORMATION
226–256

HOW TO USE THIS BOOK

*Y*ou have picked up *this book because you think that there is room for improvement in your life. You may be feeling a little tired and "run down;" you may have members of your family who are ill; you may have niggling little symptoms that are taking the joy out of life, but your physician tells you all is well; you may yourself be chronically sick. In all of these situations, and many more,* The Complete Illustrated Guide to Nutritional Healing *is just what you are looking for!*

It is important to stress that the suggestions offered in this book are not intended to replace appropriate medical investigation and treatment. The supplements that are recommended for any particular disorder should be discussed with your medical physician or nutritional therapist.

The book is divided into five parts:

● **Part One** gives you a general idea of the basic principles that are at the foundation of nutritional healing.

● **Part Two** takes you deeper into the whole concept of optimum nutrition by explaining what is really meant by the term "balanced diet." You will find a wealth of information in this section on a basic, wholesome, well-balanced program of eating, along with detailed information on fats, proteins, carbohydrates, vitamins, and minerals, as well as up-to-date information on antioxidants and phytochemicals.

● **Part Three** enables you to carry out self-assessment questionnaires which will lead you to a greater understanding of how to regain or optimize your health.

● **Part Four** is a section entirely devoted to specific conditions that are likely to be helped by nutritional healing – simply turn to the section most applicable to your present need.

● **Part Five** specifically deals with nutritional help for common female problems as well as providing important advice about preconception, nutrition during and after pregnancy, and nutritionally based problems with children and adolescents.

● **The Appendices** contain the nutritional programs and recipes recommended to treat your condition. Appendix Six lists the foods, supplements, herbs, and aromatic oils that you might consider keeping in your family's medicine chest.

Main text outlines the basic principles behind nutritional healing and explains how humanity has sacrificed its health for the sake of convenience, progress, and profit

Full color illustrations and self-contained panels demonstrate and explain the benefits of a wholesome diet

Advice is given in Parts One and Two on how to achieve optimum health, build the immune system, and increase energy levels, so even those who are free from any "named" disorder will benefit.

Questionnaires help you take an analytical view of certain disorders. Do not be concerned that some of the symptoms are similar in different questionnaires

Main text explains the origins of common disorders and suggests ways of modifying your diet to help deal with the causes

Part Three helps you assess your health and diet using questionnaires. It is important to go through this section sequentially, and be led to the correct nutritional program by your answers.

Specially commissioned photographs illustrate the symptoms of each disorder

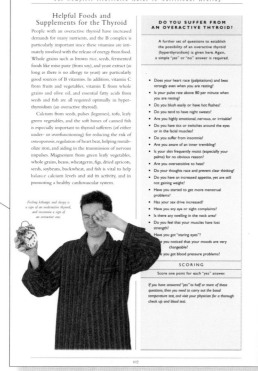

Parts Four and Five detail specific disorders, and how they can be treated by good dietary planning and nutritional supplementation.

Introductory and main text details the origins of each complaint

Lists are given of the nutritional factors which should be taken into account when treating this complaint

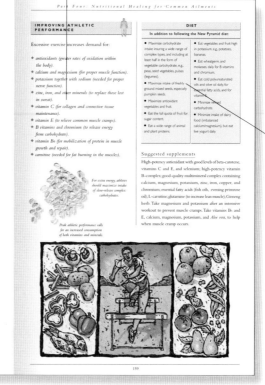

Each complaint is accompanied by a diet recommending foods that should form the bulk of your nutritional program, together with helpful food supplements

INTRODUCTION

T HIS BOOK IS DESIGNED *to be used by anyone wishing to improve their health by nutritional means. A complete understanding of the theory of food chemistry and nutrition is not necessary in order to use this type of healing effectively and safely. The short overview given here provides a brief introduction to the theory behind nutritional healing.*

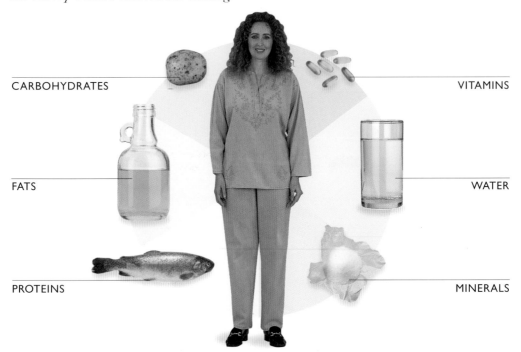

CARBOHYDRATES

VITAMINS

FATS

WATER

PROTEINS

MINERALS

Everyone can improve their well-being by understanding the nutrients required for optimum health.

The human body is a complex, bio-chemical machine which has specific requirements for health. In addition to proteins, fats, carbohydrates, energy, and water, there are some 40 different vitamins, minerals, essential fatty acids, and other components needed by our body, for it to remain healthy. We also need oxygen (from air), warmth, shelter, sunlight, and companionship. If we are deprived of any of these, we would soon wither.

A deficiency, however, in any one of the essential nutrients will result in anything from mild, almost imperceptible, ill-health through a wide range of symptoms and diseases to eventual death. (Deficiency diseases kill; subclinical diseases lead to illness and breakdown in body chemistry homeostasis.) Single deficiencies tend to be rare, but multiple deficien-cies often occur, particularly in people who are already unwell. Multiple subclinical deficiencies are common in individuals who eat a typical Western diet, char-acterized by its many excesses alongside its lack of essential nutrients, which leads to biochemical chaos and so to poor health.

Moreover, nutrient-deficient diets and those which also include large and frequent amounts of common allergens (wheat, yeast, milk, eggs, citrus, alcohol, etc.) can impair digestion, irritate the gut lining, and lead to a range of food intolerances in susceptible people. Further attack by environmental pollutants, and the common use of antibiotics and other drugs, may cause changes in the body chemistry which can affect our ability to absorb and assimilate nutrients.

The amalgamation of these differing aspects of sub-optimum nutrition, especially if further compro-mised by an unhealthy lifestyle of insufficient exercise, smoking, high stress levels, and lack of proper rest and relaxation, may eventually take us along the road to chronic ill-health and degenerative disease.

A good place to start redressing ill-health and lack of vitality is by encouraging proper digestion and increasing the amount of nutrient-dense, additive-free food in the diet, so that the body can receive the raw materials it needs. This book will take you on a journey of self-discovery to help you develop a system of nutritional healing which is right for you.

THE ROAD TO GOOD HEALTH

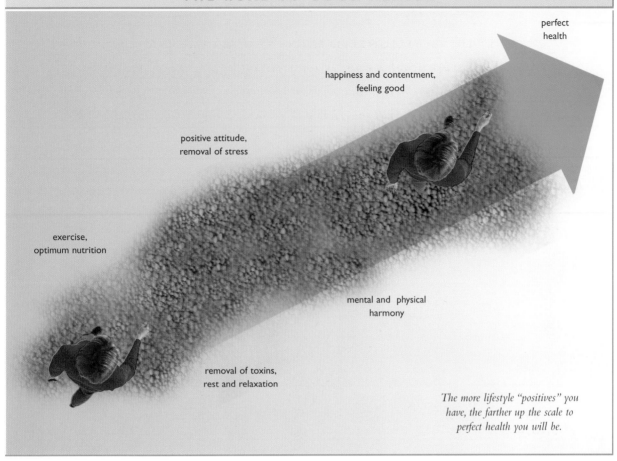

perfect
health

happiness and contentment,
feeling good

positive attitude,
removal of stress

exercise,
optimum nutrition

mental and physical
harmony

removal of toxins,
rest and relaxation

*The more lifestyle "positives" you
have, the farther up the scale to
perfect health you will be.*

THE ROAD TO BAD HEALTH

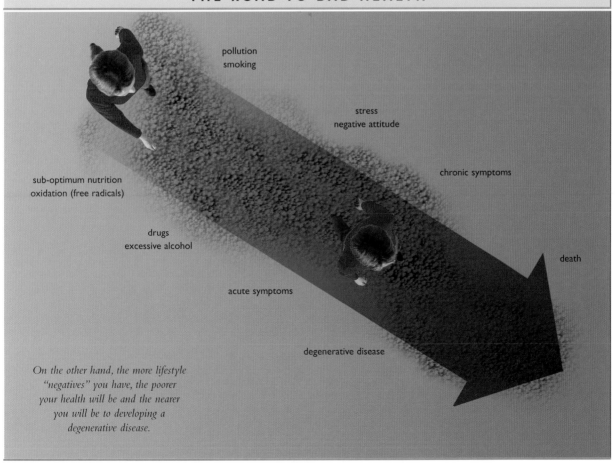

pollution
smoking

stress
negative attitude

chronic symptoms

sub-optimum nutrition
oxidation (free radicals)

drugs
excessive alcohol

death

acute symptoms

degenerative disease

*On the other hand, the more lifestyle
"negatives" you have, the poorer
your health will be and the nearer
you will be to developing a
degenerative disease.*

PART ONE

THE BASIC PRINCIPLES

WHAT IS NUTRITIONAL HEALING?

NUTRITIONAL HEALING WORKS *on a principle that is so simple that it is generally overlooked: that what you absorb into your body must affect how it functions. "You are what you eat" is obviously not the whole truth, but what you eat cannot help but contribute to how you are.*

Nutritional healing is a practical way of overcoming illness and promoting health naturally without the use of toxic drugs. During the process, the whole body is encouraged to heal itself so that:

◆ *the cause of the disease/illness is treated and not just the symptoms;*
◆ *additional health problems are addressed simultaneously; and,*
◆ *general health is improved and opportunistic infections are likely to be prevented.*

As with all reputable therapies, the holistic and individual approach is vital. Any person truly wishing to improve his or her state of health will want to encourage healing in the "whole" body and not just the part of it that is presently malfunctioning. Also, since each person has a body chemistry which is unique to them (arising from their genetic inheritance, their constitution, and their environment), it is obvious that each individual must be treated according to his or her own symptoms. This treatment is likely to be quite different from that given to another individual who would traditionally be diagnosed as having the same disease. Nevertheless, the initial stages involved in loss of health are caused in nearly all cases by several common factors (see Factors Affecting our State of Health, opposite).

Good health is essential to our well-being and underpins our whole enjoyment of life.

Nutritional healing bases its success in five main areas of dietary change (*see* Five Ground Rules for Restoring Health, opposite). Dietary improvements can be introduced gradually at your own pace and fitted into your lifestyle. Gradual change in diet leads to better success and a more permanent improvement in health. Rapid change in diet is likely to be abandoned soon after it has started. Gradual improvement means, of course, that the benefits of nutritional healing do not occur as rapidly as treatment given by a more conventional medical approach, and some degree of patience is required.

The Complete Illustrated Guide to Nutritional Healing has nothing to do with "fad" diets, and there is no need to be a "health freak" to partake of this natural system of healing. Vegetarianism is an option but not a necessity, though all healing diets will contain optimum amounts of vegetables and fruit.

The timescale for improvement of health by change in diet depends on many things; for example, how long you have had the symptoms, how committed you are to your new regime, the types and quality of the supplements you use, and the improvement in other areas of your lifestyle. In general, you should begin to reap the benefits in two to four weeks. In some cases of deeply entrenched ill-health it may take a little longer, since repair of digestive function, removing toxins, and nourishing

Bananas provide
essential minerals

Grapes are good for
cancer protection

Apples are a good
source of fiber

*The daily consumption
of fresh fruit is an essential
part of a healthy diet.*

the body properly require time. A set of symptoms, or some specific health problem, may have been decades in the making, and instant recovery is not very likely, but if you persevere with your new system of eating, your whole sense of well-being is likely to reach new heights.

This book will help you to investigate your own levels of health, point you in the direction of your own particular nutritional requirements, and guide you to the correct eating plan for your metabolism.

FACTORS AFFECTING OUR STATE OF HEALTH

Nutritional therapists believe that most states of ill-health, barring accidents and trauma, are brought about by one or more of four main factors.

🖙 Poor digestion because of stomach acid insufficiency and/or poor digestive enzyme production/or stress effects.

🖙 Food intolerance and allergy because of the frequent consumption of irritating foods.

🖙 Nutrient deficiency because of sub-optimum intake and/or poor absorption.

🖙 Toxic overload because of an inability to eliminate and excrete various substances.

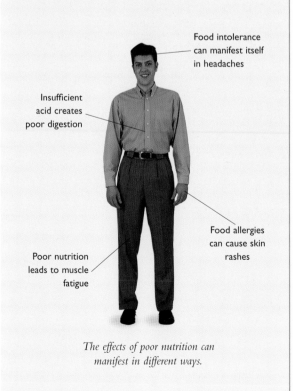

Food intolerance
can manifest itself
in headaches

Insufficient
acid creates
poor digestion

Food allergies
can cause skin
rashes

Poor nutrition
leads to muscle
fatigue

*The effects of poor nutrition can
manifest in different ways.*

FIVE GROUND RULES FOR RESTORING HEALTH

The nutritional therapists' five ground rules for restoring the body to health are:

1. Correct faulty digestion and eliminate food intolerances by combining appropriate foods, and by observing reactions to different food groups.

2. Decrease toxic overload by increasing the amount of nutritious, organic food, and decreasing the amount of rich and overprocessed foods.

3. Release healing energy for elimination of toxins by making balanced choices from foods that are part of your food culture.

4. Rebalance the intestinal bacteria in order to encourage conditions that improve absorption of important minerals, vitamins, amino acids, essential fatty acids, and other components.

5. Identify and support weakened, overburdened or exhausted organs by correct supplementation.

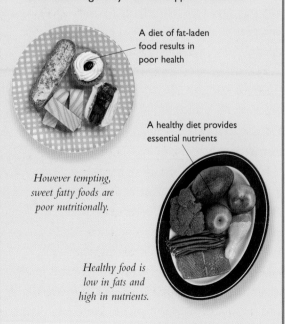

A diet of fat-laden
food results in
poor health

A healthy diet provides
essential nutrients

*However tempting,
sweet fatty foods are
poor nutritionally.*

*Healthy food is
low in fats and
high in nutrients.*

NUTRITIONAL HEALING AND OUR FOOD CULTURE

O N THIS PLANET THERE *are billions of people consuming different diets and having different disease patterns. It is amazing that the health and lifespan of those who are underfed, or indeed overfed, are not worse than they are. This only goes to show that the body is a remarkably tough machine, one which withstands considerable changes in food supply and is still able to maintain and reproduce itself. However, its ability to do this does not mean it is being optimally fed, or that it is doing anything more than just "surviving" on its so-called "healthy diet."*

It is probable that no human group or race has lived on a completely healthy diet for any great length of time. Changes in climatic conditions, disease of animals and plants which are used for food, and disruptions caused by war and natural disasters have meant that there has never been a long-lasting period within which any one group of people can be truly described as being optimally fed.

However, the rapidity of change in Western eating habits is unprecedented and undoubtedly accounts for many diseases affecting Western man. Dietary changes occurred only slowly before the modern technological age, but now agricultural research, modern farming methods, and food production processes in general have made it possible to create large amounts of new, highly processed, genetically engineered, chemically adulterated food.

This massive change in the type of food we eat now, as compared to only two or three hundred years ago, has put an enormous strain on the metabolism and biochemistry of the human body. Modern Western diets contain many substances which our

Today people in the West can take for granted a choice of foods deriving from an international range of different cultures.

body chemistry is not equipped to metabolize properly. Subtle changes in the natural food supply could probably be accommodated over a number of generations, but the rate of change and degree of chemical interference with food has been too rapid for this assimilation to be achieved easily in the present population.

Many sweet drinks contain artificial colors and flavorings

Cakes contain high levels of fat

Candies are mainly sugar

Our bodies need sugar, but "treat" foods deliver far too much.

Since individuals have different body chemistries it may take some time for whole populations to become accustomed to a specific diet. However, it is likely to be the case that the longer a group of people remain on their "cultural" diet, despite their biochemical diversity, the more each individual within the population will adapt, so long as the diet contains a good, balanced range of basic nutrients and very little "chemical" interference. A high salt intake, for example, is not universally associated with high blood pressure. Another example is provided by those people who are predisposed to kidney stones if they eat a diet that is high in sugar and dairy foods, and low in fiber and magnesium. Such a diet in other people may be tolerated well and would not necessarily produce stones.

Large amounts of evidence for "cultural eating" are displayed by groups of people who have changed their diet dramatically on moving from one part of the world to another. For example, Japanese people leaving their homes and their typical Japanese diet for America and the typical Western diet start to develop degenerative diseases never incurred in their own culture.

We can see, therefore, that our cultural roots dictate, to some degree, the type of basic diet on which we would thrive. This does not mean, of course, that we may never again taste the wonderful delights of foods from different nations, but only that we may need to consume the majority of our foods in a way that is based in our own culture for an initial healing period.

This pattern of eating foods related to our own origins has been seriously eroded within the last three or four decades as various interesting foods have been

Awareness of healthy foods has increased in recent years and they are now readily available.

incorporated into the Western diet from other cultures. We only have to look at the number of different types of restaurant and the enormous variety of specialist foods found in the supermarket to realize this. It is my belief that this rapid change in basic diet, coupled with the ever increasing "novel" methods of food production, preparation, and preservation, has been the main reason for our decreasing standards of general health and fitness. Since there is no longer a basic American, Australian, or British diet for consumption by the majority of each population, our individual biochemical differences are beginning to play a much greater part in the see-saw balance of our general health.

A failure to appreciate these individual variations in biochemistry has resulted in many members of the medical profession dismissing diet as a potential factor in disease. Yet more and more evidence is coming to light that indicates the involvement of basic nutrition in healing many of the chronic diseases of our time, such as heart disease, diabetes, arthritis, cancer, and many others.

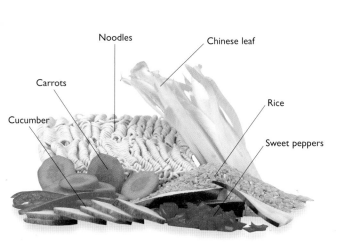

Traditional Chinese cooking has become popular in many other countries.

Ingredients widely used in Italian cooking are now popular throughout Europe and North America.

MODERN DIET
AND ITS IMBALANCES

*I*T SEEMS UNBELIEVABLE *that those of us who live in the prosperous West enjoy a standard of living unparalleled in history, but at the same time poor nutrition is widespread. Nevertheless it is true, for the reason that much of the food that we eat is of the wrong kind, and our diets are unbalanced.*

In spite of the megabillions of dollars and pounds spent on health care, degenerative diseases are still on the increase in the Western world. By using proper nutrition and maintaining a healthier lifestyle, many of these diseases would be preventable, and, perhaps, even curable.

For example, many millions of people die annually from cardiovascular diseases, including heart disease, arterial damage, and high blood pressure. The underlying causes of these diseases suggest that the actual cause of death might more accurately be written as one or more of the following:

A POOR DIET

A poor diet in which there is a high intake of fat, sugar, sodium and chemicals, and/or a low intake of fiber (from vegetables, fruit, and whole grains), essential fatty acids (from fish, seeds, vegetables, and fruit), vitamins (mainly C, E, and the B-complex), and minerals (mainly magnesium, calcium, selenium, zinc, and chromium).

INSUFFICIENT EXERCISE

A sedentary lifestyle in which there is very little exercise, or even, none at all.

STRESS

A stressful lifestyle in which there is too much worry, tension, anxiety, and depression as well as insufficient rest and relaxation.

INGESTING TOXINS

Pollution from environmental toxins found in air, water, and food, and those voluntarily taken in through tobacco-smoking, drugs, and alcohol.

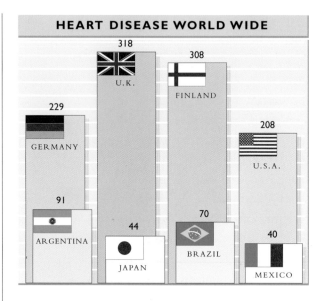

HEART DISEASE WORLD WIDE

318 U.K.

308 FINLAND

229 GERMANY

208 U.S.A.

91 ARGENTINA

44 JAPAN

70 BRAZIL

40 MEXICO

Heart disease is much more common in the industrialized West than in other countries. These figures show deaths per 100,000 of population.

It is fairly well established now that a nutrient-deficient or excessive calorie diet is a major risk factor in heart disease and cancer – two of the Western world's primary killers. In addition, loneliness, depression, and anxious, tense behavior are all known to contribute to heart disease, cancer, and early death.

The current high intake of meat and dairy products in the Western world is, I believe, a major cause of cancer, heart disease, and osteoporosis. If meat and dairy foods can disrupt bodily functions so much that they can cause major diseases, are we to believe anyone who says that large amounts of these foods are good for us?

Large-scale food processing, for example the refining of flour, can be detrimental to the nutritional quality of food, which may have long-term consequences for our health. When flour is refined, dietary fiber, essential vitamins, in particular B vitamins, and minerals are removed, which are needed by the body to turn starchy food into energy. Not only are

WESTERN DIET

Simply put, the typical Western diet contains:

☞ Too much animal fat but insufficient good-quality essential fatty acids.

☞ Too much "salt" but an insufficient range and amount of mineral salts.

☞ Too much sugar and refined carbohydrate products but insufficient fiber.

☞ Too many processed foods with their consequent vitamin loss.

☞ Too many stimulants: tea, coffee, and alcohol.

☞ Potentially harmful insecticides, pesticides, herbicides, colorings, preservatives, etc.

essential nutrients being removed from food during food processing, but in order to make food easier for transport, distribution, and preparation in the home, "new" foods – convenience foods – that would otherwise not exist have flooded onto the market. To make these "new" foods look more colorful and appealing (since their natural flavors and colors have been processed out), substances are added by the manufacturers. Many of these substances can be harmful to susceptible individuals. Moreover, although we are assured that each food additive has undergone rigorous tests to insure its safety, most present-day food additives have not been tested in groups (as they would appear in the food) and therefore their synergistic (combined) effects are mostly unknown.

It has been said that many people in the West are overfed and undernourished. The reasoning behind this statement is that although our total energy intake is excessive, the quality of food is often so poor that the nutrient intake in terms of vitamins and minerals is inadequate. This is in contrast to some developing countries where there simply is not sufficient food of any kind to sustain healthy life. True under-nutrition is seldom found in the West except

in people with anorexia nervosa or certain severe illnesses. What we suffer from is malnutrition, and throughout this book we shall be looking at ways in which we can combat the effects of this modern dilemma with a good nutritional program.

Many of the diseases from which we suffer in the West have been linked with excessive fat, sugar, or salt, and government agencies, educational establishments, and the media have gone a long way to get this message across. However, the additional problems of over-processed/nutrient-deficient food, combined with what nutritional therapists believe to be a widespread incidence of deficient digestion and poor assimilation of nutrients, is yet to be recognized fully. This means that the population is not yet sufficiently well informed to make more wholesome choices.

The idea that our Western diet is excellent and healthy needs to be "debunked." Some misconceptions are still widely held, even by many in the medical profession. For example:

◆ *large amounts of animal protein are essential for optimum health.*

◆ *nutrient deficiencies do not exist in individuals consuming a "balanced" diet.*

◆ *milk is an essential food for all age groups.*

◆ *maximum amount of fat (of all types) must be removed from the diet.*

◆ *consuming low-cholesterol food will reduce the incidence of heart disease.*

◆ *vegetarians and vegans run the risk of major nutrient deficiency.*

Many of these "myths" will be exposed in the various sections of this book, allowing you to gather more nutritional information in order to make your own healthy choices.

We can see, then, that the Western diet leaves a lot to be desired, and when compared to a "natural" diet, there are enormous differences to be found.

The traditional, wholemeal loaf of bread is worlds apart from the factory-produced, over-refined concoction that has overtaken it.

OUR FUTURE
IS ON OUR PLATE

BLATANTLY BAD NUTRITION *brings about serious clinical symptoms quickly. However, in Western society our marginal diet more commonly encourages subclinical deficiencies that do not surface as diagnosable problems until years have passed. We are familiar with this in the case of heart disease, cancer, and osteoporosis.*

A person with no symptoms but with abnormally high cholesterol in their blood is at risk of eventually developing heart disease. A person with no symptoms but abnormally high platelet aggregation (stickiness of blood cells) is at greater risk of suffering a stroke or some other circulatory disorder. A person with a low selenium or low vitamin A level in the blood is possibly at greater risk from cancer. A person with low tissue and blood calcium and other minerals is at greater risk of developing osteoporosis.

What people eat today may not affect them now, but it is likely to affect them greatly in the future. I remember waiting at the school gates along with a mother who was feeding her three-year old child chips, chocolate, and candy. When I made a comment about the healthiness of such food for our children, the mother said that it did not seem to be doing her children any harm whatsoever! This is just one example of how people can expect effect to follow cause instantaneously.

Cumulative poor nutrition creates diseases that are not recognized as nutrition-related disorders. But this is exactly what they are. Even if symptoms are not immediately present, subtle problems become monumental disasters if allowed to continue for years. Long-term subclinical (mild) deficiency of vitamin C may produce anything from heart disease to gallstones. Long-term subclinical deficiency of chromium and zinc may bring about poor glucose tolerance and blood sugar problems later in life.

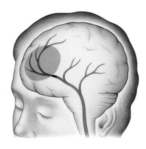

Damage to the frontal area of the brain is caused by circulatory disorders.

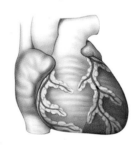

Excess cholesterol can block an artery in the heart which destroys heart muscle.

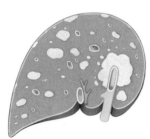

Cancerous tissue – the lighter areas – in a cross-section of the liver.

A lack of calcium in the diet leads to osteoporosis.

Nutritional therapists believe that an adequate intake of vitamin E and essential fatty acids, among other nutrients, helps to prevent heart disease, lung damage from air pollution, cancer, premenstrual syndrome, and premature senility, which have been on the increase for several decades. I would speculate that long-term deficiencies of vitamin E probably eventually surface as common degenerative diseases, such as heart disease, cancer, senility, allergies, cataracts, premenstrual syndrome, and premature aging, rather than a neat and concise vitamin-deficiency disease. Modern research is now going beyond early work in nutrition, wherein nutrient deficiency came to be associated with specific problems, such as a lack of vitamin C leading to scurvy.

How much proof is necessary in order to convince both scientific and lay communities of the value of nutrition? Chronic disease has often been linked to poor nutrition; however, intellectuals continually point out pedantic limitations in research. Meanwhile, innocent people suffer and die needlessly because some people refuse to admit that they might have been wrong about the link between poor nutrition and disease. Personally, I am more impressed with the wisdom acquired from thousands of years of natural healing with herbs and nutrients, than with five or so years of scientific, double-blind, placebo studies on a few hundred patients, all of whom will, in any case, vary in their biochemistry.

How much evidence is enough? Many scientists and professionals in the medical world are demanding an unrealistic degree of proof before they will consider changing their beliefs.

It is foolish to assume that giving any animal species a diet different from that which was present during the major part of its evolution will not result in certain individuals within that species developing health problems. But this is what has happened in the Westernized world over the last century or so. We are now paying the price for this. The largest uncontrolled, unscientific trial ever undertaken is occurring with us as the guinea pigs.

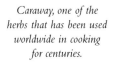

Caraway, one of the herbs that has been used worldwide in cooking for centuries.

Herbal medicines were commonly used in the Middle Ages, and still are in many non-Western cultures.

Kidney beans – drying beans has long been a natural form of preservation

Pumpkin seeds, a good source of essential fatty acids

Eggplant (aubergine) is a relative newcomer to most diets

Walnuts – nuts have always featured in the human diet

Oats are one of the most nutritious grains

Sweet peppers are very high in vitamin C

Brown rice still has the roughage that has been removed from white rice

A modern healthy diet can be built around the same types of nutritious foods to which we adapted during the course of our evolution.

DIET AND EVOLUTION

The foods that humans evolved on are the foods most likely to contain the nutrients that keep us healthy. Knowing which foods humans ate for hundreds of thousands of years can, I believe, give us a better idea of our ideal diet. Comparing our modern diet with our native food pattern shows how far we have deviated, and may help us understand why we have become so unhealthy.

EARLY HUMANS	HUNTER-GATHERERS
25,000 B.C.E.	3,000 B.C.E.

Over 25,000 years ago our diet consisted of meat, nuts, and berries. As the animals eaten were wild and free to roam, their meat was lean.

With the development of agriculture humans began to cultivate and develop grains and keep animals for consumption of their milk.

Millions of years ago the earliest mammals ate insects and plant foods (including roots, tubers, shoots, buds, flowers, nuts, seeds, and gums). The earliest humans, however, were primarily meat eaters, but the wild game that these individuals consumed was very low in fat (around 5 percent, as opposed to our present day "domesticated" meat which is around 30 percent fat), and contained around five times the level of polyunsaturated fats. Moreover, it may have been consumed raw, with virtually no nutrient loss, and it was certainly uncontaminated by pollutants and additives. Seeds, nuts, fruit, and roots were eaten at times when game was scarce.

Modern agricultural methods are geared to monoculture, the massive production of a single crop.

Fish and other seafood was probably introduced to our native diet around 25,000 years ago, and it is generally thought that around 20,000 years later these early hunter-gatherer humans became farmers and started to utilize grains. This primitive diet probably had a polyunsaturated fat content of around three times the saturated fat content. This situation is reversed today, when we eat three times more saturated fat than polyunsaturated fat.

Studies on early humans also indicate that the mineral potassium was consumed in far greater amounts than sodium was: probably around 10 to 15 times more, whereas present-day humans consume around five times more sodium than potassium. Further studies estimate that only one-third of the calcium and one-third of the fiber that was eaten then is eaten now, and only one-tenth of the amount of vitamin C eaten by those people is consumed by the average modern person.

With these comparisons in mind, we can perhaps begin to understand why the diet of modern man has brought ill-health upon the population in such epic proportions. Early humans, of course, simply ate the food that was there. It is probable that their intake of nutrients was not "optimum" but, nevertheless, we can use this information as a rough guideline for "healthy" nutrient intake. This early "cave-man" diet can be taken as a basis for our present-day nutritional needs, and can be further modified, in the light of current scientific knowledge, to produce a finely tuned optimum-nutrition program.

THE MIDDLE AGES	PRESENT DAY
1500	1990

In the Middle Ages in Europe the range of vegetables increased and consumption of both freshwater and saltwater fish became more widespread.

In the modern age the range of foods an individual can eat is limited only by preference and by the size of his or her budget.

WESTERN DIET COMPARED TO THAT OF EARLY HUMANS

Present-day Western man was not determined by evolution to thrive on a continuous intake of refined sugar, hydrogenated fat, high-fat meats, dairy food, salt, pastry, white flour, diet drinks, coffee, and "convenience" foods, yet these have become the staple foods of the modern diet. Humans evolved as omnivorous grazers of a semi-vegetarian diet, eating lean meat, fish and other seafood, seeds, nuts, fruit, and vegetables. It is likely that our survival over millions of years was at least partly due to the fact that the diet provided high-quality nutrients with a minimum of pollutants. The high dietary levels of essential fatty acids is believed to be the origin of man's intelligence. Yet we expect, nowadays, to feel healthy and "vital" on a highly refined, nutrient-depleted diet too rich in animal fats, salt, sugar, and additives. Moreover, because of the current frightening levels of drugs, alcohol, tobacco, stress, and pollution, our diet needs to be even higher in essential nutrients than that of primitive man to combat these excesses.

Perhaps what is truly amazing is not the high level today of nutritionally related disease but the fact that so many of us manage to survive for as long as we do.

Where primitive agricultural methods prevail, the quality of food is often better, even if there is less of it.

OPTIMUM NUTRITION AND SUPER NUTRITION

MODERN LIVING BRINGS *with it pollutants in air and water, additives in food, and toxic chemicals. These substances are, in the greater part, "foreign" materials. They are likely to put an increased demand on our metabolism because they have to be rendered harmless and eliminated. Potentially, therefore, we require even greater amounts of the essential nutrients than we ever did before.*

In addition to combating pollution and stress with optimum intake of nutrients, some people's nutrient requirements are above average. Inherited defects in metabolism, advancing age, excessive exercise, illnesses, pregnancy, and lactation; all of these factors, plus others, may also elevate nutrient needs.

Nutritional therapists believe that certain nutrients taken at high levels of intake can become "disease-beaters" and develop "supernutrient" powers. For example, 15mg niacin (vitamin B3) per day is the reference nutrient intake (R.N.I.) for general health, but when five or more times that amount is consumed, niacin becomes an effective dilator of blood vessels. These large doses of niacin can normalize the levels of fats in the blood which may help people who have had heart attacks or who are at risk, genetically, from furring up of the arteries.

Extremely high doses of vitamin A and vitamin C (only under supervision) help to protect the body against the destructive (but potentially helpful) effect of chemotherapy.

High doses of vitamin E (400–800IU per day) reduce breast tenderness in premenstrual women, in addition to thinning the blood and improving circulation in individuals with circulatory disorders.

High doses of zinc (15–30mg per day) and vitamin C (1–3g per day) boost immune function and wound healing.

Thus what we describe, at the present time, as "normal" levels of nutrients, may be different for different people depending on many factors of their lifestyle and state of health, sex, age, etc. What we can say, then, is that "normal amounts" of nutrients will be those levels which are sufficient to maintain "normal" health, while nutritional therapists believe above-normal amounts of nutrients appear to have "supernutrient" abilities for use in extreme healing situations.

THE EFFECTS OF NIACIN

Certain nutrients have a special capability beyond their food value. For example, vitamin B3 (niacin) taken at five times the level usually needed helps dilate clogged-up blood vessels, which is useful to those with coronary disease.

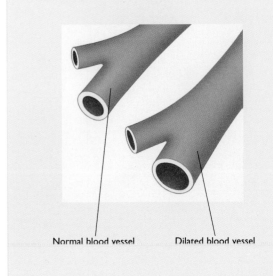

Normal blood vessel   Dilated blood vessel

Nutritional support can also increase the effectiveness of more conventional health treatments such as drugs, surgery, and cancer therapy. To speed healing, Guy's and St. Thomas's, two major teaching hospitals in London, automatically give vitamin C and zinc to those undergoing operations. Many medical techniques are less effective than they could be because these aggressive procedures create stress in the body and elevate nutrient needs at a time when the patient is less likely to eat well. Malnutrition, then, reduces the benefit of the therapy and retards healing while increasing the risk of complications. Optimum nutrition at these stressful times allows the patient's own natural healing forces to assist in the medical treatment.

Optimum nutrition can also prevent future disease by elevating a person from subclinical (mild) deficiency into a healthy "saturation state" for all essential nutrients. While you may not be obviously ill now, you may be suffering borderline deficiency that could cause problems later on. As we have seen, subclinical deficiencies are difficult to detect, but may lead to eventual lowering of immune function, and to degenerative diseases.

Therefore, optimum nutrition, and in some instances supernutrition, will raise many people above an average health status into a far more desirable level of physical and mental well-being.

Modern life, with its relentless pace, its constant emphasis on consumption, its pollution, and its ready use of chemical cures for all ailments, leaves us subject to many stress-induced illnesses.

Extra vitamins and minerals are often advisable for patients, such as this man undergoing chemotherapy.

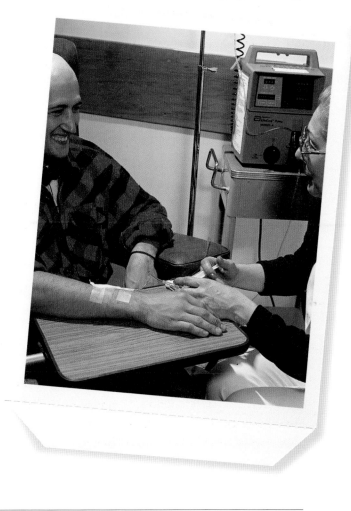

Good health is apparent in the body's whole appearance.

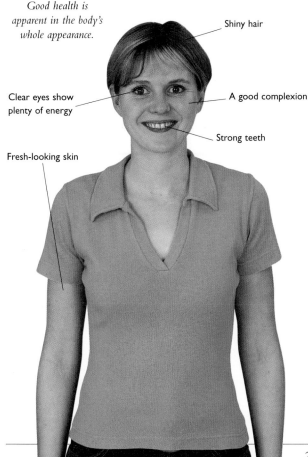

Shiny hair

Clear eyes show plenty of energy

A good complexion

Strong teeth

Fresh-looking skin

PERSONAL NUTRITION STATUS

IN ORDER TO FORMULATE *your own optimum nutrient intake, you must first consider those factors which determine how much nutrition your body is really getting: the quality and quantity of the food you eat, and also the efficiency of your digestion, absorption, and assimilation.*

Modern farming methods have triumphed in their ability to produce quantity, but the price paid is often poor quality, degradation of the soil, and environmental pollution.

THE QUALITY OF FOOD

Food grown on poor soil can be deficient in certain nutrients. A good-quality soil will contain all the necessary nutrients, including trace elements, and will not be contaminated with chemical fertilizers or pesticides. Good crops grown on this soil will not have been treated with chemical sprays, but with natural fertilizers such as compost and manure. Healthy livestock will have been raised in areas where they have access to uncontaminated, natural foods and will not have been treated with drugs, antibiotics, and growth enhancers. The only way to insure your food meets these criteria is to consume organic produce.

However, if you live in an area where organic produce is difficult to obtain, and you are unable to grow much yourself, then there are still several things you can do to reduce the chemical load on your body, such as washing all vegetables and fruit thoroughly, and having less meat and dairy produce in your diet.

THE QUANTITY OF FOOD

As we have said, in the Western world, undernutrition tends not to be a problem, but malnutrition is rife. If nutrient-dense foods such as vegetables, fruit, pulses (legumes), whole grains, fish, nuts, and seeds are used to replace refined foods that have been stripped of essential nutrients, there will be an improvement in the nutritional status of the person who eats them. New research by Barry Sears has suggested that diets high in grains, rice, pastas, and breads (even of the wholegrain type) play havoc with blood-sugar levels and cause tiredness, brain "fatigue," and constant hunger. Diets low in grains are likely to establish "true hunger" feelings and allow a consequent decrease in overall input of food (because cravings related to blood-sugar swings have been abolished). Furthermore, the results of several scientific studies now confirm that eating a diet high in nutrients but low in calorific content helps prevent signs of aging, and increases life span.

Fruit, vegetables, nuts, and grains are rich in nutrients, especially if produced organically.

FACTORS AFFECTING NUTRITIONAL STATUS

There are four main factors
that influence nutritional status:

☞ The quality of the food we eat.

☞ The quantity of the food we eat.

☞ The efficiency of the whole digestive process.

☞ Biochemical individuality *(see page 28).*

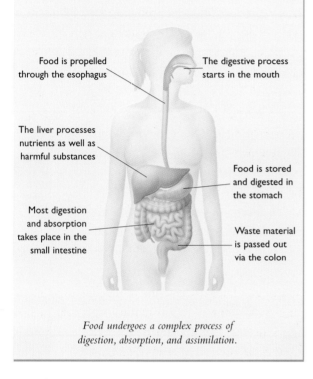

Food is propelled through the esophagus

The digestive process starts in the mouth

The liver processes nutrients as well as harmful substances

Food is stored and digested in the stomach

Most digestion and absorption takes place in the small intestine

Waste material is passed out via the colon

Food undergoes a complex process of digestion, absorption, and assimilation.

DIGESTION

An individual whose digestive system is inefficient is more likely to have a poor nutritional status than someone with an efficient digestion. This might seem an obvious fact, but it is almost totally overlooked by health professionals. Inefficient digestive systems may be caused by insufficient production of hydrochloric acid in the stomach, or poor digestive enzyme production by the pancreas and other enzyme-secreting glands.

Even if your present diet is optimum, if you are not digesting the fats, carbohydrates, and proteins properly, then essential fatty acids, energy-giving sugars, and essential amino acids will not be released in sufficient quantities for absorption into the blood. The result is nutrient starvation.

You will be given information and questionnaires in Part Three of this book to enable you to assess your digestive capabilities.

ABSORPTION

In addition to poor digestion, if for some reason the end products of digestion are not being absorbed properly, because of poor membrane function, intestinal irritation, or a condition such as celiac disease, then the nutritional status of that individual will again be compromised. Furthermore, the presence of some substances in the diet can prevent certain nutrients from being absorbed efficiently. For example, both tea and coffee reduce the absorption of iron and zinc, and certain types of fiber, such as cereal bran, and substances like phytic acid (found commonly in grains) can prevent the absorption of many minerals, especially calcium, iron, and zinc. Therefore, any coffee and tea you drink would be best taken between meals rather than with meals; supplements containing minerals are best taken at meals which do not contain cereals.

ASSIMILATION

Even if digestion and absorption are working reasonably, there is still a third possibility which may be having an effect upon nutritional status. This is the efficiency with which nutrients are used (assimilated) by the body. For example, an individual who excretes large quantities of nutrients in the urine will have a higher nutritional requirement than someone who uses these more effectively. Other individuals have metabolic faults (as a result of a genetic defect, food intolerance, other nutritional deficiencies, food toxins, and environmental pollutants) that prevent the body from efficiently utilizing nutrients that are already there in adequate amounts. For example, children, in particular, are affected badly by cadmium (a potentially toxic trace element and contaminant) found in tobacco smoke, and by lead in petrol fumes, which some nutritional therapists believe can cause them to develop hyperactivity or attention disorders. To check for assimilation faults, assess whether or not you have food intolerances *(see Part Three)*, and consider an initial detoxification program, or assess your need to cut down on household pollutants.

Coffee reduces the body's ability to absorb the vital element, zinc.

BIOCHEMICAL INDIVIDUALITY

INDIVIDUAL BIOCHEMICAL MAKE-UP *is a fundamental concept in understanding the factors that determine whether a person remains healthy or becomes sick. There is an optimum range of nutrient intake for each one of us, but because this range is so wide, it is almost impossible to have a clearly defined amount calculated for each of the 50 or so nutrients we know of. National tables of reference nutrient intakes (R.N.I.s) give specific levels of many nutrients, but nutritional therapists believe that they do not give enough consideration to our unique individual nutritional requirements, since our nutrient levels are influenced by age, stage of growth, gender, state of general health, degree of stress, activity, and toxic levels.*

As we grow older we need to consume more essential nutrients.

AGE

As we age, we may need greater amounts of essential nutrients both to combat the wear and tear of an aging metabolism and digestive system, and to counteract the nutrient-depleting effect of medication. To complicate matters, calorific intake conversely needs to be reduced as we age.

GENDER

Nutrient requirements are different between men and women, and even between boys and girls. The nutritional requirements of women can vary throughout the menstrual cycle, and lack of certain nutrients may contribute to P.M.S., and so on.

GROWTH

Young children have different nutritional requirements from adults since a growing body has a greater need for some nutrients. Protein, essential fatty acids, and certain minerals, such as zinc, are required in greater amounts by children at puberty than are required by adults.

Calcium is important for the baby's bone formation

A pregnant woman should take increased amounts of minerals.

PREGNANCY AND LACTATION

A woman who is pregnant or breastfeeding has different nutritional requirements from one who is not. In particular she needs to be taking in increased amounts of calcium (while breastfeeding) and other minerals for development of the child's skeleton.

STATE OF GENERAL HEALTH

Nutritional requirements vary greatly in health and disease. Many conditions severely deplete resources of certain nutrients: for example, protein loss (loss of amino acids) after surgery; zinc and vitamin C loss after extensive skin burns, etc. However, force-feeding a sick person can put his/her metabolism under greater stress. Eating to "keep your strength up" is not always the best advice. Each case will be different and no one strategy is applicable to all cases.

Women's nutritional needs change during their monthly cycle.

PSYCHOLOGICAL AND EMOTIONAL STRESS

Certain types of stress may increase requirements of some nutrients, such as vitamin C and the B-complex of vitamins, calcium, magnesium, and zinc. Stress of any kind can influence food choices and appetite adversely.

*Athletes need to remember that iron
and zinc are lost in perspiration.*

ACTIVITY LEVEL

Anyone who exercises frequently to the point of sweating profusely may have an increased requirement for the minerals iron and zinc, since these are lost in the sweat. Also, since metabolism is enhanced during these times, general nutrient requirement will be increased. Obviously, exercise is good for the body, but any excesses will need additional nutrients to replace those lost in sweat and to refill the stores of nutrients decreased by the temporarily elevated metabolism.

DRUGS AND TOXIC LEVELS

Even fairly social activities like tea- and coffee-drinking can increase nutrient requirement for thiamine (vitamin B1), and the minerals iron and zinc. Smoking and drinking alcohol increase body requirements for zinc, magnesium, the B group of vitamins, and vitamin C. Any person on prescribed or recreational drugs, or living and working in a polluted environment, will find their nutritional requirements greatly increased because the body (and the liver in particular) needs help to detoxify these chemicals.

SUMMARY

It is therefore evident that each individual has different nutritional requirements, and that these needs vary during a lifetime. If we imagine that the body has a reservoir of each essential nutrient and that many situations – digestive distress, food intolerance, poor nutrient absorption and assimilation, an aging body, growth, gender, pregnancy and breastfeeding, stress, wound recovery, infection, and increased exercise – "drain" the reservoirs more quickly than usual, then optimum or "supernutrition" will make sure that each reservoir is kept well stocked.

On some occasions, these elevated nutrient needs cannot be satisfied even with a "superdiet" and nutritional supplements may be needed. Nutritional therapists believe your system can be more finely tuned to its biochemical demands.

Try acting on the advice gained by completing the questionnaires in Part Three in order to:

◆ *Improve digestion and absorption.*
◆ *Remove food intolerances.*
◆ *Detoxify the body and assess your pollution levels.*
◆ *Balance blood-sugar levels.*
◆ *Combat stress.*
◆ *Help the thyroid gland.*
◆ *Enhance metabolism.*
◆ *Remove excess weight.*

**SEVEN INITIAL STEPS TO
YOUR NEW WAY OF EATING**

1. Eat a "culturally based" diet of fish, shellfish, game, lean meats, seeds, nuts, fruit, roots, leaves, and whole grains.

2. Eat nutrient-dense food to combat present ill-health and to protect against future disease.

3. Guard against overeating.

4. Eat organic food and drink filtered, distilled, or bottled water to cut down on pollutants.

5. Remove as many environmental pollutants as possible.

6. Avoid processed food, refined food, and food additives, and replace them with wholefoods.

7. Cut down on stimulants (tea, coffee, salt, sugar, alcohol, and soft drinks) to prevent unnecessary loss of nutrients.

HOW NUTRITIONAL IMBALANCES LEAD TO DISEASE

Much of the information *bandied about in the media would have us believe that vitamins are the all-important dietary factor for good health, whereas, although vitamins are important for an efficient metabolism, minerals and trace elements are at least as important and in some cases more important in the workings of our biochemistry.*

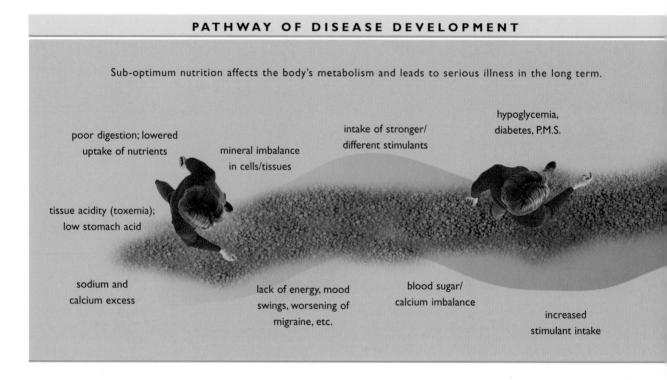

PATHWAY OF DISEASE DEVELOPMENT

Sub-optimum nutrition affects the body's metabolism and leads to serious illness in the long term.

poor digestion; lowered uptake of nutrients

mineral imbalance in cells/tissues

intake of stronger/ different stimulants

hypoglycemia, diabetes, P.M.S.

tissue acidity (toxemia); low stomach acid

sodium and calcium excess

lack of energy, mood swings, worsening of migraine, etc.

blood sugar/ calcium imbalance

increased stimulant intake

Despite the chemical similarity of certain pairs of minerals, such as calcium and magnesium, and sodium and potassium, their biochemical activity is very different. This is illustrated by the fact that most body cells actively collect potassium and excrete sodium, and similarly, many actively bring in magnesium and throw out calcium. The first step along the road to poor health seems to originate in body tissues failing in this basic "separation" principle, which leads to acidity (or toxemia) of the tissues. There are parts of the body where the environment needs to be acid: the stomach, for the digestion of food; the colon for microbial balance and nutrient absorption; the skin for bacterial control. But in all other areas the acidity/alkalinity of the tissues should remain neutral, or within a very narrow range around it, with the small intestine tending toward the alkaline side of neutral for digestive enzymes to work efficiently.

As nutrient intake falls below optimum, nutritional therapists believe that the general ability of body cells to retain a range of nutrients, especially minerals, within the cell, and to remove others to different areas, starts to fail. Energy levels drop and tissues become more acid (toxic), which in turn reduces the acidity of those areas which need to be acid. If, for example, the acidity of the stomach is reduced, then food, and particularly protein, will not be broken down to a suitable state for digestive enzymes to act upon it in the small intestine. As undigested or partly digested food travels through the gut, nutritional therapists believe that it will irritate certain areas, prevent the uptake of digested end products (since there are fewer available), and encourage the wrong type of bacteria and other micro-organisms in the bowel. The overall effect is then a decrease in body energy, an inefficient metabolism, and the beginnings of malfunction.

If, at the same time, the diet contains too much sodium (from "salt" and convenience foods) and calcium (from excess of dairy foods, where the calcium is poorly balanced because of low levels of magnesium), it is speculated that cellular imbalance and the degree of tissue acidity may be further encouraged. The first signs that something is wrong are lack of energy, mood swings, and the worsening of any existing condition like migraine or asthma. Underlying these (very common) symptoms is a change in the body's homeostatic (regulatory) mechanisms so that blood-sugar control and calcium metabolism become unbalanced. It is believed that as symptoms worsen, we find ourselves attracted to stronger and different stimulants. This is the point where we take more sugar and salt in our diet or are tempted to consume more refined and sugary foods. We may find ourselves drinking more (and stronger) alcohol, coffee, and tea, and perhaps smoking more. The result is that the body becomes even less capable of good maintenance and control, and what was a subtle collection of minor symptoms becomes

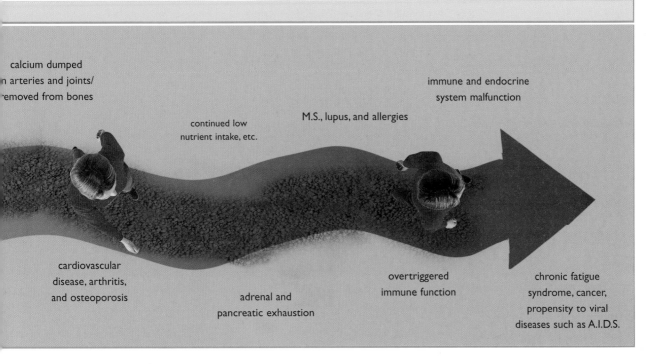

calcium dumped
in arteries and joints/
removed from bones

continued low
nutrient intake, etc.

M.S., lupus, and allergies

immune and endocrine
system malfunction

cardiovascular
disease, arthritis,
and osteoporosis

adrenal and
pancreatic exhaustion

overtriggered
immune function

chronic fatigue
syndrome, cancer,
propensity to viral
diseases such as A.I.D.S.

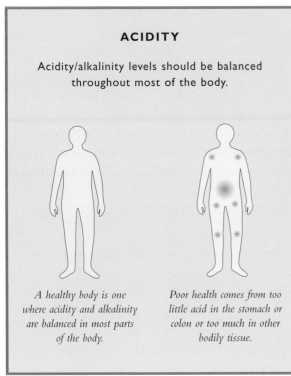

ACIDITY

Acidity/alkalinity levels should be balanced
throughout most of the body.

*A healthy body is one
where acidity and alkalinity
are balanced in most parts
of the body.*

*Poor health comes from too
little acid in the stomach or
colon or too much in other
bodily tissue.*

disease. Calcium may be "dumped" in inappropriate places such as the arteries and the joints, giving rise to cardiovascular disease and arthritis. It may fail to reach the bones, producing osteoporosis. As the body tries desperately to cope with a sub-optimum intake of essential nutrients and an unbalanced system, various endocrine (hormonal) glands become over-stressed, leading to possible adrenal and pancreatic exhaustion. When this happens, it is speculated that autoimmune diseases such as multiple sclerosis, lupus, and common allergies appear, which in turn leads eventually to a trigger-happy immune function. The downward spiral continues and, because the immune and endocrine systems are failing, nutritional thera-pists believe that diseases such as chronic fatigue syndrome and cancer appear, and viral diseases such as A.I.D.S. are made worse.

The next section will look at how to begin to reverse the disease process and reach optimum health.

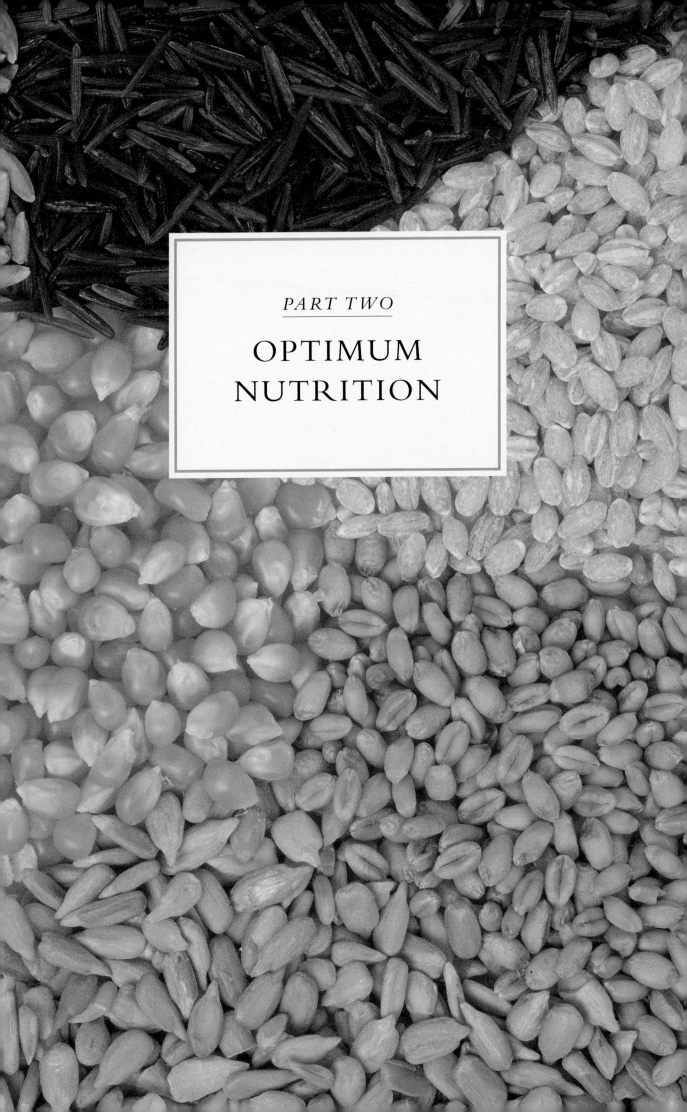

PART TWO

OPTIMUM NUTRITION

WHAT IS A WELL-BALANCED DIET?

THE OLD BELIEF *that "as long as you eat foods from the four main food groups (meats, dairy foods, fruit/vegetables, and carbohydrates) and eat three good 'square' meals a day, you are receiving all the nutrients you need" is quite inadequate. It makes no mention of the types and variety of foods within each group that are necessary for a healthy balance; makes no mention of possible nutrient depletion in "processed foods;" and takes no account of the biochemical uniqueness, changing needs, or state of health of the individual.*

Because of our modern food-production and preservation techniques, even fruit and vegetables do not contain the levels of nutrients they did in the past. Analysis of nutrient levels has indicated, on average, a decline of around 22 percent in mineral content of fruit and vegetables over the last 50 years. It has even been found that some supermarket oranges contain no vitamin C whatsoever.

Surveys carried out in Britain on tens of thousands of people have indicated that more than seven in every ten people are borderline deficient or severely deficient in B vitamins. Also, Nutrition Reviews carried out in 1992 demonstrated that it is impossible to get sufficient vitamins from the regular American food supply.

Furthermore, nutritional therapists believe that many modern diseases have their basis in acidosis (toxemia) of the tissues (*see* Part One). Very small changes in pH (acid/alkali balance) of the blood in the order of 0.01 pH points appear to be significant as to whether a person is ill or not. The healthy norm is pH 7.46, with 7.49 being extremely alkaline and pH 7.40 being extremely acid. However, conventional medical authorities continue to maintain that nutrition does not play a part in the acid/alkaline balance of the body because they consider the normal range of blood pH to be 7.4 to 7.5. Even wide fluctuations in eating patterns are unlikely to produce scores outside this range.

Fruit and vegetables have declined in nutritional value since World War II.

Under normal conditions, symptoms of over-acidity (which nutritional therapists believe to be poor mental function, fatigue, arthritic disorders, muscle aches and pains, and so on) should not occur because the body is able to "buffer" any excess acid via alkaline reserves in blood and bone.

Modern living, however, can exhaust this buffering capacity. For example, meat is a very concentrated source of protein and if eaten three times a day over a period of several days it can, nutritional therapists believe, generate a state of acidity which has to be neutralized by, primarily, the bicarbonate buffer system. This requires sodium and calcium. When blood reserves are used up, the body calls on calcium from the bones.

We can see the link, then, between excessive protein consumption and bone-density loss, putting a very large question mark over the necessity for large amounts of protein in a healthy diet. However, a healthy diet must contain sufficient protein to meet bodily demands, and this needs to be balanced adequately with carbohydrates.

Another example is where alcohol, which is detoxified by the liver, is taken in excess amounts. It overwhelms the detoxifying enzyme systems in the liver, and instead of alcohol being metabolized to carbon dioxide and water it is converted to acetaldehyde. This is an extremely toxic substance and gives rise to "ketoacidosis" which manifests itself as the symptoms of a hangover, putting an even greater

ALKALI-FORMING AND ACID-FORMING FOODS

Nutrition plays a critical part in achieving the correct balance of acid and alkali in the body – and the balance is a fine one. What is important here is what is left behind after any particular food has been metabolized, what is known as the "ash." The nature of this ash is not necessarily what you might assume from the nature of the food in its undigested form.

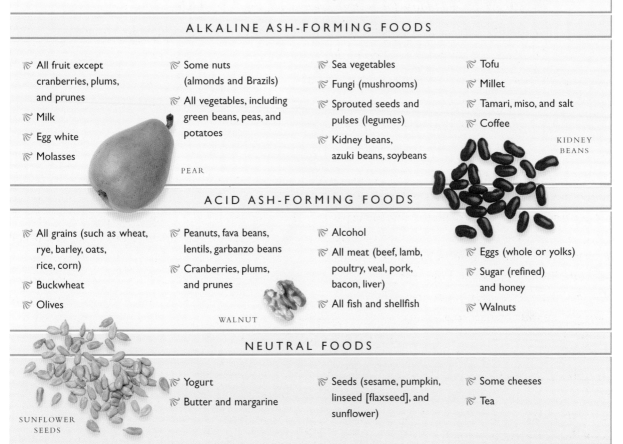

ALKALINE ASH-FORMING FOODS

- All fruit except cranberries, plums, and prunes
- Milk
- Egg white
- Molasses

- Some nuts (almonds and Brazils)
- All vegetables, including green beans, peas, and potatoes

PEAR

- Sea vegetables
- Fungi (mushrooms)
- Sprouted seeds and pulses (legumes)
- Kidney beans, azuki beans, soybeans

- Tofu
- Millet
- Tamari, miso, and salt
- Coffee

KIDNEY BEANS

ACID ASH-FORMING FOODS

- All grains (such as wheat, rye, barley, oats, rice, corn)
- Buckwheat
- Olives

- Peanuts, fava beans, lentils, garbanzo beans
- Cranberries, plums, and prunes

WALNUT

- Alcohol
- All meat (beef, lamb, poultry, veal, pork, bacon, liver)
- All fish and shellfish

- Eggs (whole or yolks)
- Sugar (refined) and honey
- Walnuts

NEUTRAL FOODS

SUNFLOWER SEEDS

- Yogurt
- Butter and margarine

- Seeds (sesame, pumpkin, linseed [flaxseed], and sunflower)

- Some cheeses
- Tea

strain on the acid/alkali balancing system. Therefore, since these acid-buffering systems depend on a sufficient supply of alkaline minerals, it is imperative that our diets contain enough foods to supply these.

We need to know the difference between the natural acidity of a food and its ability to become "acid-forming." When a food is metabolized a mineral "ash" remains and when this ash is rich in calcium, magnesium, sodium, and potassium, it is "alkaline-forming," but when the ash contains large amounts of chlorine, phosphorus, and sulfur, it becomes "acid-forming." Basically most fruit (even lemons), all vegetables, millet, and some pulses (legumes) and nuts, produce an ash rich in the alkaline minerals, and are, therefore, alkaline-forming, whereas, meat, fish, grains, and other pulses (legumes), produce an ash rich in the acid minerals, and are, therefore, acid-forming. It can be seen, then, that even vegans and vegetarians are likely to be "over-acid" if they rely too heavily on certain grains and pulses (legumes).

To counteract the tendency toward acidosis and its ensuing symptoms, the diet needs to be made up of 80 percent alkali-forming foods, and only 20 percent acid-forming foods, something not even hinted at in the conventional "balanced diet" advice.

When you have made further discoveries about your own dietary needs, you will be suitably equipped to formulate for yourself the best eating plan ever – a plan which accurately suits your body's metabolism. Only then will you be consuming a "balanced diet."

However, to get you on the right track immediately, we need to re-shuffle and extend the "four food groups," and give more precise information on the relative amounts of each type. This eating program developed out of the U.S. Department of Agriculture's "The Food Guide Pyramid," which visually displayed the ratio of all the important foods in one diagram. This idea has been altered somewhat in the light of more recent evidence on blood-sugar mechanisms. We will call this new eating program the New Pyramid.

THE NEW FOOD PYRAMID PROGRAM

E VERY MEAL SHOULD *be a balance of carbohydrate, protein, and essential fatty acids, and at the same time attempt to achieve 80 percent alkaline-forming and neutral foods to 20 percent acid-forming foods. The tables on page 39 should give you a rough guide to help you achieve a healthy balance of foods.*

The New Pyramid diet looks at foods from the point of view of their true role in promoting good health. The space given to it in the pyramid indicates how much of the diet should come from each of the food groups.

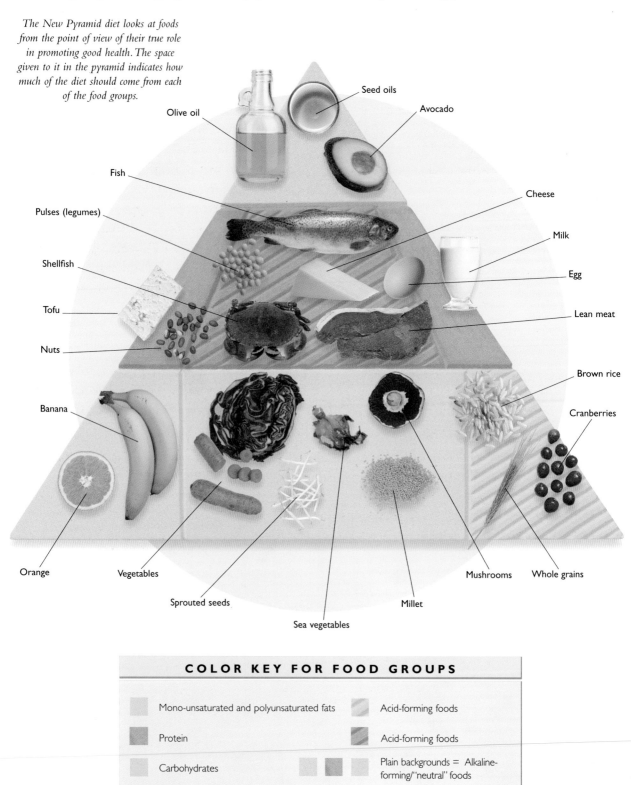

Olive oil
Seed oils
Avocado
Fish
Cheese
Pulses (legumes)
Milk
Shellfish
Egg
Tofu
Lean meat
Nuts
Brown rice
Banana
Cranberries
Orange
Vegetables
Mushrooms
Whole grains
Sprouted seeds
Millet
Sea vegetables

COLOR KEY FOR FOOD GROUPS

Mono-unsaturated and polyunsaturated fats

Protein

Carbohydrates

Acid-forming foods

Acid-forming foods

Plain backgrounds = Alkaline-forming/"neutral" foods

New Pyramid Carbohydrates

At the base of the pyramid, and therefore making up the largest portion of your food, are the fruit, vegetables, and whole grain carbohydrates. They should constitute around 40 percent of your calorie intake. Bear in mind that refined carbohydrates (white bread, sugar, sugar-rich cakes and cookies, pastries) have no place here, and that to insure a good mixture of the important minerals and vitamins within these "complex" carbohydrates, you should select a variety of them for your diet and not stick to only one or two. Try to keep acidity/alkalinity in balance.

Grains (including bread, pasta, rice, millet, breakfast cereals, buckwheat, etc.) and starchy vegetables (called "high glycemic index food," *see* pages 51 and 92) need to be kept at a low level to prevent blood sugar imbalances. This is reflected in the serving sizes. Having only minimal amounts of wholegrain carbohydrate will also keep acid-forming foods at a low level. However, since whole grains contain many essential vitamins and minerals, it is important that they are not cut from the diet altogether.

This is particularly true of rice, which is high in essential nutrients. In addition to a whole host of vitamins and minerals, it contains antioxidants called tocotrienols, which are related to vitamin E, and may help to reduce blood cholesterol. Furthermore, rice has no digestive inhibitors, which are sometimes found in grains and beans, so that it is digested more completely than related foods and prevents the formation of gas in the intestines, making it an ideal food for weaning infants. The rice bran (rice husk), too, is broken down into short chain fatty acids by the intestinal bacteria. These fatty acids are extremely useful in healing the gut lining, and helping to prevent the growth of toxic bacteria. However, there is one drawback with brown rice, which is that the bran contains lectins. In some individuals these cause an allergic reaction. White rice can be used in these circumstances, and although the nutritional benefits of the husk are lost, at least some of the grain's useful properties are retained.

Use the tables on page 39 to compile the ratio of carbohydrates in your meals and snacks, and the balance between vegetables and fruit on one hand and whole grains and potatoes on the other.

Most fruit is alkali-forming.

Green beans, are a good source of carbohydrate.

Cranberries are acid-forming.

Seeds are a source of fat to which our bodies are well adapted.

Whole grain cereals are essential, but intake should be limited.

New Pyramid Proteins

The middle level contains the proteins. These should make up around 30 percent of your calorie intake. Select a good range from (in descending order of importance) oily fish, lean meat, tofu, lentils, beans, seeds, nuts, milk, cheese, and eggs. Always have an equal balance of animal and plant protein if you are a meat eater, and for two or three days a week take your protein quota from the pulses (legumes), seeds, nuts, and tofu. If you are a fish- and dairy-consuming vegetarian, just omit the meat; if you are a strict vegetarian or a vegan, take equal amounts of tofu and pulses, with smaller amounts of nuts and seeds.

An important factor in protein choice for all concerned is to insure that alkaline-forming or neutral vegetable protein like tofu, almonds, Brazil nuts, seeds, and pulses (legumes) is balanced with the many acid-forming proteins (*see* page 35). However, this is a difficult task since protein is, by its biochemical nature, usually highly acid-forming, and it is probably easier simply to obtain most of your alkaline-forming food from vegetables and fruit. This automatically means cutting down on grains. Use the table opposite to compile the ratio of protein in your snacks and meals.

New Pyramid Fats and Oils

The top of the pyramid accounts for around 30 percent of your calorie intake, but since fats and oils contain more than twice the number of "calories" of either protein or carbohydrate, you need to make sure that you have very small servings. For example if you are having a meal containing 3oz (75g) of fish (or tofu) plus a large salad, then your fat quota would be obtained from half a teaspoon of olive oil, or a few seeds. Seeds (sunflower, sesame, etc.) and their oils supply the essential Omega-6 fatty acids, and pumpkin and linseed contain some Omega-3 acids. Any butter or margarine you may like to use (very sparingly) is included in this level, as are fish oils (from your fish intake, which supplies E.H.A. and D.H.A.) and mono-unsaturated oils, the best of which is olive oil.

Again, use the tables opposite to compile the ratio of oils/fats in your meals and snacks.

NEW PYRAMID TREATS

A diet without any treats is not going to be adhered to for very long and the odd cake, chocolate, or glass of wine is going to do you no harm, but bear in mind that the health-giving foods within this program are meant to become your major choices. When you do treat yourself, count it as part of your carbohydrate quota for the day.

Nuts should feature even in the diets of meat-eaters.

Though a fruit, avocado is a good source of fat.

Oily fish is an excellent source of protein.

Olive oil is far healthier for cooking than animal fat.

THE NEW PYRAMID SERVING SIZES

To establish your personal daily food requirements according to the New Pyramid program, use this table in conjunction with the two tables beneath it. This first table introduces you to how much food is meant by "one serving." Within the three basic food groups (carbohydrates, proteins, and fats), there are various types of foods, and a specific weight of food is given for each type. To find out how many servings of carbohydrate, fat, and protein you should eat each day, use the table bottom left. Finally, to achieve a correct balance of foods within the three basic food groups, consult the table bottom right where codes correspond to this main table.

FOOD GROUP	FOOD	CODE	SERVING SIZE ONE
Carbohydrates	Vegetables – except potatoes; sprouted seeds; mushrooms	C1	4 ounces (100g)
	Fruit	C1	2 ounces (50g)
	Whole grains and starchy vegetables, e.g., potatoes	C2	1 ounce (27g)
Protein	Oily fish – includes 1 fat serving	P1	1½ ounces (40g)
	Shellfish	P1	1½ ounces (40g)
	Lean meat	P1	1 ounce (27g)
	Tofu	P1	3 ounces (80g)
	Dairy: cottage cheese	P1	2 ounces (50g)
	Hard cheese – includes 1 fat serving	P1	1 ounce (27g)
	Yogurt	P1	3 ounces (80g)
	Milk	P1	3 ounces (80g)
	Eggs – includes 2 fat servings	P1	2 ounces (50g)
	Nuts – includes 2 fat servings	P2	1½ ounces (40g)
	Seeds – includes 1 fat serving	P2	2 ounces (50g)
	Pulses (legumes) – includes 1 carbohydrate serving	P2	2 ounces (50g)
Fats	Olive oil; sesame oil; sunflower oil; butter	F1	½tsp (2.5ml)
	Nuts – includes some protein	F2	1 tsp (5ml)
	Seeds – includes some protein	F2	1½tsp (7.5ml)
	Peanut butter; tahini – includes some protein	F3	1 tsp (5ml)
	Avocado	F3	1 ounce (27g)
	Fish oils – included in protein list		

DAILY SERVINGS

Related to body size and levels of activity.

Small to average size, sedentary: 5 servings of each group	Greater than average size (taller or heavier), sedentary: 7 servings of each group
Small to average size, moderately active: 7 servings of each group	Greater than average size, moderately active: 9 servings of each group
Small to average size, very active: 9 servings of each group	Greater than average size, very active: 11 servings of each group

RATIO OF DAILY SERVINGS

This table shows how the servings should be made up within each food group.

DAILY SERVINGS	CARBOHYDRATES		PROTEIN		FATS		
	C1	C2	P1	P2	F1	F2	F3
5	4	1	2	3	2	2	1
7	5	2	3	4	2	3	2
9	5	4	5	4	3	3	3
11	6	5*	6**	5	4	4	3

* As serving size increases, use more millet and potato to keep acidity low

** As serving size increases, use more tofu and/or fish to keep dairy foods low

The Results of the New Pyramid Program

Eating a diet constructed in the New Pyramid way will give your body ten major healthy changes:

◆ *Saturated fat intake will be reduced, and essential fatty acids raised.*

◆ *Protein level will be more in line with the biochemical demands of the body, and will be obtained from a range of sources.*

◆ *Sugar and salt intake will be reduced, and natural sugars and mineral salts will be obtained from vegetables and fruit.*

◆ *Intake of convenience foods and, therefore, intake of artificial additives, excess sugars, and salt, will be drastically decreased.*

◆ *Intake of all necessary vitamins and minerals will be greatly increased.*

◆ *Intake of important antioxidants and phytochemicals (biologically active chemicals in food which are not strictly classed as nutrients; see pages 72–75) will be increased.*

◆ *Dietary fiber will be obtained from a range of different fiber types, with harsh wheat fiber being minimal.*

◆ *Carbohydrate intake will be well balanced and will consist of "complex" types rather than "refined" types; grains will be kept at a low level and, correspondingly, blood sugar imbalances will be minimal.*

◆ *Intake of environmental toxins and pollutants will be drastically reduced if you consume most of your food from an organic source.*

◆ *The pH balance will conform more to the 80 percent alkaline/20 percent acid ratio.*

To help you get started, there is a list of recipes for the New Food Pyramid program in Appendix Five.

When you begin your New Food Pyramid program, remember that wholefoods taste different from processed foods, which contain all sorts of flavorings and flavor-enhancing chemicals. Moreover, the taste of food depends upon your ability to detect subtleties of flavor, which in turn depends upon the quality of your diet. This essentially means that as you change to the types of food recommended here, you may find them bland at first. However, after a week or two your palate will have cleared sufficiently for your taste buds to return to their natural state, and you will begin to savor the natural flavors of these chemical-free whole foods. If you then eat any "flavor-enhanced" foods, you will experience an overpowering taste of salt and "artificialness."

A closer look at each of the food groups depicted in the New Food Pyramid shows the range of foods occurring within each group and assesses the usefulness of the different types for improving and maintaining health (*see* pages 42–53).

The New Pyramid program, with fats at the top, protein in the middle and carbohydrates at the bottom.

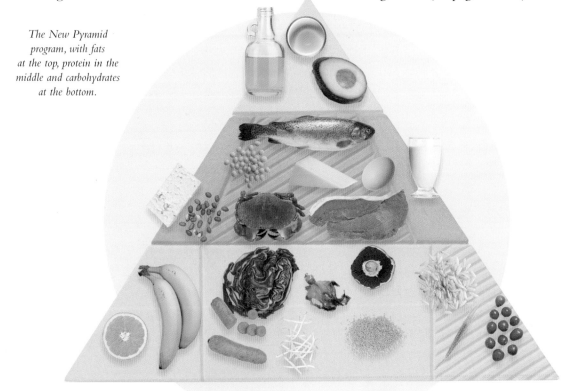

GENERAL HINTS FOR THE NEW PYRAMID PROGRAM

☞ Avoid any form of sugar (except fructose), white, refined, or processed food, or food containing additives.

☞ Minimize intake of alcohol, coffee, and tea. Instead of downing three or four glasses of cheap wine in an evening, buy a good organic wine and savor one, or at most, two glasses. Treat yourself to a really nice cappuccino, instead of drinking coffee constantly just to keep yourself going.

☞ Avoid fried (except stir-fried vegetables in a cold-pressed virgin olive oil), burned, or "browned" food, hydrogenated fats (read food labels carefully to find them), and margarines. Use saturated animal fat sparingly. Have a small amount of good quality butter as a treat.

☞ Eat organic, raw vegetables wherever possible.

☞ Keep dairy foods to a minimum. They may be catarrh-forming, and can be a cause of sinus trouble in some people. If you like to eat cheese, have one serving of sheep's, goat, cottage, or mozzarella cheese as a treat instead of meat. Swap cow's milk for rice milk, soy milk, or oat milk, and use soy cream instead of ordinary cream. Yogurt is the exception; one tub of any type of live yogurt should be eaten daily for the natural bacteria needed in the large intestine.

☞ Drink four to six half-pint glasses of water per day, plus diluted fruit juices (1:1 juice to water). Keep citrus juices to a minimum. Drink herb tea, fruit tea, rooibosh tea, or milk-free, lactose-free dandelion coffee, or other coffee substitutes.

☞ Consume most of your drinks in between meals to prevent dilution of digestive enzymes.

☞ Supplement your diet with a high-potency, good-quality, multivitamin/multimineral, and 1,000mg (1g) vitamin C a day.

☞ Eat when you are hungry and not just out of habit, or to give yourself a treat.

☞ Avoid sugar substitutes. There is some evidence that these could be involved in cancer and other degenerative diseases.

☞ Don't eat when you are in a hurry, stressed, or upset.

☞ Chew food thoroughly: this is easier if you don't drink with your meals.

☞ Treat all fats, oils, and foods that naturally contain them (nuts, seeds, etc.) with great care. Rancidity (oxidation) occurs very quickly, brought about by oxygen, heat, light, or contact with metals (which act as catalysts). Always buy the best quality unhydrogenated oils you can afford and store in tightly sealed jars and bottles in a cool dark cabinet or in the refrigerator. If using ground seeds and nuts, grind them yourself in a coffee grinder or blender, and store in a tightly sealed jar in the refrigerator. Grind small amounts at a time to keep the turnover rapid. The more oxidized foods you consume (rancid, fried, barbecued, etc.), the greater will be the free radical load on your body, the more energy will be required for detoxification, and the less energy there will be available for normalizing your metabolism. If you need to heat fats, use good quality olive oil or a little organic butter.

Healthy eating is for all the family, and it is especially advisable to get children into the habit of enjoying nutritious food as early as possible.

UNDERSTANDING THE FOOD GROUPS

F OOD FALLS INTO *four main groups: fats, proteins, carbohydrates, and fiber. The other essential component of our diet is water. To eat properly you need to understand not only how these groups work together, but also the different categories within each group and their distinctive characteristics.*

Fats

There are basically two kinds of fats. Hard fats, which are solid at room temperature, usually come from an animal source such as fatty meat and dairy food (but also coconut), and are referred to as "saturated fats." Saturated fats are so called because all their chemical bonds are "saturated" with hydrogen atoms, and this tends to make molecules of this type of fat very rigid. Conversely, oils are "liquid" at room temperature. More often than not they come from a plant source, such as seeds and nuts (but also fish), and are referred to as "unsaturated" or "polyunsaturated" fats (oils). They are "unsaturated" because not all of the chemical bonds are linked to hydrogen atoms, which allows the formation of "double" bonds within the fat molecule, giving these oils a much more flexible structure.

It is important to understand the difference between the fats so that you can choose the healthiest for your diet.

BAD FATS

Animal fats (excluding fish oils), and in particular dairy foods, are high in saturated fat. The media and medical profession alike have been telling us for some time now that we should not eat too much saturated fat, and the reasons for this advice have been fairly well documented. Many of the degenerative diseases of modern man (heart disease, stroke, obesity, M.S., and cancer) have been linked to our large intake of saturated fat, which, because of its chemical nature, clogs up arteries and interferes with the body's metabolism.

Additionally, saturated fat impedes the metabolism of good fats. It may also produce "insulin resistance," causing the blood sugar control mechanism to fail. This is where vegetarianism and veganism have the upper hand!

It is fairly easy to remove saturated fat from meat: you either trim it off or cook the meat so that the fat drains away. You can eat less beef, pork, and lamb, and more poultry. However, it is a different story with dairy foods. You are rarely any better off consuming "polyunsaturated" margarines and shortenings, or "half-fat" cheeses and "low-fat" spreads. This is because of the degree of processing these foods go through, in particular the process of "hydrogenation," where polyunsaturated oils are changed from liquid oils into solid or semi-solid fats. Not only do unsaturated oils (the good fats) then become saturated fats (the bad fats), but these artificially produced substances are not readily metabolized by the body, and nutritional therapists believe that they become toxic to the system. Consumption of hydrogenated fat has been linked to serious disorders such as cancer, heart disease, and other conditions.

Another "villain" in the fat group, if occurring in excess, is arachidonic acid, which interferes with hormonal control, and causes inappropriate clotting of the blood. Foods rich in this fat are egg yolks, organ meats (liver, etc.), and fatty red meat. These foods need to be kept low in any healthy diet. Again vegetarians and vegans benefit here.

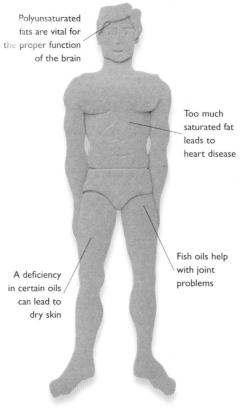

Polyunsaturated fats are vital for the proper function of the brain

Too much saturated fat leads to heart disease

Fish oils help with joint problems

A deficiency in certain oils can lead to dry skin

Fats are essential for our health, but it is important to understand the difference between "good" and "bad" fats.

SATURATED FATS

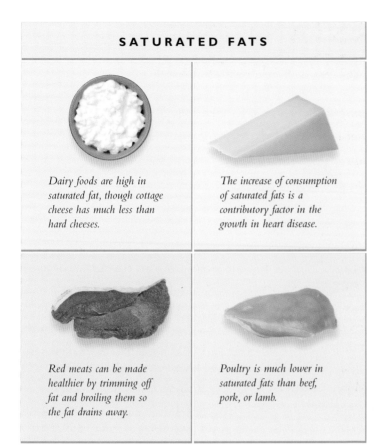

Dairy foods are high in saturated fat, though cottage cheese has much less than hard cheeses.

The increase of consumption of saturated fats is a contributory factor in the growth in heart disease.

Red meats can be made healthier by trimming off fat and broiling them so the fat drains away.

Poultry is much lower in saturated fats than beef, pork, or lamb.

Furthermore, even unsaturated oils of the very purest quality are chemically unstable and susceptible to damage by heat, light, oxygen, and presence of metals. This instability causes another problem during processing: the production of "trans-fatty acids." Fatty acids make up part of the fat molecule, and, in natural oils and unsaturated fats, these fatty acids exist in what, in chemical terms, is called the "cis" conformation. These molecules have a variable zigzag shape related to the number of double bonds in the fatty acid chain. It is this shape that gives flexibility to the membranes and other structures of our bodies when these oils are incorporated into them from the food that is eaten.

However, when natural "cis" form fatty acids are processed, their instability causes a degree of chemical rearrangement, changing them to the "trans" form. The shape of these fatty acids is very different from those of the "cis" form and this weakens the cell membranes, preventing them from engaging fully in the normal exchange of materials in and out of cells.

A vegetarian diet, especially one free of dairy produce and processed food, is very low in saturated fats.

Additionally, trans-fats accumulate in blood vessels, and, since the body finds it difficult to metabolize them, this is where they stay, collecting other bits of cell debris and excess calcium, and forming blockages.

Another reason why the "polyunsaturated" margarines and spreads do not serve to reduce heart disease is that many of them concentrate solely on using oils from the Omega-6 series (linoleic acid) as their base. The body requires the two essential fatty acids – linoleic and linolenic – to be in balance, and an intake of around a 2:1 ratio of linoleic to linolenic seems to be the best for a healthy cardiovascular system.

Any diet including even moderate levels of these imbalanced and over-processed products, therefore, is doing nothing toward preventing heart disease. It is imperative that you avoid excess arachidonic acid, and as many saturated fats, hydrogenated fats, and trans-fatty acids as possible. Read labels carefully and choose good quality virgin cold pressed oils, pure butter, and margarines which have undergone very little processing.

A diet high in seeds and nuts results in shiny hair

Brown rice and vegetables are high in nutrients and low in fat

GOOD FATS

Unsaturated fats (the so-called "good" fats) can be divided into two groups: mono-unsaturated fats, such as those found in olive oil; and polyunsaturated fats, such as those found in fish, nuts, and seeds. Mono-unsaturates appear to have a protective function against heart disease, as seen by the very good health of people living in the Mediterranean, while certain polyunsaturates are "essential." This means that the body cannot make them from other dietary fats or oils, so they must be taken into the body in their active form.

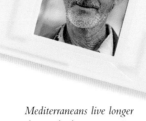

The two essential polyunsaturates are linoleic acid and linolenic acid. These belong to the Omega-6 and Omega-3 groups of oils respectively. Both these fatty acids are vital for the structure and effective working of the brain and nervous system (around half the weight of our brain is made up of essential fatty acids!), the immune system, the hormonal system, the cardiovascular system, and the skin.

Mediterraneans live longer due to the heart-protective mono-unsaturated fat in their diet.

The first indications of a deficiency in these two essential oils are a dry skin, dry eyes, and a greater than normal thirst. Seeds in general, but especially sesame and sunflower seeds are rich in linoleic acid (Omega-6), while pumpkin and flax seeds (edible linseeds) are rich in linolenic acid (Omega-3). Linoleic acid (Omega-6) is converted in the body into two further substances. These substances are known as Gamma-linolenic acid (G.L.A.) and Di-homo-gamma-linolenic acid (D.G.L.A.), which is further converted to Arachidonic acid (A.A.). Linolenic acid (Omega-3) is converted to Eicosa-pentenoic acid (E.P.A.) and Docosahexenoic acid (D.H.A.). E.P.A. and D.H.A. are also found in fatty fish (such as mackerel, herring, salmon, sardines, and so on). Furthermore, D.G.L.A., A.A., and E.P.A. go on to produce prostaglandins (*see* the tables on the functions of essential fatty acids below for more information).

These conversions do not always proceed efficiently. In fact, the following are just some of the agents able to block the process:

- *Exotoxins (pollutants, food additives)*
- *Endotoxins (some metabolites, Candida)*
- *Saturated fats*
- *Excessive cholesterol*
- *Stress*
- *High blood sugar*
- *Excessive alcohol*
- *Aging process*
- *Some viruses*
- *Radiation*
- *Protein deficiency*
- *Excessive calorie intake*
- *Deficiency of vitamin B6, biotin, vitamin C, calcium, magnesium, and zinc*

The inability for conversion to take place is so common, that adding G.L.A. (found in evening primrose oil and borage oil) and E.P.A. (found in fish oils) to the diet in supplement form is the only way to improve the health in many individuals, by producing a better balance of prostaglandins.

BALANCING ESSENTIAL FATTY ACIDS

Balancing essential fatty acids in the diet is beneficial for the following:

- Athletic performance.
- Aging.
- Weight loss.
- Cardiovascular disease.
- P.M.S. and menopausal problems.
- Hormonal and blood sugar imbalance.
- Poor immune function.
- Skin problems.
- Stress.
- Behavioral problems.
- Depression.

A balance of Omega-3 fatty acids, found in pumpkin seeds (above), and Omega-6 fatty acids is essential for health.

Prostaglandins are hormone-like molecules that function to regulate moment-to-moment cellular activities. Unlike true hormones, however, prostaglandins are found in all tissues and are not just produced only in specific glands. Also, they have their effect in the cells in which they are synthesized, whereas true hormones from glands have effects away from the cells that produce them. Prostaglandins appear to be able to alter the activity of hormones and, to date, more than 30 different molecular species

FATTY ACID PROFILE FOR VEGETABLE OILS				
FRESH PRESSED ORGANIC OIL	SATURATED FAT	MONO-UNSATURATED	LINOLEIC	LINOLENIC
Almond	9%	65%	26%	-
Flax (linseed)	9%	16%	18%	57%
Hazelnut	7%	76%	17%	-
Olive	10%	82%	8%	-
Pumpkin	9%	34%	42%	15%
Safflower	8%	13%	79%	-
Sesame	13%	46%	41%	-
Sunflower	12%	19%	69%	-
Walnut	16%	28%	51%	5%

The above table is an extract from information obtained from Lamberts Healthcare Limited, England, with their kind permission.

have been identified. These are usually grouped into three broad categories: the Series 1 Prostaglandins (P.G.1), Series 2 Prostaglandins (P.G.2), and the Series 3 Prostaglandins (P.G.3).

P.G.1s (from D.G.L.A.) have been studied in the greatest detail so far, and have an anti-inflammatory activity. They decrease platelet aggregation, cause vasodilation (increase of the internal diameter of blood vessels), act as diuretics, help insulin activity, help T-cell functioning, and regulate calcium metabolism. They are involved in preventing heart attacks (and some may slow down cholesterol production), removing excess fluid, helping lower blood pressure, relieving angina, helping control arthritis, improving nerve and immune function (which also produces a sense of well-being). Some P.G.1s prevent the release of A. A. from cell membranes, and thereby regulate the effects of P.G.2s.

Series 2 prostaglandins (from A.A.) are a mixture of anti-inflammatory and pro-inflammatory species, on balance considered to be the latter. They influence, among other things, platelet aggregation and broncho-constriction.

Although P.G.2s are needed for balance, too much activity from this group (possibly influenced by too much

A.A. in the diet) can cause inflammatory problems leading to platelet aggregation, water retention, and high blood pressure. P.G.3s (from E.P.A.) have a controlling effect on the release of A.A. from cell membranes and thereby limit P.G.2 production. This may explain why fish oils (which contain E.P.A.) help cardiovascular problems, water retention, and inflammatory ailments, such as arthritis, since these conditions are likely to be caused by excessive P.G.2 levels.

It is obvious that essential fatty acids play a vital role in health, and shows why a fat-free diet (which removes all fat, not just saturated fat) is, over a long period of time, potentially dangerous. Recent research demonstrates that even very fit marathon runners who consume only 15 percent of their daily calories from fats (instead of the recommended 30 percent) have a lowered immune function.

The good fats, then, are the essential fatty acids found in cold-pressed olive oil (mono-unsaturated fatty acid), sesame seeds, and sunflower seeds (Omega-6), pumpkin and linseeds (Omega-3), fish oils (D.H.A. and E.P.A.), and evening primrose and borage flowers (G.L.A.). For optimum health, aim to have your full daily quota of essential fatty acids.

Marathon runners and other heavy exercisers who do not consume enough fatty acids endanger their health.

CHOLESTEROL

For decades we have been told that our blood cholesterol levels are related to our risk of heart disease, and the only way to reduce the risk is to cut cholesterol-containing foods from our diet. Fortunately, there is much evidence to dispel these myths.

Firstly, low-cholesterol diets actually encourage the liver to produce cholesterol while at the same time restricting many important nutrients (for example, the lecithin found in eggs), which are needed to control cholesterol levels in the body. Lecithin is a substance needed to emulsify fats and render fat molecules small enough to be carried efficiently in the blood to the cells, thereby removing them from the blood. People with atherosclerosis tend to produce very small amounts of lecithin when compared to healthy people. This may be because bodily production of lecithin needs essential fatty acids, choline, inositol, and magnesium, most of which tend to be low in low-cholesterol diets. Therefore high blood cholesterol may be more related to lack of important nutrients, than directly to levels of cholesterol contained in the diet.

Secondly, it is the ratio of L.D.L. (low density lipoprotein) to H.D.L. (high density lipoprotein) that is important, and not simply the total amount of cholesterol in the diet that is related to the risk of heart disease. It is the L.D.L. which is the "bad" cholesterol, and H.D.L. which is the "good" cholesterol.

Thirdly, if cholesterol of any type is so bad for us, why does our body make so much of it? The reason is, of course, that it is a vital substance. It is the building material of many structural cell components (membranes), and the precursor molecule for production of steroid hormones (estrogen, testosterone, adrenaline, cortisol, etc.).

Fourthly, although high blood cholesterol levels are related to heart disease, there is still extensive heart disease in people who have moderate or low levels.

Also, in the elderly, people over 70, there is little association between high blood cholesterol and death from heart disease, or between cholesterol in the diet (from eggs and fatty meat) and blood cholesterol levels. In fact, more than 80 percent of the body's cholesterol comes from that made in the liver, and not from the diet! More importantly, patients with heart disease who are instructed to cut down severely on dietary cholesterol and saturated fat, tend to eat massive amounts of carbohydrates. Frequently these are of the refined variety, and are low in manganese, zinc, magnesium, potassium, chromium, which are the very nutrients needed to nourish a healthy heart. Such foods are usually low in vitamins, which are also required to keep the heart healthy. Consequently, the elevation of insulin levels needed by this high carbohydrate diet may lead to the production of more cholesterol.

The risk of heart disease increases as we get older, but low fat doesn't mean no fat – the body needs essential fatty acids.

FUNCTIONS OF E.F.A.S

The following list includes scientifically proven functions of essential fatty acids.

- ☞ Increase energy production by helping the body to obtain more oxygen.
- ☞ Improve energy levels and stamina.
- ☞ Increase strength and endurance.
- ☞ Speed up recovery from fatigue.
- ☞ Increase metabolic rate.
- ☞ Balance blood-sugar levels.
- ☞ Increase excess water loss via the kidneys.
- ☞ Prevent food cravings.
- ☞ Improve circulation.
- ☞ Balance hormones and prostaglandins.
- ☞ Fight infection.
- ☞ Prevent abnormal growths.
- ☞ Improve the skin.
- ☞ Reduce stress and anxiety.
- ☞ Elevate mood.
- ☞ Prevent juvenile behavior problems.

Since the effectiveness of essential oils is so easily destroyed it is important to have a fresh daily source.

RELATIVE CALORIFIC VALUE OF FOODS

Each gram (about ⅟₂₅ of an ounce) of fat or oil consumed supplies 9.3Kcals (39Kjoules) of energy. This is approximately double the calorific value of either protein or carbohydrate, which release 4.0Kcals (16.8Kjoules), and 3.75Kcals (15.8Kjoules) of energy respectively when they are metabolized. This is an additional reason for keeping fats and oils at a low level in our diet. Fortunately, the fats our bodies require, the essential "cis" fatty acids, are adequately provided by the New Pyramid program. Any fat consumed over and above what the program recommends will tend to remain as fat, leading to overweight, heart disease, and other degenerative diseases.

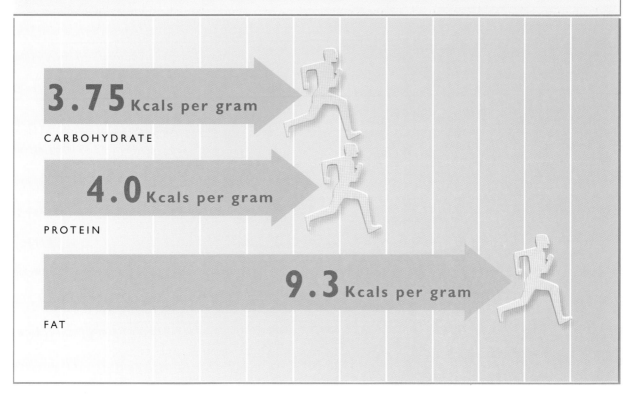

3.75 Kcals per gram
CARBOHYDRATE

4.0 Kcals per gram
PROTEIN

9.3 Kcals per gram
FAT

Cholesterol levels are much better controlled by a diet that is well balanced in protein, carbohydrates, and essential fatty acids, such as that outlined in the New Food Pyramid program.

Whether we suffer from high cholesterol or not, it is important to keep protective H.D.L.s high and reduce damaging L.D.L.s. Research shows that monounsaturates (in olive oil, peanuts, and avocados) lower L.D.L.s and raise H.D.L.s. This may be the reason for the vascular protection provided by the Mediterranean diet, high in olive oil. Poly-unsaturates on the other hand, lower both types of cholesterol, but at the same time are undeniably necessary for their essential fatty acid content. The New Pyramid serving ratios of different oils and the foods that contain them (seeds, avocados, etc.) are devised to optimize intake of monounsaturates and essential fatty acids alike, to fulfill all bio-chemical functions. In addition, the soluble fibers, particularly pectin, from fruits and vegetables, are perfectly suited to removing excess cholesterol from the intestines.

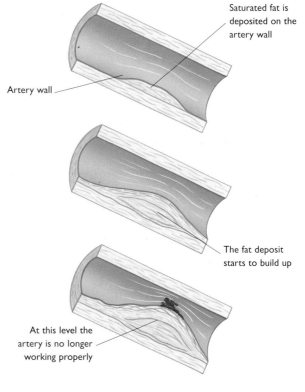

Saturated fat is deposited on the artery wall

Artery wall

The fat deposit starts to build up

At this level the artery is no longer working properly

A section across an artery showing how fat blockages typically build up and obstruct the flow of blood.

Proteins

Proteins are made up of basic units called amino acids. Around 22 amino acids exist in nature and, of these, eight are deemed "essential" for the adult human and ten for children. Amino acids are vital for growth and the repair and maintenance of body tissue; this is their structural role. Additionally, amino acids have a biochemical role in that they are the basis of many hormones, enzymes, antibodies, neuro-transmitters and carriers of oxygen, fats, and other substances within the blood.

However, protein does not need to be consumed in excessive amounts to fulfill its functions. If protein is eaten in excess of body requirements, it cannot be stored by the body in this form (apart from a minute pool of amino acids in each body cell), and has to be converted to carbohydrate or fat. This process is carried out by the liver and requires the removal of nitrogenous material which would otherwise become toxic to the system. In such circumstances the liver

Proteins consist of amino acids, of which several are essential to all human beings.

Without protein we would never grow, and our bodily tissues would not be renewed.

and the kidneys are put under stress by having to work hard to remove these waste products.

What is left of the amino acids at this stage is a carbohydrate-like skeleton which, in normal circumstances, is metabolized to produce energy. If this energy is not used it is converted to fat for storage; consequently, excess protein can cause body fat to build up. Moreover, excess protein makes the body tissues very acidic, and the body has to release calcium and other mineral salts from the skeleton to buffer this excess acidity. It follows from this, that diets high in protein are likely to be one of the possible causes of osteoporosis and other conditions affecting the skeleton. However, there is a very great difference between a diet of excessive protein intake when no limit is put on protein consumption, and a balanced protein intake as in the New Pyramid program.

As with fats, both the quantity and the quality of protein we eat is important. British government recommendations suggest we obtain around 15 percent of our total calorie intake from protein, whereas the New Pyramid program recommends a more balanced 30 percent; this is in line with recent research by Barry Sears, Ph.D. No further governmental advice is given on the types or quality of protein which would be best. However, information along these lines is vital to a successful health-giving diet. In the past animal proteins were regarded as "first class" proteins simply because each one contains all eight of the essential amino acids, which are easily assimilated. However, as you get older animal protein may become harder to digest. In addition, it is more likely to contain saturated fat, and it may also be carrying antibiotic and hormone residues, unless you eat organic meat and dairy foods.

Plant proteins are a less contaminated form of protein, especially if obtained from a pesticide-free source. However, protein from any one plant source may need to be balanced with other plant proteins to obtain the same range of amino acids as in animal protein. Furthermore, vegetable protein tends to contain additional beneficial complex carbohydrates, as in the case of beans and lentils, and is less acid-forming than fish, meat, and some dairy products.

ESSENTIAL AMINO ACIDS

Isoleucine	Tryptophan
Leucine	Valine
Lysine	Arginine*
Methionine	Histidine*
Phenylalanine	Taurine*
Threonine	*Conditionally essential

However, although fish and lean meat are high acid-forming foods, they were a major part of our ancestral diet, and are undeniably well suited to our digestive capabilities and metabolism. Fish, especially, is important for its content of D.H.A. and E.F.A. fatty acids. As a general guide, it is best to eat fish in preference to meat; to limit lean meat to three times a week; and to restrict dairy foods (since these are fairly new in evolutionary terms) to a very small amount, say 2/3 cup (150ml) of milk or 1 ounce (27g) cheese, or one small pot of (live) yogurt daily, or slightly larger amounts but less frequently. It is a complete myth to insist that milk and cheese are an essential part of the diet because of their calcium content.

All the amino acids of meat can be found in vegetables

Heavy meat eating produces acidity in body tissue

Meat eaters often assume that vegetarians always lack quality proteins, but this is a myth. Moreover, vegetarians are less likely to suffer from excess protein.

There are several reasons that show why.

- *Vegans do not suffer more than dairy-food eaters from calcium-deficiency diseases.*
- *Since milk reduces stomach acidity, it makes calcium less readily absorbed (calcium needs an acid environment for its absorption).*
- *Dairy foods (milk proteins) are allergenic in susceptible individuals.*
- *Some adults are sensitive to lactose (milk sugar).*
- *You can get all the calcium you need from seeds (especially sesame), tofu, and dark green vegetables.*

Live yogurt is probably the only dairy food that is useful. It is initially acidic so that its calcium content is readily absorbed, and the milk proteins and lactose have been "pre-digested" by the bacteria, which are themselves beneficial for topping up those in our intestines. Strict vegetarians and vegans should obtain their main protein from tofu, beans, lentils, and "seed" vegetables, supplemented by smaller amounts from nuts, grains, and seeds.

It is very easy to achieve adequate protein intake whether you are a meat-eater, a vegetarian, or a vegan, since many vegetables, such as runner beans, French green beans, peas, corn, and broccoli, supply good levels of protein. Generally, most people eat too much protein. Recent findings indicate that protein high in the essential amino acid methionine may be problematical. Excess methionine produces a substance called homocysteine which is now known to cause arterial damage leading to cardiovascular disease. Meat, dairy food, and fish are all high in methionine, while good quality plant protein has more moderate levels. Vitamins B_6, B_{12}, and folic acid have been shown to protect against homocysteine production. Ideally then, meat-eaters should consider eating vegetable protein for three or four days a week to help neutralize excess tissue acidity and prevent loss of calcium and other minerals, maximize levels of B vitamins, and prevent the build-up of homocysteine.

Carbohydrate

Carbohydrate is the main fuel for the body. Unlike fats and proteins, carbohydrate has no other function in the body than to supply it with energy, apart from a small amount of dietary carbohydrate which is vital for the structural basis of D.N.A. and other important molecules. (Indigestible carbohydrate, or fiber, is discussed on page 52.) Carbohydrate exists in nature, in two main forms: the "sugars" and the "starches." The first of these are made up of simple monosaccharide sugars, such as glucose and fructose (fruit sugar), and disaccharide sugars such as sucrose ("sugar"), maltose (malt) from germinating grain, and lactose from milk. Starches, on the other hand, are made up of polysaccharides, which are long chains of simple sugars, usually predominantly glucose.

The structure of a molecule of a polysaccharide, one of the two main types of carbohydrate. Polysaccharides, such as starch, are made up of simple sugars.

Another natural polysaccharide is cellulose, obtained from plant cell walls (and, therefore, from all fresh vegetables and fruit), and from cereal husks, and seed coats (and, therefore, from brown rice, whole oats, beans, seeds, etc.). Since humans do not possess a cellulose-degrading enzyme, cellulose becomes the "fiber" in your diet.

Starchy vegetables (potatoes, parsnips, corn, peas, broad beans) and grains (whole wheat, rye, oats, barley, rice, millet, maize) are the best source of starch. If you are gluten-sensitive, you can choose from rice, corn, millet, tapioca, amaranth, buckwheat, and quinoa, which are all gluten-free. The last three are not, in fact, true cereals at all, and, despite its name, buckwheat is not related to wheat but is a member of the rhubarb family.

Natural monosaccharide sugars (glucose and fructose), and disaccharide sugars (sucrose, maltose, and lactose), are obtained from sweet vegetables like carrots and beets, fruit, honey, malt, milk, sugar cane, sugar

Rice is a good source of starch, and for people who suffer from celiac disease it has the advantage of being free of gluten.

beet, and molasses. Other sweet foods in our diet come, predominantly, from sucrose-containing refined foods, such as cakes, cookies, pastry, candies, chocolate, puddings, custards, and alcohol. You need to be ruthless in cutting these from your diet.

Substances called glycosinolates are produced when "sugar" intake is high; the excess glucose reacts with protein and cells in the blood, to produce "advanced glycation end products" – A.G.E. proteins. These are very much related to biological aging (at least in animals) and interfere with metabolism by increasing the level of toxic substances associated with damage to the endocrine, immune, and nervous systems.

Generally, foods containing "sugar" release glucose easily and quickly into the bloodstream, whereas starches, especially when eaten as vegetables, fruit, and whole grains, take much longer to digest, passing through the digestive system more slowly, releasing their glucose a little at a time. Beware, however, of having excess bread and pasta in your diet, since even wholegrain varieties of these carbohydrate-dense foods can play havoc with insulin levels

Whole grains release energy into the system gradually

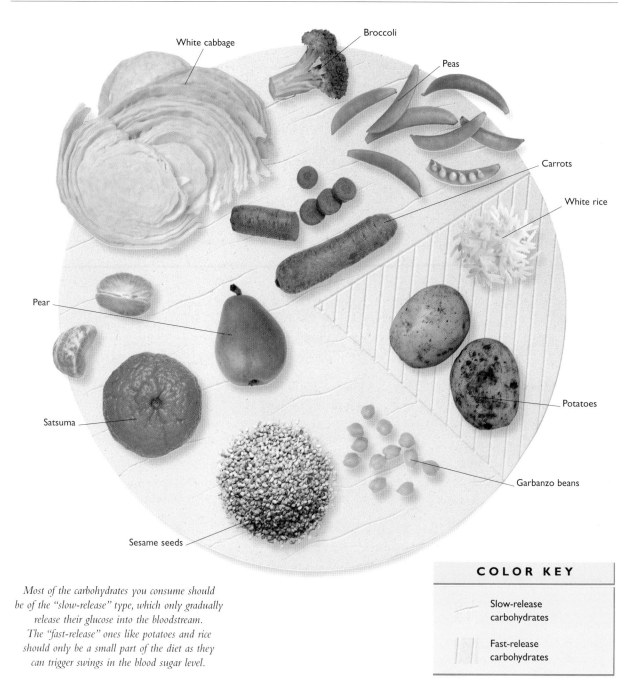

White cabbage
Broccoli
Peas
Carrots
White rice
Pear
Satsuma
Potatoes
Garbanzo beans
Sesame seeds

Most of the carbohydrates you consume should be of the "slow-release" type, which only gradually release their glucose into the bloodstream. The "fast-release" ones like potatoes and rice should only be a small part of the diet as they can trigger swings in the blood sugar level.

COLOR KEY

Slow-release carbohydrates

Fast-release carbohydrates

if you eat too much carbohydrate in proportion to protein. Fructose from fruit is released slowly, and has other characteristics which prevent it from affecting blood sugar balance adversely.

Sugars such as glucose and sucrose tend to give you a sudden burst of energy, followed by a slump, whereas starches, the "slow-releasing" or "complex" carbohydrates from vegetables, pulses (legumes), seeds, and fruit, provide more sustained energy over a longer period of time. The slow-release mechanism works to prevent drastic swings in blood sugar level. When your blood sugar level is stable, your energy level is more balanced, and you have longer relief from hunger. Refined foods like pure sugar and white flour also lack the vitamins and minerals needed for their metabolism, and are best avoided for this reason. Since

some natural foods, such as cooked carrots and parsnips, bananas, dates, and raisins, also contain sugar of the "fast-release" type (*see* Glycemic Index on page 92), it is best to keep these items at a low level in the diet, but not to exclude them completely as they are an excellent source of potassium and other important minerals and vitamins.

Slow-release carbohydrate foods such as vegetables, pulses (legumes), seeds, and fresh fruit should provide about 80 percent of your carbohydrate intake, with the remaining 20 percent of your intake provided by carbohydrate-dense foods such as potatoes, whole grains (especially brown rice), bread, pasta, and dried fruit. Sweet treats and candies should not form a regular part of the diet but should be eaten only occasionally.

Fiber

ABOVE
*Whole grains are one source
of the fiber that is essential
to the digestive tract.*

If your diet includes plenty of fresh fruit, vegetables, pulses (legumes), seeds, nuts, and whole grains, you will automatically be consuming sufficient fiber, in the form of cellulose, hemicellulose, lignin, pectins, gums, and mucilage. Insoluble fiber, which is found in wheat bran, corn, and rice, has its effect mainly by increasing the frequency of bowel movements, but it is also useful for controlling blood-sugar levels, since it prevents fast sugar release into the blood. Pectin, which is a soluble fiber found in apples and carrots, is a particularly useful chelating agent, meaning that it absorbs heavy metals and prevents their absorption in the gut. In addition, it helps prevent the build up of cholesterol (as do oats) and helps eliminate it from the body. Pectin is also involved in balancing blood sugar levels, making apples a good choice for staving off hunger.

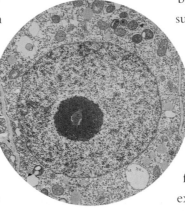

*Cellulose, the basis of dietary
fiber, is found in the walls
of plant cells.*

Fibrous foods help you to feel full for longer and hence reduce the appetite, as well as having the additional health benefits of helping to control blood sugar levels by allowing sugar to be released from food more slowly. A high-fiber diet will prevent constipation and more severe forms of bowel problem, such as diverticular disease (weakening of the colon) and even bowel cancer. Moreover, a diet high in natural fiber, with its ability to encourage efficient elimination of waste products, prevents the reabsorption of toxins in the bowel.

In most people, the body is able to recognize when the dietary intake of cholesterol is too high and it will cut back on its own production of this substance. In some people, however, this regulatory system is faulty and large amounts of cholesterol remain in the blood, eventually finding their way into the bile and from there into the intestines. If your diet includes sufficient natural fiber, particularly pectin and bran that is found in brown rice and oats, this excess cholesterol will be absorbed by the fiber and then excreted along with all the other waste materials. If not, your body will reabsorb up to 90 percent of it, and it will return to the blood system where it may build up in arteries, or it will become deposited in the gall bladder or kidneys where stones may form.

At the same time, you need to get away from the idea that having a "high fiber" diet means piling mountains of wheat bran onto your food. Wheat bran is one of the least effective fibers since it is very harsh on the digestive tract and carries with it, out of the body, not only waste materials, but also many important minerals which are attracted to it. The fiber contained in vegetables, fruit, oats, lentils and beans is much more gentle and effective. In fact, overall, the most healthful fiber is to be found, in descending order of importance, in apples, rice bran, beets, peas, brown rice, and oats.

Water

Water is not depicted in the New Pyramid program diagram, but no one would deny that it is vital for life. Despite the fact that water has no calorific value, it is an important component of the diet. Two-thirds of the body is made up of water. Approximately 6 cups (1.5 liters) of water are lost through the skin, lungs, gut, and as urine daily. This water loss is an important part of the process of eliminating toxic substances from the body. However, when carbohydrates are metabolized, about 1¾ cups (0.4 liters) per day of water is made available to the body.

To replace the difference between that lost and that gained ("metabolic" water), we can see that we need to drink just over 4 cups (1 liter) of water; though a better level of intake would be around 8 cups (2 liters). Since fresh fruit and vegetables are about 90 percent water, the New Pyramid program would provide you with around 4 cups (1 liter) of water, leaving 4 cups (1 liter) to be consumed in the form of filtered or bottled water, diluted fruit juice, herb and fruit teas, and grain "coffees." Large amounts of tea, coffee, and alcohol are not recommended as they are diuretics and cause the body to lose water.

GOOD SOURCES OF THE VARIOUS FORMS OF FIBER

CELLULOSE AND HEMICELLULOSE	LIGNIN	PECTIN, GUMS, AND MUCILAGE
Apples	Green beans	Apples
Green beans	Bran	Bananas
Beets	Muesli	Green beans
Bran (Rice)	Eggplant	Cabbage
Broccoli	Pears	Cauliflower
Brussels sprouts	Radishes	Carrots
Cabbage	Strawberries	Citrus fruit (Pith)
Carrots		Grapes
Eggplant		Linseeds (Flax Seed)
Whole grain flour		Oatmeal
Pears		Potatoes
Peas		Sesame seeds
Radishes		Strawberries
Sweet peppers		Squash

PEAR

ABOVE
Although water has no calorific value, it is essential to life.

Rice is so important a food source in Asia that farmers will reform the landscape for its cultivation.

VITAMINS AND MINERALS

Vitamins can easily be taken in pill form.

V ITAMINS AND MINERALS *are frequently referred to as the "micronutrients" in contrast to fats, protein, and carbohydrates which are called the "macronutrients." The reason for this is related to the amounts of each nutrient needed by the body. Macronutrients are required in weights that are easily measured by ordinary kitchen scales; despite being essential, micronutrients are only required in very small amounts.*

The guide to vitamins and minerals shows that there are excellent sources from both plant and animal foods. It is a complete myth to suggest that strict vegetarians and vegans are not obtaining all the essential nutrients from their diet. Where quantities of a particular nutrient are low in vegetable foods, for example zinc, it has been found that absorption rates in vegetarians and vegans are correspondingly enhanced. Nevertheless, if the diet is not optimum, it is quite possible that the digestive system of a meat-eater or vegan alike may function poorly and reduce absorption of micronutrients.

Vitamins

Vitamins are not structural components of the body, unlike some minerals (such as calcium in the bones), but they have a biochemical function in that they are needed, in conjunction with enzymes, to allow chemical reactions within the cell to proceed. For example, the transport of glucose from the blood into the cells of the body depends upon the presence of vitamins B_3 and B_6, and the actual breakdown of glucose within the cells into energy requires vitamins B_1, B_2, B_3, B_5, and C.

In addition to helping with the release of energy from nutrients within the body, vitamins are needed for a host of other essential functions to be performed effectively: to balance hormone levels, to

Copper, which can be found in seafood and in nuts, plays an important role in the production of hormones.

Bone formation and the production of red blood cells are not possible without phosphorus, which is found in meat, fish, and whole grains.

Iron is a constituent of hemoglobin, which carries oxygen in the bloodstream.

MEASUREMENTS

Most vitamins and minerals are measured by weight:

microgram	=	mcg
milligram (or 1,000mcg)	=	mg
gram (or 1,000mg) g	=	g

IU (International Units) is a measurement system for vitamins A, D, and E. Many supplements are still sold in IUs, but most scientists prefer to measure vitamins by weight.

1iu vitamin A	=	0.3mcg
1iu vitamin D	=	0.025mcg
1iu vitamin E	=	0.7mcg

boost the immune system, to strengthen the skin and connective tissue, to protect the arteries, to assist brain function and in the transmission of nervous impulses, to list but a few.

Vitamins can be divided into two categories: the water-soluble vitamins, which are not stored in the body and which must be taken daily; and the fat-soluble vitamins, which can be stored in larger amounts. The table on pages 56–58 illustrates the variety of their actions and their best food sources.

Some vitamin pills also contain iron, and will be indicated as such. Iron is important for the correct functioning of the blood.

Minerals

The essential minerals in food go to make up only around 4 percent of your body tissues. Most of this is composed of the "macro-minerals" – calcium, magnesium, phosphorus, sodium, chloride, and potassium. These are largely involved with the structural part of the skeleton and the teeth, and as electrolytic salts in the blood and tissue fluids. Correct nutrition is vital to obtain sufficient amounts of these within the body because they are not as abundant as the "macronutrients." There are also fourteen or so "micro-minerals,"

Although it is preferable to get your vitamins as part of your regular diet, they can be taken in pill form, especially when large doses are required.

commonly called "trace elements" because they are only needed in trace amounts in the body and are found in very tiny amounts in foods. It is even more crucial to insure that this latter group of nutrients is adequately supplied by the diet in order to avoid deficiency.

Minerals, like vitamins, are essential for just about every process in the body. However, unlike vitamins, some minerals become incorporated into body structures, for example calcium, magnesium, and phosphorus which are found in the bones. Others are similar to vitamins in taking an essential role in metabolism, acting as coenzymes, for example magnesium, zinc, and copper. However, other minerals have very specific functions, such as iron, which has an important role as part of the structure of hemoglobin molecules.

As with the vitamins, many minerals are co-workers, so that the absence of one mineral severely disrupts the functions of other minerals, and ultimately disrupts the body's metabolism. The table of minerals and their functions on pages 59–61 shows how they work together and lists good food sources.

MINERALS AND THE BODY

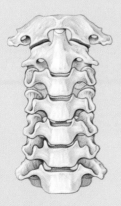
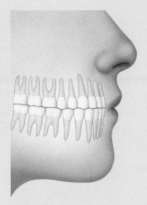

Bones require several minerals. Calcium, phosphorus, boron, fluorine, magnesium, manganese, and silicon are all essential.

Teeth, like bones, need calcium, phosphorus, and fluorine. Most calcium absorbed in the diet goes to the teeth and bones.

The production of red blood cells requires phosphorus and copper, while iron is the central element of the hemoglobin carried in the red cells.

The state of the skin is often a sign of how healthy the body's cells are overall. They depend on supplies of zinc, magnesium, iron, and other minerals.

GUIDE TO VITAMINS, MINERALS, AND TRACE ELEMENTS

Vitamin A • *Retinol and Beta-carotene*
Essential for normal vision (especially night vision), skin, mucous membranes of the respiratory, digestive, and urinary tracts, growth of bones and tissues, reproduction and immunity. It is fat-soluble.

Best food sources: Retinol – liver, fish liver oils. Beta-carotene – carrots and green leafy vegetables. Generally, the more intense the green/orange/red color of the vegetables, the higher the beta-carotene content.

Vitamin B₁ • *Thiamine*
Essential for releasing energy from carbohydrates, and for the integrity of the nervous system. It is water-soluble.

Best food sources: whole grains, seeds, beans, and nuts.

Mangoes are high in vitamin A – an essential nutrient for healthy bones and teeth.

Vitamin B₂ • *Riboflavin*
Essential for metabolizing carbohydrates, fats, and proteins. It is especially important in assisting many enzymes in the liver to enable the efficient removal of toxins. This vitamin is water-soluble.

Best food sources: kidney, liver, fish, milk, wheatgerm, broccoli, and green leafy vegetables.

Vitamin B₃ • *Niacin, Niacinamide/Nicotinamide*
Essential for releasing energy from carbohydrates, and the metabolism of proteins, fats, and polyunsaturated fatty acids. Additionally, it is vital for the formation of red blood cells and steroid hormones. It is water-soluble.

Best food sources: liver, poultry, fish, meat, peanuts, whole grains, eggs, and milk.

Green leafy vegetables are one of the best sources of vitamin B₂.

Vitamin B₅ • *Pantothenic Acid*
Essential for making glycogen (energy stores) and fatty acids in the body. Also required for making neuro-transmitter chemicals (chemicals that transfer nerve impulses from one nerve to the next), and for the steroid hormones (sex hormones) testosterone and estrogen. It is water-soluble.

Best food sources: peanuts, liver, kidney, egg yolks, fish, whole grains, beans, and nuts. Occurs in many foods.

Vitamin B₆ • *Pyridoxine, Pyridoxal-5-Phosphate*
Essential for protein and amino acid metabolism, for promoting a healthy cardiovascular system, and in producing hemoglobin (the oxygen-carrying pigment in blood). It is water-soluble.

Best food sources: wheatgerm, seeds, chicken, lamb, fish, eggs, bananas, avocados, soybeans, walnuts, and oats.

Bananas contain large amounts of B₆ which is beneficial to the heart and circulation.

Olive oil is an excellent source of vitamin E — essential for fighting the damaging effects of free radicals.

Vitamin B₁₂ • *Cyanocolbalamin*

Essential for efficient working of every cell in the body, especially those cells which undergo rapid turnover, such as red blood cells, the lining of the gut, and blood vessels. It is involved with the synthesis of D.N.A., the body's genetic material. In addition, it is essential for proper development and functioning of the nervous system, especially for the production of the myelin sheath which is found around nerves. It is water-soluble.

<u>Best food sources:</u> liver, oysters, poultry, fish, eggs, fermented foods like miso (fermented soybean paste), tempeh (fermented whole soybeans).

Folate • *Folic Acid, Folacin*

Essential for transporting co-enzymes needed for amino acid metabolism in the body. Especially needed by children during growth, and where cell turnover is rapid such as in red blood cells. It is required for the process of cell division, for a growing fetus, and is vital for development of the neural tube and the nervous system. It is water-soluble.

<u>Best food sources:</u> wheatgerm, fresh, dark-green leafy vegetables (especially spinach), beans, egg yolks, asparagus, whole wheat, lamb's liver, and salmon.

Note: Pregnant women should not use lamb's liver as a source of folate because of high vitamin A levels.

Biotin

Essential for helping enzymes in the manufacture of glycogen and fatty acids in the body, and in the production of prostaglandins (compounds involved with normal immune function). It is essential for normal growth and development of the skin, hair, nerves and bone marrow. It is water-soluble.

<u>Best food sources:</u> liver, sardines, egg yolks, soy, whole grains, nuts, and beans.

Note: Excessive intake of raw eggs can destroy biotin.

Vitamin C • *Ascorbate, Ascorbic Acid*

Essential for formation of collagen (part of the connective tissue in skin, and muscles), skin integrity, tissue repair, effective action of white cells and antibodies, and the immune system in general. Acts as an antioxidant, protecting vitamins A and E from free-radical damage. It helps to normalize blood cholesterol levels, and is involved with production of some adrenal hormones. It is water-soluble.

<u>Best food sources:</u> guava, Brussels sprouts, cranberries, blackcurrants, kiwi fruit, papaw (papaya), mango, sweet (bell) peppers, peas, broccoli, cauliflower, tomatoes, strawberries, and citrus fruit.

Vitamin D • *Cholecalciferol*

Essential for bone growth and balancing mineral levels within the body. It is needed for the proper absorption of calcium and phosphorus from the intestines. Sunlight on the skin will produce vitamin D. Like vitamin A, it is fat-soluble.

<u>Best food sources:</u> fish liver oils, fortified milk, and fatty fish. Unlikely to be deficient in the diet.

Vitamin E • *Tocopherol*

Essential as an antioxidant for protecting essential fatty acids (and, therefore, cell membranes and blood vessels) from oxidation damage due to free-radical activity. Also involved in the reproductive system. It is fat-soluble.

<u>Best food sources:</u> wheatgerm oil, wheatgerm, soybean oil, olive oil, egg yolk, liver, nuts (especially almonds and walnuts), and sunflower seeds and their oil.

Vitamin K • *Phylloquinone*

Essential for blood clotting, especially in new-born babies. It is fat-soluble.

<u>Best food sources:</u> raw cauliflower, green leafy vegetables. It is also made by the bacteria in the gut.

Raw cauliflower is rich in vitamin K, necessary for efficient blood clotting.

OTHER NUTRIENTS RELATED TO VITAMINS

Choline • *Phosphatidyl choline*

Essential as a neuro-transmitter in the brain and nervous system, and as a "fat mobilizer" in the liver.

Best food sources: soy lecithin, egg yolks, liver, fish, and whole grains. The body can make it from other nutrients.

Inositol

Essential for the normal metabolism of calcium and insulin. May also be involved in fatty acid metabolism.

Best food sources: soy lecithin, egg yolks, liver, fish, citrus fruit (except lemons), milk, nuts, and whole grains. The body can make it from other nutrients.

Eggs are a good dietary source of choline, a vitamin that is needed for the production of neuro-transmitters.

Co-enzyme Q10 • *Ubiquinone*

Essential for all energy production within the cell as part of the electron transport system, immunity, heart function, and as an antioxidant.

Best food sources: heart and other organ meats, meat, egg yolk, milk fat, wheatgerm, and whole grains.

Bioflavonoids

There are over 500 different bioflavonoid compounds and they are almost all substances needed by plants for photosynthesis. They increase the potency of antioxidants and maintain cell membranes, especially those lining blood vessels, and collagen.

Best food sources: white rind of citrus fruit, vegetables, buckwheat, and honey.

All vegetables are packed with bioflavonoids — essential for healthy cell membranes and capillaries.

Pyrolloquinolone Quinone • *P.Q.Q.*

Involved in collagen metabolism.

Best food source: fresh citrus fruit.

P.Q.Q., found in citrus fruit, is vital for the manufacture of collagen.

Carnitine

Helps in carriage of fats and fatty acids in the blood.

Best food source: lamb, chicken; animal foods in general. Can be made in the body.

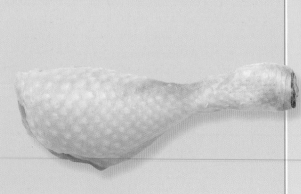

Carnitine contributes to the efficient carriage of fats in the blood — chicken is a good source.

THE MACROMINERALS

Calcium

Essential for bones and teeth, where most dietary calcium is found. The remainder moves in and out of cells allowing conduction of impulses between nerves, and the contraction of muscles. Excess calcium depresses magnesium levels.

Best food sources: cooked bones (as in canned fish), whitebait, homemade fish stock, tofu, sesame seeds, yogurt, turnip greens, broccoli, milk and dairy products.

Magnesium

Essential as a component of bone, and in general body metabolism where it is part of over 300 enzymes. It is also needed for the oxidation of glycogen for energy, muscle relaxation, and in the formation of new proteins within each body cell. Excess magnesium depresses calcium levels.

Best food sources: whole grains (especially cooked millet), lima beans, taco shells, black-eyed peas, seeds, wheatgerm, dried apricots, dark green vegetables, soybeans, buckwheat, and fish.

Phosphorus

Essential for bone formation and production of red blood cells. A vital part of A.T.P. (Adenosine Tri-Phosphate) which is the chemical energy store in every cell of the body, and D.N.A.

Best food sources: meats, fish, and whole grains.

Note: many processed foods are very high in phosphorus. When these foods make up a large part of the diet, the excess phosphorus causes imbalance with other minerals.

Sesame seeds are an excellent source of immune-boosting calcium and magnesium.

Sodium

One of the body's electrolytes, which are electrically charged atoms (together with potassium and chloride), performing essential functions in the cells. Sodium is the main cation (positively charged electrolyte) in the extra-cellular fluid. There is too much sodium in most people's diet. Even if you never use convenience foods, and never add common salt to your food, you will still obtain sufficient sodium from vegetables.

Chloride

Another of the body's electrolytes. It is the main anion (negatively charged electrolyte) in the extra-cellular fluid. Along with sodium, most diets contain too much chloride, as common salt (sodium chloride). A healthy, balanced diet, such as the New Pyramid program, will contain sufficient chloride.

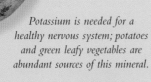

Potassium is needed for a healthy nervous system; potatoes and green leafy vegetables are abundant sources of this mineral.

Potassium

The third of the body's electrolytes. It is the main cation (positively charged electrolyte) within the cells. It interacts with sodium and chloride in maintaining an optimum environment in and around each body cell. Like other electrolytes, it allows transmission of nerve impulses, and maintains the body's water balance and normal heart rate.

Best food sources: tomato paste, dried apricots, figs, bananas, pumpkin seeds, almonds, soybeans, potatoes (especially baked), green leafy vegetables, fish, avocados, beans, fruit, and vegetables.

THE MICROMINERALS (TRACE ELEMENTS)

Boron

Essential for the manufacture of many hormones, and is involved in bone formation via its possible role in the balance of estrogen.

Best food sources: alfalfa, cabbage, lettuce, peas, soybeans, almonds, hazelnuts, apples, prunes, raisins, and dates.

Cobalt

Forms an essential part of the vitamin B12.

Best food sources: liver, kidney, oyster, meat, fish, and sea vegetables.

The beneficial amounts of copper contained in cashews help to maintain the production of blood cells and hormones.

Chromium

Essential for efficient glucose metabolism (as Glucose Tolerance Factor), insulin production, fatty acid metabolism, and protein metabolism.

Best food sources: whole grains, shellfish, liver, pulses (legumes), black pepper, and molasses.

Copper

Essential for many enzymes, especially those controlling normal production of blood cells and hormones. Too much copper will depress zinc levels.

Best food sources: organ meat, seafood, cherries, nuts (especially cashews), olives, and cocoa.

Fluorine

Important for bone and tooth structure, and may help to prevent heart disease.

Best food sources: seafood, meat, and tea.

Seafood has a high fluorine content – vital for strong bones and teeth.

Iron

The main function of iron is as the central element in the oxygen-carrying blood pigment hemoglobin.

Best food sources: cockles, molasses, cocoa, liver, meats, wheatgerm, clams, prunes, seaweed, and spinach.

Note: animal sources of iron are absorbed better than vegetable forms. Absorption of iron is enhanced by taking vitamin C at the same meal.

Iodine

Forms part of thyroxine, the thyroid hormone, which regulates energy production in the body.

Best food sources: haddock, mackerel, cod, live yogurt, seaweed, and iodized salt.

Manganese

Essential for normal formation of bone and cartilage, and for control of glucose metabolism. It is also part of the antioxidant superoxide dismutase which helps prevent free radical damage.

Best food sources: whole grains, rice bran, wheatgerm, black tea, nuts, ginger, and cloves.

Needed for the formation of bone and cartilage, manganese can be obtained from ginger.

Molybdenum

Forms part of at least three enzyme systems, and is an important antioxidant.

<u>Best food sources:</u> wholegrains, pulses (legumes), buckwheat, wheatgerm, liver, and sunflower seeds.

Selenium

Essential for many key enzymes in the body. It is an antioxidant, neutralizing free radicals.

<u>Best food sources:</u> Brazil nuts, molasses, cashews, soybeans, tuna, seafood, meat, and whole grains. Also present in many vegetables, but the amount is dependent upon the presence of selenium in the soil. Many soils are now very deficient in this mineral.

Silicon

Involved in normal bone growth, and is needed for healthy skin, hair, and membranes.

<u>Best food sources:</u> whole grains and seaweed.

Seaweed contains silicon, important for healthy skin and hair.

Vanadium

Vanadium is an interesting mineral, in that the latest research indicates its involvement in the sodium/potassium pump mechanism that is present in all cells, and may implicate the mineral in instances where there is an inability to lose weight.

<u>Best food sources:</u> black pepper, soy oil, corn oil, olive oil, olives.

Nickel

Essential for normal growth.

<u>Best food sources:</u> widely distributed in fruit and vegetables. Tiny amounts transfer from stainless steel pans.

Vital for growth, nickel is found in most vegetables.

Zinc

Essential for metabolism, as zinc forms part of many enzymes involved in cell growth, immunity, production of testosterone (the male hormone), sperm formation, and sexuality. It is also required for normal production of stomach acid. Too much zinc will depress copper levels.

<u>Best food sources:</u> seafood (especially oysters), popcorn, pumpkin seeds, sesame seeds, fish, wheatgerm, meat, and eggs.

Eat popcorn for its zinc content – essential for wound healing, and healthy growth and repair of cells.

Other minerals found in the human body include cadmium, germanium, tin, aluminium, arsenic, barium, bromine, gold, lead, mercury, and strontium. It is not yet clear whether these are actually required by the body in the minute amounts in which they are found, or whether they are truly toxic trace impurities from the environment.

Excesses of Vitamins and Minerals

As long as you obtain your vitamins and minerals from good wholesome food sources in a balanced diet (as in the "diets" in this book), there is no need to worry about possible "overdosing." However, warnings have been issued about pregnant women and high vitamin A levels in liver, where excess vitamin A has been recorded as possibly producing birth defects. However, if you follow the advice given in this book with regard to eating a range of protein types, then there is very little possibility of consuming excess vitamin A. To be on the safe side, pregnant women should avoid eating liver. Beta-carotene, the plant version of vitamin A, is non-toxic even at very high levels.

Oranges are widely thought to be high in vitamin C, but some other fruits are higher, and some supermarket oranges have been found to have none.

If, however, you wish to use supplements to enhance your diet, a table of normal levels and toxic limits is given opposite. Research to assess more accurately the toxic levels of minerals and vitamins is still underway, and in view of current uncertainty the levels here err on the side of caution.

Apart from possible vitamin A toxicity, vitamin B6 and vitamin C have also been reported to cause problems in high doses. Extensive testing of B6 for toxicity has shown that the reported effects of nerve damage when B6 is taken in excess are due to information from isolated cases, where as much as 500mg per day was taken over a period of years. All reports point to the fact that B6 (especially when taken as pyridoxal-5-phosphate with its cofactor zinc) taken on a daily basis of up to 100mg is generally considered safe. This is reflected by the amounts listed in common vitamin B6 supplements.

To be safe, pregnant women should avoid eating liver, though reasonable quantities of vitamin A (as beta-carotene) are not harmful.

With large amounts of vitamin C the reported problem is that in some cases it has been thought to have contributed to the formation of kidney stones, but most of the scientific evidence indicates that supplementation up to a level of around 3,000mg (3g) per day is safe. There is some research that suggests that vitamin C might increase the potency of the contraceptive pill, and although very recent information contradicts this, it would be wise for all women taking the pill to keep their vitamin C supplementation at the lower levels. Generally all that happens if you take a little too much vitamin C is that it acts as a laxative. A slight reduction in the daily amount will correct this.

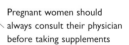

Pregnant women should always consult their physician before taking supplements

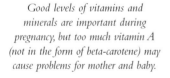

Good levels of vitamins and minerals are important during pregnancy, but too much vitamin A (not in the form of beta-carotene) may cause problems for mother and baby.

ADULT DAILY RANGES OF VITAMINS AND MINERALS

VITAMINS	OPTIMUM RANGE	MAXIMUM SAFETY LEVEL
A	5,000 – 10,000IU*	25,000IU*
B$_1$	25 – 100mg	140mg
B$_2$	25 – 100mg	140mg
B$_3$	50 – 150mg	180mg
B$_5$	50 – 300mg	400mg
B$_6$ (as Pyridoxal)	50 – 100mg	200mg
B$_{12}$	5 – 100mcg	300mcg
Biotin	50 – 500mcg	10,000mcg
Folic Acid	50 – 400mcg	2,000mcg
C	1,000 – 3,000mg	5,000mg
D	400 – 1,000IU	2,000IU
E	50 – 800IU	1,500IU

* For women during childbearing period, maximum safety level of retinol is 8,000IU; the same caution does not apply to beta-carotene. All pregnant women should discuss their supplement needs with their physician prior to taking nutritional supplements.

MINERALS	OPTIMUM RANGE	MAXIMUM SAFETY LEVEL
Boron	3 – 6mg	40mg
Calcium	400 – 800mg	2,500mg
Chromium	50 – 250mcg	500mcg
Copper	1 – 3mg	5mg
Iodine	50 – 200mcg	1,000mcg
Iron	10 – 25mg	50mg
Magnesium	300 – 500mg	1,000mg
Manganese	5 – 25mg	100mg
Potassium	100 – 500mg	5,000mg
Selenium	50 – 250mcg	450mcg
Zinc	15 – 30mg	50mg

The optimum range reflects the levels of vitamins and minerals available in nutritional supplements at the time of going to press. Maximum dosage ("maximum safety level") should be used in the short term only, and only under the supervision and guidance of a practitioner.

Vitamins and minerals come in various forms, the most popular of which are tablets, capsules, or powders.

VITAMIN E CAPSULES

POWDERED CALCIUM

Proper Use of Supplements

There is a vast range of nutritional supplements on the market, making it very difficult for the layperson to choose. As a general precaution, you would be best advised only to self-prescribe the multiformulas which cover a broad spectrum of nutrients in one capsule or tablet (minerals, vitamins, herbs, and nutritional "accessories"), since taking isolated nutrient supplements can have a disastrous effect on the fine tuning of metabolism. If you feel that your health problems require specific supplementation, it would be safer (and cheaper in the long run) to obtain the help of a nutritional therapist (*see* Useful Addresses, page 248, for registers).

There are some excellent, high-quality products on the market, and there are some that are nearly useless. Generally, you get what you pay for. Some prices may seem excessive, but usually this reflects the high level of research, preparation, and quality control that goes into their production. Furthermore, to get the very best out of your supplement regime there are a few basic principles that need to be considered. These relate to the variability in the absorption rate of different nutrients. For example, some nutrients, such as vitamin E, are very easily absorbed, while others, like manganese, may have a maximum absorption of around three percent. Additionally, almost all nutrients have other nutrients, which help their absorption (these are synergists), and some which hinder their absorption (antagonists). The way they are cooked or prepared may also affect how well they are absorbed. Absorption rates of nutrients in food and in supplements can be increased by following the simple guidelines below and opposite.

HOW TO IMPROVE NUTRIENT ABSORPTION

- Keep alcohol and supplements separate – alcohol will leach these supplements immediately. The one exception is vitamin C which can help counterbalance the effects of alcohol.

- Avoid drinking tea and coffee at meal times, or within one hour either side of taking your supplement – these beverages have a leaching effect on nutrients.

- Do not smoke for at least 30 minutes either side of a meal or taking supplements – the chemicals in tobacco smoke have a leaching effect on nutrients and use up antioxidants in the process.

- Eat slowly – stressful activities (like eating too fast) can impair digestion and prevent absorption.

- Fat-soluble vitamins are best taken with meals that contain some fat – this will help "escort" them into the body.

- Foods high in B-complex vitamins (e.g., cereals), and vitamin B-complex supplements are best taken early in the day, since they kick-start the metabolism.

- Calming supplements like magnesium, calcium, and zinc are best taken half an hour or so before bedtime.

- Take a combined multiformula supplement in the morning, but an hour after breakfast cereal.

- Never take supplements, especially those containing minerals, on an empty stomach; they may bring on nausea. Amino acids, and some probiotics are an exception to this rule.

- Never take "single" supplements except under the guidance of a nutritional therapist.

- Begin and stop taking supplements gradually to give your body time to readjust.

- Eat adequate levels of a good variety of fiber, and some live yogurt (or a probiotic supplement) to enhance absorption rates by keeping the intestines healthy.

Supplementary vitamins should not be taken within an hour of drinking tea or coffee.

HOW TO GET THE BEST USE FROM SUPPLEMENTS

Get the best out of your supplement by taking it at the appropriate time and with "helpers"
in supplement form or obtained from food if possible, which will have a beneficial effect on its absorption.

SUPPLEMENT	WHEN TO TAKE	HELPERS	HINDERERS
Vitamin A	With fatty food	Zinc, vitamins E and C	Lack of bile
Vitamin D	With fatty food	Calcium, phosphorus, vitamins E and C, sunlight	Lack of bile
Vitamin E	With fatty food	Selenium, vitamin C	Ferric iron, fried food
Vitamin B1	Early in day	Vitamin B-complex, manganese	Alcohol, stress, antibiotics, cooking
Vitamin B2	Early in day	Vitamin B-complex	Alcohol, stress, antibiotics, tobacco, cooking
Vitamin B3	Early in day	Vitamin B-complex	Alcohol, stress, antibiotics, cooking
Vitamin B5	Early in day	Vitamin B-complex, biotin, folic acid	Stress, antibiotics, cooking
Vitamin B6	Early in day	Magnesium, zinc, Vitamin B-complex	Alcohol, stress, antibiotics, cooking
Vitamin B12	Early in day	Calcium, vitamin B-complex, folic acid	Alcohol, stress, antibiotics, cooking, internal parasites
Folic Acid	Early in day	Vitamin C, B-complex	Alcohol, stress, antibiotics
Biotin	Early in day	Vitamin B-complex	Stress, avidin in raw egg white, antibiotics
Choline	Early in day	Vitamin B5	Alcohol, stress, antibiotics
Inositol	Early in day	Choline	Alcohol, stress, antibiotics
Vitamin C	Between meals	Hydrochloric acid (HCl)	Heavy metals, cooking
Calcium	With protein food or at bedtime	Magnesium, vitamin D, HCl	Tea, coffee, smoking, phytic acid
Magnesium	With protein food or at bedtime	Calcium, vitamin B6, vitamin D, HCl	Tea, coffee, smoking, alcohol, excess iron
Iron	With any food (though it will impede uptake of dietary minerals)	Vitamin C, HCl	Tea, coffee, smoking, oxalic acid, phytic acid
Zinc	With food or at bedtime	Vitamin B6 and vitamin C, HCl	Phytic acid, lead, copper, calcium, tea, coffee, alcohol, excess iron
Manganese	With protein food	Vitamin C, HCl	High dosage zinc, tea, coffee, smoking, iron
Selenium	With food	Vitamin E, HCl	Mercury, tea, coffee, smoking, excess vitamin C, excess iron
Chromium	With protein food	Vitamin B3, HCl	Tea, coffee, smoking, iron
Iodine	With protein food	Manganese	Tea, coffee, smoking
Molybdenum	With any food	Vitamin B-complex	Tea, coffee, smoking

ANTIOXIDANTS

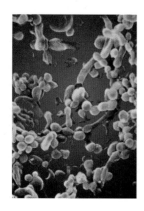

The products of oxidation help cells fight micro-organisms.

D URING THE LAST FEW YEARS *or so, research has confirmed that many of the common diseases and ailments of the 20th century (cardiovascular disease, diabetes, cataracts, high blood pressure, infertility, gum disease, respiratory infections, rheumatoid arthritis, Alzheimer's disease, some cancers, and even mental illness), are associated with tissue deficiency and/or low dietary levels of compounds called "antioxidants." From a medical context these substances are comparatively new, but in other branches of science they have been around for a long time. Oxidation is a natural occurence in the world of chemistry and biology.*

Life could not exist without the presence of oxygen; it is the basis of all plant and animal life on this planet. Without it we could not release the energy from our food, and without energy the body can do nothing. Furthermore, scavenger cells in our immune system use some of the products of oxidation as weapons against invading micro-organisms. Although it is obviously biologically necessary, oxidation is damaging to whatever is oxidized, but our bodies are forced to risk the damage to obtain the energy they need to function.

Because oxygen is chemically a very reactive element it can be highly dangerous if not regulated, producing too many "oxidized" molecules inside the body, and creating havoc. You only have to think of what happens if a fire occurs near a supply of oxygen.

During all normal biochemical reactions, oxygen reacts readily to "oxidize" other molecules in its vicinity. If there is nothing available to control this, a cascade of reactions can occur in which the oxidized molecules, which are called "free radicals," become unstable. Any damage likely to occur is kept to a minimum by an army of antioxidant substances.

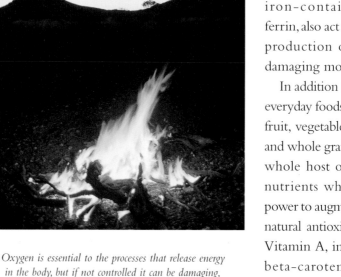

Oxygen is essential to the processes that release energy in the body, but if not controlled it can be damaging, causing deterioration of the cells, aging, and disease.

What are Antioxidants?

Antioxidants are substances which retard or prevent deterioration, damage, or destruction caused by oxidation. Fortunately, the body has an army of antioxidants for damage limitation. A family of antioxidant enzymes are provided in healthy tissue, together with substances like cysteine and glutathione. Blood constituents, like the iron-containing transferrin, also act to prevent the production of oxidative-damaging molecules.

In addition to these, many everyday foods – particularly fruit, vegetables, seeds, nuts, and whole grains – contain a whole host of antioxidant nutrients which have the power to augment the body's natural antioxidant capacity. Vitamin A, in the form of beta-carotene (found in orange and dark green fruit and vegetables), vitamin C (found in fruit and vegetables), vitamin E (found in cereals and seeds), selenium and zinc (found in nuts, seeds, and seafood) are all excellent antioxidants.

Under normal circumstances, when cells utilize oxygen and nutrients to make A.T.P. (the basic energy molecule), the free radicals generated are removed by the system of antioxidant enzymes and nutrients.

Oxygen is the basis of all plant and animal life on the planet. However, if its action is not controlled within an organism by antioxidants, it can lead to the destruction of the very life form that depends upon it.

Oxygen is essential to making the Earth the planet it is. It is a major constituent of the atmosphere, and is one of two elements that make up our most precious resource, water.

The free radicals are deactivated and then recycled by the body again. For example, hydrogen peroxide is converted into oxygen and water. If there are plentiful amounts of high-energy molecules, essential nutrients, water, and antioxidant enzymes, cell damage is minimized.

However, if any of these components are missing, cell damage, aging, and disease follow. The body will employ antioxidant nutrients, such as beta-carotene, vitamin E, vitamin C, molybdenum, selenium, zinc, and reduced glutathione, to mop up any free radicals that escape the antioxidant enzymes, but these nutrients do this several times more slowly than the antioxidant enzymes. Nevertheless, they are incredibly important in this "rear-guard" action.

Additionally, a good way to boost enzyme potential is to eat foods in their raw state. Raw vegetables and fruit contain significant amounts of enzymes which are released when the food is chewed – a good reason for chewing food thoroughly. The two main digestive enzymes are amylase and protease, which are found in many foods, but are destroyed the longer food is cooked; hence the importance of raw food in the diet. Some foods such as apples, grapes, mango, mushrooms, and honey also contain the antioxidant enzymes known as peroxidase and catalase.

Contrary to general opinion, a major proportion of food enzymes are not denatured by stomach acid and can actually remain active throughout the digestive tract, so that a good 50 percent of them reach the colon (large intestine or bowel) unaltered. At this point, they are able to bring about changes in the intestinal environment by binding any free oxygen and preventing free radical damage, reducing the potential for fermentation and putrefaction (factors linked to colon cancer), and helping to create conditions in which the beneficial lactic-acid forming bacteria, such as *Lactobacillus acidophilus*, can grow.

How Free Radicals Cause Damage

Free radicals are produced wherever combustion occurs, so they will arise from tobacco smoke, exhaust fumes, radiation, and fried or barbecued food. In addition, the "normal" oxidation processes occurring in cells will produce their own range of free radicals. Furthermore, free radicals can also arise from industrial pollution, too much sun on the skin, infection, excessive exercise, and even stress.

When free radicals are present in excess, this can lead to cellular damage, because important fatty acids and proteins in cell membranes become unstable and their "traffic-directing" effect of balancing the flow of nutrients in and out of the cells becomes ineffective. When the cell membrane is oxidized, it is either hardened so that nutrients cannot get into the cell, or it may be punctured so that the cell collapses as the cell fluid drains out.

This process leads to a very familiar sign of aging – wrinkles! The skin cells collapse and harden and this makes the skin sag and take on a leathery look.

Not only structural oils are at risk, but dietary oils are, too. Any good diet (such as the New Pyramid program) should encourage the inclusion of foods rich in polyunsaturated oils but it must, at the same time, increase the amount of antioxidant nutrients (beta-carotene, vitamins C and E, selenium, etc.) to allow some degree of protection for these oils so that they can be built up appropriately into cellular structures. For example, when stir-frying vegetables in olive oil, the addition of raw garlic (which is full of antioxidants) to the mixture may protect the heated oil. Also, when undertaking a detoxification program, foods or supplements that are high in polyunsaturated oils should be minimized because the dietary oils could produce free radicals themselves and add to the oxidative stress of such a program.

Free radicals are produced whenever anything is burned, so even a relaxing barbecue will release them.

Pollution is one of the greatest causes of free radicals at a level at which the body cannot cope.

Another common effect of oxidative damage in the body is inflammation, common forms of which are arthritis, bursitis, and gout. This inflammation occurs when free radicals gain entry to the synovial fluid inside the joint and cause it to lose its lubricating quality by oxidation of the lipids (fats) in the synovial "oil."

CELL DAMAGE

When free radicals enter cells they may damage the D.N.A. (the genetic material of the cell), causing inappropriate cell division and other changes that might lead to the development of tumors and cancers.

In chemical terms, free radicals damage cell tissue by "stealing" electrons from nearby molecules which are otherwise electrically "balanced," in order to bring themselves back into balance. The neighboring molecule which has been "robbed," then turns to its neighbor and steals further electrons to rebalance itself, and so it goes on. In biological terms, with excess free radical activity in our bodies, we are destroying more cells than we can create. Free radicals can thus cause cellular damage on a large scale; they are capable of causing arterial damage and inflammation, triggering cancer, and speeding up the aging process.

Increasing evidence demonstrates that oxidative damage is commonly behind the aging process, and diseases associated with it. Years of research have shown that free radicals are the major cause of cell damage in many of the degenerative diseases of our time. Anyone interested in keeping at bay the signs of aging and associated decline into degenerative disease would do well to increase their intake of antioxidant nutrients.

A diet that is high in antioxidant nutrients will help to combat the aging effects of free radicals.

The signs of aging are visible manifestations of cell damage, often caused by free radicals.

Overexposure to the sun and a diet high in fried food leads to premature wrinkles

Free radicals can cause inflammation of the joints

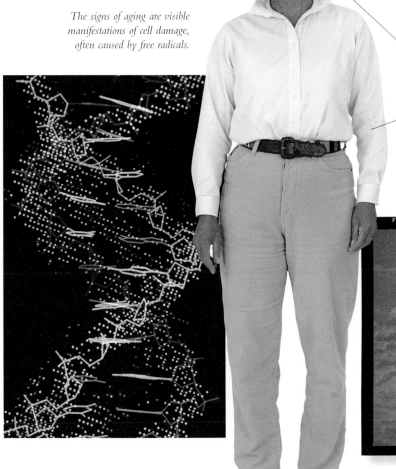

The famous double-helix structure of the DNA molecule. A cell's DNA is damaged when free radicals invade it.

The harm that too much exposure to the sun causes is now widely recognized; the sunlight creates free radicals.

The Effects of Age and Stress

As we have seen, there are several enzymes, made by the body, which control reactive free radicals. The names of some of these enzymes are superoxide dismutase (S.O.D.), catalase, glutathione peroxidase, and methione reductase. Recent research indicates that cellular production of some of these enzymes decreases markedly with age. It is becoming increasingly likely, therefore, that the balance between your body's antioxidant enzyme level (plus your intake of antioxidant nutrients and/or supplements), and your exposure to the huge variety of environmental and internally produced free radicals, is the deciding factor in whether your pathway in life is one of good health.

The unfortunate truth is that many things which cause free radical stress in our lives are unavoidable. For example, if you live in a city, it is impossible to avoid car exhaust fumes. However, one of the best ways to reduce the amount of free radical damage is to eat foods, such as vegetables, fruit, and whole grains, that contain high levels of antioxidants. We need also to remove, as far as possible, the stress in our lives, and change the way in which we react to unavoidable stress.

Each day most of us are exposed to stress. It comes in many forms, which can be divided into three major categories:

* *Chemical stress, from pesticides, insecticides, heavy metals, asbestos, polluted air, polluted water, polluted food, and sub-optimum nutrition, radioactive waste, and radiation and ozone during airplane travel.*
* *Emotional stress, from family and relationship problems, overwork, financial problems, loss of job, etc.*
* *Physical trauma, from injuries, surgery, and infection.*

The common denominator in all forms of stress is the overproduction of cell-damaging free radicals. Under normal conditions, free radicals, such as superoxides, are kept in check by antioxidant enzymes such as S.O.D. When we are exposed to any type of stress, the production of superoxides, particularly hydroxyl, increases dramatically, and the normal levels of S.O.D. may not be sufficient to neutralize their activity. The hormone melatonin, which is manufactured in the body while we sleep, can detoxify the hydroxyl free radical, giving us another good reason to insure we have our full quota of "beauty sleep."

The major way that stress harms us is by weakening our immune system. It is perhaps easy to see why people are falling prey to viruses like A.I.D.S. An overloaded immune system trying to process thousands of toxic chemicals (both from within and from outside the body) is not going to be very effective when an immune-suppressing virus like A.I.D.S. comes along. (However, even an optimum diet will not prevent the onset of A.I.D.S. if care is not taken in other areas, such as not using condoms or sharing hypodermic needles.) It is imperative, therefore, to use stress-reducing techniques in an attempt to minimize the overall level of stress in our lives. Additionally, to maintain a healthy immune system we must employ optimum nutrition and effective lifestyle changes, to combat those stress-producers in our lives which we are powerless to change.

Stress, sadly one of the common characteristics of modern life, weakens our bodies' immune systems.

Melatonin neutralizes hydroxyl, which is a common free radical. Melatonin is made by the body during sleep.

By taking you to a deeper level of rest than sleep, meditation is a powerful way of restoring balance to your life.

Most meditators find that their breathing naturally becomes easier and calmer

Meditation involves relaxing physical tension

Meditation lets mind and body come into harmony with each other

The speed of modern life makes it difficult to avoid stress altogether.

ANTIOXIDANT ENZYMES

The body creates several enzymes that combat free radicals. When they cannot control the free radicals, possibly because there are too many, then the body is prone to certain identifiable diseases and conditions.

ENZYME	FREE RADICAL ACTED UPON	DISEASES/CONDITIONS RELATED TO EXCESS FREE RADICALS
S.O.D.	Superoxide	*Arthritis, bursitis, gout.*
Catalase	Hydrogen peroxide	*Arthritis, bursitis, gout.*
Glutathione-peroxidase	Lipid peroxides and Hydrogen peroxide	*Heart disease, liver disease, premature aging, skin cancer, eczema, wrinkling, age spots, dermatitis, psoriasis.*
Methione reductase	Hydroxyl	*Poor recovery from excessive exercise, radiation damage.*

Antioxidant Nutrients

The good news is that, in addition to the antioxidant enzymes and hormones such as melatonin made by the body, we have another weapon against free radical molecules. These are the group of nutrient antioxidants, mentioned earlier, which work to protect our cells from oxidative damage. Some antioxidants are vitamins, such as vitamin A (and beta-carotene), vitamin C, and vitamin E. Others are minerals, such as selenium, zinc, and molybdenum. Additional nutrients, such as L-glutathione, N-acetyl cysteine, and Co-enzyme Q10, all display antioxidant activity. Yet others, not strictly essential to the body, nevertheless show excellent antioxidant activity. These include such compounds as anthocyanidins, bioflavonoids, lycopene, pycnogenol, and, possibly, hundreds of other recently identified natural chemicals found in common everyday fresh foods. Many herbs also contain excellent ranges of antioxidants and are now being included in the list. For example, *Ginkgo biloba* is a particularly efficient scavenger of the hydroxyl radical.

There has been a great deal of research carried out recently on a whole range of antioxidant nutrients, and the conclusions in general show that these substances have a profound effect on aging and the degenerative diseases of this modern age. As one might expect, the protective qualities of antioxidant nutrients increase with concentration of the different nutrients, and many researchers and physicians are suggesting that supplementation of the diet may be necessary to achieve this protection.

Many of these researchers and physicians are dealing with patients whose diet has been less than optimum for a number of years, so that the idea of artificial supplementation is the best way to treat them. However, anyone embarking on the New Pyramid program, especially if organic foods are consumed, is likely to have a diet much higher in these health-promoting substances. Nevertheless, supplementing the New Pyramid program with a multi-antioxidant supplement will do no harm and will probably help to speed up the healing process for many individuals. Some of the research work that has been carried out on antioxidants indicates that the risk of heart disease, cancer, and many other degenerative diseases such as arthritis and diabetes can be reduced even with short-term use. Vitamin C, together with its related bioflavonoids, beta-carotene, and vitamin E, have been given particular attention.

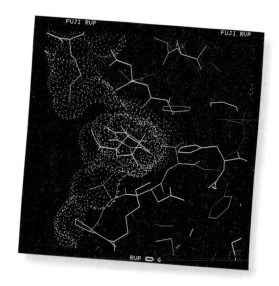

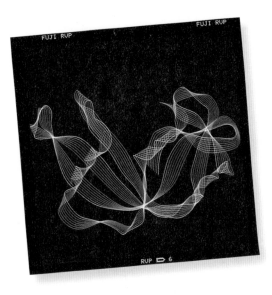

Certain herbs and plants, including Ginkgo biloba, *have excellent antioxidant levels.*

Computer graphic representations of antioxidant enzymes which help the body fight free radicals.

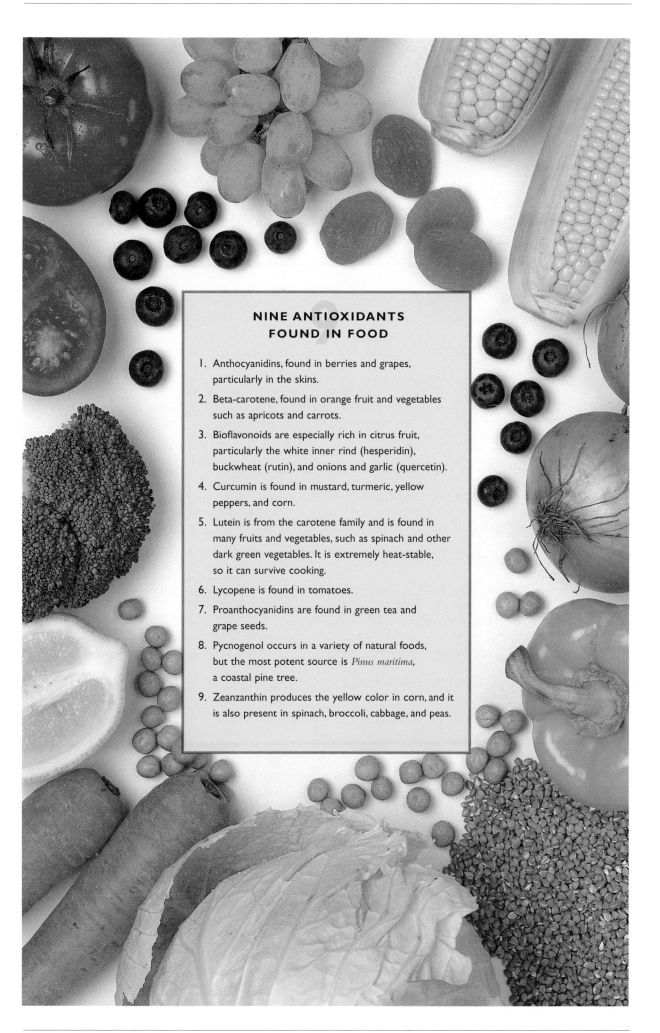

NINE ANTIOXIDANTS FOUND IN FOOD

1. Anthocyanidins, found in berries and grapes, particularly in the skins.

2. Beta-carotene, found in orange fruit and vegetables such as apricots and carrots.

3. Bioflavonoids are especially rich in citrus fruit, particularly the white inner rind (hesperidin), buckwheat (rutin), and onions and garlic (quercetin).

4. Curcumin is found in mustard, turmeric, yellow peppers, and corn.

5. Lutein is from the carotene family and is found in many fruits and vegetables, such as spinach and other dark green vegetables. It is extremely heat-stable, so it can survive cooking.

6. Lycopene is found in tomatoes.

7. Proanthocyanidins are found in green tea and grape seeds.

8. Pycnogenol occurs in a variety of natural foods, but the most potent source is *Pinus maritima*, a coastal pine tree.

9. Zeanzanthin produces the yellow color in corn, and it is also present in spinach, broccoli, cabbage, and peas.

Phytochemicals

There is one further group of substances that play a part in nutritional science. These substances are known as the "phytochemicals."

Phytochemicals are not properly classified as nutrients since our lives do not depend on them in the same way that they do with proteins, carbohydrates, fats, vitamins, and minerals. Nevertheless, they play a vital role in our body's biochemistry and, therefore, have a direct relevance to our health.

Phytochemicals are closely related to antioxidants and, in some cases, merge with them. They are biologically active compounds that are widely found in everyday foods, such as fruit, vegetables, and some grains (*see* the table below for the best food sources). So far, well over a hundred of these substances have been isolated and identified, and many of them appear to have an important effect in regulating the hormonal (endocrine) and immune systems, and hence can help prevent disease.

IMPORTANT PHYTOCHEMICALS

This table lists some of the most important phytochemicals and the food sources in which they are found, and describes their roles in healing or in the prevention of disease.

PHYTOCHEMICAL	FOUND IN	IMPORTANT FOR
Allium compounds	Garlic, onions, leeks, chives, and shallots	*Proper function of the cardiovascular and immune systems.*
Capsaicin	Hot peppers	*Protecting D.N.A. from damage; pain relief.*
Chlorophyll and carotenoids	All dark green and orange vegetables, germinated wheat grains (*wheat grass*), and seaweed.	*Healthy red blood cells, protecting against cancer, killing germs, and acting as a wound healer.*
Coumarins and clorogenic acid	Tomatoes, sweet green peppers, pineapples, strawberries, and carrots	*Preventing the formation of cancer-causing nitrosamines in the gut.*
Genistein	Soybeans	*Preventing the growth of tumors; balancing estrogen.*
Ginkgolides	*Ginkgo biloba*	*Specifically acting as an antioxidant in the brain.*
Glucosinolate	Brussels sprouts, cabbage, broccoli, and caulitlower	*Enhancing detoxification enzyme activity.*
Ellagic acid	Strawberries, grapes, and raspberries	*Neutralizing carcinogens before damage occurs.*
Isoflavones	Soybeans	*Reducing tumor formation.*
Isothiocyanates and Indoles	Broccoli, Brussels sprouts, cabbage, cauliflower, cress, kale, horseradish, mustard, radish, and turnip	*Preventing some forms of cancer (especially colon cancer) by deactivating carcinogens.*
Lentinan	Shiitake mushrooms	*Preventing cancer by stimulating the immune system.*
Lignans	Fibrous vegetables (*runner beans, carrots, etc.*)	*Normalizing estrogen activity.*
Phyto-estrogens	Soy (tofu and miso), pulses (*legumes*), citrus fruit, wheat, licorice, alfalfa, fennel, rhubarb, aniseed, and ginseng	*Binding xeno-estrogens from the environment; helping with menopausal symptoms, fibroids and other hormone-related problems; reducing the risk of breast cancer.*
Saponins (Diosgenin)	Mexican yams	*Stimulating adrenal glands, and the production of progesterone and other sex hormones.*
Sterols (Plant)	Red wine, and chocolate	*Preventing oxidation of "bad" (L.D.L.) cholesterol.*
Sulforaphane (from Glucosinolate)	Broccoli, cauliflower, kale, brussels sprouts, and turnips	*Helping to boost the production of anti-cancer enzymes.*
Tocotrienols	Palm oil, barley oil, rice oil, and rice bran	*Helping lower cholesterol.*

You now have a wealth of information at your fingertips with regard to:

- *the basics for healthy eating.*
- *a good basic diet – given in the explanation of the New Pyramid program.*
- *the nutrient composition of foods.*
- *the natural protective substances available.*
- *some knowledge of the powerful healing properties of food.*

Building on the knowledge given of how foods work in the body and the particular healing abilities of some of them, the next part of the book will show how to look at your own situation and how to identify potential improvements. The principle here is that we are each unique and cannot simply apply universal remedies. With this in mind, everyone reading this book should be able to fulfill their absolute full potential for nutritional healing.

ANTIOXIDANT/PHYTOCHEMICAL FOOD CHOICES

In order to obtain a good quantity of antioxidants and phytochemicals, choose one item from as many of these groups as possible every day. For variety, make a different choice each day. These are the best vegetables, fruit, whole grains, seeds, nuts, and so on, to eat as part of your New Pyramid program.

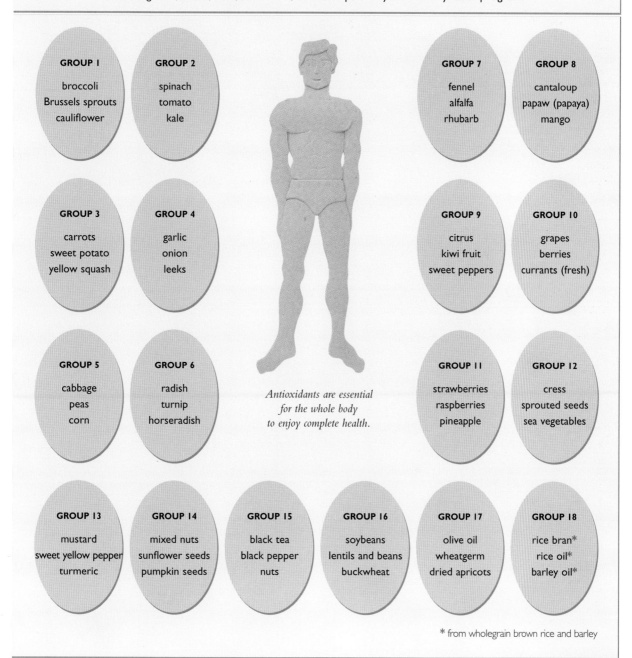

GROUP 1

broccoli
Brussels sprouts
cauliflower

GROUP 2

spinach
tomato
kale

GROUP 3

carrots
sweet potato
yellow squash

GROUP 4

garlic
onion
leeks

GROUP 5

cabbage
peas
corn

GROUP 6

radish
turnip
horseradish

Antioxidants are essential for the whole body to enjoy complete health.

GROUP 7

fennel
alfalfa
rhubarb

GROUP 8

cantaloup
papaw (papaya)
mango

GROUP 9

citrus
kiwi fruit
sweet peppers

GROUP 10

grapes
berries
currants (fresh)

GROUP 11

strawberries
raspberries
pineapple

GROUP 12

cress
sprouted seeds
sea vegetables

GROUP 13

mustard
sweet yellow pepper
turmeric

GROUP 14

mixed nuts
sunflower seeds
pumpkin seeds

GROUP 15

black tea
black pepper
nuts

GROUP 16

soybeans
lentils and beans
buckwheat

GROUP 17

olive oil
wheatgerm
dried apricots

GROUP 18

rice bran*
rice oil*
barley oil*

* from wholegrain brown rice and barley

PART THREE

ASSESSING YOUR HEALTH AND DIET

WHERE AILMENTS ORIGINATE

IN TRYING TO ESTABLISH *advisory nutritional guidelines, we have to recognize that there is no single optimum program which will suit everybody. If we imply that there is, we are denying our uniqueness and paying no attention to what is the basis of nutritional healing – biochemical individuality. We can, as has been done in Part Two, outline a general program that works well for the majority of people. The New Pyramid eating program is the way to optimum nutrition for most of us. It is an attempt to nourish our bodies from a state of average to optimum health. Further, it is an excellent way of protecting ourselves against disease.*

After reading the preceding chapters you will understand what a balanced diet is, and, if you have been following the advice given, you will be enjoying one, probably for the first time. You will also have a wealth of information at your fingertips about the good nutrients in food. However, specific ailments will still need to be addressed through the diet. Now you can take a more analytical view of where any ailments you may still have originate, and what can be done to modify the New Pyramid program to help heal their underlying causes.

There are several, critical, bodily functions which seem to be underperforming in a very large percentage of the population. Unless and until we correct these through nutritional healing our health is always going to be sub-optimum or "average." The following "in depth" analysis looks at common problems related to digestion and absorption, food allergy and intolerance, toxicity, pollution, blood sugar balance, stress, thyroid function, metabolism, and overweight. You may have some of these; you may have none of them; you may have all of them.

A single diet is not the answer to everybody's problems. Our physical types differ, and sedentary and active people have varying nutritional needs.

As well as being determined by our biochemistry, we are also affected by the pollutants in our environment, which act constantly upon us.

DIGESTION AND ABSORPTION

DIGESTION IS THE PROCESS *whereby ingested food (containing proteins, fats, and carbohydrates) is broken down in the mouth, stomach, duodenum, and ileum by a whole range of digestive enzymes made in the salivary glands, gastric glands, pancreas, and lining of the ileum. Hydrochloric acid in the stomach is also vital for digestion, especially that of protein.*

Minerals and vitamins generally do not, mostly, need breaking down before they enter the bloodstream, but the system has to be in tip-top working order to insure their maximum absorption. Fiber, of course, stays in the digestive tract to help carry away wastes. Besides these activities, there are several hormones and nervous reflex actions which orchestrate the whole system.

When any one of these many activities is impaired, our ability to digest food declines and so, I believe, begins the downward spiral to ill-health. To heal our bodies, it is important to start with digestion.

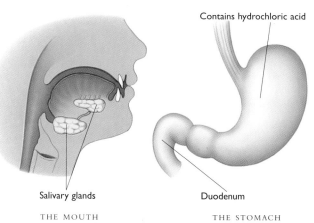

Contains hydrochloric acid

Salivary glands   Duodenum

THE MOUTH   THE STOMACH

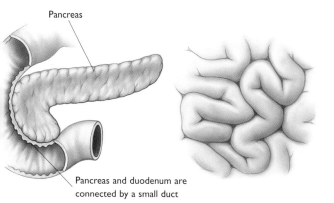

Pancreas

Pancreas and duodenum are connected by a small duct

THE PANCREAS   THE ILEUM

Food is broken down by enzymes made in the mouth, stomach, pancreas, and the part of the small intestine called the ileum.

IS YOUR DIGESTION UP TO SCRATCH?

Try the following questionnaire to see what your digestive capabilities are. Simple "yes" and "no" answers are required.

- Do you have frequent gas in the lower bowel?
- Do you suffer from psoriasis, acne, or other skin problems?
- Do you have frequent discomfort on the left side of the upper abdomen (around the lower ribs area), or under the left shoulder blade?
- Do you suffer frequently from rectal itching?
- Do you have a history of asthma, sinus problems, or hay fever?
- Do you feel as though your food "sticks" in your stomach (pain or discomfort just behind the lower part of the breast bone)?
- Do you feel nauseous frequently?
- Do you have either diarrhea or constipation most of the time?
- Do you feel bloated often?
- Do you have frequent heartburn (reflux into the esophagus), or suffer excessive belching?
- Do you have stomach pains or cramps after eating?
- Do you have much undigested food in the stools?

SCORING

Score one point for each "yes" answer.

0 – 2 *Your digestion seems fine. You may omit pages 80–81, if you wish, and continue with the next section.*

3 – 6 *You are borderline. Some of your digestive symptoms may be due to stress, and it would be well worth you continuing with this section.*

6 and over *It is likely that you have a large degree of digestive distress which needs to be dealt with as part of your optimum program, so read on.*

The Causes of Poor Digestion and Absorption

As we get older, the acid in our stomachs is produced less efficiently and can lead to poor chemical and enzymatic digestion of our food, particularly protein. Food may remain in the stomach for longer than normal; it ferments and produces gas (belching) and discomfort. Further problems occur if the pancreas and intestinal lining are functioning poorly and releasing lower levels of their specific enzymes and hormones. As the improperly digested food travels through our intestines it irritates the lining and may eventually damage the absorptive layers, resulting in what is commonly called "leaky gut." This leakiness allows fragments of improperly digested foods to pass through the lining into the blood system, and can be the starting point for the development of "intolerance" reactions to foods.

Additionally, eating a typical Western diet for several years (excess meat and dairy foods, with very few vegetables) encourages the wrong type of bacteria to proliferate in the large intestine, causing putrefaction of partially digested food and wastes. Metabolic wastes from these micro-organisms become toxic to our system. They can either set up localized irritation and infection (flatulence, bloating, discomfort, and/or pain), or cause a more widespread toxicity in the body if they are absorbed. The result of either is poor availability of essential nutrients and an irritated gut, causing the sufferer to experience low energy and general poor health.

These conditions are clearly related to what we eat, and hence nutritional healing is well equipped to deal with them. The "plan of attack" to improve digestion and absorption has three stages:

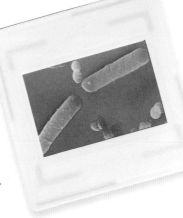

Intestinal bacteria are either rod-shaped (bacilli) *or ball-shaped* (cocci).

♦ *Correcting stomach acidity and improving digestive enzyme production.*

♦ *Promoting the healing and strengthening of the intestinal lining.*

♦ *Rebalancing the bowel flora.*

FOOD COMBINING

Many people with digestive problems, either simple discomfort, or more chronic problems, try "food combining," otherwise known as the Hay Diet (after Dr. Hay who first described this way of eating). The main principle of this regime is never to mix concentrated carbohydrates and concentrated proteins in the same meal. By using this method, you are encouraging the efficient digestion of one particular food group at a time.

The reasoning behind the diet is that the body is not wasteful in its production of digestive enzymes and juices, and if the meal contains mainly carbohydrate, then the secretions that are chiefly produced will be those containing enzymes to digest carbohydrate. On the other hand, if the meal contains mainly protein, it is the production of the gastric juice (which contains hydrochloric acid and protein-digesting enzymes) that is stimulated to the greater extent.

It is essentially true that the breakdown of carbohydrates and proteins need different conditions for their enzymes to act correctly; the breakdown of carbohydrate requires a neutral environment and that of protein takes place in an acid environment. By eating carbohydrates and proteins at different times rather than together you will be promoting ideal conditions for the complete breakdown of foods. Obviously, the human digestive tract is able to deal with digestion of all food groups at the same time in ordinary, healthy circumstances. However, food combining optimizes digestion within a body that may not be in tip-top working order.

Appendix One (*see* page 228) contains a section on Food Combining, which will help you to group your foods together correctly, should you feel like trying this method. Alternatively, there are many good books on the market which will give you a fuller picture of what the theory is all about and which give detailed advice on how to put it into practice (*see* page 250).

Black tea prevents the body absorbing nutrients fully, but herb teas are fine.

SUPPLEMENTS

There are a variety of supplements on the market to assist in digestive healing, and your nutritional therapist should be able to give you tailor-made advice. On a general level you may like to try a supplement of digestive enzymes, together with hydrochloric acid capsules (not to be taken if you have ulcers or gastric disease). If you have a specific digestive problem, refer to Part Four of this book (*see* pages 162–165) for further advice. Your nutritional therapist will also be able to arrange for urine tests to assess leaky gut levels. A dietary challenge test using lactulose and mannitol is the usual type. Also, stool samples can be taken to look for the presence/absence of pathogens, and to ascertain the degree of dysbiosis (an imbalance of helpful and unhelpful bacteria in the gut).

All colas contain stimulants, which hamper digestion.

As your food is digested more effectively, nutrient uptake will improve, and the digestive organs and glands, now in a state of improved nourishment themselves, will begin to work more efficiently. As healing continues, your digestion will improve and you will find that any irritation of the intestinal tract, or any imbalance of gut flora, you may have had will have mostly self-corrected. However, should you require a little extra help, there are many supplements available which contain good combinations of soothing herbs and nutrients to encourage further healing of the digestive tract (such as Slippery Elm, cabagin, zinc, vitamin A), and

others which will correct the bowel flora (*Lactobacillus acidophilus* and *Bifidobacterium* complex, along with butyric acid, biotin, and fructo-oligosaccharides).

Quercetin, *Ginkgo biloba*, *Aloe vera*, and antioxidant vitamins and minerals can be used to reduce any damage that might have been caused to the gut, while the amino acids L-glutamine and glucosamine, together with the mineral zinc, will help to heal the lining.

The herb Aloe vera has a healing effect on the gut.

If you are in any doubt about your symptoms, consult your physician first.

HINTS FOR A HEALTHY DIGESTION

In addition to "food combining" there are several things you must do if you are to help your body digest and absorb your food properly. These are:

1. Omit all refined foods, especially refined carbohydrates (white sugar, white flour, white pasta, etc.).

2. Omit all stimulants (including tea, coffee, colas, and chocolate).

3. Reduce sweet foods (honey, maple syrup, candy) to a minimum.

4. Reduce alcohol to a minimum.

5. Reduce fat intake to a minimum and focus fat intake around seeds, nuts, virgin cold-pressed oils, and the oils in oily fish.

6. Reduce salt intake to a minimum, if necessary cutting out regular salt and changing to one of the "low salt" alternatives.

7. Eat good-quality live (containing beneficial bacteria) yogurt every day.

8. Chew your food thoroughly; take time over eating; enjoy each mouthful.

9. Don't eat when you are upset or stressed; wait until you are calmer.

10. Don't drink fluids with your meals (this dilutes the digestive juices), or within a half hour either side of a meal. But make sure you still have a good intake of fluids each day.

Slippery elm is a gentle and soothing digestive remedy.

FOOD ALLERGY
AND INTOLERANCE

Y OUR DIGESTION MAY *be fine (only one or two "yes" answers to the diges-tion questionnaire), but you may still have some foods in your diet to which you are intolerant. Alternatively, you may have some digestive problems and be working on them, but at the same time need to assess your intolerance levels.*

Since even the best digestion is only about 50–60 percent efficient, this means that some undigested or partially digested food may be reaching the areas of absorption (mainly in the lower small intestine or "ileum"), and if the lining of this area is more porous than it should be (leaky gut), then fragments of partially digested protein can escape through to the blood where they are likely to be recognized as a "foreign invader" by the immune system. Those to whom this happens may then find they get the symptoms of an allergy or food intolerance.

In general, food allergy causes an adverse immune system reaction in which antibodies, or defensive proteins, are released to combat what the body perceives as an invasion by an enemy. A true allergic reaction can be measured by a blood test. It is usually immediate and triggered by a protein, e.g., gluten from grains or casein from milk.

Generally, we tend to call anything having an immediate reaction an allergy, while anything having a delayed or masked reaction we tend to call an "intolerance," though the situation is complicated by the allergy to gluten, celiac disease, which normally provokes a delayed response.

In this section we are mostly looking at intolerance, since this is the more difficult to weed out. The more common foods causing intolerance are wheat, dairy foods, eggs, citrus fruit, chocolate, red wine, coffee, and nuts, but could be any food. The most likely will be those foods eaten regularly each day, having a delayed response, and causing an overall feeling of "just not quite right," with a few niggling little symptoms present most of the time.

Try the checklist opposite to assess your level of intolerance. Score one point for each symptom, in any one of the groups, that you suffer from frequently.

ALLERGY QUESTIONNAIRE

Taking your score from the questionnaire opposite:

11 – 30 (with no more than three in one group)
You seem to have a small amount of food intolerance. Try cutting out the main allergenic foods (wheat, dairy foods, eggs, citrus fruit, chocolate, red wine, coffee, and nuts) for two weeks and see if your "niggling" symptoms disappear. If they do, try adding each food back into your diet, one at a time. Eat your "test" food every day for three days, then leave a gap before you reintroduce the next food. Any food bringing a return of symptoms, would be better avoided for a few months.

31 and over (or four or more in any one group)
You have a major problem with food intolerance. Try the Hypoallergenic Diet for two to three weeks; see Appendix Two, page 232.

If you continue to have problems, you might benefit from seeing a food allergy specialist.

NOTE

There are no specific questions related to digestive symptoms since they have been assessed earlier.

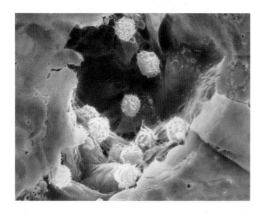

White cells may attack "foreign" protein in allergic reactions.

CHECKING FOR ALLERGIES AND FOOD INTOLERANCE

The following case study shows how you can work out if you have a reaction to a certain food or foods. You can apply the same questionnaire to yourself. Look at each group and score a point for each symptom that regularly applies to you. Then add up the totals. With less than 10 overall, and not more than two in any one group of six, you should have no worries. If you score more than 11, then follow the advice given in the box on the facing page.

Ears and eyes

Frequent itchy ears or earache/tinnitus/gritty, watery, or itchy eyes/swollen, sticky or red eyelids/permanent dark circles under the eyes/visual problems, not related to definite eye defects.

Score for this group: 2

Nose, mouth, and throat

Sinusitis, hay fever, or stuffy nose/sneezing attacks or excessive mucus production unrelated to a cold/irritating cough, not related to cigarette smoking or infection/constant sore or catarrhy throat, or hoarseness/halitosis (bad breath)/sore or cracked lips, mouth corners, tongue or receding gums.

Score for this group: 5

Lungs and heart

Chestiness, wheeziness, or asthma/shortness of breath/high blood pressure/rapid heartbeat, when resting/palpitations/general discomfort in chest area.

Score for this group: 2

Head and emotions

Headaches and migraine/insomnia or restless sleep/behavioral changes or problems/mild depression, loss of humor/frequent irritability, or aggressiveness/frequent anxiety, or nervousness.

Score for this group: 1

Mind

Frequent concentration and memory lapses/poor comprehension, or confusion/coordination problems, or learning difficulties/indecisiveness/stuttering, or inarticulation/obsessiveness or phobias.

Score for this group: 0

Skin

Nonspecific itchy skin/excessive sweating, or cold sweats/hot flashes, or "bloodshot" cheeks/nonspecific rash, or dry skin/thinning hair or sudden hair loss/acne or psoriasis.

Score for this group: 3

Energy, and activity levels

Apathy or sluggishness/unusual fatigue/lethargy/hyperactivity/inability to relax, restlessness/exhaustion after light exercise.

Score for this group: 3

Joints and muscles

Generalized joint pain or stiffness/bursitis or arthritis/deep bone pain/weak or sore muscles/generalized muscle aches and pains/frequent muscle cramps.

Score for this group: 0

Weight

Cravings (especially carbohydrates)/binge eating, compulsive eating, or comfort eating/alcohol cravings/fluid retention/weight fluctuation over a short period of time/excessive weight or underweight resistant to change in diet.

Score for this group: 1

TOTAL SCORE: 17

Tom scored 17 on the questionnaire. After eliminating dairy products from his diet he found that his symptoms disappeared.

NOTE

Many of the above symptoms can be associated with severe medical problems; always consult your own physician about anything that concerns you.

TOXIN LEVELS

EW PEOPLE THINK ABOUT *the way the everyday chemicals they encounter may affect them. But toxins reach your liver and adipose (fatty connective) tissue through a variety of ways – in the water you drink, from the air both within your home and workplace, and from outside. We eat fruit and vegetables loaded with pesticide and chemical residues, and battery-farmed animals that are dosed up with antibiotics and artificial hormones. Moreover, dioxins, one of the most toxic groups of manmade substances ever made, are turning up in our milk, eggs, and fish.*

In addition to what enters our bodies with our food, many physiological processes, particularly those reacting to stress, produce within the body metabolic by-products which themselves are toxic and would cause problems if not removed.

All of these many chemicals and metabolites in the blood supply and the tissues must be removed at a greater rate than the new ones are entering via our lungs and gut, if we are to make headway in removing some of the toxic deposits that we may have had stored in our bodies for many years.

The body is constantly working to expel toxins through the liver, lungs, kidneys, skin, intestines, bowel, lymphatic and immune systems in an attempt to achieve homeostasis (balance). The younger and healthier you are, the more effective this process is. But, as you get older or as your health deteriorates, this self-cleansing mechanism can become overloaded and you take in more toxins than you can remove.

The body cleverly makes sure that poisonous substances which it is unable to detoxify and remove from the tissues are locked away, at least initially, where they can do least damage to the effective workings of our system. This usually means surrounding them in fat and storing them away in the adipose tissue under the skin, or in fatty tissues surrounding major organs like the heart and kidneys. Some people seem to store their toxins in joints, and consequently suffer from joint and muscle pain and stiffness.

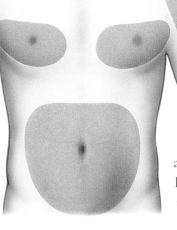

Toxins are often stored in fatty tissues under the skin, or in the joints.

As we know, a toxic system is also an acidic one and to function effectively the body needs a neutral to slightly alkaline environment. Lightening the toxic load with a full detox program (*see* page 236) will cause your body to become more alkaline and help it to restore itself.

Alternatively, you could take detoxification more slowly by carrying on with the New Pyramid program and having just one full day a week on a cleansing regime. Or you could do a type of "split" cleanse by having fresh fruit only (organic, if possible) for breakfast every morning and only filtered or bottled water, or herb tea. More fruit can be eaten throughout the morning if desired, and then from lunchtime onward, you can return to your main diet.

This "split" program is designed to fit in with your daily detoxification cycle, where for around eight hours from, say 4:00 A.M. until 12:00 noon, the body is cleansing itself naturally, so that consuming fruit only during this period encourages further cleansing. Then from around 12 noon, the next eight hours is the "intake" period when you will be eating your normal healthy diet. The last eight-hour period from around 8:00 P.M. is the "assimilation" period when your body is digesting and delivering nutrients (from the previous eight-hour period) around the body. You should try not to eat or drink anything (apart from water, herb tea, or grain coffee without milk) during this period, so that your evening meal needs to be timed to finish no later than 8:00 P.M.

Anything consumed after this period will not be efficiently digested and will tend to lie around and ferment in the system – not something that will encourage detoxification. You could have a little more fruit or raw salad vegetables if you are really hungry during this period, but the best advice is to try to resist and you will find that within a day or two you don't need anything further to eat after 8:00 P.M.

To help you along with a cleansing program, there are many good combinations of herbs and nutrients which will expedite toxin removal while at the same time damping down some of the more unpleasant healing reactions which may occur. Any good health food store will stock several high-quality preparations relating to "colon cleanse," "total cleanse," "detoxification formula," etc., or you might find it more helpful to consult a nutritional therapist (*see* Useful Addresses, page 248).

Finally, remember that a "13-day detox" is not a cure-all, but if you are feeling under par, then treating yourself to one once or twice a year will keep your body in peak condition: your mind will be sharper, your skin clearer, your eyesight and digestion will improve, and you will have more energy. Moreover, your immune system will get a boost and many minor ailments are likely to clear up.

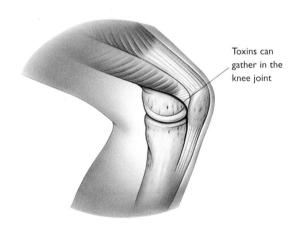

Toxins can gather in the knee joint

Toxins are sometimes deposited in the joints, creating pain and stiffness.

WARNING

There are some individuals who should not detoxify. If you have an eating disorder, a serious mental problem, are pregnant or breastfeeding, are currently taking prescription medication, or are at all concerned about any preexisting condition, do not attempt a detoxification diet without taking the advice of your medical practitioner.

WORKING OUT YOUR TOXIN LEVEL

Simple "yes" and "no" answers are required to the following questions. They assume you have done some healing work on your digestion and intestines and have worked on any food intolerances you may have had.

- Do you feel sluggish or dull-headed much of the time and find concentrating difficult?
- Is you energy level low in the morning and again about 3:00 P.M.?
- Do you have bad breath, or an unpleasant taste in your mouth most of the time?
- Do you have strong body/foot odor?
- Do you seem to need excessive amounts of sleep (more than eight hours per night)?
- Do you have a poor tolerance to alcohol?
- Do you feel the cold more than others?
- Do you often have discomfort in the right upper abdomen (around lower ribs) or under the right shoulder blade?
- Do you have bowel movements less than once daily?
- Are your stools yellow, clay-colored, or foul-smelling?
- Do you suffer from chronic constipation?
- Do you have joint pains?
- Is your skin dull/dry/greasy/spotty?
- Do you consume more than two units of alcohol per day?
- Do you develop indigestion and/or headaches in response to eating fat-based foods?
- Do onions, cucumbers, radishes, or cabbage cause digestive distress?
- Do you have a poor appetite?
- Do you feel nauseous frequently?
- Do you get itchy skin with no apparent cause?
- Do you have asthma, eczema, hay fever, or other allergic conditions?

SCORING

Score one point for each "yes" answer.

3 and over *You will need to cleanse (detoxify) your system before returning to a basic wholesome diet like the New Pyramid program. The more questions you have answered in the affirmative, the greater your need to detoxify. For full details of the Detoxification Diet, see Appendix Three (page 236). A three-day stint would suffice in a mild case or the time can be extended by two-day sessions if needed, through 11 days or, in extreme cases, 13 days.*

Detoxification and the Liver

The organ which is primarily responsible for removing these toxic products as they flow through it in the blood is the liver. If you are interested in the details of how the liver achieves this, then you can refer to any good human physiology text book to give you a clear understanding of just how important the liver is. Nevertheless, even if you are not interested in detailed physiology, it is important to mention here that detoxification in the liver is controlled by two phases.

Phase one of detoxification (oxidation) involves the activity of a special family of enzymes known as the P450s, whose job it is to activate a fat-soluble toxin and make it more able to be dissolved in bodily fluids. The nutrients needed to support a healthy oxidation phase are vitamins B2, B3, B6, B12, folic acid, vitamin C, bioflavonoids (such as rutin from buckwheat, hesperidin from citrus, and quercetin from onions and garlic), vitamin E, glutathione, branched-chain amino acids, and phospholipids, plus a good supply of antioxidant nutrients to disarm free radicals created during this phase. Some people have problems if this first phase works too well, especially if the second phase doesn't, and a lot of free radicals are produced, which are highly toxic to the body. Such people are called "pathological detoxifiers" and they can get worse when put on a supplement program, especially if polyunsaturated oils are given; so take care (detoxification phases one and two can be assessed by stool and/or urine samples taken by your nutritional therapist).

Phase two of detoxification (conjugation) is where the toxin is combined with another molecule, usually making it less destructive. This phase can also be stimulated back into activity by certain nutrients, such as the B-complex vitamins (especially B5), beta-carotene, vitamins C and E, selenium, molybdenum, manganese, copper, zinc, glutathione, and the amino acids L-cysteine, n-acetyl cysteine, L-glutamine, L-glycine, L-methionine, and taurine, plus a diet which decreases the toxic load. There are many herbs which are also extremely good at nourishing the liver tissue and increasing the activity

Onion is a source of the bioflavonoids that are necessary for proper oxidation, which is the first phase of detoxification.

of both phases of detoxification, such as Milk thistle, dandelion, yellow dock, and barberry.

The kidneys are also involved in detoxification since they filter the blood and remove toxic wastes which have not been released by the liver into the bile. There are several botanicals, such as celery seeds, alfalfa, parsley, etc., which will help strengthen the kidneys.

A qualified nutritional therapist should be able to arrange for a test to assess your phase one and phase two detoxification capacity. This is a noninvasive test where dietary "challenges" are used, and their breakdown products tested in the urine.

One further important point to mention is that the liver is unable to remove toxins stored in other body tissues and organs, since it can only remove toxins from the blood as it passes through. We need, therefore, something to remove any stored poisonous substances retained by cells and not released into the blood. This is sometimes referred to as "stage one" in the detoxification process (this is different from phase one in the liver), and a diet high in fresh organically grown vegetables and fruit, and filtered water, would usually achieve this (*see* Appendix Three, page 236). Once the toxins are out of the cells and flowing around the body in the blood, the liver (always assuming it has the energy and capacity to do this) is then able to remove them by detoxification into the bile, which then enters the alimentary canal at the duodenum. From here the toxins can travel the length of the intestines and pass out of the body.

It is, unfortunately, while we have toxins circulating around in our blood that we get symptoms of detoxification, sometimes referred to as a "healing reaction" or "healing crisis." The list of possible detoxification symptoms can be fairly long but usually includes things like a fuzzy head, coated

Milk thistle is one of several herbs that build up liver tissue.

tongue, sweating, fever, increased bowel movements and urination, rash, lowered energy levels, and weight loss. If any of these sound familiar, it is because they are similar to the symptoms of food intolerance. But intolerance to food is also a reaction which stimulates the body in trying to rid itself of these "allergens!" How do you tell the difference between the two? Am I intolerant to a food or foods in my diet, or am I toxic and going through a healing crisis?

Parsley nourishes the kidneys and hence aids detoxification.

The only thing that will give you the right answer is to look at your diet.

If you had food intolerances and you have mostly cleared them through the Hypoallergenic Diet, or an elimination diet given to you by your therapist, and you are actively engaged upon a Detoxification Diet, then your symptoms will be those of detoxification. If you have, as yet, made no attempt to remove any food intolerances you have, and are on a Detoxification Diet, then your symptoms will also be those of detoxification, since detoxification diets in general are extremely low in allergens. If you have, as yet, made no attempt to do either of these things (that is, remove intolerances or detoxify), then you may be suffering from symptoms of food intolerance and a high toxic load. Your body is just reacting to the substances (foreign substances, toxins, etc.) circulating around in your blood.

An example of a detoxification diet which is poorly balanced would be one in

CAUTION

Do not move onto a detoxification program until you have done some work on improving your digestion, healing your gut lining, rebalancing your gut flora, and removing a large proportion of your food intolerances; otherwise, toxins released in cleansing may further irritate the absorptive lining, or may be reabsorbed. If stage one of detoxification (different from phase one in the liver) is managed properly, these symptoms should be minor and short-lived as long as your diet is properly employing stage two of the detoxification process (different from phase two in the liver).

This stage involves making sure that when toxins reach the intestines with the bile, they are bound to an appropriate material which will carry them out of the body and prevent them from being reabsorbed in the large intestine. The foods that are excellent for this job are brown rice (especially short-grain organic brown rice) and organic millet.

which a fruit such as grapefruit is eaten at every meal for several days. Fruit, it has to be said, is extremely good at removing toxins from tissues; the ineffectiveness of this particular "detoxification diet" lies in the fact that there is no fibrous food passing through the intestines to enable efficient toxin removal

Grapefruit alone is not enough for detoxification.

from the body, and a large proportion of the stage one toxins are simply reabsorbed. The sufferer in this case probably goes through some unpleasant detoxification symptoms without actually clearing the system.

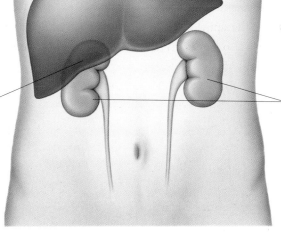

The liver processes nutrients from the intestines, as well as removing toxins from the blood

The kidneys filter out the wastes in the blood produced by the liver's work

The liver and kidneys work together in making fuel available to the body, as well as being prime centers for detoxification.

POLLUTION

IN ADDITION TO *removing toxins which may have been stored in your body for a long time, you may also like to consider the general level of pollution in your home or work place. There is not a lot of point in going through a thorough cleansing program, only to replace body toxins with environmental toxins.*

Living or working in an area where there are a large number of airborne chemicals will put your detoxification system under stress and will use up important energy which you could put to better use. Of course, there will always be a limit; there is very little we can do about general air pollution in the street, and even in our workplace there may be very little we can do to make the air we breathe less chemically laden. Thankfully, now, many offices, work areas and public places are no-smoking areas, and new governmental regulations, such as the C.O.S.H.H. (Control of Substances Hazardous to Health) in Britain, and government protection agencies, such as Environmental Protection Agency (E.P.A.) in the U.S., puts the onus onto the employer to control any chemically damaging substances.

To assess the level of airborne chemicals in your own home, carry out the following "pollution check."

POLLUTANTS QUESTIONNAIRES

Taking your score from the questionnaires opposite:

0 – 50 The chemical contamination of your home is low, and well below average.

51 – 100 You are a moderate user of chemicals, but you err on the side of having too many. Make sure you dispose, safely, of those you really don't need. Focus particularly on any products which make any members of your family sneeze or feel unwell.

101 – 150 The level of chemical contamination of your home is very high and is very likely to cause you problems. Safely dispose of those items you know you can really do without, and restrict the use of those which you feel are vital.

151 and over Your home is heavily contaminated with chemicals. Take stock of all those items you really do need, and safely dispose of the rest.

Anyone with a history of allergies should aim for a score of 40 or less.

CHECKING FOR POLLUTANTS

Using the following case study questionnaires you can work out the level of pollutants in your home. Score as indicated at the end of each question.

Questionnaire I

- Count all the aerosol sprays in your home, garage and/or garden shed (include any polishes and other cleaning materials, hair sprays, air fresheners, deodorants, shaving creams, starch laundry sprays, fabric sprays, stain-removal sprays, waterproofing products, spray paints, varnishes, dyes, fly sprays, pet flea sprays, insecticide sprays, fat sprays for use in skillets, and any other aerosols you come across).

Total number of aerosol spray cans: **10**

Score 1 point each: **10**

- Count any insecticidal pet shampoos and flea collars used in the last three months, and any pesticides or insecticides used in the garden in the last three months.

Total number of pet/garden insecticides: **2**

Score 2 points each: **4**

- Count all the times you have brought "dry-cleaned" clothes into the house, or have had any furnishings (carpets, curtains, upholstery) dry-cleaned, or used dry-cleaning treatments in the house or car, in the last six months.

Total number of dry-cleaned items: **5**

Score 2 points each: **10**

- Count the number of long-lasting air fresheners or deodorizers in the kitchen, bathroom, or car, at the present time.

Total number of long-lasting air fresheners: **2**

Score 2 points each: **4**

- Count the number of gas fires, gas heaters, a gas cooker, paraffin heaters, or bottled gas heaters you have in your house and garage.

Total number of gas appliances: **2**

Score 2 points each: **4**

CASE STUDY

After filling out this questionnaire, the Whitaker family were shocked to discover the high level of chemical contamination in their home.

• Count the number of flexible plastic items, such as shower curtains, tablecloths, etc.

Total number of flexible plastic items: **7**

Score 4 points each: **28**

• Count the number of occasions on which you have carried out any decorating in the house (especially if you did the work yourself) within the last three months.

Total number of decorating occasions: **0**

Score 5 points each: **0**

• Count how many long-lasting insecticides are used in the house, garage or car.

Total number of long-lasting insecticides: **3**

Score 5 points each: **15**

• Count the number of times you have used cellulose paints or paint/varnish strippers in the house or garage within the last 2 months.

Total number of times strippers used: **0**

Score 5 points each: **0**

• Count the number of items of plastic-covered furniture in your house or garage.

Total number of furniture items: **2**

Score 5 points each: **10**

TOTAL SCORE SO FAR: **85**

Questionnaire 2

Add on the following scores, if applicable:

• Do you have a new car? *Score 4 points:* **0**

• Do you use strong-smelling glues in the house?
Score 4 points: **4**

• Do you use biological laundry detergents (those that contain enzymes), regularly?
Score 5 points: **5**

• Do you use fabric softeners in your washing regularly?
Score 5 points: **5**

• Do you have urea-formaldehyde cavity foam insulation in your home or garage?
Score 10 points: **10**

• Can you smell gas anywhere in the house?
Score 20 points: **0**

• Have you had the woodwork in your home treated with preservative within the past year?
Score 25 points: **0**

SUB TOTAL:
(ADDITIONAL POINTS) **24**

GRAND TOTAL:
(POLLUTION POINTS) **109**

BLOOD-SUGAR BALANCE

T HE LEVEL OF *"sugar" (glucose) in the blood is under the control of a pair of hormones called insulin and glucagon. Both are manufactured in the pancreas, which is situated just underneath and behind the stomach. When the amounts of the two hormones are unbalanced, the person begins to suffer from fatigue.*

The pancreas secretes insulin into the bloodstream after a meal containing carbohydrate. The insulin travels to the liver and the muscles, instructing them to take glucose from the bloodstream and to store it as glycogen. As insulin levels increase, blood-glucose levels start to fall, but when this reaches a critical low level, it causes the brain to send for more supplies. The brain cannot exist for long without glucose. If these instructions from the brain are ignored or slow in being fulfilled, you begin to suffer the symptoms of "hypoglycemia," the first of which is usually mental fatigue. You might ask why, at this point, the liver does not replenish the blood-glucose level from its stores of glycogen. The answer is that the levels of insulin in the blood are still high, because perhaps your last meal contained too much carbohydrate, which will prevent the release of more glucose.

Under normal circumstances (where carbohydrate is properly balanced with protein) the production of insulin is not excessive, and the range over which blood-sugar moves is minimal. In this case, when a small drop in glucose occurs, the hormone glucagon is released from the pancreas and this hormone stimulates the breakdown of glycogen stores in the liver to release glucose into the blood again. So, we can see that insulin and glucagon have opposite effects, and the balance needs to be finely tuned to keep blood-sugar stable.

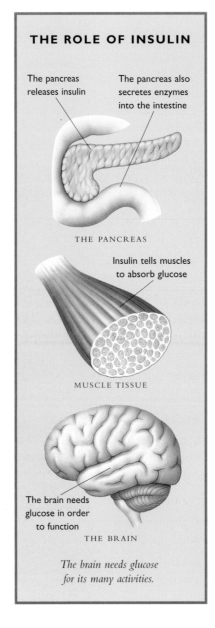

THE ROLE OF INSULIN

The pancreas releases insulin

The pancreas also secretes enzymes into the intestine

THE PANCREAS

Insulin tells muscles to absorb glucose

MUSCLE TISSUE

The brain needs glucose in order to function

THE BRAIN

The brain needs glucose for its many activities.

A possible problem arises here if you are using the Food Combining Diet where you do not eat carbohydrate and protein at the same meal. In this case, you must insure that each day you have one protein meal (preferably at lunch time), and one carbohydrate meal (preferably at supper time), and one neutral meal of low G.I. (glycemic index, *see* page 92) fruit and seeds. Blood-sugar will then be balanced out well over the day, and having protein for lunch will prevent any blood-sugar tiredness and "brain fatigue" occurring during the afternoon.

There is also a condition known as "insulin resistance," where insulin levels are elevated but blood-sugar levels remain high because the target cells cannot respond to insulin. This leads to "hyperinsulinemia" which causes accumulation of excess body fat, and may also increase the tendency toward diabetes and heart disease.

The liver releases a substance called glucose tolerance factor (composed of three amino acids, vitamin B3, and the mineral chromium) which aids glucose uptake by the target cells. However, there may be some impairment in this system in cases of insulin resistance.

In addition to the insulin-glucagon seesaw, the release of the hormone adrenaline from the adrenal glands (adrenal medulla), and the release of the glucocorticoids (hormones from the adrenal cortex) occurs as a response to stress. These hormones also raise

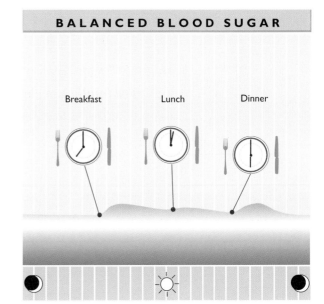

UNBALANCED BLOOD SUGAR

Breakfast

Lunch

Dinner

BALANCED BLOOD SUGAR

Breakfast

Lunch

Dinner

blood-sugar levels by further stimulation of the pancreas and liver.

Furthermore, continued high stress levels from mental, emotional, or nutritional (toxicity and/or lack of essential nutrients) sources do not require a physical response ("fight" or "flight"). The energy (glucose) which has been made available via our physiological makeup to combat the stressful situation is often not required to fight or run away, and the glucose is returned to storage as glycogen or fat.

If blood-sugar levels stay low, a part of the brain called the hypothalamus is stimulated and we feel hungry, which, of course, encourages us to find food and replenish our sugar levels in the blood. Therefore, if we constantly consume meals that are poorly balanced (too much carbohydrate in relationship to protein) the tendency will be towards destroying this fine balance in blood-sugar homeostasis.

Also, if we regularly consume sweet foods and carbohydrates with a high G.I., this will cause a surge of insulin into the blood to deal with the excess sugar by increasing target cell uptake. However, when large amounts of glucose enter the system on a regular basis, the pancreas may theoretically overreact and produce too much insulin so that it takes more glucose out of the blood than it should. Then blood-sugar levels drop below the lower level. We begin to feel very hungry and tired and may reach for something sweet to help improve the situation. Of course, this just makes the imbalance worse. Eventually the pancreas may start producing

Blood-sugar levels fluctuate wildly if we eat a great deal of high G.I. carbohydrates.

excess insulin on a regular basis, or it may become exhausted and hardly produce any. The end result of this will be diabetes.

To be confident that our diet comprises carbohydrates which are not going to overtax the pancreas or blood control mechanism, it is helpful to know something about the glycemic index of the foods we eat.

When we are stressed but not able to respond with "fight or flight," the extra glucose is converted to fat.

GLYCEMIC INDEX OF SOME
COMMON CARBOHYDRATE-RICH FOODS

High glycemic index	(over 70)	Moderate glycemic index	(50 – 70)
Glucose	100	Pancakes	70
Maltose	100	White bread	70
Cooked parsnips	97	Fresh mashed potato	70
Sports drinks/glucose drinks	95	Watermelon	70
Cooked carrots	92	Wholewheat bread	69
Boiled white rice	88	Rye crispbread	69
Honey	87	Chocolate and caramel bar	68
Baked potato	85	Soft drinks	68
Cornflakes	84	Shredded breakfast cereal (wheat)	67
Instant mashed potato	83	Granola or muesli (unsweetened)	66
Wheat breakfast cereal	75	Brown rice	66
Bagel	72	Cordial/fruit concentrate	66
Millet	71	Sucrose (sugar)	65
		Raisins	64
		Cooked beets	64
		Boiled new potatoes	62
		Ice cream (low fat)	61
		Banana	60
		Pastry	59
		Graham crackers or digestives	59
		Potato chips (full fat)	59
		Corn	59
		Basmati rice	58
		Whole boiled potato (with skin)	56
		Sultanas	56
		Rich tea cookies	55
		Oatmeal cookies	54
		Orange juice	52
		Garden peas	51
		Buckwheat	51
		Rye bread	50
		White spaghetti	50

CORNFLAKES

HONEY

WHITE RICE

SPORTS DRINK

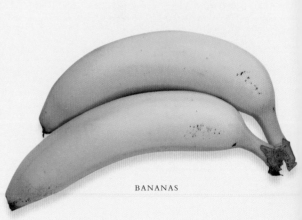

BANANAS

Low glycemic index	(under 50)
Porridge (oatmeal)	49
Natural wheat bran breakfast cereal	49
Chocolate	49
Baked beans (no sugar)	48
Dried peas	48
Sweet potato	47
Wholewheat spaghetti	42
Boiled white pasta	41
Apple juice	41
Oranges	40
Boiled wholewheat pasta	37
Butterbeans	36
Garbanzo beans	36
Apples, pears	36
Ice cream (full fat)	35
Flavored yogurt	34
Whole milk	34
Black-eyed peas	33
Skim milk	32
Haricot beans	31
Lentils	30
Kidney beans	29
Fructose (fruit sugar)	20
Soybeans	15

SWEET POTATOES

BLACK-EYED PEAS   MILK

Although the list to the left is not complete, it is intended to show you that different carbohydrate-rich foods affect blood glucose in a manner that might not be predictable from other features of the food. You can see from the list that several foods that many modern diets are based on, such as potato, rice and other grains, cooked carrots, fruit juice, and low-sugar breakfast cereals, have a high G.I., and may be causing problems with blood-sugar control.

This is not to ignore the fact that all these foods have their own excellent properties with regard to good-quality nutrient content, but at the same time, where there are problems with blood-sugar control, they must be kept at a low level in the diet for a while. Generally, the sweeter a food (with the exception of fructose) and the more it is refined or cooked, the greater will be the glycemic index.

GOOD EXAMPLES OF LOW G.I. FOODS

GRAINS	FRUIT
Pot barley, oatmeal, wholegrain rye bread, buckwheat, spaghetti.	Apple, apple juice, pears, grapes, peaches, cherries, plums, grapefruit.

VEGETABLES	PULSES (LEGUMES)
All vegetables except cooked carrots and parsnips, and corn.	Kidney beans, lima beans, soybeans, black-eyed peas, garbanzo beans, peas, lentils, peanuts.

SUGAR	DAIRY PRODUCTS
Fructose.	Milk (skim and whole), yogurt, high-fat ice cream.

Raw carrot has a lower glycemic index than cooked, and hence is less likely to produce insulin surges.

BLOOD-SUGAR QUESTIONNAIRE

To check how stable your blood sugar is, answer "yes" or "no" to the following questions.

- Do you get tired and/or hungry in the mid-afternoon?

- About an hour or two after eating a full meal that includes dessert, do you find yourself wanting more of the dessert?

- Is it harder for you to control your eating for the rest of the day if you have breakfast containing carbohydrates than it is if you only have only coffee or a meal rich in protein instead?

- When you want to lose weight, do you find it easier not to eat for most of the day than to try to eat several small diet meals?

- Once you start eating candy, starches, or snack foods, do you often find difficulty stopping?

- Would you rather have an ordinary meal that included a dessert than a gourmet meal that did not include a dessert?

- After finishing a full meal, do you sometimes feel as if you could go back and eat the whole meal again?

- Does a meal of only meat and vegetables leave you feeling satisfied?

- If you are feeling low, does a snack of cake or cookies make you feel better?

- If there are potatoes, bread, pasta, or dessert on the table, do you often skip eating vegetables or salad?

- Do you feel sleepy (with a feeling as if you were "drugged") after eating a large meal containing bread/pasta/potatoes or dessert, but on the other hand feel more energetic after a meal that consists only of protein and salad?

- Do you find it hard work trying to get to sleep without a bedtime snack?

- Do you often wake in the middle of the night feeling hungry and are unable to get back to sleep without eating something?

- If you are going to eat at a friend's house, do you sometimes eat something before you go in case dinner is delayed?

- At a restaurant, do you find yourself eating too much bread before the meal is served?

- Do you get attacks of sweating for no reason?

- When you haven't eaten for a few hours, do you ever get dizzy or shaky?

- Do you ever feel as if you are going to pass out or are unable to think clearly if you have gone without food for a few hours?

- When hungry do you mainly crave sugary things?

- Do you frequently get severe mood swings for no apparent reason?

Waking in the night and needing food is a symptom of blood sugar irregularities.

BEDTIME SNACKING

NIGHTTIME HUNGER

SCORING

Score one point for each "yes" answer.

0 – 3 *Your blood-sugar control appears to be working fairly well, and you could safely include complex carbohydrates of a high G.I. in your New Pyramid program.*

4 – 10 *It is likely that at least some of the time you have a problem maintaining the correct sugar balance, and you would do well to steer clear of sweet foods and those carbohydrates with a high G.I. for a period of around one to two months. Concentrate your carbohydrates around brown rice, buckwheat, lentils, beans, oats, wholewheat spaghetti, and low G.I. fruit and vegetables.*

11 and over *It is almost certain that poor blood-sugar control is one of the things causing your ill-health. Remove all refined and processed foods from your diet. Also avoid carbohydrate foods with a high G.I., and restrict very severely those with a moderate G.I. for a month or two. Then reintroduce moderate G.I. carbohydrates, one food at a time over a three-day period. Make sure the food is of good quality and of the complex variety. Take careful note of any of the old symptoms recurring, and if a food causes them, omit it from the diet a while longer.*

BLOOD-SUGAR CONTROL

If you have health problems that originate in poor blood-sugar control, you need to cut out from the diet all foods with a high glycemic content, and for a while also avoid those with a moderate glycemic content. After about a month or so you can reintroduce the moderate ones, but only one at a time, and giving each one three days before adding another one.

DAY 1	DAY 4	DAY 7
Rye crispbread has a glycemic index of 69	Orange juice has a glycemic index of 52	Corn has a glycemic index of 59

Helpful supplements

As with all other aspects of our physiology, certain nutritional supplements can help to nourish specific parts of the body, allowing it to recover more quickly than it does by diet alone. In the case of sub-optimum blood-sugar control, the main nutrients are the B-complex vitamins, since it is these substances that help to metabolize carbohydrates effectively within the body. Although it consists of individual vitamins that are distinguished from each other by number, the whole B-vitamin complex works in unison, which is why the vitamins are grouped together rather than put into separate classes. It is therefore unlikely to be of benefit, and indeed may cause a greater imbalance, if any of the B vitamins are taken separately from the rest of the complex. If you feel you need one specific B vitamin more than the others, it would be far better to take a B-complex vitamin, plus at the same time, extra of any one particular B vitamin that you feel you need.

The B-complex vitamins affect the blood-sugar balance.

This is not to say, however, that specific B vitamins are not useful supplements. Good examples of those that are include B6, which helps with premenstrual syndrome, and extra B5, which helps with stress.

In addition, since the glucose tolerance factor (G.T.F.) is so important in aiding the appropriate uptake of glucose by the tissues, then this can be supplemented also either in the form of additional G.T.F. or as a more general dietary supplement containing the mineral chromium.

Other useful supplements include the antioxidants (vitamins A, C, E), the minerals manganese and zinc, high potency garlic, lecithin, E.P.A. (Eicosapentaenoic acid from fish), and spirulina. If you are in any doubt about what to take, obtain advice from a nutritional therapist or your local health food store. See your physician if you are concerned about any of your blood-sugar symptoms before you start to take supplements, especially if you are diabetic, or have diabetic symptoms.

STRESS

I F YOU FEEL THAT *stress from emotional problems, relationships, or the work environment is sabotaging your nutritional healing attempts, by causing excessive (or comfort) eating, or causing you to indulge too frequently in alcohol, try the quick test below to assess to what degree you may be affected.*

HOW STRESSED ARE YOU?

Answer "yes" or "no" to the following questions.

- Is your energy level lower than it used to be?
- Are you especially competitive at work, sports, or relationships?
- Do you feel you work harder than most of your colleagues?
- Do you find yourself often doing several tasks at the same time?
- Do you get very impatient if people or circumstances delay you?
- Do you feel guilty each time you try to relax?
- Do you become angry easily?
- Do you have a constant need to be recognized or to achieve?
- Are you unclear about your goals?
- Do you have difficulty getting off to sleep, sleep poorly/lightly, or wake up with your mind racing?

- Do you find it hard to say "no" to people?
- Do you often bottle up your feelings?
- Are you always in a hurry to get somewhere, or get something done?
- Are there any long-term stressful situations in your life (parents, marriage, job, children, finances, etc.)?
- Has anyone very close to you died recently?
- Have you recently been divorced or separated from your partner?
- Have you had to leave a job recently?
- Have you moved house recently?
- Do you feel you have poor self-image, low self-esteem, or poor self-confidence?
- Do you eat to cheer yourself up, or often eat when you are not hungry?

SCORING

Score one point for each "yes" answer.

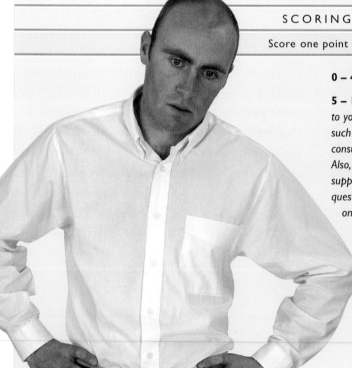

0 – 4 *Stress effects on your health are low.*

5 – 10 *Your moderate stress levels are probably contributing to your health problems. Continue with a good wholefood diet such as the New Pyramid program, and insure that you consume maximum levels of antioxidant fruit and vegetables. Also, make sure you are taking a high-potency antioxidant supplement. Read on and carry out the Adrenal Function questionnaire, to assess just how much effect stress is having on your hormonal system.*

11 and over *It is almost certain that your stressful existence is a major cause of your health problems. Continue with this section and undertake the Adrenal Function questionnaire.*

Stress often makes us eat badly, but a good diet can help us cope with stress.

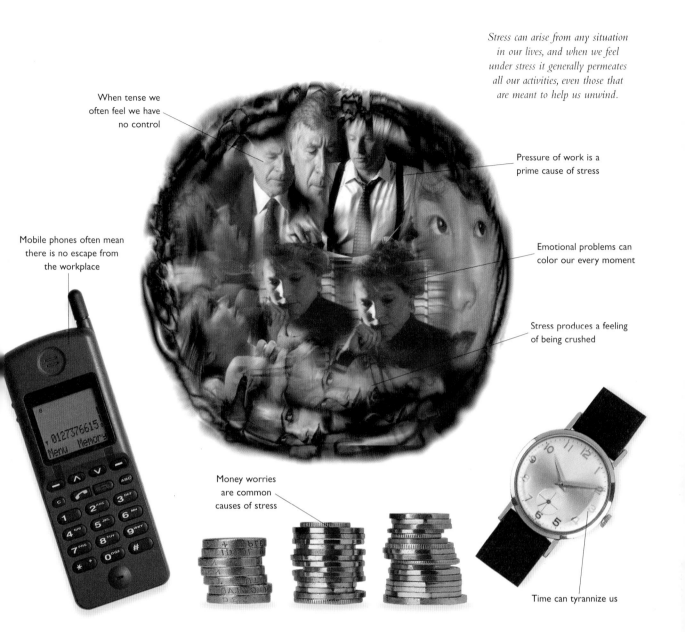

Stress can arise from any situation in our lives, and when we feel under stress it generally permeates all our activities, even those that are meant to help us unwind.

When tense we often feel we have no control

Pressure of work is a prime cause of stress

Mobile phones often mean there is no escape from the workplace

Emotional problems can color our every moment

Stress produces a feeling of being crushed

Money worries are common causes of stress

Time can tyrannize us

Stress and the Endocrine System

Our ability to deal with stress is under the control of the endocrine (hormonal) system. Stress induces a series of reactions known as the "fight or flight" mechanism. Body systems act in a coordinated fashion in order to prepare the body for physical action and energy expenditure.

The first, immediate effect is caused by the brain stimulating a part of the adrenal glands called the adrenal medulla to secrete the hormone adrenaline. This hormone acts on the liver, stimulating it to convert some of its stored glycogen to glucose, and causing it to release this into the bloodstream. Blood pressure and heart rate increase to allow this "emergency" glucose to be conveyed around the system to the target cells. The breathing rate is similarly increased in order to bring in the necessary extra oxygen to deal with the breakdown of glucose for energy release. Digestion stops as the blood supply is diverted to the muscles to prepare them to move quickly away from the "source of danger." The blood platelets get ready to aggregate quickly in case they need to form a blood clot over any cut or wound that may occur in the "fight."

In addition to this, stress stimulates the pituitary gland to release a hormone called A.C.T.H. (adrenocorticotrophic hormone), and this hormone stimulates the adrenal cortex to release a group of hormones called the corticoids (glucocorticoids and mineralocorticoids). The glucocorticoids further help in making glucose available to the cells, while the mineralocorticoids help to retain sodium (by reabsorbing this in the kidneys) which is needed by the body for increased nervous transmission and for appropriate muscle contraction.

Hormone Exhaustion and Stress Reduction

It is easy to see how these activities were necessary to enable the body to deal quickly with dangerous situations, but in modern humans, although the physiological reaction to stress remains the same, the triggers and the effect are completely different. The cumulative physiological reactions to raise blood glucose, blood pressure, heart rate, breathing rate, and blood-clotting mechanisms, which are precursors to rapid physical activity, still occur, but we rarely choose to fight or run away. The majority of our stress triggers are not those which were suffered by the dangers of a caveman existence, but are more likely to be an impossible work load, worries about money, frustrations in slow-moving traffic, demanding children, and unsympathetic partners. We rarely do anything "physical" with the extra energy we have at our disposal, except perhaps fume, swear, and shout. The cumulative effect of stress hormones, stress triggers, and a heightened response level can eventually lead to anxiety states or will simply keep the body on "red alert" even when the "danger" has passed.

All of these factors can eventually lead to exhaustion of several endocrine (hormonal) glands and in particular the adrenals. There is a slowing down of the metabolic rate as the adrenals and other endocrine glands, such as the pancreas and the thyroid, begin to function less well. This inevitably leads to a general slowing-down of the whole system, the accumulation of weight, and a worsening ability to fight off disease and cancers.

Nevertheless, it has to be said that a little stress is good for us. It keeps us sharp and on our toes, and it does stimulate metabolism in the short term. It is the amount of stress that is the problem, and the way in which we dissipate its biochemical products within the body. For example, it is well known that regular exercise is a very good de-stressor, as is proper relaxation or yoga (which is a good combination of both exercise and relaxation).

HORMONAL BALANCE

The nutritional aspects of stress reduction are based on the maintenance of hormonal output. Adrenal hormones, such as adrenaline and cortisol, are the prime contenders in stress reactions, as too are insulin from the pancreas and thyroxine from the thyroid. Another hormone called D.H.E.A. (dehydroepiandrosterone), manufactured in the body from cholesterol (as is cortisol), has received a great deal of interest over the last decade. It is intimately involved in glucose metabolism and the stress response, and has been heralded as the "youth hormone." When homeostatic equilibrium, involving all the hormones related to stress handling, is absent, there is a gradual progression through stages of chronic stress adaptation to maladaptation and through to exhaustion of many glands. Hormonal balance is of vital importance in preventing stressful events resulting in glandular exhaustion, and is best achieved by eating a well-balanced, wholefood diet as in the New Pyramid program. The omission of refined and processed foods, together with stimulants such as tea, coffee, salt, and sugar, is especially important when optimizing nutrition to combat stress. Stimulant foods and beverages are particularly detrimental to hormonal harmony since they artificially raise pancreatic activity leading to a chaotic chemical state far removed from that of healthy homeostasis.

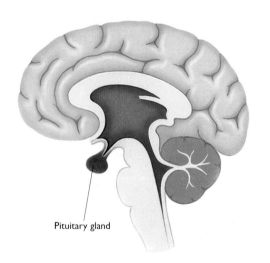

In response to stress the pituitary gland triggers a rise in glucose.

Pituitary gland

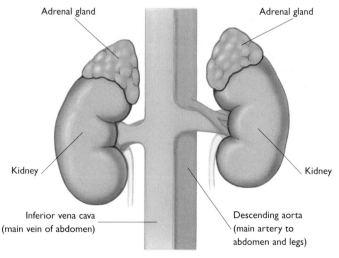

Adrenal gland

Adrenal gland

Kidney

Kidney

Inferior vena cava
(main vein of abdomen)

Descending aorta
(main artery to
abdomen and legs)

The adrenal glands, on top of the kidneys, secrete the "flight or fight" adrenaline.

ADRENAL STRESS QUESTIONNAIRE

If you feel that stress has been a big feature in your life for a long period of time, give "yes" or "no" answers to the following questions, which are based on symptoms of sub-optimum adrenal function.

- Do you have a tendency to severe emotional swings?
- Do you have a tendency to have allergies, e.g., eczema, urticaria (hives), or hay fever?
- Do you have low blood pressure, or do you feel dizzy when standing up quickly?
- Do you feel unable to get enough air, i.e., feel suffocated, and frequently sigh or yawn?
- Do you feel lacking in energy in the morning and perhaps require a stimulant such as coffee or a cigarette to "get you going"?

- Are you very sensitive to bright lights?
- Do you frequently have a dry mouth, lacking in saliva?
- Do your ankles swell, especially at night?
- Do you crave salty foods, such as chips, salty meats, salted nuts, etc.?
- Does eating foods such as cabbage, beans, or very starchy/sugary foods, give you indigestion?

SCORING

Score one point for each "yes" answer.

4 and over *It is very likely that your protracted stress levels have reduced the efficiency of your adrenal glands to some degree. Supplementing your diet with nutrients such as vitamin C, the B-complex vitamins, and additional vitamin B_5 (usually in the form of calcium pantothenate), together with special adrenal nourishing herbs like Siberian ginseng, would be of real help. If you are considering consulting a nutritional therapist, he/she will be able to take noninvasive saliva samples for analysis of your adrenal stress index. Also, a urine test to assess the ratio of sulphite to creatinine can be carried out. The lower the sulphate, the higher the stress.*

The best diet for anyone with high stress levels is the New Pyramid program, since this will not only nourish the endocrine system in general, but the feel-good factor inherent in this diet will itself promote better stress-handling. Metabolism-enhancing exercise will deal with increased levels of stress hormones as enhanced levels of endorphins, the pleasure molecules, are released.

Remember too, that high body toxicity and/or working and living in areas of high pollution will add chemical stress factors to the overall stress load. You would be well advised to combat toxicity and pollution problems first, by undergoing a detoxification program and depolluting your house. This will automatically give you more energy to deal with your emotional stress producers.

Regular exercise puts the body in a condition where moderate stress can actually make you feel good.

THYROID FUNCTION

THE RATE OF METABOLISM is controlled by the thyroid gland, which is positioned at the base of the throat. The thyroid gland produces and secretes the hormone thyroxine, in response to another hormone called T.S.H. which is made in the anterior pituitary gland. The pituitary gland, therefore, ultimately controls metabolism and will be encouraged to raise metabolism by a stress reaction, exercise, or taking a stimulant food/beverage such as chocolate or coffee. However, despite the apparent usefulness of an increase in metabolic rate by these three means, a continually stimulated pituitary will eventually begin to underfunction.

As well as raising the metabolic level, the pituitary gland depresses metabolism when the person is on a calorie-reduced diet, or is fasting. This enables the body to conserve its stores of body fat. In these conditions the pituitary reduces the amount of T.S.H. that it sends to the thyroid gland, which has the effect of lessening thyroid output.

In normal circumstances, a finely tuned system will allow proper maintenance of metabolic rate appropriate to requirements at a particular time. However, there is much information available now which indicates that around 40 percent or more of the present population have some degree of thyroid malfunction. Research undertaken on thyroid conditions has indicated that many of them are likely to be due to food intolerance. Food intolerance (particularly to the proteins in cow's milk and wheat)

may be linked to the negative effect that allergens have on the thyroid gland, preventing it from working properly and in consequence lowering metabolism.

An underactive thyroid is generally characterized by weight increase (despite a reduction in appetite), slow pulse rate, sluggish digestion, constipation, lethargy, and apathy. An overactive thyroid usually occurs because of proliferation of thyroxine-producing cells within the thyroid, and results in the speeding up of the metabolic rate. This usually brings with it a drop in weight and an increase in appetite, more rapid digestion and diarrhea, increased heart rate and blood pressure, muscular tremors, nervousness, excitability, and apprehension.

WHEAT

It is now thought that an intolerance to cow's milk can stop the thyroid working properly.

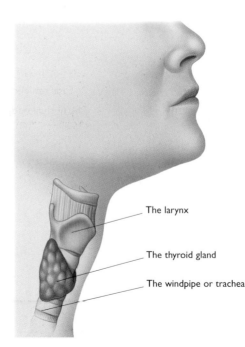

The larynx

The thyroid gland

The windpipe or trachea

The thyroid gland, which is situated in the throat, governs the rate of metabolism. If the thyroid ceases to function altogether, a person will become very tired and sluggish, and if not treated the condition will become fatal.

DO YOU SUFFER FROM AN UNDERACTIVE THYROID?

You can obtain some idea of your thyroid function by answering the following questions. Again, a simple "yes" or "no" is required, then consult the scoring box underneath.

- Do you tend to gain weight easily and fail to lose it even with a calorie-restricted diet?
- Are you chronically or frequently constipated?
- Is your skin pale, thick, dry, wrinkled, "waxy," or puffy, especially around the eyes?
- Do you feel lethargic, dull, confused, or uninterested much of the time?
- Is the hair on the outer third of your eyebrows noticeably thin or even absent?
- Do you tend to feel better in the mornings and worse in the afternoons?
- Are you very sensitive to cold, or have cold hands and/or feet?
- Do you have ringing in the ears, or have you noticed any hearing loss?

- Is your appetite very poor, yet you are not losing weight?
- Is your pulse rate slow (below 65 per minute)?
- Do you have weakness and aches in muscles?
- Is your hair thinning or falling out?
- Do you have very brittle nails?
- Do you feel depressed much of the time?
- Do you have problems with menstruation or fertility?
- Have you lost interest in sex?
- Do you have headaches with focusing problems?
- Do you have sticky eyelids, slow healing or frequent infections (especially of the throat)?
- Do you have tingling in hands and feet?
- Have you noticed any changes in skin pigmentation?

SCORING

Score one point for each "yes" answer.

If you have said "yes" to more than half of these questions, you may be suffering from an underactive thyroid (hypothyroidism). One self-test you might try before taking the matter further is to carry out the basal temperature test (see below).

If you are concerned about a large proportion of the above symptoms, and your basal body temperature is low, see your physician, who will give you a thorough examination and may carry out a blood test to assess the level of your thyroid activity.

TEMPERATURE TEST

This test must be performed before you get out of bed and before you have undertaken any form of activity. It must be done before you drink or eat anything.

1. Place a thermometer under your right arm, insuring the "bulb" of the thermometer is exactly in the center of the underarm.

2. Keep the thermometer in place for at least five minutes.

3. Record the temperature as accurately as you can, to the smallest fraction of a degree.

4. Repeat this daily. If you are a regularly menstruating female, then the best time to do this is from day one of the menstrual cycle, for about a week. If you are a nonmenstruating female or are male, you need to take your temperature over a period of two weeks.

5. Add up all your temperatures and divide by the number of readings to obtain your average (mean) basal temperature.

The normal body temperature value is 98.6° to 99°F (36.8° to 37°C), so that the more you depart from this value, the more likely there is to be a thyroid imbalance.

Underactive (hypothyroid) shows up as below the normal level, and overactive (hyperthyroid) as above the normal level.

Place the thermometer under your arm to test temperature for an underactive thyroid.

Helpful Foods and Supplements for the Thyroid

People with an overactive thyroid have increased demands for many nutrients, and the B complex is particularly important since these vitamins are intimately involved with the release of energy from food. Whole grains such as brown rice, seeds, fermented foods like miso paste (from soy), and yeast extract (as long as there is no allergy to yeast) are particularly good sources of B vitamins. In addition, vitamin C from fruits and vegetables, vitamin E from whole grains and olive oil, and essential fatty acids from seeds and fish are all required optimally in hyperthyroidism (an overactive thyroid).

Calcium from seeds, pulses (legumes), tofu, leafy green vegetables, and the soft bones of canned fish is especially important to thyroid sufferers (of either under- or overfunctioning) for reducing the risk of osteoporosis, regulation of heart beat, helping metabolize iron, and aiding in the transmission of nervous impulses. Magnesium from green leafy vegetables, whole grains, beans, wheatgerm, figs, dried apricots, seeds, soybeans, buckwheat, and fish is vital to help balance calcium levels and aid its activity, and in promoting a healthy cardiovascular system.

Feeling lethargic and sleepy is a sign of an underactive thyroid, and insomnia a sign of an overactive one.

DO YOU SUFFER FROM AN OVERACTIVE THYROID?

A further set of questions to establish the possibility of an overactive thyroid (hyperthyroidism) is given here. Again, a simple "yes" or "no" answer is required.

- Does your heart race (palpitations) and beat strongly even when you are resting?
- Is your pulse rate above 80 per minute when you are resting?
- Do you blush easily or have hot flashes?
- Do you tend to have night sweats?
- Are you highly emotional, nervous, or irritable?
- Do you have tics or twitches around the eyes or in the facial muscles?
- Do you suffer from insomnia?
- Are you aware of an inner trembling?
- Is your skin frequently moist (especially your palms) for no obvious reason?
- Are you oversensitive to heat?
- Do your thoughts race and prevent clear thinking?
- Do you have an increased appetite, yet are still not gaining weight?
- Have you started to get more menstrual problems?
- Has your sex drive increased?
- Have you any eye or sight complaints?
- Is there any swelling in the neck area?
- Do you feel that your muscles have lost strength?
- Have you got "staring eyes"?
- Have you noticed that your moods are very changeable?
- Have you got blood pressure problems?

SCORING

Score one point for each "yes" answer.

If you have answered "yes" to half or more of these questions, then you need to carry out the basal temperature test, and visit your physician for a thorough check up and blood test.

Manganese from nuts, whole grains, and black tea helps those with an underactive thyroid (hypothyroidism). It is involved in the formation of the thyroid hormone, thyroxine, and can help eliminate fatigue, improve muscle function, aid memory, and reduce nervous irritability. Similarly, iodine is a mineral which forms part of the thyroxine molecule, and since this mineral is found in seaweeds (especially kelp), supplementing the diet with kelp extract is likely to help those with hypothyroidism. Thyroxine must be converted to its active form, known as triiodothyronine, before it can act; and for this conversion the minerals zinc, copper, and iron are needed.

Manganese aids in the production of thyroxine.

Having an efficient metabolism is at the core of thyroid treatment. For our body chemistry to work well, the body's enzymes must be supplied with all the micronutrients necessary to work as co-factors. The minerals zinc, selenium, and magnesium are extremely important in this respect.

There is an increased requirement for vitamin A, as retinol, since beta-carotene is not easily converted to retinol by the liver of thyroid sufferers. Attempting to obtain good levels of this vitamin from high intakes of beta-carotene does not work. Care must be taken with any foods (e.g., liver) or supplements containing vitamin A (as retinol) if pregnant or breastfeeding, since this form can soon become toxic.

Some foods contain substances called goitrogens which interfere with the workings of the thyroid gland.

Shellfish help to nourish and rebalance the thyroid gland.

These substances occur naturally in several plants, particularly those belonging to the family Cruciferae, such as white turnip, cabbage, broccoli, cauliflower, Brussels sprouts, and mustard. Fortunately, cooking will usually inactivate goitrogens. Goitrogenic foods should, therefore, be used sparingly, or at least not eaten raw, by anyone with a thyroid complaint.

In addition to any medical care given to you by your physician, the best way to nourish your thyroid gland and enable it to rebalance is to undertake the New Pyramid program, making sure you include fish, shellfish, and seaweed regularly, along with foods high in the antioxidants beta-carotene, vitamin C, selenium, and zinc (*see* pages 66–73).

Supplement complexes specifically designed for nourishing the thyroid gland include nutrients such as calcium, magnesium, selenium, zinc, vitamin A, vitamin C, niacinamide, and other B-complex vitamins, Siberian ginseng, kelp, licorice, and possibly the amino acids L-glycine, L-tyrosine, and L-glutamine. However, take extra care with kelp supplements, or any food containing iodine. Although the thyroid gland needs iodine to make thyroxine, an excess of this mineral will interfere greatly with thyroid function, and could cause further imbalance. Ask for advice at your health food store if you are considering using supplements, or, even better, seek the professional advice of a nutritional therapist.

Seaweed contains iodine, good for those with hypothyroidism.

Oily fish is an essential part of the diet program for thyroid sufferers.

METABOLISM

Mᴏꜱᴛ ᴏꜰ ᴛʜᴇ ᴀᴍɪɴᴏ ᴀᴄɪᴅꜱ, *fats, and sugars in the bloodstream are transported to the liver after absorption from the intestines. From the liver some nutrients go directly into the circulation and are delivered to all cells of the body, and others remain in the liver. Whichever happens, their fate is basically the same. Amino acids are reconstituted to make proteins which are incorporated into the structure of the cells or become biologically active molecules such as enzymes and antibodies. Apart from a small amino acid "pool" which each cell contains, proteins cannot be stored as such, and excess protein is broken down and used to supply energy. Fats are also incorporated into cell structure as fatty acids (principally in the membrane systems found there), used as the basis for some hormones, used for energy, or put into storage. Carbohydrates are predominantly used to make energy.*

The utilization of these nutrients is called metabolism, and it occurs in every cell of the body. The chemical reactions involved in metabolism themselves require nutrients in the form of many different vitamins and minerals. Metabolism can be divided up into two parts – breakdown of nutrients (to release energy), and synthesis of new structures (to build new cells). The process of turning food into energy (breakdown) is called catabolism. Our cells oxidize carbohydrates, fatty acids, and excess amino acids to release energy. This energy is used to power the chemical processes which we know of as life. Some of the energy released is used to help build new cells.

This process of building up nutrients to form new structures and new cells (biosynthesis) is called anabolism. Catabolism and anabolism work together to keep the body functioning in accordance with information that is received from the genetic makeup of the cell. When the rate of one exceeds the rate of the other, health problems arise, the first of which is usually a change in body weight. Since a change to a lower metabolic rate is much more common, overweight and obesity are seen as prime indicators in metabolic disharmony.

The daily requirement for energy varies depending on our genes, our gender, level of activity, state of health, and other factors, but if we took an average, we would probably require around 2,500 calories (really kilocalories) or 10,500 kJ (kilojoules). Part of this energy will be used up by the body in maintaining normal body processes such as heartbeat, breathing, digestion, etc., and our body will need energy to satisfy this requirement whether we are sitting reading or doing something more active. This figure is referred to as the Basal Metabolic Rate.

Some people don't put on weight however much they eat, while others put it on easily.

TESTING YOUR METABOLIC RATE

For an idea of your metabolic rate, answer "yes" or "no" to the following questions. They are an assessment primarily for low metabolism, since this is likely to be related to more general health problems (except hyperthyroidism, for which medical help should be sought).

- Do you have less energy, or become tired more easily, than friends of similar age and lifestyle to yourself?
- Do you seem to feel the cold more than most of the people in your family or group of friends?
- Do you find that you only have to eat very little food to start gaining weight?
- Have you recently been on either a very low-calorie diet, a very low-carbohydrate diet or have taken slimming pills, such as amphetamines?
- Have you been on a calorie-restricted diet continuously over the last six months or longer?
- Do you have weak and/or poorly defined muscles?
- Is your hair thinning?
- Do your ankles swell, particularly at night?

SCORING

Score one point for each "yes" answer.

0 – 3 *You are unlikely to have a slow metabolism, and, using the New Pyramid program as a basis, you can afford to have an overall higher calorific intake.*

4– 5 *Your metabolism is on the low side, but after a few weeks on the New Pyramid program you will find your energy levels rising, and any excess weight disappearing, especially if you balance your proteins and carbohydrates correctly.*

6 and over *You would appear to have quite a low metabolic rate. Your body runs too economically and often you are quite exhausted for very little effort. You are likely to have the type of metabolism which responds quickly to food being in short supply, and if you have been trying to lose weight (especially by "yo-you" dieting) for a long time, you have probably set off your hunger/survival mechanism on several occasions and have reduced lean tissue and laid down more fat. Fat takes very little in the way of metabolic energy to keep it functioning. The New Pyramid program is ideal for you, but care must be taken to obtain most carbohydrates from vegetables and pulses (legumes).*

Symptoms of a low metabolism can include tiredness and a constant feeling of cold.

We use up additional energy units as we become more active. However, some people have a naturally low basal metabolic rate – and will have a tendency to put on weight quickly and easily. Others have a naturally high basal metabolic rate. These are the people who seem to be able to eat all the time and stay thin. Whatever the basal metabolism of our bodies may be, we are all able to maximize our potential, keep trim, and maintain our health by using nutritional healing.

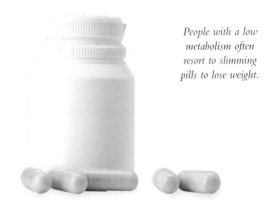

People with a low metabolism often resort to slimming pills to lose weight.

Thinning hair can also signify a low metabolic rate

Excessively cold hands are a classic sign of a low metabolism

Stimulating the System

The best way of raising the metabolic rate is to eat a metabolic-boosting diet containing fresh whole foods, and with the correct balance of nutrients.

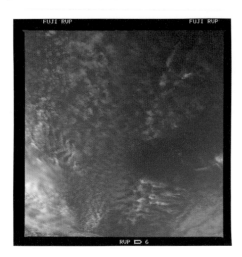

Fire does not burn with fuel alone – our dietary-induced rising metabolism needs as much oxygen as possible.

METABOLISM-BOOSTING FOODS

Since carbohydrates are the principal energy-giving foods in the diet, you may feel that all you need to do is increase the amount of these to obtain more energy and stimulate metabolism. However to metabolize carbohydrate efficiently we need a whole host of different enzymes, and these depend on many different vitamins and minerals to act as co-factors. The important vitamins are the B complex, folic acid, and biotin and the best natural sources are fresh fruit, raw

Getting the metabolism in balance has a stimulating effect and makes it easier to deal with problems.

vegetables, and wheatgerm. Seeds, nuts, and whole grains also have reasonable levels. The minerals iron, calcium, magnesium, chromium, and zinc (all found in whole grains, seeds, and nuts) are vital for the manufacture of energy within the cells. Furthermore, simply by ingesting food (particularly protein), metabolism may be raised by as much as 30 percent. This is called the "thermogenic effect of food."

The New Pyramid program incorporates all of the above, and has an excellent nutrient balance for stimulating your metabolism, but how do you know that your metabolism is improving?

◆ *You will find that you move faster and achieve more with less effort.*
◆ *You will find yourself dealing with challenges that defeated you before.*
◆ *The healing effects (via nourishment of glands and systems that had become overworked and depleted of nutrients) will show by the decrease in lots of little aches and pains and improved resistance to infection.*

The theory is that the energizing effects of good food affects your mind and body at the same time, so that when you are mentally alert, your brain's hormone balance changes and you burn food faster thereby obtaining more physical energy. Eating foods such as those in the New Pyramid program insures that your body obtains the top grade fuel it needs to turn up the thermostat on your metabolism and get it burning hotter.

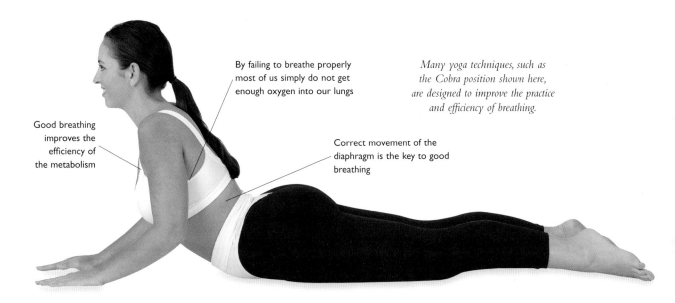

Good breathing improves the efficiency of the metabolism

By failing to breathe properly most of us simply do not get enough oxygen into our lungs

Correct movement of the diaphragm is the key to good breathing

Many yoga techniques, such as the Cobra position shown here, are designed to improve the practice and efficiency of breathing.

GETTING MORE OXYGEN

In addition to eating the wrong kinds of food, many people do not get enough oxygen into their lungs and bodies to maximize their energy levels. The biggest problem is incorrect breathing, or not breathing deeply enough (using only the upper part of the lungs), so that the total lung volume available is never approached. The modern lifestyle in the Western world is much to blame for this. Sitting at desks most of the working day, driving to and from work or during leisure hours, and flopping in front of the television most evenings. Whereas, were you to interrupt your sedentary occupations regularly by carrying out a deep breathing routine, you would keep your mental and physical energy at a higher level. There is no need to get anxious that this is time-wasting (especially at work), since the improvement in your performance will enable you to keep on top.

It is not the intention to go into great detail here about breathing routines, since there is adequate literature available. You could start to attend yoga classes, where correct deep breathing routines are an integral part of the techniques. The Alexander Technique will also help with breathing, as will being taught to sing or to act.

SMOKING

Smoking is the worst thing you can do to your oxygen levels, and therefore, your metabolism. The chemicals in tobacco smoke will damage the delicate lining of the lungs and prevent proper uptake of oxygen. Furthermore, these chemicals enter the bloodstream and are carried to every body tissue, causing many diseases that are commonly related directly (and indirectly as well) to tobacco smoking.

Some of the chemicals in tobacco have a stimulating effect and consequently will raise metabolism slightly, but there is a much healthier way, as we have learned.

If you still smoke, remind yourself that you are not only damaging your body, but that you are interfering with your body's capacity to produce energy as well. If you decide to stop smoking at the same time as starting the New Pyramid program, you will probably find that the program will help to reduce the misery of nicotine withdrawal.

They may be stimulating, but tobacco chemicals are very damaging to the body.

Damage to the lung lining prevents the proper intake of oxygen

The lungs bear the brunt of the effects of smoking, but chemicals in smoke are also dispersed through the body.

Chemicals from smoking get carried around the body via the bloodstream

Improving Metabolism with Activity and Exercise

When you reach the stage where you are beginning to feel the benefits of a healthy metabolism-boosting program (a good wholefood diet, and improved breathing), the next natural step is to look for ways of being more active. As your energy levels rise, your body begins to feel more alive. Life becomes more interesting and you want to dive into things. If you are a hardworking person with a job and family to look after, finding time to undertake additional activities may seem a daunting prospect. However, when your metabolic fires are truly burning brighter, you will begin to have much more than just a passing urge to do things and will find that you make the time.

You must congratulate yourself when you reach this stage – you are beginning to think like a healthy person. This is the time to make sure you don't miss the chance and lose all the power you have built up. Use the increased energy that is pushing for an outlet to enhance metabolism, and do it in a way that both fits in with your daily routine (run upstairs, run for a bus, walk to work, cycle to work, dance around with the vacuum cleaner, walk briskly with the baby carriage or buggy), and in ways which will interest you; scan the local press, nightschool class

You don't need a gym or running shoes; vigorous walking is good exercise.

prospectuses, gym and leisure center advertisements to find an activity that you would really like to take part in two or three times a week.

Many people who try to lose weight and improve health by exercise alone, or by a combination of diet and exercise, fail because they do not understand the metabolic processes involved.

When we begin to exercise, muscle tissue uses its local supply of glycogen, and there is a delay before any fat is mobilized or more glycogen is released from the liver. This is why warming up is so important; it helps to get this process started. Most beginners do not continue exercising for long enough to break through the warm-up barrier, and they tend to give up as their muscle glycogen stores begin to run out – just at the time when they are about to start burning any excess body fat. If you never exercise continuously for more than a few minutes, your fat reserves won't diminish and stamina won't improve. Moreover, the more this happens, the more the muscles will rely on their own stores of glycogen and the less readily will they burn fat. However, after about 10 to 20 minutes of continuous, moderate exercise, fat becomes an increasingly important source of fuel to the muscles, and the metabolism becomes more efficient.

Warm-up routines are important, as is exercising for a good length of time.

Taking regular exercise provides you with increased energy and a sense of well-being for all the other activities in life.

EXERCISE

WORK

RELAXATION

You do not need to start running marathons. The fact is that brisk walking in the fresh air, or even on a treadmill in a gym, is by far the best way to start. The longer the activity continues, the greater the proportion of fat that will be used as fuel and the fitter you will become. As you begin to exercise regularly (healthy person activity), the faster will be the switch from pure glycogen to the glycogen/fat mixture. In addition, the more you exercise, the faster the oxygen will move to the tissues, as your heart and lungs become better conditioned and operate more efficiently.

Again, it is not the intention here to give you a list of set daily exercises or to give a full list of possible activities. There are many good books available to call upon for ideas. The main advice is to get to know your body, listen to it asking to be more active, and find something to do which delights you, gives you pleasure, and makes your more creative. Enjoyable activity will not be a chore; will not be "just another pressure" on your already full life, but will encourage you to remain active. The more you do it, the easier you will find it is to fit it in.

The more active you are, the more excess fat you will shed, and the healthier and fitter you will be. Eventually you will reach a stable point where food, activity, and your whole lifestyle are in balance and at a level which is right for you. Don't compare yourself with others; each one of us has a unique biochemistry which requires a unique nutrient intake and a unique energy output.

As you get used to using your body for an increased level of energy output, so your capacity for pleasure will grow. You will become competent and will get the "buzz" that encourages you to do more. This is called positive feedback, and is one which we more readily relate to sexual enjoyment. But any physically active person is aware that similar pleasurable bodily rewards happen at many levels with differing types of activity. The more you do, the more you will be able to do and, more importantly, the more you will want to do. When you get that little bit extra from your body, your self-esteem rises, your capacity for output increases, and so your opportunities for pleasure rise further. You have reached the stage where optimum nutrition and body activity are in harmony.

Metabolism and Balancing Hormones Naturally

Finally, in addition to the changes already mentioned, your body will also begin to undergo a balancing of hormones. Our hormones, like every other part of our uniqueness, have a specific profile. The hormone profile of an unfit overweight person is different from that of a healthy slim person. With the rebalancing of your hormones, your transition will be complete. A rebalancing of your hormones will not change your sexuality. You are likely to find, however, that one of the rewards of a slim, active, healthy body is a greatly enhanced capacity for sensual and sexual satisfaction. As with all our other bodily functions, sex is improved by the correct balance of our hormonal system. Unfit, unhealthy, overweight people have lost their balance and will find that some of the spice has gone out of life.

PASSION

Hormones are intimately involved with the metabolism of fat. One hormone, growth hormone, made in the pituitary gland, is a liberator of fat from the fat stores of the body. Being active causes a rise in the level of this hormone; it has been found to increase sharply at about 10 to 15 minutes into a vigorous exercise period. If you are an adult, growth hormone will not actually cause you to increase in size (though this is the effect that it has on children), but it will promote the growth of lean tissue within your body, provided you are eating enough of the right sort of food.

Once you become more physically active, other hormone changes occur. Muscular effort, combined with the excitement of doing something you really enjoy (and this is why you need to choose your activities carefully) leads to the production of adrenaline and nor-adrenaline from the adrenal glands. These hormones make you feel active

THE RESULTS OF A DEPRESSED METABOLISM	THE BENEFITS OF A HEALTHY METABOLISM

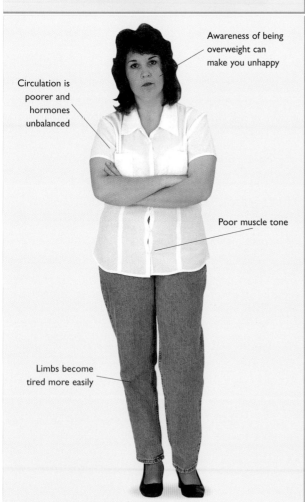

Awareness of being overweight can make you unhappy

Circulation is poorer and hormones unbalanced

Poor muscle tone

Limbs become tired more easily

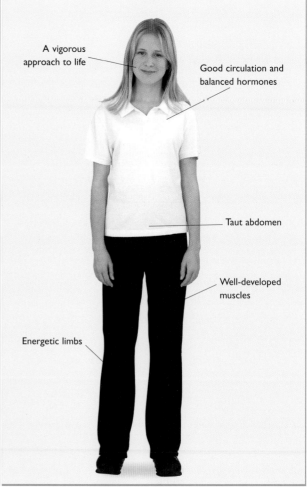

A vigorous approach to life

Good circulation and balanced hormones

Taut abdomen

Well-developed muscles

Energetic limbs

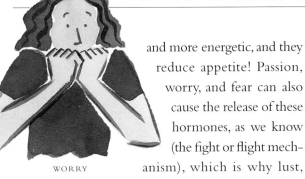

WORRY

and more energetic, and they reduce appetite! Passion, worry, and fear can also cause the release of these hormones, as we know (the fight or flight mechanism), which is why lust, love, and any other type of emotional stress can make you lose weight fast.

Insulin (from the pancreas) is another hormone important in fat metabolism, as we have seen from the section of this book on blood sugar control. As activity is increased, the production of insulin decreases. The importance of this is that, since insulin is involved in fat storage, anything that effectively balances the levels of insulin and keeps them low, will prevent fat deposition. Furthermore, the foods used in the New Pyramid program are just those that are needed to balance blood sugar properly: complex carbohydrates, such as vegetables, fruit, and whole grains, appropriately balanced with

good quality protein, such as fish, lean meat, pulses (legumes), soy, nuts, and seeds. The combined effects, then, of regular exercise and the New Pyramid program will enhance metabolism and reduce the tendency to store excess body fat, while encouraging the muscles to burn fat. When blood levels of insulin are high, muscles don't burn fat, only glycogen. Conversely, when insulin levels fall, fat can be released from fat storage to be used as fuel.

It is unfortunately true that one of the problems with a depressed metabolism is that high quantities of insulin are produced. Not only does this aid the accumulation of fat, but can eventually lead to obesity-related diabetes (mature-onset diabetes), heart disease, and other degenerative conditions.

A depressed metabolism is an extremely unhealthy metabolism; not the efficient survival mechanism it would at first appear to be.

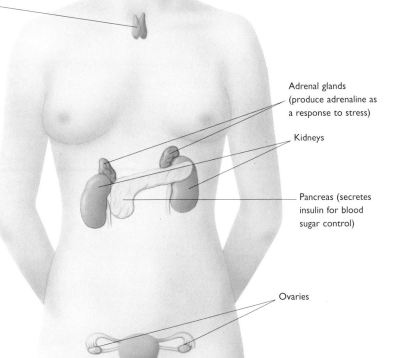

FEAR

Protracted emotional states can lead to the release of adrenaline hormones which cause weight loss.

Pituitary gland (controls the activity of other glands in the body)

Thyroid gland (regulates the body's metabolic rate)

Thymus gland

Adrenal glands (produce adrenaline as a response to stress)

Kidneys

Pancreas (secretes insulin for blood sugar control)

Ovaries

LEFT
Being slim (left) rather than overweight (far left) brings benefits that are nothing to do with resembling models in advertisements, but relate to feeling good and being healthy.

The thyroid, pituitary, and adrenal glands, together with the pancreas, secrete hormones which are important in fat metabolism.

WEIGHT GAIN AND HEALTH

B EING OVERWEIGHT CAN *be dangerous to health. Research indicates that at present more than a quarter of the population of Britain is classed as overweight – 37 percent of men and 24 percent of women. Of these, some are obese, which is defined as being more than 20 percent above your ideal weight. American research has shown a steep rise in the numbers of overweight adults from a quarter of the population between 1960 and 1980, to a third of the population between 1980 and 1991 – a 32 percent increase in 10 years. Results from a U.S. government study show that young adults (25 to 30) are getting fatter the fastest of all. At the present time, more than 20 percent of the U.S. population are clinically obese.*

MEASURING EXCESS WEIGHT

As a general rule of thumb, a B.M.I. (body mass index) between 20 and 28 can be accepted as normal, and anything over 28 is regarded as being overweight. B.M.I.s over 30 are classed as seriously overweight, with anything over B.M.I. 40 classified as obese. Anything under 20 can be regarded as underweight. The calculation disregards age and gender. It also avoids making a judgment about large or small frame. The calculation below indicates that this woman is seriously overweight. Even by this generous standard of B.M.I., in 1987, 32.6 million Americans were classified as being overweight.

FAT DISTRIBUTION

A further complication is the distribution of fat. Android type obesity (fat on the upper body and within the abdomen) is much more commonly associated with cardiovascular disease and diabetes than is the gynoid pattern (fat on the buttocks and thighs). As a guide to determine which type you are, the waist/hip circumference for women should not exceed 0.8, or 1.0 for men, regardless of the individual's B.M.I.

For example, if a woman had a waist measurement of 30 inches (76cm) and a hip measurement of 36 inches

CALCULATING YOUR BODY MASS INDEX

A simple calculation can be used to give you some idea of the dividing line between underweight, normal weight, and overweight.

It is called the Body Mass Index and is calculated as follows:

$$\frac{\text{weight in kilograms}}{\text{height in meters, squared}} = \text{B.M.I.}$$

The location of fat matters. A woman's waist should measure less than her hips.

For example, for a woman 5ft 2in tall and weighing 168 pounds, we would have the calculation:

168 pounds ÷ 2.25 *(Divide by 2.25 to give kilograms)* = around 75 kg

5ft 2in is 62 inches

62 × 0.0254 *(Multiply by 0.0254 to give meters)* = 1.58 meters

This figure has to be squared
1.58 × 1.58 = 2.5

The final calculation of B.M.I. is:
$$\frac{75}{2.5} = 30$$

A B.M.I. of 30 would suggest that the woman in this example is overweight.

(92cm), then the calculation of: 30/36 = 0.83 shows us that this woman has more fat accumulated around the waist than is healthy, and is a rather large "apple."

Although we are genetically "programed" to have either an "apple" (android) or a "pear" (gynoid) shape, good nutrition and a little exercise will go a long way to removing the extra risk of ill health that is associated with being an "apple."

Despite there being more overweight men than women, twice as many women as men are trying to lose weight. Of these women, around 17 percent are trying to shrink below a healthy weight. This is a very bad state of affairs for the women concerned, but not for the diet food industry.

However, for those individuals who are truly overweight to the point of obesity there is a substantial risk to their health from a number of diseases, such as cardiovascular disease, cancer, diabetes, etc. Conservative American estimates indicate that the cost of treating conditions relating to obesity in 1986 was $39 billion. For a significant proportion of the others, being overweight is due to a problem of image, and although this seems an unimportant aspect from a health point of view, it nevertheless causes much misery and lowering of self-esteem, which can have a disastrous effect on social life, work, and relationships, which, in turn, has an effect on our health!

Since it is women who, on the whole, suffer from a poor sense of self-image, it is women in general who

---

ACHIEVING A HEALTHY BODY WEIGHT

The conclusion to be drawn about achieving a healthy body weight and shape can be summed up as follows:

- ☞ Aim for a B.M.I. of between 20 and 28 (no more or less) by using a metabolism-boosting diet such as the New Pyramid program.
- ☞ Aim to reduce fat accumulation around the waist by good nutrition and exercise.
- ☞ Avoid smoking, amphetamines, and the excessive use of stimulant beverages.
- ☞ Attempt to find other ways of improving your self-image while you are in the process of losing weight, such as having a new hairstyle and pampering yourself with beauty treatments.

---

make up the largest percentage of slimmers at any one time. The stereotype of the slim female body is now also thought to be the reason why more teenage girls are using amphetamines and taking up smoking at an alarming rate in an attempt to "look cool" and raise metabolism, while at the same time staving off hunger pangs. Of course, both taking drugs and smoking will lead to weight loss, or at least prevent weight gain, but neither is a healthy way to go about it.

Upper body fat is more common in males – a contributory factor to heart disease.

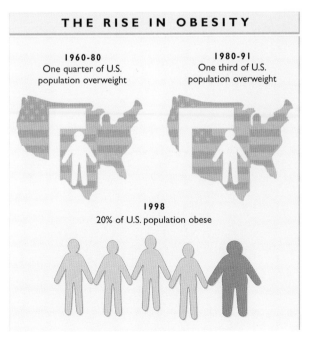

THE RISE IN OBESITY

1960-80
One quarter of U.S. population overweight

1980-91
One third of U.S. population overweight

1998
20% of U.S. population obese

The number of overweight adults in the U.S.A. has risen dramatically since 1960. Today, 20 per cent of the population are obese.

Women are more likely to develop fat on the thighs than the upper body.

Why Do We Get Fat?

Apart from any psychological reason, what biochemical changes cause us to become overweight in the first place? Why does it happen more particularly in later years? Why is it so hard to lose this extra weight? Of course, we all know that the extra weight is due to extra fat (unless we are into excessive body building) and this has obviously accumulated by eating more food than we are metabolizing. However, for years we have been spoon-fed the notion that "energy in" must always equal "energy out" or our weight will change (usually by this we mean it will increase); we see now, from the last section on "metabolism" that there is a middle bit to the equation which is rarely mentioned, giving us a more complicated formula: energy in (food) – basic body functions (or basal metabolism) = energy out (for muscular activity). This shows that losing weight is not a simple matter of "burning it off"; it also shows that we can control our weight much more effectively if we consume foods that allow for the nature of our basal metabolism.

Most diets concentrate on ways of consuming fewer energy units – such as low-fat diets, crash diets, liquid diets, meal replacement diets, mono diets (eating only one food type), high-fiber diets – while others include foods which are believed to be harder to digest, examples of these being high-protein diets, and starch/fat blocker diets. Some further types of diet concentrate on a selection of "special herbs or vegetables." Few diets have been designed to stimulate and balance the metabolism.

Furthermore, food allergy has been particularly implicated where individuals have found it very difficult to lose weight. Food allergies are likely to depress metabolism by having a negative effect on the activity of the thyroid gland. By avoiding the major food allergens (wheat, dairy foods, citrus fruit, yeast, etc.) you are likely to improve the activity level of your metabolism and lose weight. For a more analytical assessment of food allergy, various tests have recently become available in which samples are taken of the individual's blood which is then tested against a range of foods to assess any reaction.

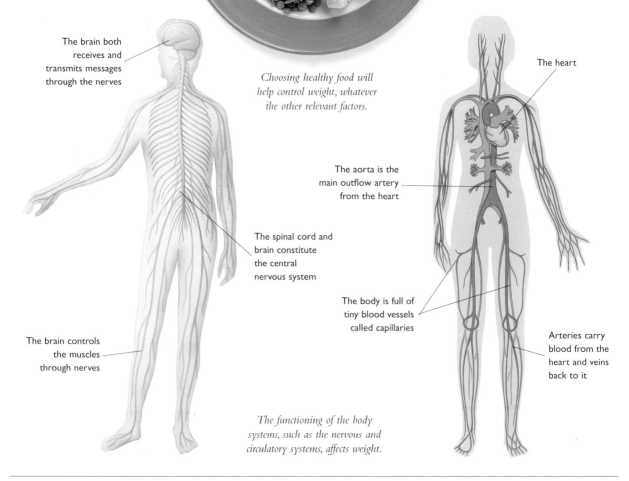

Choosing healthy food will help control weight, whatever the other relevant factors.

The brain both receives and transmits messages through the nerves

The heart

The aorta is the main outflow artery from the heart

The spinal cord and brain constitute the central nervous system

The body is full of tiny blood vessels called capillaries

The brain controls the muscles through nerves

Arteries carry blood from the heart and veins back to it

The functioning of the body systems, such as the nervous and circulatory systems, affects weight.

Unfortunately, one of the problems with diets which reduce calorie intake below 1,000 per day is that the body sees this lowered amount of food as a threat of famine and it takes action by slowing down the metabolic rate by as much as 40 percent! At this point, you need less food than you did before just to maintain your weight at the same level. When you have been on one of these very low-calorie diets for a time, the minute you return to "normal" eating, the weight will pile back on even faster than it did before. So, what's the alternative?

Research has shown that people who consume a metabolically stimulating diet (such as the New Pyramid program), even where their daily calorie consumption is 1,500 or more, have achieved a constant weight loss. Even more importantly, if you follow such a diet, since it is one that will not let you feel ravenously hungry or exhausted (just the opposite) and one which you will keep for life (with minor modifications here and there), then you have fulfilled all of the five criteria of a healthy weight-loss diet.

These criteria are:

◆ It produces WEIGHT LOSS.
◆ It is GOOD for your health.
◆ It EDUCATES you in a healthy way of eating for your whole life.
◆ It is relatively EASY to carry out.
◆ It doesn't leave you hungry or exhausted; it SATISFIES HUNGER and makes you feel ENERGETIC.

So, to answer the questions at the beginning of this section, we may become overweight because we are consuming too much food and/or exercising too little, but the main reason for overweight is that the metabolism becomes unbalanced, either because of an upset hormonal system or because of food allergy. Obviously, the older we get the worse this condition becomes, and when metabolism is reduced, it becomes much harder to lose weight.

Exercise helps keep weight down, but without the right diet is not enough to keep slim and healthy.

CALORIFIC CHART

This chart shows how many calories per minute are expended on each activity.

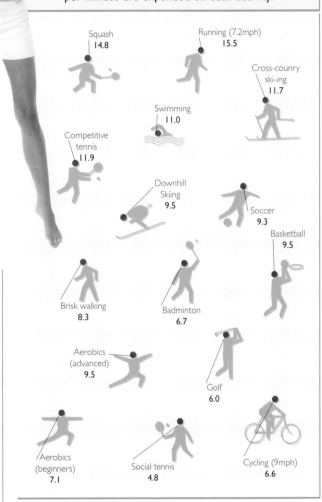

Squash 14.8
Running (7.2mph) 15.5
Cross-counry ski-ing 11.7
Swimming 11.0
Competitive tennis 11.9
Downhill Skiing 9.5
Soccer 9.3
Basketball 9.5
Brisk walking 8.3
Badminton 6.7
Aerobics (advanced) 9.5
Golf 6.0
Aerobics (beginners) 7.1
Social tennis 4.8
Cycling (9mph) 6.6

ENERGY FORMULA

Dieters are wrong in thinking that all food consumed needs to be "burned off" in order to lose weight. We need to retain some of that energy in order to stimulate our metabolism.

ENERGY IN	minus	BASIC BODY FUNCTIONS	equals	ENERGY OUT
(FOOD)		(BASAL METABOLISM)		(MUSCULAR ACTIVITY)

The Fat Connection

Concentrating on fat, for the moment, since this is what we want to lose, it may help to understand if we look at a pound of margarine (450g package). Some quick-fix diets lead us to believe that our bodies can actually lose 7 pounds (about 3kg) of fat in a week. This is ludicrous. The absolute maximum, in normal healthy circumstances, is more like 2 pounds a week, but really 1 pound is more realistic. Any more than this is likely to be water, which will easily return, or muscle tissue which would be disastrous. Since a large amount of energy is expended on lean tissue metabolism, losing any of this will quickly reduce basal metabolic rate.

Since fat is the most energy-dense (high calorific content) food group, many diets are based on reducing fat intake, and indeed, research indicates that overweight individuals, on average, consume around 8 percent more fat per day than lean people. Clearly, we need to reduce the amount of total fat, and in particular the saturated fat, but essential fatty acids must still be part of our healthy eating program.

Apart from the problems with saturated fat itself, there are the unnatural substances which occur frequently in processed fats, primarily in margarines, shortenings (and, therefore, in cakes, pastries, and cookies), chips, and confectionery (especially chocolate). These substances are the hydrogenated oils and trans–fatty acids discussed in Part Two. They are substances that will interfere with efficient metabolism and will slow weight loss considerably. They must be avoided at all costs.

Most of the fat in the average diet comes from meat, dairy produce, margarines and spreads, and high-fat processed or "fast" foods, so all of these foods need either to be kept to a very low level in any healthy diet, or eliminated altogether as in the vegan type of eating. One study, undertaken to ascertain the effects of a vegan diet on arthritis, found that there was a 9 percent reduction in body weight over three months on this diet despite the fact that it was both high

Chocolate contains substances that hinder effective metabolism.

in nutrients and high in calories; the main high calorie foods being nuts, seeds, seed and nut oils, sauces and salad dressings. A vegan diet will obviously be high in fiber (of assorted types), but it is also likely that the very high nutrient level in this study had a stimulating effect on metabolism.

Whether you want to try veganism or not, there is no need for saturated fat in any diet, but certain polyunsaturated fats, such as those found in fatty fish, nuts, and especially seeds and seed oils, are essential to optimum health. Udo Erasmus, author of *Fats that Heal, Fats that Kill*, confirms that these essential fats (Omega-3 and Omega-6) actually help to burn fat stored in adipose tissue. The best balance of fats is to cut down radically on saturated fat, but to include nuts, seeds, fish, and seed/nut oils in your diet.

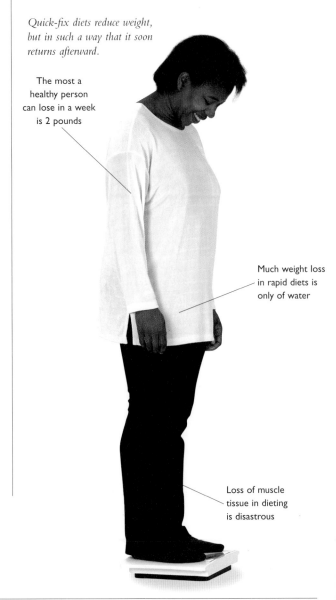

Quick-fix diets reduce weight, but in such a way that it soon returns afterward.

The most a healthy person can lose in a week is 2 pounds

Much weight loss in rapid diets is only of water

Loss of muscle tissue in dieting is disastrous

The consumption of fatty foods, especially fried ones, has to be reduced for weight loss.

METABOLISM AND FAT LOSS

Metabolism is adaptive. When food intake is moderate and constant, fat accumulation occurs only when muscle mass is small. But when food intake is reduced, metabolic processes adjust to the new input level. Fat is not necessarily lost, unless muscle tissue remains metabolically active, by exercise and a good supply of all nutrients not just energy units. Calorie (energy unit) counting on its own is not going to work.

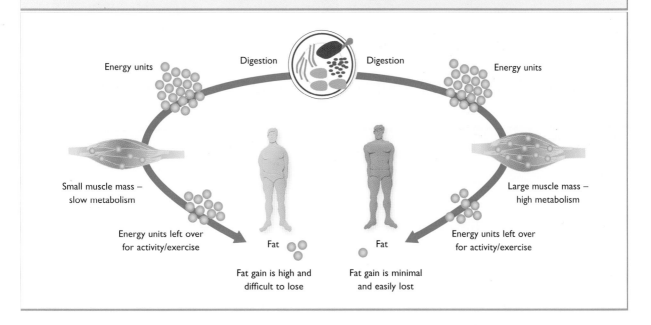

The Calorie Connection

Most nutrition books tell us that if you take what you eat and deduct what you burn off through exercise, the remainder ends up as flab round your middle; consequently, if you want to lose weight, all you have to do is to eat less or exercise more (or both of these, of course). This is a very simple theory which does not hold up in practice.

In the first place, this theory does not tell us why we overeat or under-exercise – there can be many psychological problems (stress, relationships, etc.) and physiological problems (food intolerance, allergy, side-effects of prescribed drugs, over-toxicity, poor digestion, blood-sugar swings, hormonal imbalances, etc.), and we may not be fully aware that these are part of the problem.

In the second place, this theory just doesn't work. For example, a slice of wholewheat bread is around 100 calories, and if we made sure that we kept to our diet but omitted one slice of bread every day, then over that year you would, theoretically, have lost 36,500 calories. If we take it that 1 pound (0.45kg) of fat is just over 4,000 calories, in that first year you should have lost around 9 pounds of fat, and in two years (keeping to the diet of "omitting one slice of bread") 18 pounds (8kg), and in five years just over 42 pounds (19kg), and onward. All simply by not

eating one slice of bread per day! We know, of course, that this doesn't occur but nobody has really explained why. The reason why this "calorie theory" does not add up is because we are not taking into account metabolism, or any psychological or physiological problems associated with weight conditions.

Metabolism is the overall name given to a whole host of enzyme-mediated chemical reactions that go on inside our body, and from the point of view of losing weight, part of our metabolism has the job of turning the energy units in food into energy that the body can use. We know that people vary considerably in their ability to do this and if you are one of the unlucky ones whose metabolic fires burn slow, then you will be turning more of your food into fat. Don't despair – all you need is a metabolic boost from the New Pyramid program.

Simply omitting one slice of bread a day from your diet does not produce constant weight loss.

The body works best on the complex carbohydrates, such as vegetables, pulses, nuts, and whole grains.

The Carbohydrate Connection

It isn't just the amount of food you consume but the kind of food you eat that makes the difference.

The body is designed to work properly on complex carbohydrates (carbohydrates which release their sugar units slowly) such as vegetables, lentils, beans, fruit, and whole grains. These foods, when properly digested produce a more consistent level of energy, especially when correctly balanced with protein and fat, preventing the lows and highs of blood sugar which produce our bad moods, our ravenous hunger, and the temptation to binge on the nearest morsel.

When our blood-sugar levels are more stable, our energy levels are more balanced and we have longer relief from hunger. All of these factors give the body a better chance to use up and metabolize the food properly, rather than turning it into fat. It has been estimated that possibly as many as seven out of ten overweight people have an underlying blood-sugar imbalance, and for these people following a well-balanced complex carbohydrate/protein diet with low levels of stimulants (tea, coffee, colas, alcohol, tobacco, etc.) is essential.

The Correct Macronutrient Balance

In Britain, it would appear that the average diet derives around 44 percent of energy units (calories) from fat, around 15 percent from protein and the remaining 41 percent from carbohydrates (usually of the refined white and sugary types). In the U.S., the average diet derives more than 48 percent of energy units from fat, and roughly 26 percent each from proteins and carbohydrates. Modern nutritional research, by Barry Sears Ph.D., suggests that the ideal diet should derive no more than 30 percent of calories from fat, 30 percent from protein, and the remaining 40 percent from complex carbohydrates. These new figures complement exactly what has been outlined in the New Pyramid program: slow-release, complex carbohydrates, and their relationship to protein and fat. This balance is important for sustained energy, and prevention of peaks and troughs of blood sugar. If we convert these calorific percentages to actual amounts of food, we arrive at the ratio of 4:3 carbohydrate to protein (since they supply almost the same amount of energy gram for gram). We can add on the ratio of 1.5 for total fat (since fat supplies around twice as much energy per gram as either carbohydrate or protein).

The overall ratio is then 4:3:1.5 (or 8:6:3), carbohydrate: protein: fat. For reasons explained on pages 50–51 the best types of carbohydrate are vegetables, lentils, beans, fruit, and whole grains, and not pasta, bread, and potatoes. The best (easily absorbable) protein is obtained from fish, poultry, tofu, seeds, and nuts. The best types of fats are those containing mono-unsaturated fatty acids, such as olive oil, and polyunsaturated fatty acids which are found in fish, seeds, and nuts.

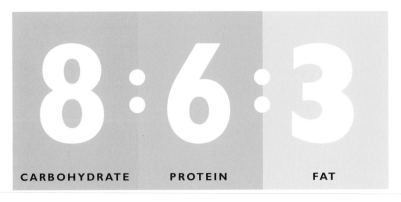

| CARBOHYDRATE | PROTEIN | FAT |

We should eat almost three times as much carbohydrate as fat, and twice as much protein as fat.

The Fiber Connection

It was back in the 1980s that the F-Plan Diet, by Audrey Eyton, was first published and appeared to be a major solution to the hunger problems encountered with low-calorie diets.

Adding fiber to the diet helps you to feel full for longer and hence reduces appetite, as well as having other health benefits. We know that a diet containing 1 ounce (27g) of fiber daily will prevent constipation, and help prevent more severe forms of bowel problems such as diverticular disease, but additionally having a diet high in natural fiber will prevent reabsorption of toxins and cholesterol.

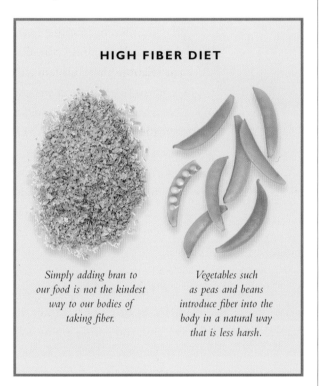

HIGH FIBER DIET

Simply adding bran to our food is not the kindest way to our bodies of taking fiber.

Vegetables such as peas and beans introduce fiber into the body in a natural way that is less harsh.

"High fiber" does not mean piling mountains of wheat or other bran onto our food. The correct way to a high fiber diet is to include fiber-rich vegetables, pulses (legumes), fruit, and some whole grains in our diet. The fiber in vegetables, fruit, lentils, beans, and oats is much more gentle and effective. Not only does fiber make food seem more on the plate and makes you feel full for longer, it also helps to control blood-sugar levels, since it releases the sugar units from the food in the intestines into the blood much more slowly and over a longer length of time.

The Protein Connection

When consumed in excess, protein is broken down to release sugar-like molecules which can be used as fuel. Otherwise, proteins would have no calorific value in energy tables. Protein has only half the calories of fat and requires more energy for its digestion than carbohydrates or fat. For these two reasons, protein would seem the ideal material for dieters. However, very high unlimited protein diets put the liver and kidneys under stress and make the body more acidic which can lead to problems.

Protein is obviously needed for building new tissues in a growing child, and for replacing and repairing worn out and damaged tissues in everyone, but we only need a moderate amount. As a rough guide, if we are of average size and sedentary, we probably need around 7 ounces (180g) of protein-rich food a day, but if we are above average in size (taller or fatter), or undergo vigorous exercise daily, we are likely to require as much as 12 ounces (320g) of protein-rich food, to maintain high amino acid turnover in lean body tissue, and replace damaged protein, as in the case of the regular exerciser. These values are not pure protein, but rather foods containing high amounts of easily available protein, such as fish, poultry, lean meat, cottage cheese, and tofu.

The recommendation is to consume the correct ratio of protein to carbohydrate and fat and to insure that animal and plant sources are well balanced.

The brain needs protein as much as the body

Body tissue is built from amino acids, which are derived from protein

Protein is essential for growth

Protein is essential to both children and adults as it provides the body's building blocks.

The Micronutrient Connection

The ability of your body to burn fat does not depend solely on the types and amounts of fat, carbohydrate, and protein in your diet. It also depends on the activity of vitamins and minerals that are consumed. These micro-nutrients are essential in controlling the careful breakdown of glucose, and other digestive end products, which in turn releases energy, together with other biochemical substances, to all our trillions of body cells. Any lack of these vital micronutrients will result in lowered physical energy and, theoretically, a tendency for the tired body to lay down fat.

The transport of glucose from the blood into the cells of the body depends upon the presence of vitamins B_3 and B_6, and the minerals chromium and zinc.

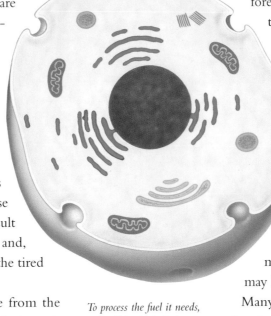

To process the fuel it needs, each cell in the body has to have micronutrients – vitamins and minerals.

The actual breakdown of glucose within the cells into energy requires vitamins B_1, B_2, B_3, B_5, C, and the mineral iron. Another substance called co-enzyme Q10 is also required. Magnesium is required for A.T.P. (energy) production. There-fore, insuring an adequate supply of these nutrients is theoretically going to increase the effec-tiveness of any weight-loss program. It is always preferable to obtain micronutrients from the food you eat, but in some cases, especially if your digestion is a little under par, or you suffer from food intolerances, supple-menting your diet with mineral and vitamin preparations may be required, at least for a while.

Many people's diet falls short of B vitamins, probably because of their easy loss from food in cooking (being water-soluble and heat-sensitive), and several studies have shown that many people have a diet which provides less than the Recom-mended Daily Allowance. Nutrient loss also occurs when food is stored for a long time.

The release of energy from cells does not only occur from the helpful B vitamins, but also by the activity of the minerals iron, calcium, magnesium, chromium, and zinc. Most average Western diets are very unbalanced where minerals are concerned, with a preponderance of calcium and generally poor levels of iron, magnesium, chromium, and zinc. A shortage of magnesium, so common in those who eat very few vegetables and fruits, often results in muscle cramps as the muscles are unable to contract and relax properly.

All in all, 22 vitamins, related substances, and minerals are needed for proper metabolism and weight control. Although our biochemical individuality means that needs will vary from person to person, the ten most important for improving metabolism and helping to break down fat are vitamins B_1, B_2, B_3, B_5, B_6, C, choline and inositol (involved in fat metabolism and transport), chromium, and zinc. Many of these are involved in other processes in addition to those already described.

Without enough vitamins and minerals the body becomes tired and may lay down fat.

Exercise

To remove excess fat effectively, we need to increase our level of activity and so increase energy output. It also tones up our muscles so that as we lose weight, our new skin fits nicely instead of sagging.

The good news is that you really don't have to be fanatically fit to lose weight. The reason behind this is that exercise, on its own without dieting, doesn't actually help to promote much weight loss; only around 300 calories are burned up by running a mile! But the effects of consistent exercise are cumulative. Each bit of exercise you take may only release a few calories, but if you do it often enough, your metabolism becomes more efficient. So, it is the frequency of exercise, not the intensity, that is more important.

As weight is lost and muscle is built up with exercise, the more oxygen the body will need to allow this extra muscle tissue to work efficiently. The best kind of exercise is, therefore, aerobic. In fact, the measurement of how hard a muscle is working is related to how much oxygen it uses up. Continuous exercise such as swimming, jogging, brisk walking or cycling are more aerobic than "stop-go" exercises such as tennis or squash. Playing tennis uses more of the "fast" muscle fibers which use glucose for fuel. You will lose weight playing tennis or squash but it will require you to play for a very long time compared to the time spent swimming, cycling, running, or walking. Since the amount of fat you carry is a far more important statistic than your weight, don't use your scales as the only means of monitoring progress; encouragement in the early days is likely to come from a reduction in "vital statistics" rather than loss of weight. As you start to exercise aerobically, you will begin to replace fatty tissue with lean muscle. With a little extra muscle you will begin to burn off excess fat faster and faster. You may not lose much weight to begin with, since muscle is heavier than fat, but you will lose inches since muscle is more compact than fat. Muscle cells are much more metabolically active than fat cells and therefore have

It is the frequency of aerobic exercise that matters, not how good you are at it. Neither does the type matter, so you can choose according to your tastes.

a much greater capacity for burning off fat. So the first thing to do is to increase your muscle tissue and this, in turn, will burn off the weight.

The additional effects of moderate exercise are probably even more important. These are that, despite popular belief, moderate exercise decreases your appetite by encouraging the appetite mechanism to work properly. Exercise also releases brain chemicals called endorphins which give you a sense of well-being (and greater determination to stick to your healthy eating regime), and, most importantly, research shows that fairly vigorous exercise will raise your metabolic rate for up to 15 hours after exercise (so you go on metabolizing on "fast burn" for a long time afterward).

ABOVE LEFT
The metabolic rate remains high for hours after vigorous exercise, so you continue to burn calories.

Running a mile burns up about 300 calories in most reasonably healthy people.

Assessing Slimming Diets New and Old

Some of the tried and tested (but not always effective) ways of weight reduction have already been mentioned. It is the intention of this section to survey, briefly, some of the major techniques around which they are constructed, to assess just how effective, or not, they are.

CALORIE COUNTING

The number of energy units in a food (calories) varies according to the food group. This knowledge has triggered a large amount of laboratory analysis of a wide range of foods (calorimetry), and out of this work "calorie guides" have been produced. The diet methods that rely on calorie counting depend upon these tables.

The main problems with calorie counting include the sheer amount of effort which has to be put in to calculate how many calories there are in any one of your meals, from the weighing to the mathematics. But by far the most important problem is that, because the usual limit is around 1,000 calories per day, these diets are very hard to stick to; hunger pangs are never far away.

Also, the mathematics of calorie counting if taken to their full extent produces some very spurious results. As we have seen, by the omission of an item of food each day (such as sliced bread) at the end of a year we will have a useful 9 pound (4.05kg) loss. So far, so good. But there is no way that simply omitting one slice of bread a day will result in a loss of 46 pounds (20.25kg) after 5 years and 91 pounds (40.5kg) after 10 years. What a frightening aspect, too, if having an extra 100 calories a day meant putting on 91 pounds (40.5kg) every 10 years!

Clearly calorie counting, though effective in the short term, pays no attention to metabolism and, consequently, is not important for our purposes. The same, of course, goes for counting fat units; the underlying principle is the same.

VERY LOW-CALORIE DIETS

These are the liquid or "milkshake" diets. Their aim is to severely cut daily calorie intake, sometimes to as low as 400Kcals (calories) for women and 500Kcals for men, but at the same time provide at least recommended daily allowances (R.D.A.s) of major vitamins and minerals. These "shakes" provide around 40g of protein for women and 50g for men. The addition of protein will allow some prevention of the breakdown of muscle tissue to produce energy, since this is what normally happens when calorie intake is greatly restricted. Weight is definitely lost on these regimes, and the high level of micronutrients in the product is probably the reason for the sense of well-being which is often encountered within the first week or so of these diets.

Very low-calorie diets reduce muscle tissue

Some fad diets are all the rage, then rapidly fall from fashion

For the studious dieter there is a wide range of diets to explore, but often the research behind them is incomplete.

Calorie counting involves weighing all your foods

There are some special high-fiber drinks on the market.

However, with such a low daily calorific intake, it is certain that lean muscle tissue, in addition to fat, will be lost from the body.

This type of "crash dieting" also lowers metabolic rate – the "famine reaction" – and since it is the lean body tissue that is the best burner of calories, the long-term results of these diets are likely to be unsatisfactory; a much smaller intake of normal food is likely to encourage the weight to return, and you have learned nothing about healthy eating into the bargain.

HIGH-FIBER DIETS

If what you are looking for is bulky food to make you feel full while still reducing your calorie intake, then you have found the answer in this type of diet.

Fiber in its natural form, found in vegetables, fruit, nuts, seeds, and grains, absorbs water and gives the feeling of fullness even though fewer calories may have been eaten. Additionally, it is fairly well documented that those cultures consuming a high-fiber diet have less risk of bowel cancer, diabetes, or diverticular disease, as well as no constipation problems.

Fiber is also fairly free of calories and for all these reasons, it is easy to see why a low-calorie, high-fiber diet is easier to follow, healthier, and more satisfying to eat than low-calorie diets without fiber.

However, this type of regime, where the main fiber is wheat bran fiber, produces fairly poor weight loss. Moreover, in some cases the diet produces an irritated colon since wheat fiber in particular is very rough on our insides. Not only that, but it is especially good at taking with it out of the body not only waste materials, but many of the important micronutrients which need to be retained. In a wholefood diet these minerals are well supplied, but on a junk food diet with added bran, we may find we are moving toward deficiencies in some minerals.

So, fiber is good for you, but you must insure that you obtain fiber from the natural sources of vegetables, fruit, pulses (legumes), seeds, and whole grains, rather than simply spooning mountains of bran onto fiber-poor food.

Just adding bran to food can create mineral deficiency

Fiber, taken in its natural form in fiber-rich foods, produces a satisfying feeling of being full.

Wheat fiber can cause an irritated colon

HIGH-FAT/LOW-CARBOHYDRATE DIETS

People who advocate high-fat, low-carbohydrate diets believe that if you don't eat any carbohydrate foods, you must burn fat instead. However, trying to burn fat without some carbohydrate present is like trying to set fire to a lump of coal without using a fire-lighter. It doesn't work easily.

Similarly, a fire which is burning inefficiently gives off a lot of smoke, and a diet that is burning off only fat releases substances called ketones into the blood. High ketone levels in the blood are extremely dangerous and these substances must be removed quickly via the kidneys. Therefore, a high blood ketone level puts the kidneys under stress.

Not only is a high-fat diet that is low in carbohydrates very difficult to produce and maintain, it causes ineffective metabolism and produces toxins, neither of which will lead to safe, healthy, and permanent weight loss. In addition your intake of hydrogenated fats and trans-fatty acids is likely to be very high. To all these drawbacks are added the problems created by saturated fats – the clogging up of arteries, and the risk of cardiovascular disease.

We certainly do need some fat in the diet (essential fatty acids together with fat-soluble vitamins) but no-one can become healthier on a diet where fat is the major energy food.

A high-fat diet hinders the metabolism, leading to tiredness.

HIGH-PROTEIN DIETS

Although this type of regime can be quite effective in the short term, consuming unlimited amounts of protein – even if it is lean meat, poultry, and fish, or even large amounts of pulses (legumes) – can have an unhealthy outcome. As we saw with high-fat diets, restricting carbohydrate intake in preference to protein also produces an ineffective metabolism leading additionally to release of ketones.

The reason protein is chosen is because it has only half the calories of the same amount of fat, and also because protein is harder to metabolize. The advocates of this approach argue that because protein is harder to convert to fuel, fewer calories are consumed by the body. Although this is undeniably true, there are, as we have seen, other problems with excessive-protein diets: liver and kidney stress and increased tissue acidity leading to osteoporosis and arthritis.

Lentils are the staple food of some high protein diets.

In addition, a diet high in non-organic animal protein is likely to carry with it a cocktail of antibiotics and hormones, both of which will interfere with optimum metabolism.

Furthermore, because protein is harder to digest, some proteins may not be digested completely before parts of them are absorbed, and in this partially digested state they may enter the bloodstream. We are then at greater risk from developing food intolerances, and, possibly, even the beginnings of auto-immune disease, such as arthritis.

So, we can see that eating a diet of excessive protein (especially animal protein) could affect our liver, kidneys, skeleton, and toxic levels adversely and may be responsible for the development of intolerances and allergies.

Our protein intake needs to be sensibly balanced with carbohydrate and fat as in the New Pyramid program.

Excess animal protein harms the liver and skeleton.

STARCH-BLOCKER DIETS

This isn't so much a specific diet of certain foods, but rather a pill, taken before each meal, containing substances which we are told will block the digestion and/or uptake of starch from our diets. The theory is that you can eat as much carbohydrate as you like without absorbing it.

Scientific analytical work undertaken on these "starch blockers" found no evidence of any effect on carbohydrate metabolism. Moreover, in addition to finding very variable levels of the starch inhibitor enzymes (which were supposed to be doing the blocking), a substance called lectin was found. This is a potentially dangerous material, though rendered harmless if cooked. It is found in beans (especially uncooked red kidney beans) from which the starch blocker is manufactured.

As well as its ineffectiveness in curbing absorption, taking these pills does nothing whatsoever to retrain the dieter in the ways of healthy eating, and may even cause toxicity. All in all, the most obvious result of diets using starch blockers is unfortunately an increase in flatulence!

Starch-blocker diets are not to be confused with the type of diets that use fiber supplements which are taken before meals. This latter approach is a means of curbing appetite before the next meal is eaten, insuring a lowered intake of food. Usually it involves taking encapsulated powdered fiber with a large glass of water 30 minutes before eating. The water then reacts with the fiber, making it swell and fill up part of the stomach. Several types of fibrous materials are used. They are usually of the soluble fiber type and are related to celluloses, pectins, and mucilages found in a range of plants, such as gels from the Plantain family, and gluco-mannan from the root of the Konjac plant which is similar to large spinach. Konjac plants have been used as a vegetable by the Japanese for 2,000 years, but its flavor is not appreciated in other parts of the world. Glucomannan fiber is now sold in a gel state as a "functional food."

Certain pills are designed to be taken with meals to stop the body absorbing carbohydrate.

FUNCTIONS OF SOLUBLE FIBER GELS

☞ Maintaining digestive regularity (by allowing the efficient movement of food through the intestinal tract).

☞ Slowing the release of sugars into the blood (which is helpful for people suffering from noninsulin dependent diabetes and hypoglycemia).

☞ Helping with some of the problems associated with irritable bowel and allergies.

☞ Improving intestinal conditions (by protecting the bowel lining and encouraging growth of healthy bowel flora).

☞ Reducing cholesterol, triglycerides, and free fatty acids in the body.

These gels and soluble fibers are not composed of the harsh fiber that is found in cereals such as wheat bran (often a component of the high-fiber diet), which can be very irritating and, in fact, does not swell to any appreciable degree. The soluble fiber in pre-meal supplements forms a gel with water in the stomach, absorbing up to 50 times its own weight and producing a feeling of fullness and decreasing the desire for food.

Therefore, when assessing starch-blocker diets we have to ascertain whether we mean one where the digestion of starches is inhibited and the normal end product of glucose is made unavailable – a process that is not recommended – or a regime where helpful soluble fibers from vegetables are used as an aid to weight loss and other health improvements. The latter starch-blocker diet would be useful for short-term use, while the digestive system is being cleaned and healed, but it is still not recommended as a long-term dietary lifestyle.

BROOM TOPS

Water-loss diets use known diuretics, often freeze-dried herbs or vegetables such as these above.

ASPARAGUS

YARROW

SLIPPERY ELM

WATER-LOSS DIETS

As with the starch-blocker diet, water-loss diets are not new regimes which might educate their followers along the lines of healthy eating. Instead they are simply ways of using freeze-dried and encapsulated diuretic herbs and vegetables, like asparagus, to rid the body of water. No one is doubting for a minute that the herbs, vegetables, or other special foods, do the job of removing water, and indeed if this is a problem for you, these preparations may work. However, they do not burn fat, and may, of course, put an extra strain on the kidneys. Using these in the short term may be beneficial, but for long-lasting weight loss which insures a healthy way of life, they go no way to break old self-defeating patterns of eating or establishing new, more healthy, fat-burning ones.

Taking a sauna is pleasant but unlikely to produce long-term weight loss.

Other techniques could be included under this heading, such as special clothing, body wraps, seaweed wraps, mud wraps, mineral baths, and saunas, all of which profess to rid the body of excess water and "impurities." Again, there is no doubt that they work in the short term, and, as they encourage sweating, a certain amount of waste material will be removed along with the water. You may feel wonderful after one of these treatments, but none of them are likely to do much about stored fat in the long term. Moreover, water-loss is soon corrected, especially as you may take in extra fluids to deal with the thirst that the treatments create.

THE DIET OF THE CARBOHYDRATE-ADDICT

This way of eating is for those individuals who feel that they cannot stick to the usual low-calorie type of regime, simply because they love their carbohydrates (grains, cakes, candies, breads, etc.). What the exponents of this diet say is that is doesn't matter how much carbohydrate you eat, nor even what type of carbohydrate you consume (this includes alcohol), as long as you eat only carbohydrate once a day within the period of about an hour before 8:00 P.M. Other meals are to be very low in carbohydrate or devoid of carbohydrate altogether. These "complementary" meals are therefore comprised of fairly large amounts of protein and fat, although you can mitigate this as the diet does allow you to chose low-fat varieties.

The theory behind this diet revolves around the excessive production of insulin which can sometimes occur in individuals who have consumed large and frequent amounts of refined carbohydrates over long periods of time. It is argued by the advocates that this hyperinsulinemia (excessive insulin production and/or insulin insensitivity) is the cause of the unsatisfied hunger. We know this to be true and that after eating a meal containing carbohydrate improperly balanced with protein and fat, too much insulin is produced and some of this remains in the blood. Consequently, there is no change in brain chemistry and the sensation of hunger remains. Moreover, it has been found that many obese individuals tend to have this insulin insensitivity, and, consequently, a poor control over blood-sugar balance.

Hence, in an attempt to control the frequency of insulin output the carbohydrate-addicted dieter only eats carbohydrate within a one-hour period in the day. However, he/she may eat any type of carbohydrate which usually means very sweet and refined types!

Most of the theory is very logical, and there is no doubt that some overweight individuals have problems with blood-sugar control. However, consuming a diet high in complex carbohydrates, which are well-balanced with protein, and omitting all refined sugars and starches is a much better way of controlling blood-sugar balance and hunger, and you can eat regularly, three or more times a day.

THE LOW-FAT DIET

Many people have had a good deal of success on this type of diet, where you are able to eat lots of carbohydrate, mostly the complex type, and moderate protein, but fat is very restricted. The "forbidden list" includes many natural wholefoods which are essential to dietary balance and providers of essential fatty acids and fat-soluble vitamins, such as seeds and seed oils, nuts, fatty fish, avocados, etc., and the omission of these foods from the diet will, in the long term, cause havoc with the endocrine (hormonal) system and immune status.

In his book *Fats that Heal, Fats that Kill*, Udo Erasmus states that low metabolic rate, excess body fats, and low tissue content of essential fatty acids all occur together. He goes on further to explain that the Omega-3 fatty acids (found in fish and linseed oils, particularly) actually increase metabolic rate, and make body and dietary fats burn more rapidly. In turn, this makes us feel more energetic, and increases the likelihood that exercise levels will increase. It is, therefore, very effective for weight loss.

Certain fats, such as those in linseed oil, are in fact essential.

Additionally, when these fatty acids are consumed in the diet they produce materials called series three prostaglandins, some of which help our kidneys get rid of excess water held in the tissues, where overweight people mainly retain it. Omega-3s help to get rid of this water naturally, as do some of the herbs and vegetables mentioned earlier.

People who eat very low-fat diets could be reducing their ability to fight infection. For example, recent investigation into blood samples from competitive marathon runners indicated that those who had been getting their energy from a 15 percent fat diet, as opposed to a more reasonable 30 percent, had fewer infection-fighting white cells in their blood after exercise when compared to athletes on the higher-fat diet. This fact alone could leave those on the very low-fat diet more open to infection. Also, scientific research has indicated that people with lower than normal blood cholesterol levels are more prone to cancer. This could be because cholesterol itself is an antioxidant, i.e., a chemical which protects our tissues from free radical damage (oxidative damage).

People on low-fat diets have fewer white blood cells, so run the risk of making themselves susceptible to infections.

White blood cells are needed to fight infection

"Diet" versions of high-fat foods are of little nutritional value.

Why Dieting Doesn't Work

Conventional dieting regimes assume that if you reduce your input of food and go hungry, you will lose fat. National statistics have disproved this on a massive scale, since decade by decade we have been eating less, yet on average, we weigh more. Looking at it another way, in the past 20 years or so there have been dozens of new miracle weight-loss diets which have been followed by millions of people; many of these diets also include exercise programs, yet very few dieters have reached their goal and maintained a healthy weight. Part of the problem stems from our unique biochemistry. Each person, as we know, has their own individual nutrient needs, and it is, therefore, impossible to set out a single simple diet that will guarantee success.

METABOLISM

It is very likely that one of the reasons for people becoming fatter is the basic problem of low or inefficient metabolism caused by either a low intake of the micronutrients needed to assist metabolic enzymes, and/or a high level of pollutants entering the body and causing a greater amount of energy to be channeled into removing these metabolic-blocking substances. In the calorie-counting process, 1,000 calories a day from refined and processed food will have nowhere near the micronutrient content of 1,000 calories from a diet comprising whole grains, fresh vegetables, fruits, lean meats, fish, seeds, nuts, and pulses (legumes). Both dieters may initially lose weight, but the wholefood dieter will be much healthier, more vital, and will be able to continue to lose weight without flagging or becoming hungry because their body is optimally supplied with all the essential metabolism-boosting ingredients it needs.

White rice

Processed and refined foods lack the vital nutrients required by the body to maintain good health and well-being.

Cookies

Sponge cake

THE DIETING EQUATION

Another reason for the rise in obesity is that the simple-minded use of the input/output equation is based on false assumptions. While under some circumstances excess input may be converted to fat, the reverse is not true. Excess fat cannot be shed simply by reducing input. Moreover, if input goes down, output cannot go up, because of insufficient energy. If the dieting equation were correct, any one of the many special diets around would have solved the fat problem for all time, because no matter what the advertising material says, nearly every new diet relies on reducing calorie input for it to be effective. (Some hinder nutrient absorption, but this comes to the same thing in the end.) Every diet reduces the amount you eat, even if it denies the fact, by encouraging

Everyone has a unique biochemistry. A healthy young man, for example, will have a different metabolism from an overweight fifty-year-old.

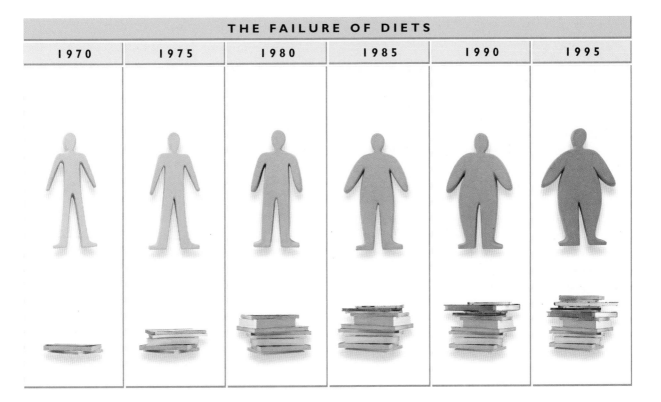

THE FAILURE OF DIETS					
1970	1975	1980	1985	1990	1995

you to eat as much as you can but limiting your choice. In practical terms it becomes apparent that simply relying on "dieting" can never achieve all that is necessary to lose fat permanently. Furthermore, it seems very likely that any way of eating which causes you to be chronically hungry will tend to make you fat. How can such a thing be true? Television pictures of hungry people in the Third World show clearly that they are not fat. However, it is important to distinguish here between hunger and starvation. People who are starving are losing both fat and lean tissue. Eventually they die since they are either too weak to resist attack by disease-causing microbes or because the lack of essential

The years since 1970 have seen a large number of new specific diets, popularized in magazines and in increasing numbers of books. But as the amount of literature has grown, so too has the number of overweight people.

nutrients causes a vital part of their system to fail. Feelings of hunger occur when you do not get enough of, or not a full complement of, the correct nutrients that your body requires for its continued maintenance. In addition to slimming diets, it can be caused by poverty (simply not having enough to eat), or, at the other end of the scale, by excesses. In the latter case people may eat too much on a regular basis but still experience hunger because the types of food they are eating do not contain the right balance of nutrients to balance blood sugar and meet their bodily needs. Hunger is, of course, purely a message from your brain, telling you to find more or different food for your body's requirements.

The modern Western diet has become far too high in sugar and saturated fat.

Ice cream consists mainly of fat and sugar

Sweet drinks are high in sugar

Hamburgers contain saturated fats

Chips contain fat and usually artificial flavorings

French fries are high in fat

Manufactured snacks leave your body short of essential nutrients.

How Can Hunger Make You Fat?

When you feel the sensation of hunger, whether it is caused by your being a dieter or because you are malnourished, your body receives the clear message that it is to "prepare for famine."

The particular dietary deprivation you are experiencing can be one thing or a combination of things. You may not be getting enough minerals and/or vitamins, or you might have an imbalance of carbohydrates, proteins, and fats. If you frequently eat any type of convenience food, it is likely that you have deficiencies and imbalances at all levels.

Whatever your particular "deficiency" or "imbalance" is, your metabolism will register the shortage and the signal it is likely to be sending to your brain is "eat more," making you feel hungry. Therefore, the hunger pangs most dieters have experienced at one time or another may not, in fact, be a signal to consume any food, but may be the body asking for more iron, or zinc, or vitamin B, or protein, to carry out its chemical processes (metabolism) optimally. For example, if your body is unable to maintain a proper metabolic balance because of a deficiency of, say, chromium, your blood sugar swings wildly, causing fat deposition when it rises and hunger as it falls. Moreover, the longer you inflict hunger upon yourself while on a calorie-restricted diet, especially if it involves any kind of "convenience" food, the more your metabolic rate will fall and your body will begin to utilize lean tissue as well as fat. You will lose weight, but most of this will not be fat, you will be losing muscle tissue and materials from vital organs.

FAMINE MESSAGE

To your body, this makes sense. After all, you don't need muscles when you haven't got the energy to use them, and a shutting down of metabolism does not require great cardiac output or efficient detoxification. Since lean muscle tissue has a higher metabolic rate than fat, reducing the former saves on running costs and cuts back on repair bills. Fat will be saved until the last because when your system becomes totally exhausted, the remaining fat will provide just enough energy to keep the vital spark of life burning in the hope that the "famine" will soon end. Also, the more often you go on a "diet" and feel hunger, the quicker your body will respond by conserving fat.

This in turn means that when your weight goes down, your fat goes up; and when your weight starts to come back, fat returns faster than lean tissue. It is thought by some experts that lean tissue loss can take years to be made up, unless you eat in a way which will prevent the "famine" message from getting through and encourage your lean body mass, via sensible exercise and well-balanced dietary protein, to be retained and improved upon.

Restricted diets lead to a deficiency of vitamins and minerals, and your body will respond with a feeling of hunger.

Severe dieting upsets the metabolism

Some diet foods lack minerals or vitamins

Because of all the problems with the modern Western diet, it comes as no surprise that our bodies are constantly hungry for the micronutrients that are missing, while at the same time piling on fat from the excesses of refined (and micronutrient-stripped) carbohydrates and fats.

Even those people within the population who would never consider a weight-reducing diet are likely to suffer nutrient deprivation if they eat normal Western food. Many individuals – and a large percentage of these are children – consume junk food with its "empty calories" because this is what the chemiculture food industry delivers.

Hunger, therefore, can make you fat. Frequent "dieters" will be carrying more fat than would be possible if their diets really worked. Nondieters are eating less, yet getting fatter decade by decade.

Although it may seem that the food industry, the slimming industry, and the media are conspiring to make you fat, there is a way out. It is, in fact, quite possible to avoid hunger and all its pitfalls. It is quite possible to be naturally slim and healthy, while at the same time eating as much as your body needs, without having to suffer the famine/fat reaction.

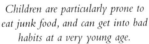

Children are particularly prone to eat junk food, and can get into bad habits at a very young age.

Think and Behave Like a Slim Person

The shedding of fat becomes automatic when you start to live in a way that makes fat a disadvantage to your body, and not a survival necessity. The essence of success is to think and behave like a slim person, no matter what size you are now. The New Pyramid program helps you do this, and its benefits are listed in the box at the bottom of this page.

Successful dieting isn't just trying to find what works for you if you stick to it, it's about what you can stick to that works! We all know that short-term results are usually fairly easy to achieve, no matter what diet we follow, but how do we make ourselves stick at it? And, if it is an artificial way of eating, should we be thinking of doing it long term anyway? You surely cannot imagine spending the rest of your life drinking very low-calorie milkshakes, and what are the consequences if you do? The best way by far is the New Pyramid program. If you feel that supplements are necessary, the most appropriate would be a high-potency multivitamin/multi-mineral complex, together with essential fatty acids such as fish oils (E.H.A. and D.H.A.) or evening primrose oil.

THE NEW PYRAMID PROGRAM AND DIETING

Although it is intended for all, and not just for slimmers, the New Pyramid program is excellent for all who want to lose weight because it confers many benefits. It will help you:

- Eat more good-quality food relieved of its chemical load and bursting with micronutrients, antioxidants, and phytochemicals; eat the correct balance of protein, carbohydrate, and fat; eat when you are hungry and not just for comfort. (Slim people always appear to be truly in tune with their food requirements and naturally stop eating when their bodily requirements are fulfilled.)

- Use your increasing metabolic capacity to burn fat through increased activity; use exercise to breath more effectively and increase oxygen levels. (Most slim people are on the go most of the time, usually sporty, and always enthusiastic and interested in "doing" things.)

- Get your body into hormonal balance so that the controlled burning of your excess fat will maintain you as a naturally slim person.

- Prevent obsession with food (which itself will cause stress and a slowing of metabolism). Whenever you have to eat out, it is not necessary to decline all the "fattening" foods. Since your basic, everyday eating plan is becoming healthier, you are able to have the odd "normal" food without causing too much disruption to your overall fat loss.

Essential Fats

Despite what we know about fats and their links with excess weight, we must not forget that some fats, the essential fatty acids (E.F.A.s), are indispensable to the body. Nerve cells and brain tissue are insulated (like electric wire) with fat, and the membranes around every cell in our body require fatty acids to control the entry and exit of materials. Enzymes would not be able to work without these membranes. Cholesterol is one of the fats that make up the membranes, and cholesterol is also one of the fats that form the basis for many hormones, including those produced by the adrenal glands and the sex glands. In addition, some fat/protein (lipoprotein) molecules are important as carriers within the blood.

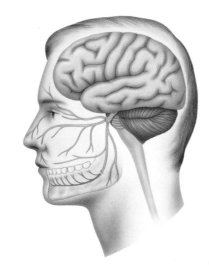

Fats are essential – the brain tissue and the nerve cells have a protective outer layer of fat.

It is quite obvious then that fats are a necessity and that even the leanest tissues require them. However, these fats are mainly those which include a good proportion of the essential fatty acids, and are not based on saturated fat.

Additionally, for those of us living in the temperate zone of the world, far from the sub-tropical climate where humans evolved, there is a need to adapt and cope with a variable climate. This means we are able to put on fat very quickly when food is plentiful and the weather becomes colder. On the other hand, we are designed to lose it only slowly and cautiously as needed or when warmer weather returns. Even with modern compensations like central heating, we are still conditioned by thousands of years of evolution, and most people who are aware of their bodies will find a little fat going on in the winter and coming off in the spring as part of a natural cycle. If your metabolism is working optimally, this slight amount of winter fat will disappear without effort in the early summer. Carrying a few extra pounds in the colder months is normal and not something that should worry the shape-conscious.

SHAPING FAT

In addition to these essential biochemical and structural fats, there is the fat that is found in women which is specifically associated with the female body shape. We are talking here about true adipose tissue – the fatty layer under the skin. It has distinct extra functions in females, and ignoring these differences can lead to dieting failure no matter how hard you try.

This fat gives women their sexually attractive shape and it develops as girls approach maturity. To the adult male this signals that the female is mature and ready to be approached, and to the adult female it is a signal that she should be treated as an equal, mature female. This fat is of biological necessity for procreation, and attraction between the sexes, and is the reason why on average women have quite a lot more fat then men.

As well as real clothes, our bodies put on their own "clothing" of extra fat to keep us warm in winter.

REPRODUCTIVE FAT

Women, during their reproductive years, will have a body that considers a store of fat desirable; this is over and above that required for insulation and body shaping. Biologically, once a young female has become shapely and attractive, pregnancy is the next step. Their bodies need to insure that there is a large enough energy store to keep mother and baby well through the nine months of pregnancy and on into a year or so of breastfeeding. Amenorrhea (lack of menstruation) occurs when female fat falls below a certain level.

So, while women are sexually active, their metabolism encourages a little extra fat deposition. Although frequent sex and a heightened emotional state can speed up the metabolism, at some point the body may over-compensate once desire is fulfilled, and as sexual exercise decreases, fat may accumulate. On top of this, if your emotional life is stressful, you may turn to food for comfort. Having a good look at how your metabolism is reacting to changing circumstances will enable you to work with your body instead of against it.

TOXIN STORE

One further function of fat, which has only been touched upon briefly in relation to losing weight, is that of toxin storage. Many of the substances in our environment are poisonous, and the majority of these are fat-soluble. If your body is unable to metabolize and remove these materials, they tend to become stored away in the fatty tissue. Indeed, the body may even manufacture fat especially for storage of dangerous substances. Because of the relatively low metabolism of fatty tissue, once toxins are stored here they are likely to remain undisturbed, and the body becomes very reluctant to have them circulate again.

The fat becomes persistent. Further fat tends to get dumped in these places because the metabolism has "learned" to do this with a wider range of substances it doesn't like.

If your weight problem is fat retention to protect against toxins, it will become apparent as you lose weight; you will begin to experience some of the symptoms of detoxification, such as a furry tongue, headaches, fever, rash, and tiredness. The only way you will successfully shed fat, especially if you are carrying a lot of it, is by attending to the pollution levels around you and carrying out periodic gentle detoxification regimes (one day a week, a weekend every month, a week every six months, and so on), in between which you can return to a normal eating plan according to the New Pyramid program.

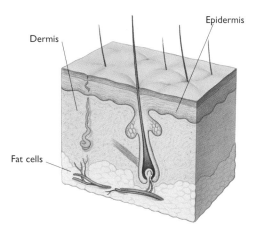

Fat cells are found in the skin in the layer below the dermis.

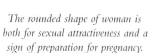

The rounded shape of woman is both for sexual attractiveness and a sign of preparation for pregnancy.

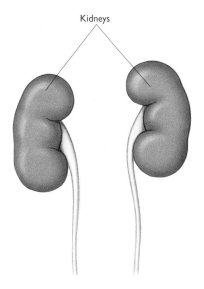

Toxins that the kidneys cannot deal with are stored in fat.

How Drugs Cause Weight Gain

Although no-one is suggesting that anyone with a weight problem should simply blame it on any medication they have to take – and it must be stressed that anyone on drugs prescribed by their physician must continue to take them – nevertheless it is important to know what the side effects of any drugs are. Your physician or pharmacist will give you details.

However, as a general guide, the groups of drugs listed on the opposite page may be making it harder for you to lose weight, either because of a tendency to encourage fluid retention, or by interfering with metabolism. This knowledge should not dishearten you, but should encourage you to eliminate the excess metabolic wastes produced, by eating a diet high in vegetables, fruits, and fiber, and learn to maximize metabolism and regain health. In addition, you can improve detoxification by a moderate increase in exercise, while those unable to exercise will find that "dry skin brushing" or a weekly aromatherapy massage can help

Prescription drugs can have an adverse affect on the metabolism.

with toxin drainage via the lymphatic system.

Even if you lose weight more slowly than a similar person who does not have to take medication, you can be positive that you are in control. It gives away our power when we blame other things for accumulated weight, but by positively seeking the healthier lifestyle, and this obviously includes diet, we can guarantee success and remain in charge.

Many of the people who come to see me for help with their diet are being treated by conventional medicine. They may already be taking any one of the drugs mentioned opposite. Several of them are concerned about their excess weight, and feel it may have something to do with the medication that they are taking. Many are fully resigned to the fact that they will never be able to lose any weight. Most are generally pleasantly surprised when, after an initial period of detoxification or change to a program containing a much higher level of nutrient-dense foods, as supplied by the New Pyramid program, they find that they are losing weight. This is likely to be

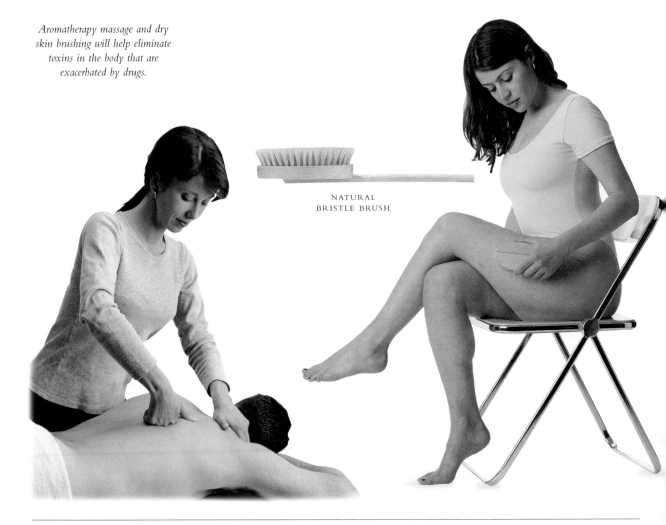

Aromatherapy massage and dry skin brushing will help eliminate toxins in the body that are exacerbated by drugs.

NATURAL
BRISTLE BRUSH

Tell your physician if you are taking supplements in addition to prescribed drugs.

due to a re-energized system as a result of spring cleaning the digestive tract, improving digestion and absorption, eliminating more wastes (including the breakdown products from the medication they are taking), and greater nourishment of the body with all nutrients but especially the micronutrients. Side effects of drugs are almost always a product of a unique interaction between the nature of the substance and the individual metabolism of the person who takes them. So, if weight gain is listed as a side effect of your drugs, this does not automatically mean it has to apply to you. Drug manufacturers are obliged to list all the possible side effects of the drugs they manufacture.

Drug groups on the list opposite will not cause weight gain in all those who take them, nor will every preparation within one group have weight gain as a side effect. This is just a general guide, so that if you feel your medication needs further investigation, you can make arrangements to be better informed by seeing your physician or pharmacist.

Most of the conditions requiring the tabulated types of medication are likely to improve considerably with nutritional healing (brought about by using any of the wholesome diets in this book). After a while you are likely to reach a stage where your physician may consider

PRESCRIPTION DRUGS AND WEIGHT GAIN

The prescription drugs that can have weight gain as a direct effect are:

- Hormones, such as oral contraceptives, hormone replacement therapy, and male sex hormones.
- Drugs for diabetes.
- Drugs acting on the central nervous system, such as antidepressants, and tranquilizers.
- Drugs for prevention of migraine.
- Drugs for heart disease and high blood pressure, such as beta-blockers, and cholesterol-reducing drugs.
- Anti-inflammatory drugs.
- Antihistamines.

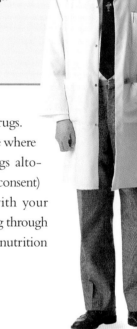

reducing the levels of your drugs. You may even get to the stage where you are able to avoid drugs altogether (with your physician's consent) and therefore continue with your journey to perfect well-being through no more than wholesome nutrition and a healthy lifestyle.

If you are taking prescription drugs and find you put on weight, talk to your physician.

The New Pyramid diet looks at foods from the point of view of their true role in promoting good health. Eating according to this program may improve your condition to the extent that you no longer need to take prescription drugs.

FATS

PROTEINS

CARBOHYDRATES

Fluctuations in Women's Appetites

If you are female and find that even on the New Pyramid diet you have times of the month when your appetite increases and you go out of control, this section is just for you. It applies to women who are, at present, experiencing a regular menstrual cycle (whatever the length). It is not suitable for individuals who have had ovaries or uterus removed, for anyone suffering absence of periods (for whatever reason), for post-menopausal women (though some may benefit), or for those on H.R.T. or steroid hormones.

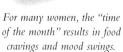

For many women, the "time of the month" results in food cravings and mood swings.

How many times have you heard, or you may even experience this yourself, that for two or three weeks of each month a woman is a normal confident person who finds it relatively easy to stick to a good healthy diet in her battle to lose weight? However, a week or ten days before her period is due she begins to feel fat and ugly and eats everything in sight. Because she gets depressed, grumpy, and very tired, and begins to believe and think she is fat and ugly, her diet goes out of the window. She may feel bloated and feel she wants to pick constantly at chocolate, bread, and cookies.

There seems to be a very fine dividing line between true P.M.S. and how a woman normally feels as her menstrual cycle unfolds, but in any case, these monthly appetite swings can ruin even the best diet, especially since it is during the increased-appetite phase that we feel less inclined to exercise. As we approach menopause, we may find that we exchange symptoms of P.M.S. for those of "the change," but even in many post-menopausal women, a regular cycle of mood swings and appetite changes still seem to occur.

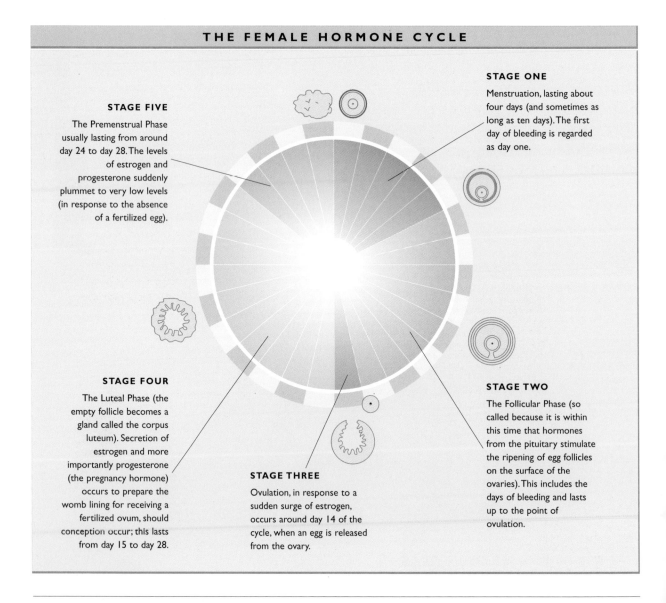

THE FEMALE HORMONE CYCLE

STAGE ONE
Menstruation, lasting about four days (and sometimes as long as ten days). The first day of bleeding is regarded as day one.

STAGE TWO
The Follicular Phase (so called because it is within this time that hormones from the pituitary stimulate the ripening of egg follicles on the surface of the ovaries). This includes the days of bleeding and lasts up to the point of ovulation.

STAGE THREE
Ovulation, in response to a sudden surge of estrogen, occurs around day 14 of the cycle, when an egg is released from the ovary.

STAGE FOUR
The Luteal Phase (the empty follicle becomes a gland called the corpus luteum). Secretion of estrogen and more importantly progesterone (the pregnancy hormone) occurs to prepare the womb lining for receiving a fertilized ovum, should conception occur; this lasts from day 15 to day 28.

STAGE FIVE
The Premenstrual Phase usually lasting from around day 24 to day 28. The levels of estrogen and progesterone suddenly plummet to very low levels (in response to the absence of a fertilized egg).

UNDERSTANDING THE FEMALE CYCLE

The female hormone cycle consists of five stages (see previous page). Although the surge of estrogen around day 14 of the cycle can sometimes bring on an "estrogen headache," most of the problems that we associate with periods occur during stage four and intensify in stage five when both estrogen and progesterone are very low. This time of the month is commonly associated, even in the healthiest of women, with mood changes, tearfulness, and irritability. It is also the time when appetite increases along, obviously, with food intake. Food cravings seem to intensify at this time also.

Scientific research has found that although a woman's daytime resting metabolic rate does not change much throughout her cycle, nevertheless at night it is increased in the ten nights before each period by up to 10 percent. This obviously means your body burns off calories more efficiently in the second half of your cycle than the first half, and is the likely reason for the increase in appetite. Linked to this increase in metabolic rate is a slight temperature rise of about $2\frac{1}{2}°F$ ($1°C$), occurring just prior to ovulation, and this fact has been used as one of the "natural" methods of birth control for some time.

We can use the above information to our advantage by constructing an eating plan which dovetails our calorific intake to our metabolic levels.

Most of the problems associated with periods come together at the end of the menstrual cycle.

Mood swings commonly occur toward the time when the period is due

Cravings are usually for chocolate or carbohydrates

HOW ARE YOU AFFECTED BY YOUR HORMONAL CYCLE?

Give simple "yes" or "no" answers to the following questions.

- Are there certain times of the month when dieting is a real struggle for you, or you may give up altogether?
- Do you find yourself craving chocolate, stodge, carbohydrate, or sweet things a few days before a period is due?
- Do you become depressed and think that you will never be slim?
- Are you fed up with your weight constantly going up and down?
- Has there been any reduction in normal sexual interest?
- Do you suffer from emotional swings, tearfulness, etc. in a regular cycle?
- Do your breasts become tender at the same time each month?
- Does your skin change to become drier or greasier in a regular cycle?
- Does your energy level drop considerably just before a period is due?
- Does your appetite increase just before a period?

SCORING

If you have said "yes" to one or two only of the above, then your system would appear to be only mildly affected by hormonal cycles, and you may consider that time-tabling changes in calorific content of your diet may be unnecessary. If, however, you have said "yes" to all, or nearly all of these questions, it may be that you have P.M.S. and are quite strongly affected by your hormonal cycles, so much so that the Cyclical Diet would suit you.

Unfortunately, candies will only exacerbate the symptoms of P.M.S.

THE CYCLICAL DIET

It has been apparent for some time now that bodily changes occur in a rhythmic way throughout the day, month, and season. The controlling mechanism occurs at the base of the brain in the hypothalamus. This part of the brain is very near to both the pituitary gland, which is the master endocrine gland orchestrating all of the other endocrine glands in their hormonal secretion and regulatory processes, not least of which is that of menstruation, and the centers controlling appetite and sleep.

The body-rhythm center in the hypothalamus releases chemical messengers in timed sequences which affect other centers in the hypothalamus and pituitary gland, resulting in a series of processes which are switched off and on depending on the unique biological rhythm or "biorhythms" of the body. These relate to the thousands of fluctuations in body chemistry that occur naturally, not only in humans but also in animals and plants, each day, month, and year. Biorhythms are not always regular and they can be thrown into chaos by all sorts of events, from emotional upheaval involving partners, family, or work to the onset of a cold, overindulgence in alcohol, or jetlag. As far as women are concerned, the most important rhythm related to appetite and weight is the menstrual cycle. Metabolic rate, particularly at night, is elevated from around day 15 to the end of the menstrual cycle. The Cyclical Diet attempts to finetune these biorhythmic changes into three stages related to variability of energy requirement.

The basis of this type of eating regime is to have a diet that follows the hormonal cycle.

During the first 14 days of your cycle (starting with day one being the first day of bleeding) you are able to restrict your eating more than you can later in the month, since your appetite will be lower, in line with your metabolism.

During the phase from day 15 to day 23 you may increase the amount of food if you feel your appetite increasing. More complex carbohydrate can be eaten, as long as it is appropriately balanced with protein, or you could increase the number of healthy snacks, such as seeds, fruit, nuts.

DEPRESSION

NERVOUS TENSION

WEIGHT GAIN

FOOD CRAVINGS

The mood swings and weight fluctuations that some women experience through the menstrual cycle can be addressed by vitamin and mineral supplements.

During the phase from day 24 to day 28, when appetite has really increased, you can indulge even more according to your appetite, and will not feel guilty about it, since you have allowed for this increase in energy content of your diet by having two lean weeks at the beginning of your monthly cycle.

If you think that this eating plan would suit your needs, turn to Appendix Four where you will find more information on the Cyclical Diet.

As well as suffering from the above symptoms, many women these days appear to experience estrogen excess. Men also seem to be suffering from this. New research indicates that high environmental estrogen levels may be responsible for the observed reduction in sperm counts. In women, estrogen excess is partly due to an imbalance in the amount of estrogen and prog-

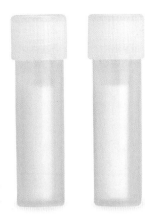

Commercially produced kits are now available with which you can test your estrogen level.

esterone, but we are hearing more and more in the press and on television that estrogens in the environment, from the breakdown products of certain plastics and pesticides, are getting into our water and our food. There are many symptoms associated with estrogen excess (estrogen dominance), but one or two are worth a mention within the context of weight problems. Estradiol (an estrogen) naturally stimulates breast tissue, increases the proportion of body fat, causes salt and fluid retention, and interferes with thyroid hormone activity, as well as affecting blood-sugar control, whereas natural progesterone generally has the opposite effects.

Since estrogen dominance can occur either because of excess estrogen, or because of lowered progesterone, we might find that stimulating the body to balance estrogen and progesterone more effectively would help. This can be achieved by consuming more foods containing these hormone-like materials (phytoestrogens) such as soy, sweet potato, etc., or obtaining the same substances from a plant/vegetable concentrate, as in freeze-dried encapsulated supplements. There are several good herbal combinations on the market that contain a natural form of plant progesterone, and the best of these is wild yam extract. Also, many excellent nutritional supplement manufacturers produce herbal combinations for premenopausal and postmenopausal women. Check for these with your herbalist or local health food store.

Additionally, you can now obtain, through nutritional therapy practitioners, noninvasive testing kits which you can use at home (usually involving a simple saliva collection) to assess, over one complete monthly cycle, the levels of estrogens, progesterone, and other hormones.

SUPPLEMENTS TO ALLEVIATE P.M.S. SYMPTOMS

Supplements can help to reduce the effect of severe swings in body rhythms:

🖎 If your symptoms are mainly centered around nervous tension, mood swings, irritability, and anxiety, then supplementing your diet with the B group of vitamins, especially vitamin B6, would help, together with the mineral magnesium.

🖎 If your symptoms are mainly those of weight gain, swelling of the extremities, breast tenderness, and abdominal bloating, then in addition to those supplements mentioned above, taking a modest amount of vitamin E would help.

🖎 If your symptoms are mainly those of headaches, craving for candy, increased appetite, palpitations, fatigue, fainting, and dizziness, then in addition to those supplements mentioned above, you might find that taking the mineral chromium would help.

🖎 If your symptoms are mainly those of depression, forgetfulness, confusion, insomnia, and crying, then, in addition to those supplements mentioned above, you might find that taking some of the minerals zinc and iron would help.

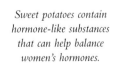

Sweet potatoes contain hormone-like substances that can help balance women's hormones.

PART FOUR

NUTRITIONAL HEALING FOR COMMON AILMENTS

SELF-HELP FOR COMMON AILMENTS

T HIS SECTION COMPRISES A *general guide to self-help for many common diseases, but it does not give the unique treatment an individual would receive from a nutritional therapist. See Useful Addresses, pages 248–9, for registers.*

Where lists of "Suggested Supplements" are quoted, it is not intended that all the supplements be used at the same time; simply that these are preparations which have been found to be helpful. The level of each vitamin and mineral supplement will be as indicated in the tables found in Part Two, or as depicted on the product labels. Any supplements not appearing in these lists, such as botanicals, amino acids, and nutrient accessories, are best taken at the levels indicated on those labels. Never self-prescribe herbs, amino acids, or non-standard/single nutritional accessories; obtain the help of a nutritional therapist, or purchase them as part of a standardized nutritional supplement. If you self-prescribe multi-formulas, pay careful attention to any contraindications for any existing health conditions you may have.

NUTRITIONAL ACCESSORY SUPPLEMENTS

NUTRITIONAL ACCESSORY	HELPFUL FOR	NUTRITIONAL ACCESSORY	HELPFUL FOR
N-acetyl glucosamine	Poor integrity of intestinal mucous membranes	Grapefruit seed extract	Parasitic/fungal infections of the gut
Anthocyanidins	Inflammation and oxidation/high uric acid levels/capillary fragility/poor eyesight	Green-lipped mussel	Osteoarthritic pain and stiffness
		Hesperidin	Poor collagen integrity/poor gut lining/ capillary fragility/ menopausal problems
Antioxidants	Inflammation and oxidation		
Beet extract	Toxicity/poor blood function	Hydrochloric acid (betaine hydrochloride)	Gastric infections/poor mineral absorption/allergy
Bioflavonoids	Circulatory problems/capillary fragility/ poor healing and repair of tissue/poor collagen maintenance	Lactobacillus acidophilus	Poor gut flora/candida overgrowth
		Lecithin	Poor fat metabolism/nerve problems
Bromelain	Poor protein digestion/food sensitivity	Lipoic acid	Cataracts/ glaucoma/diabetes
Butyric acid	Dysbiosis/irritated gut lining	Licorice root	Ulcerated gut lining
Cabagin	Peptic ulcers/dysbiosis	Manuka honey	Indigestion/peptic ulcers
Caprylic acid	Candida albicans infestations	S-methylmethionine	Intestinal irritation/dysbiosis
Cellulose	Constipation	Octacosanol (wheatgerm oil)	Poor nerve insulation
Charcoal (activated)	Flatulence/poor fatty acid levels in gut		
Chondroitin sulphate	Poor cartilage formation/joint problems	Pectin	Constipation/high cholesterol
		Peppermint oil	Bowel irritation/flatulence
Cranberry	Cystitis	Phosphatidyl serine	Poor memory
Digestive enzymes (lipase, amylase, protease)	Poor digestion	Propolis	Poor immune function
		Rooibosh tea	Intestinal irritation
		Spirulina (algae)	Poor nutrient levels (especially amino acids)
Evening primrose oil	Inflammation/hormonal problems		
Fish oils (D.H.A. and E.P.A.)	Inflammation/poor circulation/ heart problems	Starflower (borage)	General inflammation/ hormonal problems
Fructo-oligosaccharides	Poor gut flora/low levels of *Bifido* bacteria	Tea tree oil (external)	Skin infections/ringworm/pulled muscles
		Tocotrienol	High cholesterol
Gamma-oryzanol	Poor stomach muscle tone/gastritis	Wild yam	Female hormone imbalance/ menopause
Glycosamino-glycans	Atherosclerosis/thrombosis		

AMINO ACIDS USED IN NUTRITIONAL HEALING

NUTRITIONAL ACCESSORY	HELPFUL FOR	NUTRITIONAL ACCESSORY	HELPFUL FOR
L-alanine	Prostate problems	L-glutamine	Intestinal lining problems/poor thyroid function/alcoholism/poor muscle tone
L-argenine	Poor sperm production	L-glutathione	Detoxification
Aspartic acid	Imbalance of cellular minerals/low energy	L-glycine	Prostate problem/detoxification
L-carnitine	Heart and circulatory problems	L-lysine	Cold sores/shingles/genital herpes
L-cysteine	Poor detoxification and absorption, especially vitamin B6/poor hair growth.	L-methionine	Poor detoxification of protein by-products/nerve problems
L-cystine	Heavy metal toxicity/poor healing after trauma	DL-phenylalanine	Generalized pain
Glutamic acid	Prostate problems	Taurine	Gall stones/hyperactivity/poor brain function

BOTANICALS USED IN NUTRITIONAL HEALING

NUTRITIONAL ACCESSORY	HELPFUL FOR	NUTRITIONAL ACCESSORY	HELPFUL FOR
Agnus castus	Premenstrual/menstrual problems	Ginseng (Siberian)	Stress/poor adrenal function/impotence
Alfalfa	Fluid retention/urinary and colon problems	Golden seal	Constipation/upset stomach/toxic liver
Aloe vera	Inflammation/skin problems/burns/arthritis	Gota kola	Poor memory/high blood pressure
Astragalus	Poor immune function/interferon insufficiency	Grapefruit seed extract	Gut parasites
Bilberry	Menstrual cramps/poor collagen formation	Hawthorn	Stress/insomnia/high cholesterol/diarrhea
Berberis	Dysbiosis/gut spasms/poor immune function/poor liver function	Hops	Insomnia/high uric acid and fluid levels
Boswellia (boswellic acid)	Muscle and joint pain/stiffness	Kelp	Low iodine levels/low thyroid function
Cat's claw	Poor immune function	Licorice	Stomach and intestinal irritation/poor mucus production
Celery seed	Excess acid/fluid retention/arthritis/high blood pressure	Marshmallow	Epithelial irritation
Cinnamon	Intestinal cramps	Motherwort	Menstrual and menopausal problems
Clove oil	Spasm of intestinal tract	Passiflora (passion flower)	Stress/insomnia
Cranberry	Bladder and urethral infections	Pau d'arco	Fungal infections in intestinal tract
Dandelion	Poor hepatic balance/poor bile production/blood problems	Pygeum africanum	Prostate problems
Devil's claw	Arthritic pain and stiffness	Psyllium	Constipation/toxicity of colon
Echinacea	Poor immune function/flatulence/dysbiosis	Rhubarb	Low levels of phytoesterols
Elderberry extract	Poor immune function/influenza	Rutin	Eye problems/capillary fragility
Feverfew	Headaches/migraine	Sanguinaria (blood root)	Bronchial infections/periodontal disease
Garlic	Poor immune function/circulatory problems/high cholesterol	Saw palmetto	Prostate problems
Ginger	Travel sickness/gut irritation/hot flashes/menstrual cramps	Silymarin (Milk thistle)	Toxic liver/alcohol misuse/poor hepatic balance
Ginkgo biloba	Poor brain and peripheral circulation/tinnitus/asthma	Slippery elm	Toxic and irritated intestinal tract
		St. John's wort	Depression and anxiety
		Valerian	Stress/insomnia/irritated intestinal tract
		White willow	Pain/inflammation/stomach irritation

DISORDERS OF THE HEART, CIRCULATION, AND BLOOD

*T*HE CIRCULATORY SYSTEM IS *an amazing and complicated network consisting of a pump (the heart) and its connecting tubes (arteries, arterioles, capillaries, venules, and veins). Over the course of an average lifetime, the heart will pump 55 million gallons of blood through around 60,000 miles of blood vessels. The whole purpose of this system is to deliver supplies of oxygen, nutrients, and other substances to the body's 60 trillion cells, and to remove carbon dioxide and wastes. The capillaries, where the actual exchange of nutrients and wastes takes place, are so small in diameter that blood cells must squeeze through one at a time.*

CAUSES OF CARDIOVASCULAR DISEASE

Most diseases of the cardiovascular system stem from a too high intake of saturated and hydrogenated fats, which attach to the walls of blood vessels and form atheromatous plaques, constricting the flow of blood. A dietary excess of sugar and refined carbohydrates can also create plaques, because of the conversion of excess sugar to fat. High levels of refined carbohydrates also raise blood triglyceride levels and increase platelet adhesiveness. Additionally, the clotting time of the blood may be reduced, leading to a higher risk of blood clots forming and blocking blood vessels completely. Lack of essential fatty acids, on the other hand, can lead to "stiffened" red blood cells, which are unable to squeeze through the fine capillaries, and may lead to chronic fatigue. Furthermore, diets high in salt can cause fluid retention and other problems which lead to high blood pressure (hypertension). Increased capillary fragility occurs when diets are high in refined and processed food, a condition exacerbated by smoking, excess alcohol, and lack of exercise.

The main circulatory system of the blood.

The red blood cells need various nutrients to keep them working properly, including essential fatty acids, several vitamins (especially the B vitamins) and minerals (especially iron). If any of these nutrients are low, anemia and other blood diseases can develop.

HEART DISEASE AND CIRCULATORY DISORDERS

For heart disease, atherosclerosis, thrombosis, phlebitis, stroke, angina, circulatory disorders, chilblains, Raynaud's disease, restless leg syndrome, and platelet aggregation, the following factors should be taken into account:

- *excess saturated fats.*
- *excess use of hydrogenated, overheated, or oxidized vegetable oils (too many free radicals).*
- *trans-fatty acids.*
- *excess refined carbohydrates and sugars.*
- *high intake of foods fortified with vitamin D (vitamin D excess).*
- *excess dairy products.*
- *vitamin and mineral deficiencies.*
- *excess coffee and alcohol.*
- *high homocysteine levels.*
- *overweight.*

DIET

In addition to following the New Pyramid diet:

● Eat predominantly vegetable protein, with oily fish taken two or three times a week. ● Maximize foods for nourishment of blood vessels, such as dark green and orange vegetables, peas, oats, onions, garlic, fresh wheatgerm, mixed seeds, sprouted seeds, lecithin granules.	● Minimize intake of alcohol (maximum two units once or twice a week), all dairy food except live yogurt. ● Avoid salt, coffee, sugar, refined grains, hydrogenated fats and trans-fats, fried foods, fatty or processed meats, full fat milk and cheese, cream, and foods fortified with vitamin D.

Suggested supplements

A multivitamin/multimineral containing vitamin A, vitamin B-complex (especially B6) with folic acid, vitamin C, bioflavonoids especially quercetin, vitamin E (100iu per day only if on blood-thinning drugs), magnesium, selenium, chromium, and copper; a high-potency garlic supplement; *Ginkgo biloba*; *Aloe vera*. Additionally, L-carnitine, fish oils, linseed (flax seed) oil, and lecithin would help fat carriage in the blood vessels. Glycosamino-glycans can help in the treatment of thrombosis.

HIGH BLOOD PRESSURE AND CHOLESTEROL LEVELS

For hypertension (elevated blood pressure) and elevated cholesterol, the following nutritional considerations should be taken into account:

◆ *Excess salt, sugar, tea, and coffee.*
◆ *saturated fats, hydrogenated fats, and trans-fatty acids.*
◆ *excess alcohol.*
◆ *poor calcium/magnesium balance.*
◆ *low fiber intake.*
◆ *obesity.*

DIET	
In addition to following the New Pyramid diet:	
● Eat foods containing pectins, such as apples and carrots. ● Eat alfalfa sprouts and other sprouted seeds and beans, regularly (to lower serum cholesterol) Insure a large proportion of potassium-rich foods (see Macrominerals, page 59). ● Balance the Omega-3 and Omega-6 fatty acids; add ground linseeds (flax seeds) to your seed mixture of sunflower, pumpkin, and sesame.	● Eat basically a vegetarian diet for three to six months, but include a little oily fish twice a week, and live yogurt daily. ● Avoid salt, coffee, alcohol, sugar, refined grains, hydrogenated fats and trans-fats, fried foods, meat, full fat milk and cheese, cream. ● Avoid grapefruit juice if on calcium channel blockers (drugs which are often used to treat high blood pressure).

Suggested supplements

Vitamin C with bioflavonoids (or anthocyanidins, such as grape seed, bilberry, and pine bark, which inhibit lipid peroxidation), or a high-potency antioxidant including beta-carotene, vitamin C, vitamin E, and selenium; vitamin B6; magnesium; fish oils or edible linseed (flax) oil; garlic; lecithin; *Aloe vera*; palm oil or rice bran tocotrienols.

ANEMIA

A proper clinical diagnosis by a physician must be obtained before embarking on any self-help treatment. The following nutritional considerations should be taken into account:

◆ *insufficiency of iron, vitamins B6, B12, C, E, and folic acid.*
◆ *zinc-induced copper deficiency.*
◆ *excess onion/garlic/root ginger.*
◆ *excess alcohol.*

DIET	
In addition to following the New Pyramid diet:	
● Eat mineral- and vitamin-rich liver and other organ meats once or twice a week (but not if pregnant or planning a pregnancy), along with fish and/or vegetable proteins (pulses [legumes], nuts, seeds). ● Include plenty of green leafy vegetables and dried fruit such as apricots and figs, and molasses. ● Reduce level of onions and garlic, if normally eaten in large amounts.	● Increase amount of freshly ground mixed seeds, especially linseed (flax seed), and wheatgerm. ● Avoid foods and drinks which inhibit iron absorption, such as, coffee, tea, alcohol, wheat bran; or those processes that cause loss of vitamins B and C, such as incorrect storage, long cooking times, consumption of diuretics.

Suggested supplements

Multivitamin/multimineral with a good supply of all B vitamins, but not including iron (iron inhibits absorption of other nutrients), plus a separate iron supplement taken, in chelated form, at a different meal; vitamin C; *Aloe vera*.

Beansprouts and other sprouted seeds can help lower blood pressure and cholesterol.

Vitamin- and mineral-rich nuts will help combat anemia.

DISORDERS OF
THE IMMUNE SYSTEM

T̲HE IMMUNE SYSTEM IS *that part of our body which protects us against infectious disease and tissues which grow to become non-self tissues (such as cancers and tumors). There are many different types of micro-organism (prions, viruses, bacteria, yeasts, molds, protozoa) which have the power to cause us harm.*

To counteract these activities, the body has two lines of defense. The first is to prevent their entry to the body in the first place. For this we need a healthy covering of skin, normal acid levels in the stomach, and ciliated cells and mucus lining the airways to trap and inactivate any incoming microbes. The second line of defense is to disarm those that inevitably do enter. It is really this latter defense mechanism which is known as the Immune System, wherein the main army is composed of various types of white cells, which can engulf microbes, release antibodies to deactivate them, or release substances to kill them or neutralize the toxins that they emit. These amazing cells are found lining the digestive system and lungs, and in the blood and the lymphatics; a system closely related to the blood system, which returns excess tissue fluid back into the main blood vessels.

Many different nutrients are involved in keeping the immune system at peak function, and an eating plan such as the New Pyramid diet will go a long way to insure these essential nutrients are supplied. Additionally, when infections strike, taking immune boosting nutrients and herbs (such as vitamins A and C, and zinc, Echinacea herb, Astralagus herb, and so on) can make an enormous difference to the speed of the healing process.

The formation of cancers and tumors tends to be a lengthier process involving not only sub-optimum nutrition, but also other substances which are called carcinogens. Common carcinogens include cigarette smoke, barbecued and smoked food, nistrosamines, free radicals, pollutants, environmental estrogens, insecticides, pesticides, and radiation. Where a body tissue has to deal with an excessive carcinogenic load, cell division goes out of control. If left unchecked by roving members of the immune system, particularly in areas of the body where oxygen is low, this rapidly dividing group of cells becomes a growth. It is important to avoid as many carcinogens as possible by eating good wholesome food devoid of additives and pesticides, and make other lifestyle changes, such as giving up smoking. The foods in the New Pyramid diet contain large amounts of antioxidant nutrients which help greatly in the fight against free radicals and other carcinogens from interfering with cell division. Recent research indicates that many modern cancers could be prevented by proper nutrition and improved lifestyles. Moreover, nutrition is not just preventive: more and more evidence is now accruing which suggests that several types of cancer can be held in check by consuming a nutritious diet and taking various nutritional supplements.

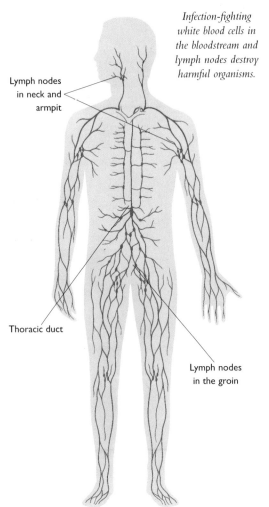

Infection-fighting white blood cells in the bloodstream and lymph nodes destroy harmful organisms.

Lymph nodes in neck and armpit

Thoracic duct

Lymph nodes in the groin

A.I.D.S. AND H.I.V.

For Acquired Immune Deficiency Syndrome (A.I.D.S.) and H.I.V., the following nutritional considerations should be taken into account:

♦ *low intake of antioxidant nutrients.*
♦ *low intake of essential fatty acids.*
♦ *generalized vitamin (especially B1 and C) and mineral deficiencies.*
♦ *dysbiosis of gut (especially overgrowth of molds and yeasts) – may need Detoxification Diet.*
♦ *food allergy/intolerance – may need Hypoallergenic Diet.*
♦ *acidosis.*
♦ *excess refined carbohydrates and sugar.*
♦ *dairy products.*

DIET

In addition to following the New Pyramid diet:

• Maximize intake of anti-oxidant vegetables and fruit, especially dark-green and orange vegetables and fruit, shiitake mushrooms, and garlic.
• Aim for a 80 percent/20 percent alkali-forming to acid-forming diet.
• Eat at least some raw vegetables and sprouted seeds and pulses (legumes) daily.
• Maximize intake of freshly ground mixed seeds, especially pumpkin seeds.

• Minimize intake of sweet foods, even fruit (to prevent proliferation of molds and yeasts).
• Eat unpolluted, oily fish, soy products (tofu), lean meat, pulses (legumes), and seed vegetables for their protein content.
• Eat live soy yogurt daily.
• Avoid refined carbohydrates (white flour) and sugar, dairy foods, fatty meats, alcohol, and common food allergens.

Suggested supplements

High-potency antioxidant formula; vitamin A; maximum levels of vitamin C; high-potency vitamin B-complex, with good levels of B1; evening primrose (or starflower) oil and fish oils or linseed (flaxseed) oil; N-acetyl glucosamine (to raise levels of glutathione); lecithin; grapefruit seed extract (if candidiasis is present); *Aloe vera*; tea tree, applied externally, for skin lesions.

Garlic has been used for centuries as an aid to disease resistance.

POOR DISEASE RESISTANCE AND WOUND HEALING

Since infection of any type (colds, catarrh, coughs, sore throats, influenza, slow/poor wound healing, and immune deficiencies) concerns the activity of micro-organisms, the following nutritional considerations relate to items which reduce immunity and allow the virus or bacteria to multiply.

♦ *low levels of vitamin C, bioflavonoids, antioxidants, and zinc.*
♦ *excess toxins in food and water.*
♦ *excess refined carbohydrate; excess carbohydrate generally (especially sweet foods).*
♦ *excess animal proteins, especially those from dairy food.*
♦ *excess alcohol.*

DIET

In addition to following the New Pyramid diet:

• Increase vegetables and fruit high in vitamins A and C, bioflavonoids and antioxidants.
• Increase amount of garlic and onion.
• Increase amount of freshly ground mixed seeds, especially pumpkin seeds.
• Eat organic produce.
• Drink elderberry cordial (especially for influenza).
• Minimize grain carbohydrate (but not carbohydrate from vegetables).
• Avoid alcohol, candy, tea, coffee, milk, and cheese.

Elderberry cordial is an excellent flu remedy.

Suggested supplements

Vitamins A and C, and zinc, at maximum levels (zinc and vitamin C lozenges for sore throats); vitamin B-complex; high-potency garlic; propolis; Echinacea herb; Astragalus herb; *Aloe vera*; elderberry extract.

COLD SORES, GENITAL HERPES, AND SHINGLES

For all these conditions, the following nutritional considerations should be taken into account:

- ◆ *excess arginine-rich foods (cereals — especially wheat, almonds, peanuts, chocolate, bacon, chicken).*
- ◆ *citrus.*
- ◆ *acid diet.*
- ◆ *generalized low levels of vitamins.*

DIET	
In addition to following the New Pyramid diet:	
• Increase vegetables and fruit high in vitamins A and C (but not citrus fruit), bioflavonoids, and antioxidants. • Increase amount of garlic and onion.	• Reduce amount of carbohydrate. Avoid arginine-rich foods (wheat, almonds, peanuts, bacon, and chicken). • Avoid alcohol, candy, tea, coffee, milk, and cheese.

Suggested supplements

Lysine (appears to inhibit replication of the virus); vitamins A and C, selenium, and other antioxidants; Echinacea herb; *Aloe vera*.

GUAVAS

Foods and drinks that are high in vitamin C, such as cranberries, guavas, and chili peppers, boost the immune system.

CRANBERRIES

CANDIDIASIS AND THRUSH

For both these conditions, the following nutritional considerations should be taken into account:

- ◆ *excess refined carbohydrate, and sweet foods (including fruit).*
- ◆ *foods containing yeast.*
- ◆ *poor gut levels of* Lactobacillus *bacteria.*
- ◆ *deficiency or poor absorption of vitamin B-complex (especially B6 and biotin).*

DIET	
In addition to following the New Pyramid diet:	
• Increase vegetables and fruit high in vitamins A and C, and antioxidants. • Increase the amount of raw vegetables. • Increase the amount of garlic, olive oil, and oily fish. • Drink three to four glasses of cranberry juice a day.	• Minimize the amount of meat and dairy foods. • Avoid all sugar (and sweet fruit, initially), refined foods, alcohol, tea, coffee, smoked/pickled meat or fish, and fermented foods.

Suggested supplements

Vitamins A, B-complex including biotin; additional B6; vitamin C; vitamin E; zinc; high-potency garlic; *Lactobacillus acidophilus*; fructo-oligosaccharides; grapefruit seed extract; *Aloe vera*; digestive enzymes; magnesium.

CHILI PEPPERS

TUMORS AND CANCERS

To help prevent tumors and cancers, the following nutritional excesses and deficiencies should be taken into account:

◆ *lack of nutrient-dense food.*
◆ *saturated, hydrogenated fats, and trans-fatty acids.*
◆ *low dietary fiber.*
◆ *excess refined food and sugar.*
◆ *excess alcohol.*
◆ *excess smoked, pickled, and salt-cured food (these contain nitrosamines which are carcinogenic).*
◆ *"soft" water (hard water protects against digestive cancers).*
◆ *chlorinated water (may be related to bladder cancer).*
◆ *polluted food and water (containing toxins, pesticides, xeno-estrogens, etc.).*

DIET

In addition to following the New Pyramid diet:

● Maximize intake of antioxidant nutrients (beta carotene, vitamins C and E, and minerals zinc and selenium).

● Eat tomatoes, broccoli, Brussels sprouts, hot peppers, onions, apples, grapes, pink grapefruit, watermelon, guava, raspberries, strawberries, wheatgrass (or sprouted seeds), shiitake mushrooms, soy, and beans for their phytochemical component.

● Maximize intake of raw and lightly-cooked vegetables, especially dark green and yellow-orange types.

● Maximize intake of freshly ground mixed seeds.

● Insure a good intake of low gluten grains, e.g., brown rice and millet, for fiber.

● Reduce intake of animal protein, and consume a little oily fish and plant proteins, e.g., pulses (legumes) and especially soy.

● Drink bottled water, green tea, and some black tea which is thought to reduce the possibility of cancers in the digestive tract.

● Avoid all saturated fats, processed fats/oils (hydrogenated fats and trans-fatty acids), refined food, sugar, smoked/ pickled/salt-cured foods, coffee, tea with milk, and alcohol.

Suggested supplements

Anthocyanidins (very powerful antioxidants); natural beta-carotene; vitamins B6, folic acid, C and E; magnesium; selenium; zinc; co-enzyme Q10; *Lactobacillus acidophilus*; butyric acid; Omega-3 oils; high-potency garlic; *Aloe vera*.

CHRONIC FATIGUE SYNDROME (M.E.)

For this condition, the following nutritional considerations should be taken into account:

◆ *food allergy/intolerance – may need Hypoallergenic Diet, and/or Food Combining Diet.*
◆ *poor level of nutrients (poor digestion and absorption).*
◆ *poor immune function (overgrowth of Candida etc.).*
◆ *poor intake of essential fatty acids.*

DIET

In addition to following the New Pyramid diet:

● Maximize intake of lightly steamed vegetables.

● Maximize intake of antioxidant nutrients.

● Maximize intake of freshly ground mixed seeds.

● Focus protein on tofu, millet, quinoa, "seed" vegetables, seeds and some nuts, and fish.

● Minimize foods that are difficult to digest, e.g., meat, dairy, some grains and pulses (legumes).

● Avoid all stimulants (tea, coffee, alcohol, colas), "rich food," common allergenic foods, food additives, refined food and sugar.

Suggested supplements

BROCCOLI

A high-quality multivitamin/multimineral; maximum vitamin B12, vitamin C, magnesium and zinc; antioxidants; maximum levels of fish oils or linseed (flax seed) oil; maximum levels of evening primrose oil; coenzyme Q10; Echinacea herb; digestive enzymes.

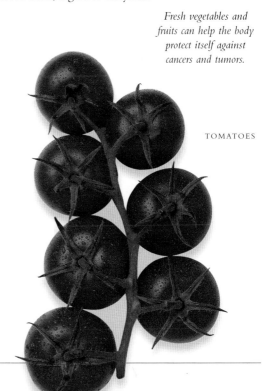

Fresh vegetables and fruits can help the body protect itself against cancers and tumors.

TOMATOES

DISORDERS OF THE NERVOUS SYSTEM

*T*HE CENTRAL NERVOUS SYSTEM *comprises the brain and spinal cord.*
*It is intricately connected to the peripheral nervous system, which comprises all
the nerve fibers (neurones) throughout the body. External stimuli are received, converted
into an electrical message and sent via sensory neurones to the brain. Automatic
actions occur within the autonomic nervous system to deal with homeostatic regulators
which may require electrical messages being sent from the brain via motor neurones
to the effector organs (the glands etc.). Voluntary actions similarly occur when the
brain sends electrical messages to our muscles, causing contraction and movement.*

The electrical messages occur because of the activities of the minerals sodium, potassium, calcium, and magnesium. Pollutants, such as drugs and heavy metals like lead, mercury, cadmium, and aluminum can interfere with the intricate electrical pathways. We need to be careful of heavy metals in our environment and our diet, to try and prevent diseases such as Alzheimer's, Parkinson's, and multiple sclerosis.

For the nervous system to work correctly many different substances are required. One of the main neuro-transmitters contains choline, which is found in the substance lecithin. If too much or too little neuro-transmitter is produced, this may lead to depression. Phosphatidyl serine, related to lecithin, has been shown to improve memory. If the body has low levels of the minerals involved in transmission, e.g., sodium, potassium, calcium, and magnesium, then nerve tissue cannot work effectively.

The "insulation" around nerves, called the myelin sheath, is made up of very specific types of fatty acids. Reduction of this insulation layer causes nerves to misfire or to fail in transmitting the impulse to its destination. These effects can be seen in diseases such as multiple sclerosis. The symptoms of multiple sclerosis can be helped by having a diet low in saturated fats, but high in essential fatty acids.

Since the way we think and behave is ultimately a reaction to what is going on in the brain and nervous system, a nutritional program which supplies them with all the nutrients they require should have a good effect on emotions and behavior.

The plant extract *Ginkgo biloba* has been found to help blood flow to the brain. This plant also has tremendous antioxidant qualities, which are important in protecting the brain against free radicals and their effects.

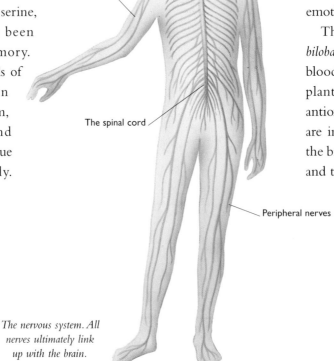

The brain

Peripheral nerves

The spinal cord

Peripheral nerves

*The nervous system. All
nerves ultimately link
up with the brain.*

DEPRESSION AND OTHER PROBLEMS OF THE MIND

For problems of the memory, mind, emotions, behavior, and depression, the following nutritional considerations should be taken into account:

- *food additives, especially colorings, preservatives, and artificial sweeteners.*
- *excess white sugar.*
- *excess refined and processed food.*
- *foods high in tyramine (e.g., cheese and red wine).*
- *caffeine.*
- *generalized mineral and vitamin deficiencies, from poor diet or poor digestion and absorption, low stomach acid, low levels of digestive enzymes – may need Food Combining Diet.*
- *essential fatty acid deficiency.*
- *alcohol and drugs.*
- *food allergy/intolerance – may need Hypoallergenic Diet.*
- *heavy metal toxicity in food, water, and air (e.g., lead, cadmium, mercury) – may need Detoxification Diet.*

DIET	
In addition to following the New Pyramid diet:	
• Maximize intake of raw and lightly cooked vegetables, and fish. • Eat fresh and dried fruit as the only sources of sugar. • Maximize intake of freshly ground mixed seeds, including linseeds. • Eat organic produce whenever possible.	• Avoid refined foods, foods containing additives (especially colors, preservatives, and artificial sweeteners), sugar, alcohol, tea, coffee, colas, cheese, and red wine (and other tyramine-containing foods), drugs (other than those prescribed by your physician).

Suggested supplements

A good-quality multivitamin/multimineral (containing maximum levels of vitamin B-complex and folic acid, vitamin C, calcium, magnesium, and zinc); vitamin C to total maximum level; lecithin; L-carnitine; DL-phenylalanine; phosphatidyl serine; evening primrose oil; *Ginkgo biloba*; methionine (to detox the liver). Additionally, for helping with depression, St. John's wort herb.

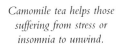

Camomile tea helps those suffering from stress or insomnia to unwind.

STRESS, INSOMNIA, AND GENERALIZED PAIN

For all these conditions, the following nutritional considerations should be taken into account:

- *excess refined and processed foods.*
- *food additives, preservatives, and colorings.*
- *low intake of magnesium and calcium.*
- *vitamin B-complex deficiency or poor absorption.*
- *low intake of antioxidant-containing foods.*
- *overeating.*
- *excess caffeine (especially when taken late in the day – insomniacs).*
- *excess sodium (salt) and iodine.*
- *alcohol (especially when taken just before bedtime).*
- *food allergy/intolerance – may need Hypoallergenic Diet.*
- *toxic heavy metals in food, water, air (e.g., lead, cadmium, mercury) – may need Detoxification Diet.*

DIET	
In addition to following the New Pyramid diet:	
• Maximize intake of antioxidant-containing fruit and vegetables. • Maximize intake of raw dark-green vegetables. • Add extra wheatgerm or oatgerm to cereals. • Maximize intake of ground mixed seeds, especially sesame (or use	sesame oil in salads) • Eat live yogurt daily • Drink camomile or passion flower teas. • Avoid refined and processed foods, caffeine-containing beverages (e.g., tea, coffee, colas), food additives, overcooked food, table salt, alcohol, and overeating.

Suggested supplements

Vitamin B-complex including B3, additional B5 (taken early in the day); vitamin C with bioflavonoids; antioxidants (especially selenium and zinc); lecithin; calcium/magnesium balanced formula (take 1 hour before bedtime for insomniacs); Siberian ginseng; herbal combinations (taken for short periods of time only), e.g., valerian/passionflower; hops; camomile; *Aloe vera*; fish oils; and DL-phenylalanine for generalized pain.

MULTIPLE SCLEROSIS

ALZHEIMER'S DISEASE AND DEMENTIA

The following nutritional considerations should be taken into account for this condition:

- *excess intake of saturated fat/low intake of essential fatty acids.*
- *excessive meat and dairy food consumption.*
- *gluten-containing grains.*
- *yeast.*
- *low intake of antioxidants.*
- *alcohol.*
- *food allergy/intolerance – may need Hypoallergenic Diet.*

DIET

In addition to following the New Pyramid diet:

- Maximize intake of raw and lightly cooked vegetables.
- Maximize intake of antioxidant-containing vegetables.
- Maximize intake of freshly ground mixed seeds (balance sunflower, pumpkin and sesame with linseed).
- Maximize intake of good-quality polyunsaturated oils, olive oil, and oily fish.

- Eat gluten-free grains (brown rice, millet, buckwheat).
- Eat some sprouted seeds daily (e.g., alfalfa sprouts, bean sprouts, etc.).
- Eat live soy yogurt daily.
- Avoid refined and processed food, saturated and hydrogenated fats and trans-fatty acids, gluten grains, meat and dairy products, yeast, and alcohol.

Suggested supplements

A high-quality multivitamin/multimineral containing good levels of vitamin B-complex, and vitamin C, calcium, magnesium, selenium and zinc; high-potency fish oils or linseed (flax seed) oil; evening primrose oil; *Aloe vera*; betaine hydrochloride (for nutrient absorption problems).

SEED OIL

Too much refined food and fat can contribute to Alzheimer's disease, so maximize your intake of whole grains, vegetables, and seeds.

The following nutritional considerations should be taken into account for these conditions:

- *low-serum vitamin B (especially B12) levels.*
- *excess refined and processed food.*
- *low intake of vegetables, fruit, and whole grains.*
- *excess saturated fat/low essential fatty acids.*
- *poor nutrient absorption (low stomach hydrochloric acid) – may need Food Combining Diet.*
- *food allergy/intolerance – may need Hypoallergenic Diet.*
- *aluminum toxicity (from environment, especially aluminum cooking utensils) – may need Detoxification Diet.*

DIET

In addition to following the New Pyramid diet:

- Maximize intake of raw and lightly-cooked vegetables, and of fruit.
- Maximize intake of antioxidant-rich vegetables (especially garlic) and fruit.
- Maximize intake of seeds, seed oils, and nuts.
- Increase level of fermented foods (yogurt, miso, tempeh).
- Sip cider vinegar with at least one meal (the largest) each day (this improves the acidity of the stomach and thus allows proper digestion and absorption).

- Take wheatgerm or oatgerm, and molasses daily.
- Avoid refined, processed, and overcooked foods, alcohol, saturated fat, aspartame, medicines and toothpastes containing aluminum, and aluminum kitchen utensils and cookware.

BROWN RICE

Suggested supplements

A good multivitamin/multimineral with maximum levels of B vitamins (especially B3, B12, and folic acid), calcium, magnesium, zinc, silica; high-potency antioxidants (beta-carotene, vitamins C and E, and selenium); *Ginkgo biloba*; phosphatidyl choline (lecithin); phosphatidyl serine.

CARROT

PARKINSON'S DISEASE

The following nutritional considerations should be taken into account:

◆ *amino acid imbalance/deficiency.*

◆ *low levels of folic acid, vitamin B1, B6, vitamin C, vitamin E.*

◆ *low levels of iron.*

◆ *manganese toxicity.*

◆ *food intolerance – may need Hypoallergenic Diet.*

◆ *heavy metal toxicity (aluminum, mercury) – may need Detoxification Diet.*

A Ginkgo biloba supplement may help those suffering from Parkinson's disease or Alzheimer's.

DIET

In addition to following the New Pyramid diet:

● Maximize intake of a wide range of vegetable and wholegrain carbohydrates (exclude wheat).

● Maximize intake of cold-pressed seed oils, olive oil, and nuts.

● Maximize intake of wide range of fruit and vegetables.

● Eat plenty of freshly ground mixed seeds.

● Eat organic produce (to minimize environmental pollutants and heavy metals).

● Minimize overall high protein foods; take these only at the evening meal.

● Avoid all refined and processed food, sugar, aspartame, alcohol, aluminum-containing toothpastes, and cooking utensils.

Suggested supplements

A high-quality multivitamin/multimineral with good levels of calcium, magnesium and silica, but without manganese; vitamin B complex; vitamins C and E; selenium; octacosanol (wheatgerm oil); iron; high-potency antioxidant; *Aloe vera*; *Ginkgo biloba*.

Sipping cider vinegar with food aids digestion and absorption.

PRODUCTS THAT CONTAIN ALUMINUM

PRODUCT	ENTRY INTO BODY BY
Aluminum foil (absorbed into food)	Ingestion
Aluminum pots and pans	Ingestion
Antacids	Ingestion
Antidiarrheal agents	Ingestion
Antiperspirant sprays	Inhalation/skin contact
Aspirin (buffered)	Ingestion
Cake mixes	Ingestion
Douches	Skin contact
Drinking water	Ingestion
Flour (self-rising)	Ingestion
Hemorrhoidal preparation	Skin contact
Pickles	Ingestion
Processed cheese	Ingestion
Roll-on deodorants	Skin contact
Room deodorizers	Inhalation
Toothpastes	Ingestion

DISORDERS OF
THE SKELETAL SYSTEM

T HE SKELETAL SYSTEM IS *made up of 206 bones (including the skull),*
differing greatly in size from the tiny ossicles in the ear to the femur of the leg.
To enable the many bones to articulate with each other correctly and to translate into
movement of the body, we have joints which are held in place by ligaments. Muscles
are attached to bones by tendons, and cartilage insures they work smoothly. All of
these tissues — bones, ligaments, tendons, and cartilage — are made up of proteins such
as collagen and elastin and a whole host of different minerals (calcium, magnesium,
phosphorus, fluoride, boron). For some of these minerals, vitamins are required to help
their absorption from food into our bloodstream.

Calcium and other minerals are also required by the blood, and body tissues in general, for efficient metabolism, and when calcium is low in these tissues, then the body will extract the calcium it needs from the bones. Conversely, when calcium is in excess (either because of a simple excess, or because of insufficient magnesium), it may be deposited in inappropriate places, such as plaques in arteries, lumps and bumps in joints, and in soft tissue such as muscle and liver.

Diets low, or imbalanced, in essential minerals and vitamins and high in acid-forming foods might lead to diseases of the skeletal system like arthritis and osteoporosis. Furthermore, certain common food allergens such as wheat and cow's milk may cause further irritation of the synovial membranes of the joints. Free radical damage is believed to play a part in joint problems too, so that foods high in antioxidants should be taken in order to counteract them. Many types of arthritis are now described as being auto-immune diseases; in other words, the body identifies some of these tissues as foreign, and attacks them. Improving digestion, preventing leaky gut, and rebalancing gut flora is essential for preventing food allergy and arthritic pain.

Much can be done by nutritional means to alleviate pain, and allow healing of the bones and joint tissues. A good wholefood diet with an appropriate acid-alkali balance which also omits common food allergens, especially wheat and cow's milk, will go a long way to help in this respect. Some foods like those belonging to the nightshade family (tomatoes, potatoes, eggplants, sweet peppers) can be a particular problem in arthritic conditions, and are believed to contribute to them. In some cases of bone and joint disease nutritional supplements are required to rebalance the system quickly and encourage the healing powers of the body. Supplements which act as antioxidants, such as boswellic acid, and others which help heal the lining of the joints, such as glucosamine, are now becoming popular. Others, like fish oils, have always been, and still remain, very useful for helping with skeletal problems. Also, celery seed extract has been found to be of use in removing excess acidity from the tissues.

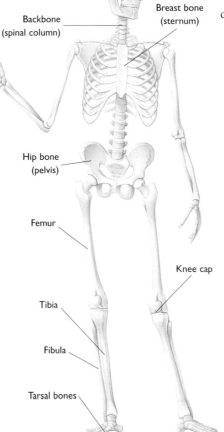

Skull

Breast bone
(sternum)

Backbone
(spinal column)

Hip bone
(pelvis)

Femur

Knee cap

Tibia

Fibula

Tarsal bones

The human skeletal
system consists of 206
separate bones.

ARTHRITIS AND FIBROMYALGIA

The following nutritional considerations should be taken into account:

◆ *red meat.*
◆ *dairy foods high in lactic acid.*
◆ *saturated fat.*
◆ *excess intake of calcium and/or vitamin D.*
◆ *excess sodium (salt), and salty foods, and pickled foods.*
◆ *acidosis (high tissue acidity).*
◆ *refined carbohydrates and "acid-forming" foods.*
◆ *insufficient intake of raw vegetables.*
◆ *food additives.*
◆ *acid fruit (citrus, strawberries, etc.).*
◆ *stimulants (tea, coffee, sugar-based drinks).*
◆ *food allergy (particularly to gluten and nightshade family of foods – tomatoes, potatoes, sweet peppers, eggplants) – may need Hypoallergenic Diet.*
◆ *dysbiosis of gut.*
◆ *excess weight.*

DIET

In addition to following the New Pyramid diet:

- Eat mainly a vegetarian diet with a little oily fish two or three times a week.
- Aim for an 80 percent alkaline, 20 percent acid diet.
- Maximize intake of antioxidant vegetables and fruit, and bioflavonoids.
- Maximize intake of raw and lightly cooked vegetables.
- Eat Jerusalem artichokes (and their flour). Drink vegetable juices, e.g., carrot and celery, or watercress, celery and parsley, instead of fruit juice.

- Drink soy milk or brown rice milk instead of "dairy" milks.
- Maximize intake of freshly ground mixed seeds, including linseeds.
- Minimize intake of potatoes, tomatoes, sweet peppers, and eggplants (nightshade family) and wheat.
- Avoid red meat, dairy foods, saturated fat, salty or pickled foods, food additives, acid fruit (such as berries, and citrus fruit), fried foods, tea, coffee, sugar, soft drinks, and highly alcoholic drinks like whiskey.

Suggested supplements

Vitamin B-complex (especially B3, and B5); vitamins C and E; high-potency antioxidants; boron; fish oils (including both E.P.A. and D.H.A.); glucosamine sulphate; *Lactobacillus acidophilus*; fructo-oligosaccharides; bromelain; green-lipped mussel extract; devil's claw herb; boswellic acid; *Aloe vera*; *Gingko biloba*.

CARPAL TUNNEL SYNDROME

For this condition, the following nutritional considerations should be taken into account:

◆ *low levels of B vitamins, especially B2 and B6.*
◆ *excess refined carbohydrate and sugar.*
◆ *excess vitamin D/calcium.*
◆ *excess alcohol and other stimulants.*

DIET

In addition to following the New Pyramid diet:

- Add extra wheatgerm or oatgerm to food.
- Maximize intake of antioxidant fruit and vegetables.
- Maximize intake of freshly ground mixed seeds.
- Take molasses daily.

- Minimize intake of stimulants (alcohol, coffee, tea).
- Avoid meat, refined carbohydrates, sugar, and dairy foods (except live yogurt), and "nightshade" vegetables (potatoes, tomatoes, sweet peppers, eggplants).

GRAPES

Suggested supplements

A high-potency vitamin B-complex; calcium and magnesium balanced formula (2:1 magnesium to calcium); fish oils or linseed (flax seed) oil.

Antioxidant fruit such as grapes should be eaten by those with skeletal disorders.

SESAME SEEDS

NOTE

Sufferers of arthritis and fibromyalgia should avoid supplements containing calcium and magnesium (they will be getting all their body needs from the seeds).

GOUT

For this condition, the following nutritional considerations should be taken into account:

- *excess meat.*
- *excess refined carbohydrates and sugar (both increase acid levels).*
- *excess alcohol.*
- *excess coffee.*
- *excess purine-containing foods (organ meats, fish, shellfish, oats, yeast, and spices).*
- *lack of fresh vegetables and fruit.*
- *acidosis.*

DIET

In addition to following the New Pyramid diet:

- Maximize intake of antioxidant vegetables and fruit.
- Eat low-acid forming grains (brown rice, millet, corn, and buckwheat).
- Drink plenty of fluid (to prevent build up of uric acid crystals).
- Eat deep-sea white fish as opposed to mackerel, sardines, salmon, etc.
- Eat free-range eggs, low-fat cheese, goat's milk, and yogurt, as opposed to meat and other dairy foods.
- Avoid refined carbohydrates and sugar, meat, offal, alcohol, and purine-rich food.

Suggested supplements

High-potency antioxidants including maximum levels of vitamins A, C, and E; bioflavonoids; vitamin B-complex with additional folic acid and B5; lecithin; bromelain; linseed (flax seed) oil; *Aloe vera*.

Gout sufferers should eat eggs (free-range) and white fish instead of meat.

OSTEOPOROSIS

For this condition, the following nutritional considerations should be taken into account:

- *excess protein, fat, dairy food.*
- *poor calcium absorption.*
- *poor levels of vitamins C, D, magnesium, boron.*
- *poor levels of gut bacteria (from excess antibiotics).*
- *excess candy, refined carbohydrates, and salt.*
- *stomach acid (hydrochloric acid) deficiency/ digestive enzyme deficiency – may need Food Combining Diet.*
- *excess alcohol and coffee.*
- *excess phytic and oxalic acids from some cereals, and some vegetables.*
- *excess levels of sodium fluoride in water.*

DIET

In addition to following the New Pyramid diet:

- Maximize the intake of vegetables and fruit.
- Maximize intake of freshly ground mixed seeds, especially sesame and pumpkin.
- Minimize the intake of refined carbohydrate and sweet foods.
- Increase the amount of raw vegetables in the diet and eat pulses (legumes) and freshly sprouted seeds (for their enzyme content, as well as for their high levels of minerals and vitamins).
- Sip a small amount of cider vinegar or fresh lemon juice with at least one meal a day.
- Eat live yogurt daily.
- Minimize intake of cereals and nightshade foods (tomato, potato, eggplant, sweet peppers), use more pulses (legumes), vegetables, and fruit for carbohydrate, and a little brown rice and millet.
- Minimize intake of animal proteins; fish can be eaten three times a week, plus soy and nuts.
- Use filtered or a range of different bottled waters.
- Aim for a diet that is 80 percent alkali-forming, and 20 percent acid-forming.
- Avoid animal protein (except fish and yogurt), coffee, alcohol, refined carbohydrates, and candy, and fluoride-containing toothpaste.

Suggested supplements

A good-quality multivitamin/multimineral with vitamin B-complex, vitamin C (maximum level), vitamin E, zinc, copper, iron, and balanced magnesium/calcium, (ratio of 2:1 magnesium : calcium), boron (prevents calcium loss and bone demineralization), silica and molybdenum; *Lactobacillus acidophilus*; fructo-oligosaccharides; digestive enzymes.

TENDONITIS

For bursitis, tennis elbow, and frozen shoulder, the following nutritional considerations should be taken into account:

- *toxic system – may need Detoxification Diet.*
- *food allergy/intolerance – may need Hypoallergenic Diet.*
- *foods fortified with vitamin D (i.e., excess vitamin D).*
- *excess calcium.*

DIET	
In addition to following the New Pyramid diet:	
• Maximize intake of fresh antioxidant vegetables and fruit, and freshly ground mixed seeds. • Minimize intake of meat but eat fish.	• Eat a vegetable and brown rice diet for a few days to remove toxicity. • Avoid dairy foods.

Suggested supplements

Vitamin C; vitamin E; beta-carotene; *Aloe vera*.

SPRAINS

For this condition, the following nutritional considerations should be taken into account:

- *low levels of vitamin C.*
- *low levels of antioxidants.*
- *excess calcium.*

DIET	
In addition to following the New Pyramid diet:	
• Maximize levels of vegetables and fruit, especially those rich in vitamin C (for healthy collagen formation). • Maximize levels of antioxidant nutrients.	• Maximize levels of fresh ground mixed seeds, especially sesame and pumpkin. • Minimize levels of meat and dairy food. • Minimize levels of alcohol and coffee.

Suggested supplements

High-potency antioxidants; maximum vitamin C; silica; glucosamine (n-acetyl glucosamine); *Aloe vera*.

LOW BACK PAIN AND SCIATICA

For this condition, the following nutritional considerations should be taken into account:

- *obesity.*
- *protein and/or calcium deficiency (poor intake, or poor absorption).*
- *poor level of stomach acid – may need Food Combining Diet.*
- *insufficient intake of dark green vegetables.*
- *low intake of vitamin C (poor collagen integrity).*
- *excess refined carbohydrates.*
- *alcohol (mineral leaching).*

DIET	
In addition to following the New Pyramid diet:	
• Maximize intake of dark green vegetables. • Maximize intake of fruit and vegetables containing vitamin C. • Eat more plant proteins (soy, pulses [legumes], seed vegetables), and a little oily fish.	• Drink a little diluted freshly squeezed lemon juice, or cider vinegar with main meal of the day. • Minimize intake of dairy foods and red meat. • Avoid alcohol, refined carbohydrates and sugar.

Suggested supplements

High-potency vitamin B-complex, containing good levels of B_1 and B_{12}; vitamin C and bioflavonoids; a balanced calcium/magnesium complex (1:2 calcium to magnesium), with boron; bromelain; digestive enzymes; DL-phenylalanine (as a painkiller).

Sipping diluted lemon juice, or cider vinegar, helps digestion.

STRENGTHENING THE MUSCULAR SYSTEM

D EPENDING ON HOW ATHLETICALLY *endowed you are, your muscular system could compose 40 percent or more of your body weight. While the average person is usually content with normal muscular performance, the athlete seeks optimum health in order to excel at his or her event. Optimum health has to be supported by optimum nutrition. Everyone correlates the aesthetically pleasing body of the athlete with being well nourished, but this is, unfortunately, not necessarily so. While athletes have higher-than-normal nutrient needs, they often eat the same as, or even worse than, the normal person.*

For the muscles to work efficiently we need many of the nervous system nutrients, such as calcium, magnesium, potassium, and sodium, in the correct proportions for swift passage of messages along the nerves and strong muscle contraction. Additionally, a good source of fuel is needed in the muscles, together with a superb oxygen supply to allow maximum combustion and release of energy. The main fuels of the muscles are glycogen and fatty acids. A good supply of high-quality carbohydrate foods, together with all the B vitamins, carnitine, and chromium, are needed to insure a high level of energy release. Exceptional muscular activity requires large amounts of oxygen to be taken into the body by the lungs. This means there is automatically a greater rate of oxidation and the production of free radicals, making a good supply

of antioxidant nutrients essential. Sweat will be produced in copious amounts to cool the body, and many essential nutrients, especially iron and zinc, are lost along with the sweat. These minerals, together with lost water, need to be replaced quickly. To insure adequate repair and maintenance of protein in muscles and for collagen maintenance, the diet must supply good levels of vitamin B6, and vitamin C. Extra vitamin E, magnesium, and calcium are vital to prevent damage and cramp. Extreme levels of exercise also take their toll on the endocrine (hormonal) system, and in women athletes, this often results in amenorrhea (lack of menstruation). The immune system, too, takes quite a beating from excessive exercise, so that eating to optimize this system is an important criterion in athletic performance.

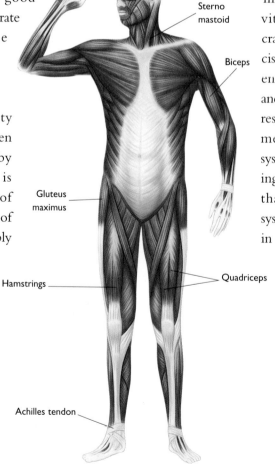

Sterno mastoid

Biceps

Gluteus maximus

Hamstrings

Quadriceps

Achilles tendon

The muscular system makes up over a third of the weight of an adult.

IMPROVING ATHLETIC PERFORMANCE

Excessive exercise increases demand for:

♦ *antioxidants (greater rates of oxidation within the body).*
♦ *calcium and magnesium (for proper muscle function).*
♦ *potassium together with sodium (needed for proper nerve function).*
♦ *zinc, iron, and other minerals (to replace those lost in sweat).*
♦ *vitamin C (for collagen and connective tissue maintenance).*
♦ *vitamin E (to relieve common muscle cramps).*
♦ *B vitamins and chromium (to release energy from carbohydrate).*
♦ *vitamin B6 (for mobilization of protein in muscle growth and repair).*
♦ *carnitine (needed for fat burning in the muscles).*

For extra energy, athletes should maximize intake of slow-release complex carbohydrates.

Peak athletic performance calls for an increased consumption of both vitamins and minerals.

DIET

In addition to following the New Pyramid diet:

● Maximize carbohydrate intake insuring a wide range of complex types, and including at least half in the form of vegetable carbohydrate, e.g., peas, seed vegetables, pulses (legumes).

● Maximize intake of freshly ground mixed seeds, especially pumpkin seeds.

● Maximize antioxidant vegetables and fruit.

● Eat the full quota of fruit for sugar content.

● Eat a wide range of animal and plant proteins.

● Eat vegetables and fruit high in potassium, e.g., potatoes, bananas.

● Eat wheatgerm, and molasses, daily for B vitamins and chromium.

● Eat cold polyunsaturated oils and olive oil daily, for essential fatty acids, and for vitamin E.

● Minimize refined carbohydrate.

● Minimize intake of dairy food (imbalanced calcium/magnesium), but eat live yogurt daily.

Suggested supplements

High-potency antioxidant with good levels of beta-carotene, vitamins C and E, and selenium; high-potency vitamin B-complex; good-quality multimineral complex containing calcium, magnesium, potassium, zinc, iron, copper, and chromium; essential fatty acids (fish oils, evening primrose oil); L-carnitine; glutamine (to increase lean muscle); Ginseng herb. Take magnesium and potassium after an intensive workout to prevent muscle cramps. Take vitamins B6 and E, calcium, magnesium, potassium, and *Aloe vera*, to help when muscle cramp occurs.

DISORDERS OF
THE ENDOCRINE SYSTEM

WHILE THE NERVOUS SYSTEM relays information quickly around the body in an "electrical" fashion, the endocrine (hormonal) system relays information in a slower, more sustained way by using various chemical messengers called hormones. Hormones are produced by glands in different parts of the body and are released directly into the bloodstream from where they pass to target organs.

The master gland – the pituitary – produces hormones to control the secretions of the other endocrine glands, such as the thyroid which produces thyroxine (regulates metabolism), the pancreas which produces insulin and glucagon (regulates blood sugar levels), the adrenals which produce adrenaline and corticosteroid hormones (involved in stress management, inflammation, and infection), and the gonads (ovaries in women; testes in men) which produce estrogen, progesterone and testosterone (regulating secondary sexual characteristics, and menstruation and pregnancy in women).

Like all body systems, the endocrine system can only work as efficiently as the programming in the genes will allow. Nevertheless, effective working of the system also depends on receiving the raw materials for its maintenance and from which to synthesize its products. Any sub-optimum diet will eventually have an effect on the endocrine system. Thyroid problems can be a result of obesity and/or insufficient iodine in the diet. Adrenal insufficiency/exhaustion may be brought on by poor diet and stress. Sex hormone problems, such as P.M.S. in women and impotency in men, may be exacerbated, or even caused by, poor nutrition and/or pollutants.

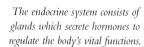

The endocrine system consists of glands which secrete hormones to regulate the body's vital functions.

The good news is that by returning to an essentially wholefood diet containing a good supply of essential fatty acids for prostaglandin synthesis, the body starts to receive the basic nutrients it requires to stimulate normal activity of the endocrine glands.

BLOOD-SUGAR PROBLEMS

If you currently have diabetes, see your medical adviser before embarking on a self-help program. For adult-onset diabetes, hypoglycemia, and blood-sugar swings (including P.M.S. [*see* page 192]), the following nutritional considerations should be taken into account:

◆ *excess refined carbohydrates and sugar.*
◆ *excess saturated fat.*
◆ *vitamin and mineral deficiencies, or poor absorption – may need Food Combining Diet.*
◆ *excess coffee and alcohol.*
◆ *obesity.*
◆ *toxicity – may need Detoxification Diet.*
◆ *food intolerance/allergy.*

DIET
In addition to following the New Pyramid diet:

● Maximize intake of a wide range of vegetables, and include watercress, Jerusalem artichokes, Brussels sprouts, cucumbers, garlic, and avocado.	● Eat mainly plant proteins, e.g., soy products (tofu, etc.), vegetables with seeds (green beans, etc.), pulses (legumes), mixed seeds (and fenugreek seeds and tea), and nuts, with some live yogurt, fish, chicken, or a free-range egg.
● Eat complex carbohydrates regularly, especially fibrous vegetables, oatmeal or oat flour products, brown rice (not over-cooked), millet, and buckwheat.	● Minimize the intake of alcohol, fruit, and fruit juices (at least initially).
● Eat five or six small meals (containing some complex carbohydrate and a small amount of protein) per day to even out blood-sugar swings.	● Avoid all refined and high G.I. foods, food additives, sugar, very sweet fruit, dried fruit, candy, pastry, white flour products, white rice, cow's milk and other common allergens, red meat, and caffeine.
● Take spirulina powder/grains in warm water two or three times a day.	

Suggested supplements

A high-quality multivitamin/multimineral containing good levels of vitamins A, B-complex, C plus bioflavonoids, and E, magnesium, chromium, zinc, copper, manganese and potassium; evening primrose oil; lecithin, and high-potency garlic; *Aloe vera*; lipoic acid.

THYROID IMBALANCE

See Part Three (pages 100–103) for a fuller investigation into thyroid problems. For both hypothyroid and hyperthyroid problems, the following nutritional considerations should be taken into account:

- ◆ *iodine deficiency.*
- ◆ *zinc deficiency.*
- ◆ *selenium deficiency.*
- ◆ *vitamin A deficiency.*
- ◆ *vitamin B6 deficiency.*
- ◆ *vitamin E deficiency.*
- ◆ *excess alcohol.*
- ◆ *fluoride and chlorine contained in tap water.*
- ◆ *overweight/obesity.*

DIET

In addition to following the New Pyramid diet:

- Maximize intake of vegetables, especially watercress, radishes, garlic, and seaweed (kelp etc.), and fruit, including dried yellow fruit, e.g., apricots.
- Insure all carbohydrate is unrefined and of a wide range of types, mostly from vegetables, pulses (legumes), and soy.
- Add extra wheatgerm or oatgerm to cereals.
- Maximize intake of freshly ground mixed seeds, especially linseeds and pumpkin.

- Eat one or two Brazil nuts daily.
- Eat vegetable protein, e.g., tofu and pulses (legumes), with fish, seafood, and poultry.
- Eat sprouted seeds and beans regularly.
- Use cold-pressed virgin seed oils and olive oil on salads.
- Use bottled or filtered water.
- Minimize intake of meat, and full-fat dairy foods.
- Avoid all refined foods, food additives, sugar, fatty meats, and alcohol.

Suggested supplements

A high-quality multivitamin/multimineral including vitamin A plus beta-carotene, vitamin B-complex, vitamin C, vitamin E, zinc, copper, iodine, iron and selenium; octacosanol (wheatgerm oil); tyrosine (helps nourish the thyroid gland in cases of hypothyroid). You must take great care to observe the label directions if you decide to supplement with concentrated kelp, as large amounts will inhibit metabolism. Note: If thyroid disease exists, see your medical advisor before embarking on a supplement program.

STRESS

For a full explanation of the effects of stress see the information and questionnaire in Part Three (pages 96–99). For adrenal exhaustion, the following nutritional considerations should be taken into account:

- ◆ *low levels of B vitamins, especially B5.*
- ◆ *low levels of antioxidant nutrients.*
- ◆ *excess refined and processed food.*
- ◆ *polluted food, water, and air.*
- ◆ *excess alcohol, tea, and coffee.*

DIET

In addition to following the New Pyramid diet:

- Maximize intake of a wide range of vegetables and fruit, especially those containing the antioxidant nutrients.
- Maximize intake of freshly ground mixed seeds.
- Use molasses and wheatgerm (or oatgerm) daily for B vitamins and a range of minerals.

- Use bottled or filtered water.
- Buy organic produce wherever possible.
- Minimize intake of alcohol, tea, and coffee.
- Avoid refined and processed food, especially white flour products, and food additives.

Suggested supplements

A high-potency B vitamin complex; additional vitamin B5; vitamin C; maximum levels of magnesium; essential fatty acids, and evening primrose oil; Siberian ginseng.

Those with stress should include a good proportion of fruit in their diet.

DISORDERS OF THE DIGESTIVE SYSTEM

O NE ASPECT OF NUTRITION *involves understanding how the raw materials from the diet end up as components of the human body. This process starts with ingestion of food, continues with digestion, and ends with expulsion of waste material. An endless array of plant and animal material is broken down into the 50 or so nutrients that our body requires. There are many areas in this system where that initial act of food choice has an almost immediate effect, and the list of disorders relating to the chewing, swallowing, digesting, and assimilating of food is endless.*

For our purposes we can limit this to three major areas: poor digestion (low stomach acid and poor digestive enzyme production), food intolerances (undigested food gaining entry to the blood through a "leaky" gut), and poor absorption (accumulated waste material in the large bowel, and the tissues). Therefore, healing the digestive system encompasses not only the introduction of good-quality food but also insures that this good food is going to be digested and absorbed correctly. With this in mind, it is necessary to take time to improve the production of stomach acid and digestive enzymes; remove irritant foods and heal the gut lining, and remove toxins and wastes from the system.

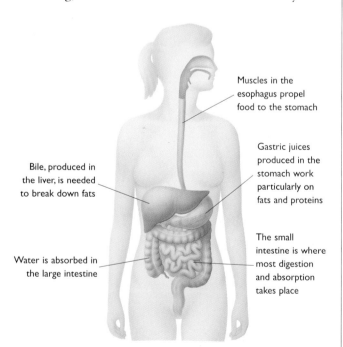

All parts of the digestive system need to work well for good nutrition.

Muscles in the esophagus propel food to the stomach

Gastric juices produced in the stomach work particularly on fats and proteins

The small intestine is where most digestion and absorption takes place

Water is absorbed in the large intestine

Bile, produced in the liver, is needed to break down fats

GALLSTONES

For these, the following nutritional considerations should be taken into account:

◆ *excess cholesterol.*
◆ *excess calcium.*
◆ *excess saturated fat.*
◆ *excess refined food and sugar.*
◆ *low fiber.*
◆ *food allergy/intolerance – may need Hypoallergenic Diet.*
◆ *low stomach acid – may need Food Combining Diet.*
◆ *excess weight.*

DIET	
In addition to following the New Pyramid diet:	
● Maximize intake of vegetables, seeds, nuts, and pectin-containing foods.	● Sip freshly squeezed lemon juice or cider vinegar with at least one meal a day.
● Eat more vegetable protein such as soy, seed vegetables, pulses (legumes).	● Use seed oils and olive oil daily on salads.
● Eat foods containing a range of vegetable fiber (cellulose) and minimize cereal fiber.	● Avoid saturated fat, refined foods, common food allergens, dairy foods, sugar, eggs, and pork.

Suggested supplements

Phosphatidyl choline (lecithin); vitamin C taken at the maximum level (*see* page 63); vitamin E; psyllium seeds or whole linseeds; taurine; ginger.

POOR DIGESTION

For indigestion, leaky gut syndrome, and food intolerance, leading to migraine, bloating, rashes, lethargy, fatigue, diarrhea, constipation, etc., the following nutritional considerations should be taken into account:

- *food allergy/intolerance – may need Hypoallergenic Diet.*
- *insufficient stomach acid and/or digestive enzymes*
- *poor blood-sugar control.*
- *incorrectly combined foods – may need Food Combining Diet.*
- *poor gut flora/presence of gut parasites/overuse of antibiotics.*
- *toxic system – may need Detoxification Diet.*
- *low fiber.*
- *excess sugar.*
- *use of sugar substitute, e.g., aspartame (headaches and migraine).*
- *excess alcohol.*
- *excess tea and coffee.*

DIET	
In addition to following the New Pyramid diet:	
• Maximize intake of fibrous vegetables, pulses (legumes), and rice and barley bran (as whole grain). • Maximize intake of antioxidant foods. • Eat a small pot of live yogurt daily (if allergic to dairy milk, use live soy yogurt). • Sip cider vinegar with meals.	• Add Jerusalem artichokes to your vegetables. • Avoid all allergenic foods, "rich" foods, and high glycemic index foods. • Avoid refined foods, sugar, alcohol, and caffeine. • Avoid mixing concentrated starches and concentrated proteins in the same meal. • Avoid sugar substitutes.

Suggested supplements

High-quality multivitamin/multimineral complex containing good levels of vitamins A, B3, B5, B6, B12, folic acid, C and E, calcium, magnesium, selenium, zinc, and potassium; peppermint oil; digestive enzymes (lipase, protease, amylase); betaine hydrochloride; bromelain and papain; *Lactobacillus acidophilus*; fructo-oligosaccharides; L-glutamine and glucosamine; linseed (flax seed) oil or fish oils; whole linseeds and psyllium (for constipation); aspartic acid (for fatigue); feverfew herb (for migraine).

HEPATITIS

This disease is made worse by:

- *alcohol and animal protein.*
- *saturated, fried, and hydrogenated oils and fats.*
- *refined foods and sugar/low fiber.*

DIET	
In addition to following the New Pyramid diet:	
• Maximize intake of cellulose- and pectin-containing vegetables and fruit, and antioxidant vegetables. • Focus the diet on vegetable protein with a little fish.	• Minimize dairy foods/eggs. • Avoid fried food, hydrogenated and saturated fats, trans-fatty acids, refined food, sugar, alcohol, animal flesh (except fish).

Suggested supplements

Lecithin; psyllium; high-potency antioxidants; Silymarin (Milk thistle); *Aloe vera*.

DIVERTICULITIS

For this condition, the following nutritional considerations should be taken into account:

- *low intake of fiber and excess refined carbohydrates, sugar, honey, and salt.*
- *poor bowel flora/dysbiosis/food intolerance – may need Hypoallergenic Diet.*

DIET	
In addition to following the New Pyramid diet:	
• Have an initial three-day cleanse of steamed vegetables, diluted vegetable juices and/or grape or apple juice; drink slippery elm tea, marshmallow tea, spirulina powder in water.	• After the fast: maximize intake of fresh fruit and vegetables. Eat a mixture of vegetable carbohydrates, nuts, pulses, and mixed seeds. Avoid spicy food, wheat, wheat bran, tea, coffee, red meat, dairy foods and salty or refined foods.

Suggested supplements

Lactobacillus acidophilus; fructo-oligosaccharides; psyllium; vitamins A and C; zinc; ginger (especially if nauseous); cinnamon; n-acetyl-glucosamine; *Aloe vera*.

ULCERS (PEPTIC, STOMACH, DUODENAL), HIATUS HERNIA

If you currently have any of these conditions, see your physician before embarking upon a self-help program. The following nutritional considerations should be taken into account:

◆ *food intolerance – may need Hypoallergenic Diet.*
◆ *aspirin.*
◆ *low fiber.*
◆ *wheat fiber.*
◆ *refined carbohydrates and sugar.*
◆ *stimulants (tea, coffee, alcohol, colas, chocolate).*
◆ *strong spices.*
◆ *excess saturated fat.*
◆ *stomach acid imbalance – may need Food Combining Diet.*

DIET
In addition to following the New Pyramid diet:

• Maximize intake of cellulose and pectin fiber (omit wheat bran and other harsh cereal fibers).	• Avoid, wheat, wheat bran, alcohol and other stimulants (including decaffeinated coffee), common allergenic foods (dairy, oranges, etc.), aspirin, saturated fats.
• Maximize intake of all vegetables, fruit, and freshly ground mixed seeds.	
• Take Manuka honey, and Rooibosh tea daily (for their antiseptic properties).	• Avoid mixing concentrated carbohydrates and proteins in the same meal.
• Drink cabbage water or cabbage juice each day.	

Suggested supplements

High-strength multivitamin/multimineral containing good levels of vitamins A, C, and E, and calcium, magnesium, and zinc; digestive enzymes; deglycyrrhinized licorice; S-methylmethionine; cabbage extract (cabagin/vitamin U); *Aloe vera* (especially for duodenal ulcers).

Cabbage – red, white, or green – and cabbage juice or water are recommended for ulcer sufferers.

BOWEL DISEASES

For inflammatory bowel disease (I.B.D.), Crohn's disease, ulcerative colitis, I.B.S., and spastic colon the following factors should be taken into account:

◆ *many deficiencies (poor absorption)/enzyme insufficiency – may need Food Combining Diet.*
◆ *food allergy/intolerance – may need Hypoallergenic Diet.*
◆ *red meat and eggs (arachidonic acid).*
◆ *refined carbohydrates (especially white wheat flour), wheat bran, and sugar.*
◆ *low intake of soluble fiber.*
◆ *fried foods, coffee, spices, salt, and other irritants.*
◆ *aluminum cookware.*
◆ *intestinal parasites/poor gut flora.*

DIET
In addition to following the New Pyramid diet:

• Maximize intake of antioxidant vegetables and fruit.	• Eat oily fish and a little chicken, and plant protein such as tofu and soy yogurt.
• Maximize intake of water and other fluids in between meals.	
• Maximize intake of freshly ground mixed seeds, especially pumpkin seeds.	• Avoid all refined food, sugar, coffee, spices, salt, fried, red meat, common food allergenic foods such as dairy foods, food additives, and aluminum cookware.
• Maximize intake of cellulose fiber and pectins, together with a minimal amount of cereal fiber; omit wheat fiber.	

Suggested supplements

Supplements with high levels of vitamins A, B-complex – especially B5 – C, and E, calcium, magnesium, zinc, iron, potassium, and selenium; high-potency garlic; *Lactobacillus acidophilus*; fructo-oligosaccharides; glucosamine; fish oils and/or linseed (flax seed) oil; *Aloe vera*; golden seal; marshmallow root; peppermint oil; slippery elm; ginger; cinnamon; glucosamine; herbal antispasmodic containing, e.g., valerian, hops, hawthorn, passiflora; ginger; cinnamon.

HEARTBURN AND ESOPHAGITIS

For heartburn (gastritis) and esophagitis, the following nutritional considerations should be taken into account:

- *excess alcohol, tea, coffee, and milk.*
- *refined carbohydrates and sugar.*
- *saturated and hydrogenated fats, and chocolate.*
- *orange juice, tomato juice, or other acidic beverages.*
- *spicy foods, salt, and food additives.*
- *over-large meals.*
- *drinking liquid with meals (dilutes gastric juices).*
- *excessively hot or cold foods, and beverages.*
- *food allergy/intolerance – may need Hypoallergenic Diet.*
- *eating too quickly/eating late at night.*
- *eating incorrectly combined meals – may need Food Combining Diet.*
- *high or low stomach acid (both conditions can produce heartburn), or low levels of digestive enzymes.*
- *excess weight.*

DIET	
In addition to following the New Pyramid diet:	
• Eat five or six small meals per day.	• Eat at least some of your vegetables raw, and some sprouted seeds and beans for their natural enzyme content.
• Drink plenty of bottled or filtered tap water, in between meals (try not to take any liquid with meals – this will encourage you to chew your food more thoroughly).	• Avoid eating hurriedly, eating late at night, eating concentrated carbohydrates and proteins at the same meal, foods and beverages that are too hot or too cold, saturated and hydrogenated fats, spicy food, spirits, milk, refined carbohydrates, sugar, food additives, common food allergens (wheat, dairy, etc.)
• Minimize stimulants and acidic foods (tea, coffee, alcohol, colas, chocolate, sugar, orange and tomato juices).	
• Have a little Manuka honey.	

Suggested supplements

High-potency antioxidants; vitamin B-complex, especially B12; vitamin C (as sodium ascorbate if overacid, and ascorbic acid if hypoacid); bromelain and digestive enzyme complex; glucosamine; silica; *Aloe vera*; camomile tea; ginger; golden seal; peppermint; slippery elm.

CELIAC DISEASE

For this condition, the following nutritional considerations should be taken into account:

- *gluten intolerance and food allergy/intolerance.*
- *vitamin B6 deficiency.*
- *digestive enzyme deficiency/stress.*

DIET	
In addition to following the New Pyramid diet:	
• Maximize freshly ground mixed seeds and nuts.	• Avoid alcohol, refined foods, additives, and modified starches.
• Eat some vegetables raw, and include sprouted seeds.	• Avoid all gluten-containing grains (wheat, oats, rye, barley); use brown rice, millet, corn, buckwheat, quinoa, sage, tapioca, and arrowroot.
• Eat a wide range of vegetable protein, with a little fish and lean meats.	

Suggested supplements

A hypoallergenic multivitamin/multimineral with vitamins A, B-complex, C, D, and E, calcium, magnesium, zinc, and selenium; extra vitamin B6 as pyridoxal-5-phosphate; essential fatty acids; lecithin; digestive enzymes.

ALCOHOLISM

If you suffer from alcoholism, see your physician before embarking on a supplement program.

DIET	
In addition to following the New Pyramid diet:	
• Maximize intake of anti-oxidant vegetables, fruit, and freshly ground mixed seeds.	• Eat a good balance of fiber (cellulose, pectin).
• Eat oily fish, live soy yogurt, and pulses (legumes) as main protein sources.	• Avoid saturated and hydrogenated fat, refined food, sugar, alcohol.

Suggested supplements

A multi-complex containing vitamin B-complex; vitamin E, zinc, selenium, calcium, magnesium; extra vitamin C; evening primrose oil and fish oils or linseed (flax seed) oil; Silymarin (Milk thistle); amino acids L-glutamic acid, L-cysteine, glycine, L-glutathione and Taurine.

DISORDERS OF THE EXCRETORY SYSTEM

THE EXCRETION OF WASTE *materials arising from cell metabolism is carried out by the lungs (removal of carbon dioxide), the skin (removal of uric acid and other materials in sweat), and the kidneys (removal of nitrogenous waste and used hormones, and so on). This section is concerned with nutritional help for the kidneys and their associated tubules.*

A diet that is high in animal protein, animal fat, and refined foods will put an enormous strain on the kidneys. So too will a diet with mineral imbalances and excessive intake of salt. The focus for helping alleviate this stress is to remove as much animal produce as possible from the diet, and to aim for a good alkali-forming/acid-forming ratio diet (80 percent alkaline/20 percent acid). This means consuming plenty of fruit and vegetables and vegetable carbohydrates. However, this has to be approached carefully to insure that the dietary change is gradual, otherwise extra pressure may be put upon the kidneys for a time as they attempt to excrete a build-up of acid waste material.

Using the New Pyramid diet, with gradual change from meat and dairy products to vegetables, pulses (legumes), some wholegrain cereal, and a little fish, will do much to improve the health of this system and increase elimination of wastes. As the system becomes stronger, urinary infections will also decrease in occurrence.

URINARY TRACT INFECTION AND CYSTITIS

For these conditions, the following nutritional considerations should be taken into account:

- *low acidity of urine (imbalance of certain minerals).*
- *excess sugar.*
- *low levels of fruit and vegetables.*

DIET

In addition to following the New Pyramid diet:

- Maximize antioxidant fruit and vegetables.
- Eat mainly plant protein, with a little oily fish, poultry, and lean meat.
- Increase fluid intake to around 8 cups (2 liters) a day, between meals.

- Drink cranberry juice in between meals (helps to remove E coli, a cause of urinary tract infections, from the bladder wall).
- Minimize intake of dairy foods, especially milk.
- Avoid refined foods and especially sugar and alcohol.

Suggested supplements

Concentrated cranberry extract; vitamin C; selenium; fructo-oligosaccharides; Echinacea herb; high-potency garlic.

Renal cortex

Medulla and renal cortex contain nephrons which make urine by filtering the blood

Renal pelvis acts as a funnel where urine collects

Ureter conducts urine to the bladder

LEFT
The kidneys play an essential role in the waste-elimination system of the body.

RIGHT
Uric acid and other waste material are excreted through the skin in the sweat.

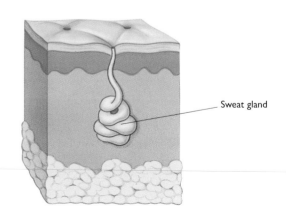

Sweat gland

KIDNEY STONES

See your physician before embarking upon a program of self-help. The following nutritional considerations should be taken into account:

- *excess animal protein and fat.*
- *low potassium.*
- *excess sodium chloride (salt).*
- *excess calcium.*
- *excess dairy foods.*
- *sugar.*
- *low magnesium.*
- *low intake of vegetables and fruit.*

DIET
In addition to following the New Pyramid diet:

• For oxalate stones, reduce intake of oxalic acid (found in tea, coffee, cocoa, parsley, spinach, rhubarb, and beets). • For uric acid stones, maximize intake of citrus fruit and alkaline-forming vegetables. • For both types of stones: drink plenty of bottled or filtered water in between meals.	• Minimize intake of animal protein; take more lentils, seed vegetables, and soy. • Avoid salt, refined carbohydrates, sugar, coffee, alcohol, red meat, and dairy foods.

Suggested supplements

Magnesium citrate/potassium citrate complex, vitamin B6 as pyridoxal-5-phosphate; selenium; cranberry juice/extract.

GREEN LENTILS

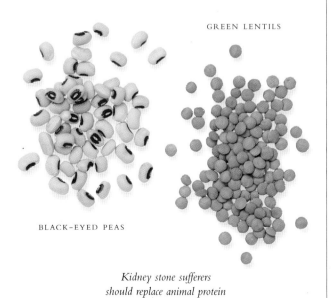

BLACK-EYED PEAS

Kidney stone sufferers should replace animal protein with pulses (legumes).

Oxalate-containing Foods
HIGH OXALATE FOODS
BEANS
CHARD
COCOA
COFFEE (INSTANT)
PARSLEY
RHUBARB
SPINACH
TEA
MODERATE OXALATE FOODS
BEET TOPS
CARROTS
CELERY
CHOCOLATE
CUCUMBERS
GRAPEFRUIT
KALE
PEANUTS

Rhubarb should generally be avoided by people with oxalate stones.

NEPHRITIS

For this condition, the following nutritional considerations should be taken into account:

- *excess free radicals.*
- *cow's milk.*
- *excess animal protein.*

DIET
In addition to following the New Pyramid diet:

• Maximize intake of antioxidant fruit and vegetables, especially garlic, carrots, kale, asparagus, parsley, watercress, celery, potato (skins), horseradish, cucumber, parsnips, watermelon, papaya, apples, and pears. • Eat varied plant protein.	• Take Manuka honey and goat's milk (if not intolerant) daily. • Drink cranberry juice daily in between meals. • Avoid cow's milk and other common food allergens, red meat and other animal protein.

- *food allergy/intolerance – may need Hypoallergenic Diet.*

Suggested supplements

High-potency antioxidants, with selenium; vitamin B-complex; vitamin C plus bioflavonoids; magnesium;

DISORDERS OF THE MALE REPRODUCTIVE SYSTEM

S INCE THIS IS A BOOK *on nutritional healing, it is concerned primarily with correct functioning for cell generation (sperm production) and delivery. Any nutritional help for these areas will also allow nourishment of the brain and the endocrine system, which in turn will improve libido, lift emotions, and remove stress. Again, a basic wholefood diet such as the New Pyramid diet is the place to start. Many of the current problems associated with poor sexual function and infertility are based in poor intake of essential nutrients, but also involve the increasing number of pollutants and estrogens in the environment.*

Male reproduction problems are mostly focused around the ability to initiate and maintain an erection. Most erectile dysfunction stems from stress and overwork, but where it originates in poor circulation, hormonal imbalance, or overuse of alcohol, nutritional therapy has much to offer.

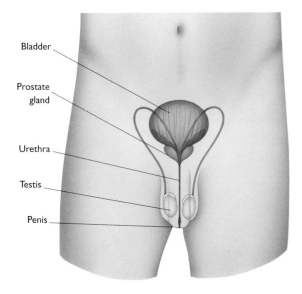

Of the male reproductive organs, nutritional healing is mostly concerned with the testes, as sperm production is easily affected by the quality of the diet, but good eating habits can also help with impotence and prostate problems.

Bladder

Prostate gland

Urethra

Testis

Penis

Oysters may not be aphrodisiacs, but they are good for the prostate and testes.

PROSTATE ENLARGEMENT

For this condition, the following nutritional considerations should be taken into account:

◆ *alcohol.*
◆ *caffeine from tea and coffee.*
◆ *low intake of foods containing zinc.*
◆ *low intake of antioxidant nutrients.*
◆ *excess saturated and hydrogenated fat.*
◆ *excess refined foods and sugar.*
◆ *low fiber.*
◆ *cadmium toxicity – may need Detoxification diet.*

DIET

In addition to following the New Pyramid diet:

● Maximize intake of antioxidant fruit and vegetables, especially tomatoes, watermelon, and guava.	● Eat oily fish and shellfish (especially oysters), freshly ground mixed seeds (especially pumpkin), and nuts.
● Maximize intake of cellulose and pectin fiber along with some cereal fiber.	● Minimize intake of alcohol and caffeine.
	● Avoid red meat, full-fat dairy foods, refined carbohydrates, sugar, saturated and hydrogenated fats.

Suggested supplements

Zinc; evening primrose oil; fish oils; amino acids complex – glycine, alanine, and glutamic acid (to help improve urine flow); Saw palmetto; Pygeum africanum.

IMPOTENCE

For this condition, the following nutritional considerations should be taken into account:

- ◆ *excess alcohol.*
- ◆ *excess saturated and hydrogenated fat.*
- ◆ *excess calcium.*
- ◆ *excess dairy food.*
- ◆ *excess refined carbohydrates and sugar.*
- ◆ *low intake of zinc-rich foods.*
- ◆ *generalized poor intake of nutrients.*
- ◆ *excess weight.*

DIET

In addition to following the New Pyramid diet:

- ● Maximize intake of antioxidant vegetables and fruit.
- ● Maximize intake of a variety of fibers (cereal, cellulose, pectins).
- ● Maximize intake of freshly ground mixed seeds, especially pumpkin seeds.
- ● Eat oily fish, shellfish, occasional eggs, soy, pulses (legumes), and seed vegetables as main proteins.

- ● Minimize intake of animal fats, dairy food, and alcohol.
- ● Avoid sugar, and refined carbohydrates.

PUMPKIN SEEDS

Suggested supplements

High-potency vitamin B-complex, with good levels of B3 and B6; zinc; fish oils or linseed (flax seed) oil; *Ginkgo biloba*; high-potency garlic.

BRAZIL NUTS

PARSLEY

BEAN SPROUTS

MALE INFERTILITY

For low or defective sperm production, and poor sperm motility, the following nutritional considerations should be taken into account:

- ◆ *generalized low intake of essential nutrients.*
- ◆ *toxicity – may need Detoxification Diet.*
- ◆ *excess refined carbohydrates.*
- ◆ *excess food additives.*
- ◆ *excess alcohol.*

DIET

In addition to following the New Pyramid diet:

- ● Maximize intake of a wide range of vegetables and fruit, eating at least some of them raw.
- ● Maximize intake of freshly ground mixed nuts and seeds.
- ● Eat sprouted seeds, such as sprouted alfalfa, daily.
- ● Minimize intake of coffee and tea.

- ● Minimize animal protein except for poultry and fish, and eat more soy, beans, and seed vegetables.
- ● Avoid refined carbohydrates, artificial additives, alcohol, fatty meat, non-organic food, and hydrogenated oils.

Suggested supplements

A broad-spectrum multivitamin/multimineral complex, containing good levels of vitamin B-complex, especially B6, B12, and folic acid, vitamin E, iodine, and selenium; vitamin C; zinc; amino acids – especially L-arginine and L-carnitine.

An increased intake of raw fruit and vegetables, mixed nuts and seeds, and sprouted seeds may help to counteract male infertility.

MANGO

DISORDERS OF THE SENSORY SYSTEM

WE LIVE IN A CONSTANTLY *changing environment. Our sense organs allow us to detect these changes, program their usefulness, and then take appropriate action. With our eyes we obtain stereoscopic, wide-angle technicolor vision; with our ears we have stereophonic sound; with our olfactory organs we can detect the faintest odors; with our taste buds tiny differences between sour, sweet, salt, and bitter; and with touch we can sense pressure, pain, and pleasure.*

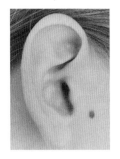

To keep all of these exceptional organs healthy we need vital nutrients to provide for maintenance and effective metabolism. A good-quality wholefood diet is essential to supply the necessary raw materials for these activities. In some cases there are special nutrients that are vital to function, such as vitamin A (retinol) for production of "visual purple" the pigment in the retina. More generally, the sensory system is very sensitive to poor peripheral blood flow

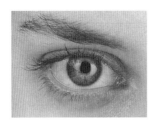

and the presence of free radicals, so that a diet containing foods which strengthen the fine capillaries and minimize oxidation reactions is essential. Extracts from the plant *Ginkgo biloba* may help strengthen and nourish peripheral circulation. Many infections of sensory organs, such as conjunctivitis, mouth ulcers, and ear infections, can be prevented by good nutrition to boost the immune system. Nourishing one part of the body with a good wholefood diet, and nutritional supplements where appropriate, has tremendous effects on all other parts.

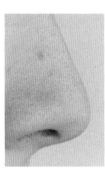

A diet high in vital nutrients will keep our hearing, vision, sense of smell, and tastebuds in top condition.

Eyes

CATARACTS

For this condition, the following nutritional considerations should be taken into account:

- *excess free radicals.*
- *low intake of antioxidant nutrients, especially vitamins beta-carotene, C, and E.*
- *high intake of saturated fats.*
- *excess weight.*
- *milk and other dairy food (lactose).*

DIET
In addition to following the New Pyramid diet:

● Maximize intake of antioxidant vegetables and fruit, especially those rich in carotene, such as carrots, and broccoli. ● Maximize intake of vegetables and fruit rich in vitamin C. ● Maximize intake of freshly ground mixed seeds.	● Eat organic foods where possible. ● Use a cold-pressed extra virgin olive oil, daily, for vitamin E content. ● Avoid fried, barbecued, and refined foods, saturated and hydrogenated fats, dairy foods, and fatty meat.

Suggested supplements

Anthocyanidins (grape seed, bilberry, pine bark extract); natural beta-carotene; vitamin B2; vitamin C and bioflavonoids; vitamin E; selenium; zinc; *Ginkgo biloba*; lipoic acid (an antioxidant found in yeast and liver).

NIGHT BLINDNESS

For this condition, the following nutritional considerations should be taken into account:

- *low intake of vitamin A.*
- *low levels of antioxidants.*
- *excess fat.*
- *excess alcohol.*

DIET	
In addition to following the New Pyramid diet:	
• Maximize intake of antioxidant vegetables and fruit, especially those containing beta-carotene (carrots, broccoli, apricots), and anthocyanidins (bilberries, blueberries).	• Eat liver once or twice a week (not if pregnant), plus a little fish – otherwise keep animal protein at a low level. • Avoid alcohol, artificial sweeteners, fatty meat, saturated and hydrogenated fats.

Suggested supplements

High-potency antioxidants; bilberry extract; vitamin A; vitamin C; zinc; *Ginkgo biloba*; lipoic acid.

CONJUNCTIVITIS

For this condition, the following nutritional considerations should be taken into account:

- *poor nutritional intake (or poor absorption), resulting in lowered immune function.*
- *low intake of vitamin C.*
- *food intolerance – may need Hypoallergenic Diet.*

DIET	
In addition to following the New Pyramid diet:	
• Maximize intake of antioxidant fruit and vegetables.	• Maximize intake of freshly ground mixed seeds. • Avoid wheat and dairy products.

Suggested supplements

Maximum vitamin C plus bioflavonoids; zinc; Echinacea herb; bilberry extract.

CORNEAL ULCERS AND RED (IRRITATED) EYELIDS

For these conditions, the following nutritional considerations should be taken into account:

- *low intake of antioxidants.*
- *low intake of B vitamins.*

DIET	
In addition to following the New Pyramid diet:	
• Maximize intake of antioxidant vegetables and anthocyanidin-containing berries. • Take blackstrap molasses and oatgerm daily.	• Eat several portions of whole grains, such as oats, rice, and millet, each week. • Add extra wheatgerm to cereals, salads, and soups (unless intolerant).

Suggested supplements

High-potency vitamin B-complex containing B_2, B_6 and B_5; vitamin C.

GLAUCOMA

For this condition, the following nutritional considerations should be taken into account:

- *excess meat and dairy products.*
- *general vitamin and magnesium deficiency.*
- *low intake of fresh vegetables and fruit.*
- *food intolerance – may need Hypoallergenic Diet.*

DIET	
• Maximize intake of fresh vegetables and fruit. • Maximize intake of freshly ground mixed seeds. • Minimize intake of meat and dairy foods; concentrate on	cold-water fish and vegetables (tofu, beans, seed vegetables) for protein. • Avoid refined foods, caffeine, sugar, common allergenic foods, and alcohol.

Suggested supplements

Anthocyanidins (grape seed, bilberry); vitamins B-complex, C, and E; bioflavonoids; natural beta-carotene; magnesium; rutin; lipoic acid; *Ginkgo biloba*; *Aloe vera*.

Ears

TINNITUS

For this condition, the following nutritional considerations should be taken into account:

- *food allergy/intolerance – may need Hypoallergenic Diet.*
- *low levels of antioxidants.*
- *alcohol.*

DIET

In addition to following the New Pyramid diet:

• Maximize antioxidant vegetables and fruit.	• Avoid alcohol and common food allergens.

Suggested supplements

High-potency antioxidants; *Ginkgo biloba*; zinc; vitamin C.

INNER EAR DYSFUNCTION AND MENIÈRE'S DISEASE

For this condition, the following nutritional considerations should be taken into account:

- *excess intake of saturated and hydrogenated fats.*
- *excess cholesterol.*
- *excess dairy food.*
- *refined carbohydrates and sugars.*
- *food allergy/intolerance – may need Hypoallergenic Diet.*

DIET

In addition to following the New Pyramid diet:

• Maximize intake of antioxidant vegetables and fruit.	• Avoid saturated and hydrogenated fats, fried foods, sugar, refined carbohydrates, alcohol, coffee, salt, and common allergens.
• Maximize intake of freshly ground mixed seeds.	
• Eat fibrous pectin-containing fruits and vegetables, and oats (if not allergic).	• Avoid mucus-forming dairy food, pork, and bananas.

Suggested supplements

Vitamins A, B-complex, D, C, and E; iron; zinc; ginger; *Ginkgo biloba*; *Aloe vera*.

Mouth and Nose

HALITOSIS

For bad breath, the following nutritional considerations should be taken into account:

- *digestive enzyme deficiency.*
- *hydrochloric acid deficiency.*
- *food intolerance – may need Hypoallergenic Diet.*
- *overeating.*
- *low fiber.*
- *excess animal protein.*
- *excess refined carbohydrates.*
- *excess dairy foods.*
- *toxicity – may need Detoxification Diet.*
- *candidiasis of the digestive tract.*

DIET

In addition to following the New Pyramid diet:

• Maximize intake of a variety of whole grains and fiber-rich vegetables and fruit.	• Sip freshly squeezed lemon juice, or vinegar in a little water with at least two meals a day.
• Eat mainly plant protein, such as soy, tofu, pulses (legumes), seed vegetables, with a little fish, poultry, and live yogurt.	• Avoid drinking large amounts of fluid with meals.
• Eat at least some raw salad vegetables and sprouted seeds daily.	• Avoid refined carbohydrates, sugar, alcohol, meat, dairy foods, caffeine, common food allergens, and overeating.
• Eat five or six small meals a day instead of three larger ones.	
• Drink at least 8 cups (2 liters) of bottled or filtered water a day between meals.	

FRENCH GREEN BEANS

Suggested supplements

Vitamin A; high-potency vitamin B-complex; vitamin B6 (as pyridoxal-5-phosphate); zinc; digestive enzymes; *Lactobacillus acidophilus*; fructo-oligosaccharides; caprilic acid and psyllium (if constipated). Chew any of the following: anise, cardamom, caraway and fennel seeds; parsley; whole cloves; peppermint.

SINUSITIS, CATARRH, LOSS OF SMELL AND TASTE

For these problems, the following nutritional considerations should be taken into account:

- ◆ *excess dairy foods, starch and sugar.*
- ◆ *high acid-forming diet.*
- ◆ *low intake of dark green vegetables.*
- ◆ *milk allergy.*
- ◆ *food intolerance – may need Hypoallergenic Diet.*
- ◆ *toxicity (toxemia).*
- ◆ *liver congestion – may need Detoxification Diet.*
- ◆ *alcohol.*
- ◆ *low intake of zinc-rich foods.*

DIET
In addition to following the New Pyramid diet:

- Maximize intake of vegetables (some raw), dark green vegetables, and fruit.
- Maximize intake of freshly ground mixed seeds, especially pumpkin seeds.
- Eat high-zinc food (fish, shellfish, edible seaweed) three times a week.
- Increase intake of onions and garlic (steamed onions are very beneficial).
- Drink some freshly pressed vegetable juice daily.

- Aim for an 80 percent alkaline to 20 percent acid diet by eating more alkali-forming foods.
- Minimize intake of starchy carbohydrates from grains, and instead use pulses (legumes) and seed vegetables (green beans).
- Avoid dairy produce, strong spices, common food allergens, pork, eggs, alcohol, refined carbohydrates, sugar, and bananas.

Suggested supplements

Vitamin A; high-potency vitamin B-complex; vitamin C (maximum); high-potency garlic; dandelion herb; Echinacea herb; zinc.

Drink some freshly pressed vegetable juice daily to help sinusitis.

CARROT JUICE

PERIODONTAL DISEASE (GINGIVITIS), MOUTH ULCERS

For these conditions, the following nutritional considerations should be taken into account:

- ◆ *excess animal protein.*
- ◆ *saturated and hydrogenated fats.*
- ◆ *excess gluten, especially wheat.*
- ◆ *refined carbohydrates and sugar.*
- ◆ *nutrient deficiencies, especially B vitamins.*
- ◆ *alcohol.*
- ◆ *low vegetable fiber and antioxidants.*
- ◆ *low stomach acid.*
- ◆ *metal toxicity (amalgam fillings) – may need Detoxification Diet.*
- ◆ *food allergy/intolerance – may need Hypoallergenic Diet.*

DIET
In addition to following the New Pyramid diet:

- Maximize intake of antioxidant vegetables and fruit.
- Maximize intake of freshly ground mixed seeds, especially sesame and pumpkin seeds.
- Increase amount of cellulose and pectin fiber.
- Sip freshly squeezed lemon juice or cider vinegar with at least one meal a day.
- Take oatgerm and/or blackstrap molasses regularly.
- Minimize intake of gluten grains.

- Minimize intake of animal protein (except fish) and fat; eat pulses (legumes), soy, tofu, and seed vegetables.
- Avoid refined carbohydrates, saturated and hydrogenated fat, sugar, alcohol, food additives, red meat, wheat, and other common allergenic foods.

Suggested supplements

High-potency vitamin B-complex, folic acid, vitamin C and bio-flavonoids (for wound healing and collagen synthesis); calcium; zinc; co-enzyme Q10; Sanguinaria (bloodroot); *Aloe vera*; Echinacea.

STRAWBERRIES

TOFU

Those suffering from periodontal disease and mouth ulcers are advised to avoid meat and eat vegetable protein and fresh fruit.

DISORDERS OF THE RESPIRATORY SYSTEM

Y OU CAN LIVE WEEKS *without food and four to five days without water, but you can only survive a few minutes without air. The function of the respiratory organs – the lungs, respiratory muscles, and diaphragm – is to provide us with a set of "bellows" to bring oxygen into close contact with the blood supply. This area of close contact has, of necessity, to be moist, delicate, and fragile in order to allow maximum exchange of respiratory gases: oxygen in, and carbon dioxide out. Any disease restricting the intake of air greatly affects the general health.*

Any disease which prevents the intake of air, or the exchange of respiratory gases, has a great effect on the working of the body, not least of which is its energy production. Such serious conditions as lung cancer and emphysema are common, and are usually found in people exposed to air pollution and/or cigarette smoke. Fortunately, in addition to a good basic diet, there are several special nutrients which are capable of helping to protect the membranes in the lungs from environmental pollutants. Many of these nutrients are antioxidants, which neutralize any free radicals. In addition, the antioxidant nutrients are often useful in boosting the immune system to prevent infections in the respiratory tract. Nutritional therapists also believe that there are some foods, such as dairy food and refined carbohydrates with mucus-generating ability, which can impede the flow of air through these passages. Because the airways are also the first point of contact for any airborne allergens, it is possible to find allergic symptoms in these organs. It would seem that in addition to attempting to remove air pollutants from the home and work environments, cutting out common allergenic foods may help to reduce the severity and frequency of allergy symptoms in some people.

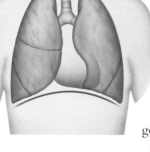

The respiratory organs: lungs, trachea (windpipe), mouth, and nose.

ASTHMA

For asthma, the following nutritional considerations should be taken into account:

◆ *excess salt (increases sensitivity to histamine).*
◆ *food allergy/intolerance – may need Hypoallergenic Diet.*
◆ *sulphite sensitivity.*
◆ *dairy foods and wheat.*
◆ *insufficiency of stomach acid – may need Food Combining Diet.*

DIET

In addition to following the New Pyramid diet:

• Maximize intake of vegetables and fruit, but avoid common allergens, such as citrus.	• Drink plenty of diluted fruit juices and bottled or filtered water between meals.
• Maximize intake of freshly ground mixed seeds, especially pumpkin seeds.	• Minimize meat, fish, eggs, coffee, tea, and chocolate.
• Eat mainly vegetable protein such as tofu and beans.	• Avoid wheat, refined carbohydrates, dairy foods, sugar, salt, sulfured fruits, food additives, and piped water.
• Sip diluted cider vinegar at least with the day's main meal.	

Suggested supplements

A high-dose multivitamin with B6, and B12; a high-dose multimineral with balanced magnesium and calcium (in 2:1 ratio), and good levels of zinc, molybdenum and selenium; vitamin C with bioflavonoids; fish oil or linseed (flax seed) oil; *Ginkgo biloba* extract; anthocyanidins.

BRONCHITIS

In addition to improving immune function (see pages 146–9), the following are important:

◆ *excess carbohydrates.*
◆ *acid-forming diet.*
◆ *excess dairy products.*
◆ *vitamin A deficiency.*
◆ *toxic system – may need Detoxification Diet.*
◆ *food allergy/intolerance – may need Hypoallergenic Diet.*

DIET	
In addition to following the New Pyramid diet:	
• Maximize intake of a good variety of vegetables, fruit, millet, buckwheat, and some pulses (legumes) to insure a more alkaline-forming diet. • Maximize intake of beta-carotene from red-orange vegetables and fruit (carrots, apricots). • Maximize intake of freshly ground mixed seeds, especially pumpkin seeds.	• Minimize intake of animal fat and animal protein, except for a little oily fish, and organic lamb's liver occasionally. • Minimize intake of all grain carbohydrates. • Avoid refined carbohydrates, sugar, alcohol, dairy produce, common food allergens, and "rich" foods.

Suggested supplements

Vitamin A (not if you are pregnant) and natural beta-carotene; high-potency vitamin B-complex, with B6; vitamin C; high-potency garlic; zinc; Sanguinaria (blood-root); onion syrup; *Aloe vera.*

HAYFEVER

For hayfever (allergic rhinitis), the following nutritional considerations should be taken into account:

◆ *food allergy/intolerance – may need Hypoallergenic Diet.*
◆ *excess carbohydrates, especially refined types.*
◆ *excess sugar.*
◆ *wheat.*
◆ *dairy foods.*

DIET	
In addition to following the New Pyramid diet:	
• Maximize intake of antioxidant vegetables and fruit (except allergenic types, e.g., citrus). • Maximize intake of millet, buckwheat, pulses (legumes), and seed vegetables. • Maximize intake of freshly ground mixed seeds, especially pumpkin seeds, and nuts.	• Minimize intake of grain carbohydrates. • Minimize intake of animal protein, dairy food, and stimulants (coffee, tea, alcohol, colas). • Avoid wheat, refined carbohydrate and sugar, cow's milk and other common allergenic foods.

Suggested supplements

Vitamin A (as beta-carotene if you are pregnant or planning a pregnancy); high-potency B-complex vitamin with B5 and B6; vitamin C plus bioflavonoids; digestive enzymes, containing proteases; zinc; propolis.

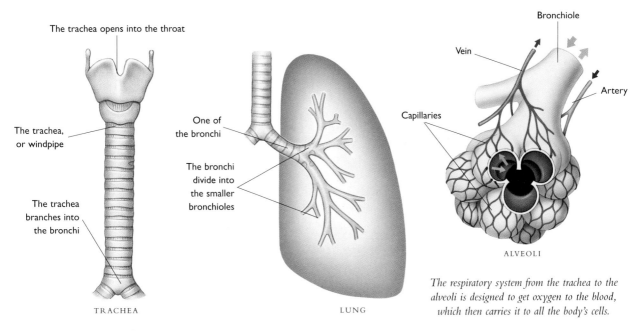

The trachea opens into the throat

The trachea, or windpipe

The trachea branches into the bronchi

TRACHEA

One of the bronchi

The bronchi divide into the smaller bronchioles

LUNG

Bronchiole

Vein

Artery

Capillaries

ALVEOLI

The respiratory system from the trachea to the alveoli is designed to get oxygen to the blood, which then carries it to all the body's cells.

SKIN, HAIR, AND NAIL PROBLEMS

T HE SKIN IS THE BIGGEST *organ we have, and any poor lifestyle or nutritional habits will affect the skin to an enormous extent. A stressful lifestyle, lack of sleep, and a diet low in the essential vitamins and minerals will eventually show up in your complexion. Recently, greater emphasis has been placed on treating skin problems from the inside (by nutrition), than by the use of creams and lotions from the outside.*

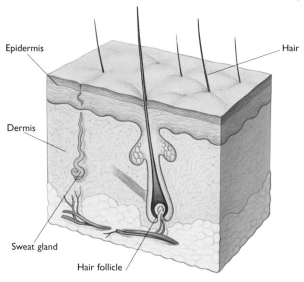

Skin and hair problems are closely related because of the presence of hair follicles over most of the skin.

Epidermis

Dermis

Sweat gland

Hair follicle

Hair

Skin

The most common agents affecting skin integrity are the free radicals that attack it, both externally from cigarette smoke, pollution, and ultra-violet light, and internally from a diet low in essential nutrients and high in hydrogenated fats, trans-fatty acids, fried food, barbecued food, and highly processed foods. These rogue molecules cause cross-linkage between collagen fibers, and encourage the formation of wrinkles as elasticity decreases. The antioxidant vitamin C is of particular importance in maintaining a youthful skin since it is an essential nutrient for the formation and maintenance of collagen.

A lifestyle that reduces the level of free radicals, together with a good basic diet of wholefoods and antioxidant-rich vegetables and fruit, will prevent and heal some of the greater part of damage. Anthocyanidins have become the main focus of researchers' attention, alongside investigation into nutrients involved in collagen integrity.

GENERAL SKIN PROBLEMS

For wrinkles, dry skin, oily skin, itchy skin, cold sores, stretch marks, and ulcers, the following nutritional considerations should be taken into account:

- *stress-generated free radicals requiring additional nutritional antioxidants.*
- *excess refined carbohydrates and sugar.*
- *excess saturated and hydrogenated fats.*
- *low intake of vegetables and fruit.*

DIET

In addition to following the New Pyramid diet:

• Maximize intake of antioxidant-containing fruit and vegetables, and those containing anthocyanidins. • Maximize intake of freshly ground mixed seeds. • Eat some raw vegetables and sprouted seeds and sprouted pulses (legumes) daily. • Eat a good balanced mixture of wholegrain carbohydrates and vegetable carbohydrates.	• Minimize intake of red meat, fatty meat, and dairy products, and consume mainly vegetable protein, such as tofu and pulses (legumes), with a little oily fish, poultry, and occasional egg. • Avoid refined carbohydrates, sugar, saturated and hydrogenated fat, alcohol, food additives, polluted food and unfiltered piped water, and common allergenic foods (wheat, dairy, citrus fruits).

Suggested supplements

High-potency antioxidant formula; extra vitamins C and E (vitamin E, together with zinc, helps with stretch marks); anthocyanidins (bilberry, etc.); evening primrose oil (for dry skin); high-potency B-complex vitamins (for an oily skin); iron (useful for itchy skin); lysine for cold sores; application of *Aloe vera* gel.

SUNBURN

Follow the New Pyramid diet.

Suggested supplements

Use for two or three weeks before sunbathing: vitamin E, beta-carotene, vitamin C, selenium. Use *Aloe vera* gel or cream or tea tree oil for treating mild sunburn. Treating burned skin with plain live yogurt or *Aloe vera* gel will encourage healing of infected parts.

ACNE

For acne, the following nutritional considerations should be taken into account:

◆ *poor gut flora (overuse of antibiotics).*
◆ *excess saturated fats and fried foods.*
◆ *low fiber.*
◆ *excess refined carbohydrates and sugar.*
◆ *dairy foods.*
◆ *food intolerance, especially to chocolate, some nuts, and cola drinks – may need Hypoallergenic Diet.*

DIET	
In addition to following the New Pyramid diet:	
• Maximize intake of antioxidant nutrients. • Maximize intake of mixed seeds, especially pumpkin seeds. • Increase intake of soluble fibers (fruit and vegetables).	• Eat live yogurt daily. • Minimize saturated fat. • Avoid refined carbohydrates, common allergenic foods, dairy food (except yogurt), and fried foods.

Suggested supplements

High-potency multivitamin/multimineral containing good levels of vitamins A, B6, C, and E, selenium, zinc, and chromium; Echinacea herb; *Lactobacillus acidophilus*, fructo-oligosaccharides; evening primrose oil; application to the skin of *Aloe vera* gel or cream, or tea tree oil.

Kiwi fruit, like other fruit high in vitamins, helps alleviate acne.

BODY ODOR

For this condition, the following nutritional considerations should be taken into account:

◆ *excess saturated fats and hydrogenated fats.*
◆ *meat, dairy products, fried foods.*
◆ *toxicity – may need Detoxification Diet.*
◆ *low intake of zinc-rich foods and essential fatty acids.*

DIET	
In addition to following the New Pyramid diet:	
• Maximize intake of fresh seeds, especially pumpkin seeds. • Eat fish, shellfish, and nuts several times a week. • Eat organic produce.	• Avoid saturated/hydrogenated fat, fried foods, fatty meats, refined and dairy foods (except live yogurt), additives, and environmental pollutants.

Suggested supplements

A colon and liver cleanse complex; magnesium; zinc; fish oils or linseed oil; evening primrose oil; lecithin.

ECZEMA

For eczema, the following nutritional considerations should be taken into account:

◆ *food allergy/intolerance – in particular cow's milk, egg, wheat, red meat, sugar, tea, coffee, and alcohol.*
◆ *low stomach acid – may need Food Combining Diet.*

DIET	
In addition to following the New Pyramid diet:	
• Maximize intake of ground seeds (especially pumpkin). • Sip diluted vinegar with main meal of day. • Drink plenty of bottled or filtered water between meals.	• Eat tofu and vegetable proteins, and a little oily fish. • Avoid saturated/hydrogenated fat, refined food, additives, chlorinated water, and all allergens listed above.

Suggested supplements

Evening primrose oil; fish oil or linseed (flax seed) oil; a multiformula containing good levels of zinc, vitamins A and C; anthocyanidins; liver and colon cleanse complex; vitamin E oil can be applied to the skin.

HIVES

For hives (urticaria), the following nutritional considerations should be taken into account:

◆ *chlorine in drinking water.*
◆ *toxicity — may need Detoxification Diet.*
◆ *food allergy/intolerance — commonly shellfish, milk, eggs, wheat, pork, onions, some fruit — may need Hypoallergenic Diet.*
◆ *stomach acid deficiency — may need Food Combining Diet.*
◆ *food additives (color and preservatives).*
◆ *coffee.*
◆ *alcohol.*

DIET

In addition to following the New Pyramid diet:

● Maximize intake of freshly ground mixed seeds, especially pumpkin seeds.

● Drink plenty of bottled or filtered water between meals.

● Increase intake of oily fish (herring, mackerel, and salmon) and vegetable protein (soy) instead of meat, poultry, and dairy proteins.

● Sip diluted cider vinegar with main meal of the day.

● Avoid saturated fat, hydrogenated fat, refined foods, food additives, coffee, chlorinated water, all allergens above, and alcohol.

PUMPKIN SEEDS

Suggested supplements

Vitamin A; vitamin B-complex (especially with B6 and B12); vitamin C; calcium.

PSORIASIS

For this condition, the following nutritional considerations should be taken into account:

◆ *low fiber.*
◆ *excess meat.*
◆ *possible copper-induced zinc deficiency.*
◆ *food allergy/intolerance — may need Hypoallergenic Diet.*
◆ *poor acid/alkaline balance.*
◆ *low intake of essential fatty acids.*
◆ *sub-optimum liver function — may need Detoxification Diet.*

DIET

In addition to following the New Pyramid diet:

● Maximize intake of alkaline-forming vegetables and fruit.

● Maximize intake of freshly ground mixed seeds, especially pumpkin seeds.

● Maximize intake of vegetable fiber and pectin (apples, carrots).

● Eat at least some raw vegetables daily.

● Concentrate on brown rice, millet, and buckwheat as main cereals.

● Drink filtered water or bottled mineral water.

● Minimize intake of animal protein (except oily fish and shellfish); use soy, and pulses (legumes).

● Avoid citrus fruit, tomatoes, red meat, saturated fats, hydrogenated fats, candy, alcohol, and refined carbohydrates.

Suggested supplements

A high-potency antioxidant formula including zinc and selenium; Milk thistle herb; magnesium fumarate; B-complex vitamins; linseed (flax seed) oil; fish oils; *Aloe vera* juice; herbal colon cleanse; lipase.

CARROTS

Fruit and raw vegetables help with the skin conditions, psoriasis and hives.

PAPAW
(PAPAYA)

NOTE

If you have psoriasis, please see your physician before embarking on a supplement program.

IMPETIGO

For impetigo (staphylococcal infection), the following nutritional factors should be taken into account:

- *toxicity – may need Detoxification Diet.*
- *low intake of protein.*
- *excess sweet food and fruit.*
- *excess acidity.*
- *low intake of dark-green vegetables.*
- *dairy foods.*

DIET

In addition to following the New Pyramid diet:

- Maximize intake of dark green vegetables.
- Maximize intake of freshly ground mixed seeds, especially pumpkin.
- Aim for an 80 percent alkaline to 20 percent acid diet.

- Eat mainly plant protein, such as soy, pulses (legumes), and seed vegetables, with a little oily fish.
- Minimize intake of fruit and honey.
- Avoid alcohol, sugar, refined carbohydrate, saturated and hydrogenated fats, meat, and dairy foods.

Suggested supplements

Vitamins A and C; high-potency garlic; zinc; essential fatty acids (fish oils/linseed oil, and evening primrose/starflower oil); golden seal herb; tea tree oil for external application.

ROSACEA (ACNE ROSACEA)

For this condition, the following nutritional considerations should be taken into account:

- *alcohol.*
- *low levels of stomach acid.*
- *low levels of digestive (pancreatic) enzymes.*
- *low intake of B vitamins.*
- *coffee, tea, chocolate, and spices (capillary dilatents).*

DIET

In addition to following the New Pyramid diet:

- Maximize intake of freshly ground mixed seeds, especially pumpkin seeds.
- Increase intake of alkaline-forming and antioxidant vegetables and fruit.
- Add wheatgerm to cereals, salads, and soups.

- Eat at least some raw vegetables and sprouted seeds daily (for natural enzymes).
- Sip diluted freshly squeezed lemon juice or diluted cider vinegar with main meal of the day.
- Avoid coffee, tea, alcohol, chocolate, food additives, and spices.

Suggested supplements

Betaine hydrochloride; digestive enzymes; high potency vitamin B-complex; zinc; fructo-oligosaccharides.

Sipping diluted lemon juice with the main meal helps treat poor stomach acid, which contributes to rosacea.

TOMATOES

BRUSSELS SPROUTS

Antioxidant vegetables can help treat the symptoms of rosacea.

LEMON

WARTS AND VERRUCAE

Although warts and verrucae are localized infections caused by a virus, the following nutritional information is important:

- *low intake of nutrient-dense foods.*
- *low intake of vitamin A-containing foods.*

DIET
In addition to following the New Pyramid diet:

• Maximize intake of immune-boosting antioxidant vegetables, and fruit, and sea vegetables.	• Eat at least some raw vegetables and sprouted seeds daily.
• Maximize intake of mixed seeds, particularly pumpkin seeds.	• Avoid immune-lowering foods such as refined and processed foods, wheat, food additives, excess carbohydrates, dairy food, alcohol, and common allergenic foods.
• Maximize intake of foods high in vitamins A, B-complex, and C.	
• Maximize intake of zinc-containing foods, such as fish, shellfish, and pulses (legumes).	

Suggested supplements

High-potency antioxidant formula containing good levels of vitamins A (as beta-carotene if you are pregnant or planning to become pregnant) and C, selenium and zinc; high-potency B vitamin complex, containing good levels of B6; high-potency garlic. Apply tea tree oil directly onto the wart or verruca.

Edible seaweeds are good sources of the zinc needed to combat warts.

Hair

Since the hair is a product of the skin, poor hair integrity or scalp disorders will be a direct cause of problems with the skin. Healthy hair is dependent upon good blood circulation and upon the level of nutrients occurring within the blood.

ALOPECIA (BALDNESS), GENERAL HAIR LOSS

For these conditions, the following nutritional considerations should be taken into account:

- *poor nutrition of the glandular system, especially the thyroid, adrenals, and pituitary.*
- *single or multiple deficiencies of vitamin B-complex, especially B6, biotin, folic acid, inositol, and P.A.B.A. (para-aminobenzoic acid).*
- *refined food, especially sugar.*
- *alcohol.*
- *nicotine.*
- *heavy metal poisoning – may need Detoxification Diet.*
- *foods low in antioxidants (needed to combat free radicals made by stress).*
- *crash and "yo-yo" dieting.*

DIET
In addition to following the New Pyramid diet:

• Maximize intake of antioxidant containing fruit and vegetables.	• Eat oily fish, and lean meat, in balance with lots of soy products, and pulses (legumes) for protein.
• Maximize intake of freshly ground mixed seeds.	• Avoid all refined food, sugar, food additives, polluted food (eat organic when possible), and alcohol.
• Add wheatgerm to salads and soups.	
• Take blackstrap molasses daily.	

Suggested supplements

A high-potency multivitamin/multimineral containing good levels of vitamins A (as beta-carotene if you are pregnant or planning a pregnancy), C, B (especially B3, B5, B6, B12 and P.A.B.A., biotin, and folic acid) and E, and the minerals iron, zinc, and selenium, iodine; lecithin (inositol/choline); essential fatty acids as fish oils or linseed (flax seed) oil, and evening primrose oil or starflower (borage) oil; *Ginkgo biloba*; digestive enzymes; lysine; cysteine.

DANDRUFF

For this condition, the following nutritional considerations should be taken into account:

- *acid diet.*
- *excess carbohydrates and sugar.*
- *excess alcohol.*
- *salt.*
- *excess citrus – a common cause of dandruff.*
- *low intake of dark green vegetables, especially antioxidant vegetables.*
- *excess saturated fats and hydrogenated fats.*
- *food allergy/intolerance, especially to wheat and dairy foods – may need Hypoallergenic Diet.*
- *low intake of essential fatty acids.*
- *low intake of foods containing vitamins A, B-complex, E, and zinc.*
- *low activity of digestive enzymes.*

DIET	
In addition to following the New Pyramid diet:	
• Maximize intake of orange and dark green vegetables.	• Increase amount of fish, shellfish, and pulses (legumes).
• Maximize intake of antioxidant fruit (except citrus) and vegetables.	• Minimize intake of grain carbohydrates. (This, along with increase in vegetables should produce an alkaline-forming diet.)
• Maximize intake of freshly ground mixed seeds, especially pumpkin seeds, nuts, oatgerm, and avocados.	• Avoid refined food, saturated and hydrogenated fats, alcohol, salt, sugar, citrus, wheat, dairy foods, and common allergenic foods.
• Eat at least some raw vegetables and sprouted seeds daily.	

Suggested supplements

Vitamin A (as beta-carotene if pregnant); vitamin B-complex (with B6, B12, and folic acid); evening primrose oil; zinc; digestive enzymes; lecithin.

Dandruff can be treated by eating plenty of the antioxidant foods, including avocado.

DULL HAIR, DRY HAIR, LUSTERLESS HAIR

For these conditions, the following nutritional considerations should be taken into account:

- *low intake of vitamin A, protein, and essential fatty acids.*
- *excess refined carbohydrates and saturated fats.*

DIET	
In addition to following the New Pyramid diet:	
• Maximize intake of vitamin A-containing vegetables and fruit (carrots, apricots, mango, broccoli).	• Eat plenty of fish, soy, pulses (legumes), and lean meat for protein.
• Maximize intake of mixed seeds.	• Avoid refined carbohydrates and saturated fats.

Suggested supplements

Fish oils, linseed oil, and evening primrose oil or starflower oil; zinc; vitamin B-complex; *Aloe vera; Ginkgo biloba.*

Nails

Any problem of poor blood circulation, or low levels of nutrients in the blood, will adversely affect the structure of the nails. Additionally, if nails are not supplied with optimum levels of nutrients, fungal and other diseases can invade the nail bed. Any acute period of ill-health will often be evident in the nails, where bumps and striations (grooves or streaks) indicate a period of poor nutrient supply to the nail bed. Low levels of iron may produce "spoon-shaped" nails.

DIET	
In addition to following the New Pyramid diet:	
• Maximize all foods which enhance the immune system and provide the body with a good acid/alkaline balance, such as antioxidant vegetables	and fruit, some (but not excessive) whole grains, good-quality proteins, seed vegetables), and seeds .

Suggested supplements

A high-potency multivitamin/multimineral complex containing good levels of all the major nutrients (and especially iron, zinc, and selenium); *Ginkgo biloba.*

PART FIVE

NUTRITION AND FEMALE HEALTH

DISORDERS OF THE FEMALE REPRODUCTIVE SYSTEM

T HERE ARE VARIOUS AILMENTS *that only apply to women. Breast disease, P.M.S., menstrual abnormalities, fibroids, endometriosis, and female infertility are prevalent among women of menstruating age. Postmenopausal women also suffer from a similar number of ailments associated with the winding down of the female reproductive process, but additionally, the effects on health can be more widespread, resulting in conditions such as osteoporosis and circulatory disorders.*

Breast Tissue

The mammary or breast tissue is composed of secretory cells and ducts. The ducts of the breast, which terminate at the nipple, branch through the breast tissue and are connected to glands called the alveoli (which secrete breast milk). A number of hormones, including estrogen, progesterone, human chorionic gonadotrophin, human chorionic somatomammotrophin, prolactin, and growth hormone stimulate breast development during pregnancy. Under the influence of these hormones, the breasts increase in size, and the ductal system and alveolar structures become more complex. Breast tissue is, therefore, periodically very active. It is stimulated into preparatory mode by menstruation and pregnancy. Sometimes this periodic switching on and off of activities leads to breast disease. At least

A healthy lifestyle may help reduce the risk of cancer.

20 percent of premenopausal women have noncancerous lumpy, tender breasts, often the result of fibrocystic breast disease. The condition may be stable, or may worsen before menstruation. The more fat in the diet, the greater the risk of benign breast disease.

When women with menstrual cycle-related breast symptoms reduce total dietary fat but retain adequate levels of essential fatty acids, breast tenderness, swelling, and lumpiness is reduced. Avoidance of methylxanthines (in coffee, chocolate, colas, some teas, and some drugs) may also be beneficial.

Though benign breast disease is not usually serious, some breast changes that cause these symptoms are precancerous and increase the risk of developing breast cancer. Adhering to a good diet and healthy lifestyle may reduce symptoms of benign breast disease, and prevent breast cancer.

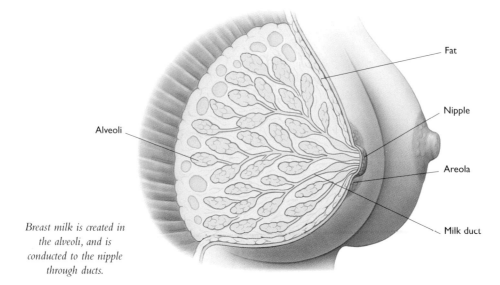

Fat

Nipple

Areola

Milk duct

Alveoli

Breast milk is created in the alveoli, and is conducted to the nipple through ducts.

BENIGN AND FIBROCYSTIC BREAST DISEASE

For these conditions, the following nutritional considerations should be taken into account:

♦ *processed foods.*
♦ *excess saturated fat.*
♦ *excess dairy foods.*
♦ *excess refined carbohydrates.*
♦ *low intake of vitamins (especially vitamin E) and minerals (selenium and iodine).*
♦ *presence of methylzanthines – caffeine and theobromine – (in coffee, chocolate, cola beverages, some teas, and some drugs, such as painkillers, muscle relaxants, "alertness" tablets, diuretics, and cold/allergy remedies).*
♦ *food allergy/intolerance – may need Hypoallergenic Diet.*
♦ *estrogen excess/hormonal imbalance (high intake of environmental estrogens) – may need Detoxification Diet.*

DIET

In addition to following the New Pyramid diet:

• Maximize intake of antioxidant vegetables, fruit, and sea vegetables.

• Maximize intake of seeds and nuts.

• Balance animal protein (fish and lean meat) with vegetable protein (soy and pulses).

• Drink plenty of bottled or filtered water between meals.

• Use olive oil (for vitamin E content) along with other seed oils (sesame, sunflower) on salads.

• Add wheat or oatgerm to salads and soups.

• Minimize dairy food, but eat live ewe's, goat's, or soy yogurt daily.

• Avoid refined carbohydrates, saturated and hydrogenated fats, trans-fatty acids, methylxanthines, food additives and pesticides (eat organic produce whenever possible), and common food allergens.

• Avoid plastic food containers.

Suggested supplements

High-potency multivitamin formula containing good levels of vitamins A (as beta-carotene if pregnant or planning a pregnancy), B (especially B1 and B6), C, and E; balanced calcium/magnesium formula; selenium; evening primrose oil or starflower (borage) oil; fish oils or linseed (flax seed) oil; kelp, or iodized salt.

BREAST CANCER

To help prevent this, the following nutritional considerations should be taken into account:

♦ *low fiber intake.*
♦ *obesity.*
♦ *excess saturated and hydrogenated fats and trans-fatty acids.*
♦ *excess animal protein.*
♦ *excess dairy foods.*
♦ *excess refined carbohydrates and sugar.*
♦ *xeno-estrogens in water and food.*
♦ *estrogen dominance (from a long period on the contraceptive pill and/or hormone replacement therapy).*
♦ *low intake of antioxidants (needed to combat high stress levels).*
♦ *sub-optimum liver activity – may need Detoxification Diet.*

DIET

In addition to following the New Pyramid diet:

• Maximize intake of all antioxidant fruit and vegetables.

• Maximize intake of mixed seeds.

• Eat foods containing phytoestrogens (tofu, tempeh, miso, celery, fennel, rhubarb, oats, and rye).

• Eat foods containing anti-cancer nutrients (cabbage, sprouts, cauliflower, broccoli).

• Balance animal protein (fish and lean meat) with vegetable protein (soy, nuts, and pulses).

• Eat a pot of live soy yogurt daily.

• Use cold-pressed virgin olive oil daily, for its antioxidant content.

• Minimize intake of dairy foods, especially milk (even skim) and hard cheeses, and stimulants (tea, coffee, alcohol, colas).

• Avoid saturated fats, hydrogenated fats, shortenings, etc., containing trans-fatty acids, unfiltered tap water, refined carbohydrates, and sugar.

Suggested supplements

A good-quality multivitamin/multimineral formula; high doses of vitamin C; an antioxidant formula containing good levels of selenium, zinc, and lipoic acid; chromium; *Lactobacillus acidophilus*; co-enzyme Q10; Siberian ginseng; wild yam extract.

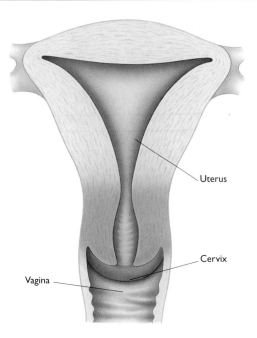

The cervix is the neck of the uterus and protrudes into the upper section of the vagina.

The Cervix

Although, strictly speaking, the ovaries are the reproductive organs because they are the place where ova (eggs) are stored, matured, and released, it is important to look at the cervix, uterus, fallopian tubes, and vagina, since these organs play a part in conception and pregnancy. If whole-body nutrition is poor, these organs can often become damaged. The ovarian tissue can become fibrous and give rise to cysts or, occasionally, ovarian cancer; and the cervix can become damaged, leading to abnormal cell growth.

The cervix is the lower tip of the uterus that extends into the vagina. When a gynecologist takes a "smear" during a routine examination, cells from the surface of the cervix are taken for examination under a microscope. Cervical dysplasia is the medical term for abnormal cell development and shows up as cellular changes in the smear test. Any cellular changes are of concern, because they may be pre-cancerous. Fortunately, once the diagnosis of cervical dysplasia is made, effective treatment can prevent the development of cervical cancer. Again, a good wholesome diet, and healthy lifestyle, will complement any medical treatment.

The female reproductive system is both complex and finely-tuned; fortunately, the majority of problems that can occur respond well to treatment with nutrition.

CERVICAL AND OVARIAN PROBLEMS

For cervical dysplasia and the prevention of cervical cancer, ovarian cysts, and ovarian cancer, the following nutritional factors should be taken into account:

- *excess animal protein.*
- *stimulants (tea, coffee, sugar, salt, alcohol).*
- *refined and overcooked foods.*
- *contraceptive pill (encourages folic acid deficiency).*
- *deficiency of fresh fruit and vegetables.*

DIET

In addition to following the New Pyramid diet:

- Balance animal protein (fish only) with vegetable protein (seeds, nuts, beans, and tofu).
- Maximize intake of antioxidant and phytochemical-containing vegetables and fruit.
- Eat at least some raw vegetables, wheatgerm, and sprouted seeds, daily.
- Drink fresh carrot, or other vegetable, juice daily.
- Avoid tea, coffee, alcohol, salt, sugar, refined carbohydrates, saturated and hydrogenated fats and trans-fatty acids, wheat, processed food, food additives, and common food allergens.

Suggested supplements

A high-potency antioxidant formula containing good levels of beta-carotene, vitamin C, and selenium; a high-potency vitamin B-complex containing good levels of B12 and folic acid.

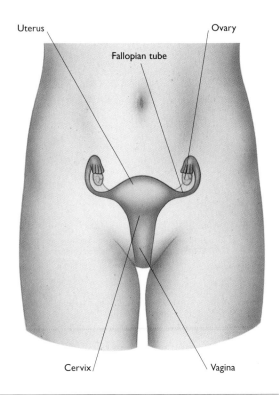

The Vagina

Many harmless, micro-organisms are normally found in the vagina, and they consist of a very large number of yeasts and bacteria. Some of these coexisting organisms are essential to normal vaginal health, such as certain species of *Lactobacillus*. The diversity of vaginal flora is controlled by several factors. The most important of these is the amount of glucose present in vaginal secretions, the acid/alkali balance of the body, and the hormonal state. Infections such as candidiasis or trichomoniasis occur when this natural balance is upset, allowing these yeasts and/or bacteria, and, sometimes, protozoa to flourish. Normal vaginal secretions contain a large amount of glucose, and this gives a high pH (alkaline) quality to these discharges. The organisms that cause vaginal infections thrive on glucose. Fortunately, the healthy bacterial inhabitants of the vaginal mucous membranes convert this glucose to lactic acid. This causes a lowering in pH, making the secretions more acid, which in turn prevents pathogenic microbes from taking over.

Diets high in refined carbohydrates and sugar, especially when hormonal imbalance is present (whether because of a medical condition or because of high stress levels), will tend to allow overgrowths of unfavorable microbes. Antibiotics kill pathogenic bacteria and helpful bacteria indiscriminately. This means they not only kill off the good bacteria in the intestinal tract, but also remove the beneficial acid-producing bacteria in the vagina. When this happens, there is no system of control for the invasion of pathogenic bacteria and yeasts. If antibiotic use is necessary, the body can be reinoculated with good bacteria by eating live yogurt and taking probiotic supplements (*Lactobacillus acidophilus*). Sometimes, large populations of the pathogenic microbes continue to thrive, and in these cases prior treatment with grapefruit seed extract may be needed to "clear" the system before reinoculating with the good bacteria.

Live yogurt encourages the growth of beneficial bacteria in the vagina.

VAGINITIS

Although vaginal thrush (candidiasis) is caused by an overgrowth of a fungus, and trichomoniasis is caused by a parasitic protozoan, the dietary suggestions below can help. For both conditions, the following nutritional considerations should be taken into account:

◆ *damaged gut ecology (dysbiosis), by antibiotics.*
◆ *contraceptive pill (causing pH changes and possible vitamin B6 deficiency).*
◆ *blood sugar problems.*
◆ *low intake of vitamin B-complex, especially B6.*
◆ *excess refined carbohydrates and sugar.*
◆ *low intake of antioxidant nutrients (needed for neutralizing stress-induced free radicals).*
◆ *food allergy/intolerance – may need Hypoallergenic Diet.*

DIET

In addition to following the New Pyramid diet:

• Maximize intake of antioxidant-containing vegetables. • Maximize intake of vegetable protein, seeds, nuts, soy, pulses (legumes), and seed vegetables. • Maintain a high alkaline-forming diet. • Take care with excess fruit, avoiding sweet and dried fruit. • Add wheatgerm or oatgerm to cereals, salads, and soups.	• Eat five or six small meals a day, each containing a little protein (oily fish, lean meat, soy, cottage cheese, nuts, seeds, beans, or seed vegetables). • Eat a small pot of live soy yogurt daily. • Avoid refined carbohydrates, sugar, alcohol, yeast-containing foods (e.g., vinegar, wine, pickles, etc.), and common food allergens.

Suggested supplements

A high-quality multivitamin/multimineral complex, containing good levels of vitamins A (as beta-carotene if pregnant), B-complex (especially B6), C, E, and zinc; high-potency garlic; *Lactobacillus acidophilus*: grapefruit seed extract (taken at a different time of day from the probiotic); fructo-oligosaccharides; *Aloe vera*; evening primrose oil; treat the affected area with plain live yogurt or some tea tree oil diluted with a little almond oil.

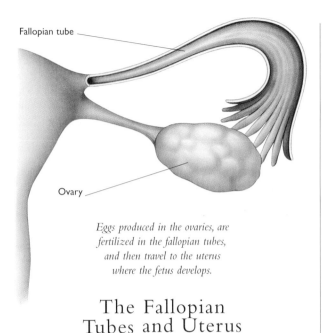

Fallopian tube

Ovary

Eggs produced in the ovaries, are fertilized in the fallopian tubes, and then travel to the uterus where the fetus develops.

The Fallopian Tubes and Uterus

The fallopian tubes (and the ovaries) are open to the outside world – with all its foreign infective agents – via the vagina and uterus. However, these delicate inner passageways and glands are protected by in-built self-defense mechanisms and barriers. The vagina, being normally acidic in nature, prevents pathogens from flourishing; the thick mucous plug of the cervix acts as a mechanical barrier to any invading bodies; and hairlike cilia in the uterus and fallopian tubes constantly waft any debris or bacteria back down toward the cervix and vagina. However, these protective measures fail during menstruation as at this time the vagina becomes relatively alkaline and the cervical plug is removed. Fortunately, a healthy menstrual flow will usually prevent infection getting through, and, in fact, most cases of fallopian tube problems occur following a birth or abortion rather than in normal menstruation.

A copper I.U.D. can also be a major cause of problems, due either to infection at the time of insertion, or to mechanical irritation and congestion, which creates a more favorable environment for bacterial growth. An I.U.D. may also increase the amount of copper in the body, which can lead to low levels of zinc. Sub-optimum nutrition, especially if immune-boosting nutrients are minimal, can allow these conditions to continue. Additionally, nutritional therapists think a mucus-forming diet (excess animal products, especially dairy foods, and excess carbohydrate) can thicken the fluids in the fallopian tubes, causing blockages. Making these dietary changes may allow clearing of the blockage, together with the removal of infectious agents.

SALPINGITIS AND SALPINGO-OOPHORITIS

Although salpingitis (inflammation and congestion of the fallopian tubes) and salpingo-oophoritis (inflammation of the ovaries) are rarely, if ever, caused by nutritional deficiencies, there are several dietary aspects involved in their healing (for example, the removal of the catarrhal state). The following nutritional considerations should be taken into account:

◆ *excess carbohydrates.*
◆ *excess sugar.*
◆ *excess dairy products.*
◆ *low intake of immune-boosting nutrients.*

DIET
In addition to following the New Pyramid diet:

• Maximize intake of antioxidant fruit and vegetables. • Eat only a few whole grain carbohydrates, e.g., brown rice, millet, buckwheat, oats, and limit their daily amounts – increased vegetables and fruit will provide fiber.	• Maximize intake of seeds, and vegetable protein such as soy, pulses (legumes), nuts, and seed vegetables. Eat oily fish from an unpolluted source twice a week. • Avoid all refined carbohydrates, sugar, dairy food, and common allergenic foods.

Suggested supplements

A high-potency antioxidant containing good levels of vitamins A (as beta-carotene if you are pregnant or planning a pregnancy), C, E, and the minerals selenium and zinc; golden seal (unless pregnant); Saw palmetto; wild yam extract; *Aloe vera* juice; evening primrose and fish oils.

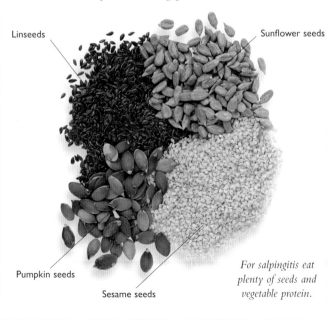

Linseeds

Sunflower seeds

Pumpkin seeds

Sesame seeds

For salpingitis eat plenty of seeds and vegetable protein.

ENDOMETRIOSIS

This is a condition in which the womb lining (endometrium) grows in sites outside the uterus (in the ovaries, fallopian tubes, ligaments, bowel, or bladder). Once in place, this tissue responds to the natural hormone cycle and sheds blood within these body cavities, often causing inflammation, pain, and, in extreme cases, infertility. Women suffering from this condition may exhibit any of a wide range of symptoms, including pain on ovulation, pain during or after sexual intercourse, heavy or irregular bleeding, depression, painful bowel and bladder movements, and intestinal upsets.

One theory suggests that endometriosis may be caused by malabsorption of nutrients caused by disruption of the gut following long-term treatment with antibiotics or steroids. Certainly, there seems to be a higher incidence of allergy-related symptoms among women with endometriosis than is normal, and many nutritional therapists believe that the tissue in the digestive tract may be involved. Ensuing nutritional deficiencies may then play a part in adversely affecting the body's ability to deal with excess levels of estrogen, which itself causes cell proliferation. Women suffering from endometriosis should follow a diet relatively low in arachidonic acid (from animal fats), but high in essential fatty acids from vegetable sources and from fish oils.

It is important to seek a proper medical diagnosis before embarking on any self-help measures.

The following nutritional considerations should be taken into account:

◆ *generalized low nutrient intake or poor absorption – may need Food Combining Diet.*
◆ *excess animal protein and animal fat.*
◆ *gut dysbiosis (overuse of antibiotics and/or steroids, stress).*
◆ *food allergy/intolerance – may need Hypoallergenic Diet.*

DIET

In addition to following the New Pyramid diet:

- Balance your animal protein (fish only) with plant proteins (seeds, nuts, soy, pulses [legumes], and seed vegetables).
- Eat live soy yogurt daily.
- Eat two helpings of dark green leafy vegetables daily.
- Sip diluted freshly squeezed lemon juice or diluted cider vinegar with the main meal of the day.
- Minimize intake of animal foods.
- Avoid animal fats, dairy foods, red meat, refined foods, and common allergenic foods.

Suggested supplements

A high-potency vitamin/multimineral formula containing good levels of all the major nutrients and especially vitamin B-complex, vitamin C, and the minerals magnesium, zinc, and selenium; an additional magnesium/calcium balanced complex; DL-phenylalanine (as a natural pain-killer); probiotics and digestive enzymes; evening primrose and fish oils.

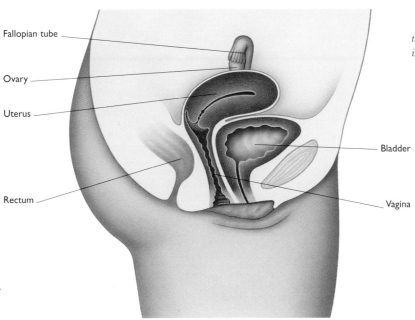

In those suffering from endometriosis the lining of the uterus (the endometrium) is found in places outside the uterus, such as the bladder, fallopian tubes, or bowel.

Fallopian tube
Ovary
Uterus
Rectum
Bladder
Vagina

Menstruation

The tissues and organs involved in menstruation undergo periodic changes under the regulation of hormones such as estrogen and progesterone. There is the possibility of problems occurring with the endometrium (the lining of the womb) as this is being constantly built up and then removed.

The first consideration in dealing with menstrual disorders is always to look for any disease that may be the

During the monthly cycle, as the lining of the uterus grows and is shed, hormone output also rises and falls.

cause. Any bleeding between periods should be investigated by your physician for possible cancer, fibroids, or cervical lesions. However, menstrual problems are most likely to be caused by hormonal imbalances, and various tests can be undertaken to assess the levels of F.S.H. and L.H. (pituitary hormones controlling the menstrual cycle). In addition, it should be remembered that hormonal production and regulation are affected by stress, so any lifestyle problems need to be addressed.

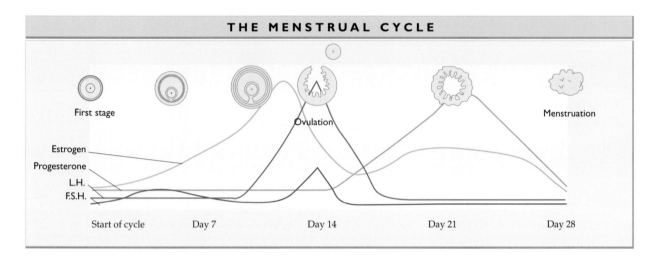

THE MENSTRUAL CYCLE

First stage

Ovulation

Menstruation

Estrogen
Progesterone
L.H.
F.S.H.

Start of cycle   Day 7   Day 14   Day 21   Day 28

NUTRITIONAL LEVELS AFFECTED BY THE PILL

The contraceptive pill can upset the hormonal balance of the body, and consequently can have a profound effect on the nutrients the body needs and how it treats those that are absorbed.

NUTRIENT	INFLUENCE OF THE PILL	NUTRIENT	INFLUENCE OF THE PILL
Vitamin A	Increases circulating levels of vitamin A, which take around three months to return to normal; prudent to stop taking the pill at least three months before trying to conceive.	Folic Acid	Possibly interferes with blood cell formation by reducing folic acid status (and B_{12} status). Since folic acid deficiency is now closely linked to neural tube abnormalities in babies, supplementing with folic acid for several months before trying to conceive is important (see page 199).
Vitamin B_1	Increases requirements for this vitamin.		
Vitamin B_2	Increases requirements for this vitamin.		
Vitamin B_6	Alters vitamin B_6 status and this may be linked to depression, impaired glucose tolerance, poor digestion, and increased risk of cancer of the urinary tract.	Vitamin C	Increases requirement for vitamin C, but avoid taking more than 1,000mg per day – excess vitamin C may change a low-dose estrogen pill to a high-dose one, and thereby increase the adverse effects of the pill.
Vitamin B_{12}	Adversely influences levels of B_{12} but without producing anemia; may be related to psychiatric symptoms not relieved by B_6.	Copper	Increases serum copper levels – which may lower levels of zinc.
Vitamin E	Lowers vitamin E levels by about 20 percent – this may be one of the reasons why the contraceptive pill increases the risk of blood clots in the legs.	Iron	Lowers serum iron in some women, but, because of reduced menstrual blood loss in others, iron status may increase.
Vitamin K	Increases vitamin K in the blood. As vitamin K is a coagulant, this may be another reason why the contraceptive pill is related to formation of blood clots.	Magnesium	Possibly lowers levels of magnesium.
		Zinc	Lowers plasma zinc – possibly because of high copper levels.

Probably the most effective way to upset the entire hormonal balance is to take the contraceptive pill. This convinces the body that it is pregnant, and after stopping taking the pill many women fail to regain normal periods for lengths of time varying from months to years. Taking the pill may also affect the adrenal glands (which produce 20 percent of the total estrogen output). Since the adrenals are very sensitive to changes in blood-sugar level any further imbalance caused by the pill may seriously disrupt hormonal output.

Extreme diets such as very low-protein diets, very strict weight-loss regimes, or excessive exercise, often cause absence of periods. On restricted diets, the levels of circulating hormones fall until a normal menstrual cycle is no longer possible.

From a nutritional point of view, excessive dieting, excessive exercise, protein deficiency, hypoglycemia, nutritional anemia, stress (causing an increase in free radicals), and generalized vitamin and mineral deficiencies, will all contribute to menstrual problems. Redress the balance by eating optimally, and many symptoms are likely to disappear.

POSSIBLE SIDE EFFECTS OF ORAL CONTRACEPTIVE PILL

- Increased risk of developing cancer of the cervix, breast, and liver.
- Blood clots in the legs.
- Stroke and heart attacks.
- Increased blood pressure.
- Increased risk of developing diabetes.
- Gallbladder disease.
- Migraine.
- Food allergies.
- Fluid retention.
- Weight increase.
- Vaginal thrush.
- Depression.
- Change in metabolism, affecting the way the body uses and needs certain vitamins and minerals.

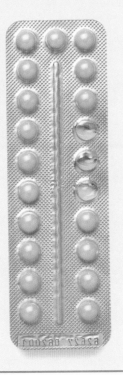

The pill can be harmful, for all its contraceptive benefits.

MENSTRUAL DISORDERS

For amenorrhea (absence of periods), dysmenorrhea (painful periods), metrorrhagia (bleeding between periods), and oligomenorrhea (infrequent or scanty menstruation), the following nutritional considerations should be taken into account:

- *excess refined food.*
- *excess intake of stimulants (coffee, tea, colas, salt, sugar, alcohol).*
- *excess intake of animal protein and animal fat.*
- *low intake or poor absorption of calcium and magnesium.*
- *generalized nutritional deficiencies.*
- *hormonal imbalance (sometimes due to excessive exercise and/or stress).*
- *toxicity – may need Detoxification Diet.*

DIET	
In addition to following the New Pyramid diet:	
• Balance animal proteins (oily fish and lean meat) with vegetable proteins (seeds, nuts, soy, pulses [legumes], and seed vegetables).	• Maximize intake of freshly ground mixed seeds, especially sesame and pumpkin seeds.
• Maximize intake of a wide range of fruit and vegetables, especially dark green vegetables because they have a high phytochemical, calcium, and iron content.	• Have five or six small meals a day, eating a small amount of protein to balance the carbohydrate at each meal. • Avoid refined foods, coffee, salt, sugar, and alcohol.

Suggested supplements

A multivitamin/multimineral formula with good levels of vitamins A (beta-carotene if contemplating pregnancy), B-complex (especially B3, and B6), C, D, and E, and the minerals calcium, magnesium, iron and zinc – it may be more prudent to obtain a complex formula omitting iron, and taking iron as a separate supplement at a different meal time (to insure maximum absorption of all minerals); anthocyanidins (bilberry extract, etc.) – especially for dysmenorrhea and bloating; lecithin; high-potency garlic; kelp; evening primrose oil or starflower oil; fish oils; protein (amino-acid) complex; digestive enzymes; wild yam extract; a probiotics-balanced herbal formula designed for menstrual problems.

PREMENSTRUAL SYNDROME (P.M.S.)

P.M.S. is very widespread, affecting one in three menstruating women. It can also be very serious; the hormonal deficiency of progesterone that often accompanies P.M.S. has been shown to increase the risk of breast cancer. The psychological effects may occasionally be extreme enough to make women feel suicidal or violent/aggressive. The symptoms can be many and varied; they include radical mood swings, tender breasts, acne, fluid retention, weight gain, cravings and binge eating, insomnia, crying, dizziness, fainting, headaches, palpitations, confusion, lethargy, abdominal bloating, depression, anxiety, and fatigue. When these symptoms occur together, P.M.S. becomes a severely debilitating condition.

Although it is widespread in the Western world, it is actually quite uncommon in more primitive societies, and this suggests that diet and lifestyle play a large part in the problem. P.M.S. is associated with an increased intake of refined carbohydrates and, specifically, a greatly increased intake of sugar. Since carbohydrates enhance mood by the synthesis of serotonin (a neuro-transmitter), women feeling anxious and depressed premenstrually often increase their intake of these substances to make themselves feel better. However, eating large amounts of sweet food can cause fluid retention, hypoglycemic symptoms, and loss of magnesium, among other things. Also, low dietary fiber will prevent the appropriate removal of excess estrogen, and the ensuing increase in the estrogen to progesterone ratio can lead to anxiety. Complex carbohydrates are more supportive to the body. Salt, alcohol, excess fat, caffeine, and low protein intake have all been implicated in P.M.S. symptoms. For anyone suffering from P.M.S., the following nutritional considerations should be taken into account:

- *excess animal fat.*
- *excess sugar and refined carbohydrates (related to hypoglycemia).*
- *stimulants (tea, coffee, chocolate, colas, alcohol, salt, caffeine-containing medicines).*
- *dairy products.*
- *generalized low intake (or poor absorption) of nutrients (may be related to smoking, contraceptive pill, etc.) especially B vitamins in general, vitamin B6, vitamin C, and magnesium.*
- *estrogen dominance/xeno-estrogens.*
- *poor levels of digestive enzymes – may need Food Combining Diet.*
- *low intake of foods high in magnesium, e.g., seeds and dark green vegetables.*
- *poor ability to metabolize linoleic acid.*
- *essential fatty acid deficiency.*
- *lead toxicity – may need Detoxification Diet.*

P.M.S. is more common in Western industrialized society, an indication that junk food and pollution exacerbate the symptoms.

DIET

In addition to following the New Pyramid diet:

- Maximize intake of fruit and vegetables, especially dark green vegetables such as cabbage and broccoli.

- Maximize intake of ground mixed seeds (sunflower, sesame, pumpkin, and linseed).

- Eat fish, poultry, pulses (legumes), and soy (soy milk, tofu) as your main sources of protein. Minimize intake of red meat.

- Eat five or six small meals a day and include a little protein with each one (to even out blood-sugar swings); if you must have something sweet, eat fruit, or a fruit soy yogurt; if you must have a sweet drink, use dilute fruit juice. Drink bottled or filtered water between meals (to avoid xeno-estrogens in piped water).

- Eat at least some raw vegetables and sprouted seeds and beans daily – this will also increase your daily fiber intake.

- Avoid buying and/or storing food wrapped in plastics or polythene.

- Avoid alcohol, refined carbohydrates, sugar, salt, saturated and hydrogenated fats, trans-fatty acids, dairy products, food additives, pesticides in food (buy organic produce whenever possible), and stimulants.

Suggested supplements:

A high-potency multivitamin/multimineral complex containing good levels of vitamin B-complex (especially B3, B6, and biotin), vitamin C, and the minerals magnesium, calcium, all trace elements (especially zinc and chromium); an additional balanced calcium/magnesium complex may be required; evening primrose oil or starflower (borage) oil; fish oils; vitamin E (especially where breast tenderness is a problem); fructo-oligosaccharides; L-methionine; L-tyrosine (where irritability and depression are a problem); wild yam extract; Dong quai; Milk thistle; *Ginkgo biloba*; digestive enzymes.

PARSLEY

Some women experience emotional as well as physical symptoms with P.M.S.

Some women suffer headaches, even fainting

Feelings of fatigue

Tender breasts are common

MUSHROOM

To alleviate the symptoms of P.M.S., eat some green vegetables and some raw vegetables each day.

BEAN SPROUTS

Piped water may contain xeno-estrogens, so drink bottled water instead.

Infertility requires medical consultation, but women are more likely to get pregnant if they are neither under- nor overweight.

Infertility and Recurrent Miscarriage

There are many physical and medical causes of infertility outside the scope of this book. In general, however, women who wish to become pregnant for the first time are more likely to succeed if they regulate their diet so that they are neither excessively underweight nor overweight. Studies show that around 12 percent of women who are infertile for ovulatory reasons are equally divided between being overweight and underweight.

Miscarriage can happen to any woman because of a chance event or some ongoing stressful condition, but recurrent miscarriages (three or more) are a different matter. There are many and varied causes and they should be investigated thoroughly by a gynecologist. Sometimes a miscarriage occurs at around the third month, when the placenta fails due to hormone imbalance. Other causes include diabetes, thyroid problems, fibroids, chromosomal abnormalities, anatomical problems with the womb, and particular infections such as chlamydia and herpes.

EATING FOR IMPROVED FERTILITY

To increase your chances of becoming pregnant, boost your immune system by consuming antioxidant fruit and vegetables, and switch from animal sources of protein to vegetable proteins such as seeds, pulses (legumes), and nuts. Vitamin deficiency, especially in folic acid, is particularly associated with low levels of fertility.

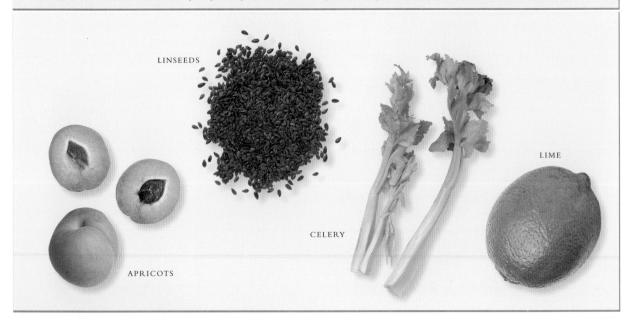

LINSEEDS

LIME

CELERY

APRICOTS

FACTORS AFFECTING FERTILITY

Alcohol may reduce a woman's fertility by increasing the level of the hormone prolactin, raised levels of which in the blood cause menstrual cycle dysfunction and infertility. Caffeine, however, may reduce levels of prolactin; low levels are also associated with infertility. Nutrient deficiencies associated with infertility include folic acid deficiency, vitamin B12 deficiency, vitamin B6 deficiency, vitamin A imbalance (either excess or deficiency), and zinc deficiency. When remedied by diet or supplementation (or by healing the gut lining and improving absorption), fertility may improve. Nutritional considerations to take into account are:

♦ *low levels of body fat (prevents menstruation).*
♦ *excessive slimming and/or excessive exercise.*
♦ *obesity.*
♦ *alcohol and caffeine.*
♦ *imbalance of vitamin A.*
♦ *low intake (or poor absorption) of B vitamins, especially B6.*
♦ *toxicity and acidity – may need Detoxification Diet.*
♦ *excess animal protein and fat.*

DIET	
In addition to following the New Pyramid diet:	
• Maximize intake of immune-boosting fruit and vegetables, particularly antioxidant types and those containing phytochemicals. • Maximize intake of mixed seeds and nuts. • Eat mostly vegetable protein, e.g., soy, pulses (legumes), nuts, seed vegetables, with a little fish and organic lean meat.	• Add wheatgerm or oatgerm to salads and soups (for extra folic acid). • Increase foods high in beta-carotene (carrots, apricots, dark green vegetables). • Minimize intake of grain carbohydrates. • Avoid red meat, liver, refined carbohydrates and sugar, caffeine, artificial additives, pesticides, alcohol, saturated and hydrogenated fat.

Suggested supplements

A good-quality multivitamin/multimineral complex containing beta-carotene, vitamin B-complex (especially B6, B12, and folic acid), and E and the mineral zinc; evening primrose or starflower (borage) oil and fish oils.

NUTRITIONAL DEFICIENCIES LINKED WITH MISCARRIAGE

Nutritional therapists think that certain nutrient deficiencies, such as those of zinc, manganese, essential fatty acids, and vitamin E, as well as toxic overload, are linked to an increased tendency for spontaneous miscarriages. After a thorough medical examination has been carried out, or while medical investigations are proceeding, it is well worthwhile embarking upon an optimum diet to deal with these, if your physician or obstetrician agrees.

The following nutritional considerations should be taken into account:

♦ *toxicity – may need Detoxification Diet, which should be undertaken before another pregnancy is planned (not if you are trying to get pregnant).*
♦ *excess refined carbohydrates.*
♦ *artificial additives.*
♦ *alcohol.*
♦ *generalized vitamin and mineral deficiencies (low intake or poor absorption).*

DIET	
In addition to following the New Pyramid diet:	
• Maximize intake of antioxidant fruit and vegetables. • Maximize intake of freshly ground mixed seeds (sunflower, pumpkin, sesame, and linseed). • Balance animal protein (fish, poultry, and occasional free-range egg) with plant proteins (soy, pulses [legumes], nuts, seed vegetables).	• Take fiber in a variety of forms (oats, brown rice, cellulose, and pectins). • Avoid refined carbohydrates, sugar, artificial additives, alcohol and other stimulants, pesticides in food, and liver.

Suggested supplements

A good-quality multivitamin/multimineral complex with good levels of the B-complex, vitamin E, zinc, selenium, and manganese; evening primrose oil or starflower (borage) oil and fish oils. Insure that the multiformula does not have vitamin A present, but has a good amount of beta-carotene.

PRECONCEPTION NUTRITIONAL CONSIDERATIONS

T HE NUTRITIONAL STATUS OF *the father and mother in the weeks and months preceding conception can influence the outcome of a pregnancy. In addition, the correct development of the fertilized egg (fetus) into a baby during the first eight weeks of pregnancy is crucial, and the mother's health can be a critical factor.*

There is a lot going on during this time: many women can be eight weeks pregnant without realizing it, and their nutritional and toxic status during these critical weeks can determine whether or not the baby will develop normally. Similarly, the quality of the father's sperm can be influenced by both nutritional and toxic factors. Excessive intake of toxic metals (lead, mercury, and cadmium) can adversely influence the quality of the sperm, and smoking and alcohol can increase the number of sperm abnormalities as well as lowering the overall sperm count.

Preconceptual Care

Hundreds of other substances capable of causing genetic mutations in both ova and sperm have now also been identified. Mutations have been linked to cannabis, diesel engine smoke, overheated cooking oils, barbecued and chargrilled meat, coal dust, some tranquilizers, paracetamol and other drugs, and viruses. More importantly, it seems that such genetic damage is made worse by nutritional deficiencies of, for example, folic acid, B vitamin complex, vitamins C, E, and zinc. There are many foods which have been shown to have antimutagenic (and anti-cancer) properties, including carrots, broccoli, cabbage, parsley, apples, pineapples, grapes, the freshly extracted oils of some nuts and seeds, and olive oil, though these properties are reduced when the foods are cooked. During the preconceptual period it is crucial that food is eaten as fresh as possible. Ova are most vulnerable to mutation in a period of about a week starting three or four days

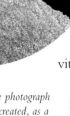

An electron microscope photograph of the moment life is created, as a sperm enters an egg.

before ovulation, and sperm during the two to three months before conception. Extreme deficiencies of some nutrients usually result in infertility, but there is a gray area between the extremes of poor nutritional status and infertility, and good nutritional status with fertility and normal reproduction, where women may be fertile, but are at risk of producing an abnormal child. It is this area that is the target of nutritional intervention in preconceptual care.

Since vitamins, by definition, are necessary for maintaining normal growth, a severe deficiency of any vitamin may cause birth abnormalities. So too may excesses of toxic metals such as lead, cadmium (from cigarette smoke), and copper. In addition to toxic metals, some normally healthy nutrients need to be handled with care during preconception and pregnancy. One such nutrient is vitamin A, which in excessive amounts has been related to congenital malformations. However, deficiencies of choline and vitamin E have been shown to enhance the toxicity of vitamin A. So a general rule of thumb is to avoid vitamin A, but have adequate beta-carotene (if using a nutritional supplement) and insure that choline and vitamin E are well supplied either in supplement form or by diet.

Essential fatty acids are vital for correct fetal development, since they are intimately involved in the development of cell membranes, and therefore each body cell, and for proper brain function (half the weight of the brain is made up of essential fatty acids).

Neural tube defects (such as spina bifida) have been strongly linked to inadequate levels of folic acid in the mother's diet. It is likely that the lack of other nutrients is also related to this type of birth defect. Recent research has indicated that those women who supplement their diet with a multivitamin, including folic acid, during the first six weeks of pregnancy have a significantly lower chance of having a baby with neural tube defects.

Furthermore, the incidence of spina bifida seems to be correlated to low folic acid levels occurring specifically within the first trimester, when many women may not even know they are pregnant. It is extraordinary that the acceptance by the medical profession of folic acid supplementation for prevention of spina bifida has not led to concern about nutritional deficiency in general as a potential cause of birth defects.

Cleft palate is a congenital abnormality which is relatively common. It has been shown that women who have had a previous child with this condition can reduce their risk substantially of having further children with cleft palates by taking a high-quality multinutrient formula supplement in the week prior to conception and throughout pregnancy.

As yet, there is no concrete evidence at all that preconceptual vitamin and mineral supplements can prevent a child being born with Down's syndrome. However, good nutrition will always be a woman's best safeguard against congenital malformation of the fetus and increase the likelihood of the baby developing normally. Some of the toxins known to be associated with the development of birth defects are toxic metals such as mercury, lead, and cadmium; and other substances such as organochemicals, D.D.T., dioxin, agent orange, P.B.C.s, drugs (anticonvulsants, thalidomide, and others). Heavy metals have been associated with the development of congenital malformations, increased rates of miscarriage, and stillbirths. It is quite possible that mothers and fathers, if exposed to high levels of any of these heavy metals and other substances, could produce children who have congenital malformations and/or defective mental development.

*Both the father's and the mother's
nutrition have a bearing on the
chances of conception, and
on the health of the fetus.*

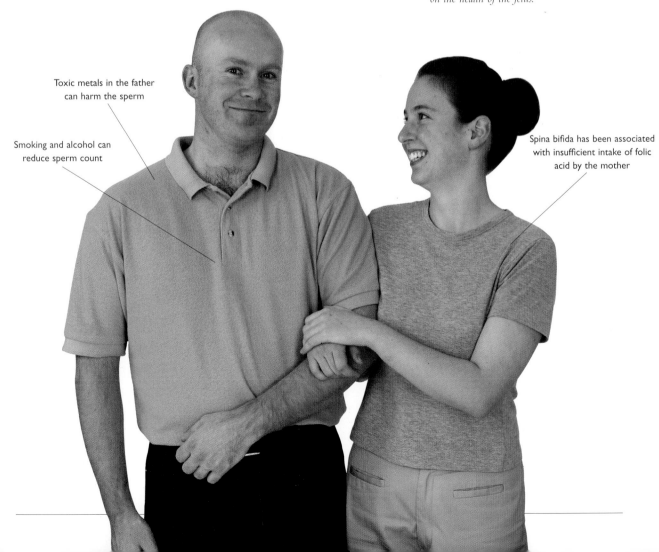

Toxic metals in the father
can harm the sperm

Smoking and alcohol can
reduce sperm count

Spina bifida has been associated
with insufficient intake of folic
acid by the mother

Preconceptual Nutrition

Sexual chemistry is designed to make sure that the egg and sperm meet and mingle their different genes. The endocrine organs of the female should then produce the hormones which insure that the developing baby is being well nourished. However, optimum nourishment can only occur if there are the raw materials present in the mother's body to enable this to happen. If, prior to conception, the woman's diet has been poor or at very best sub-optimum, then there will not be the required levels of nutrients available for the initial part of development of the fetus, even if the new mother immediately embarks upon a better diet.

Certain nutrient levels may be more affected than others. For example, if the contraceptive pill has been used for any length of time, there is the distinct possibility that zinc and magnesium will be deficient. Also requirements for the B vitamins, vitamin C, vitamin E, and iron are all likely to have been increased by taking the pill. All these nutrient deficiencies need to be rectified before conception. Any changes in diet and lifestyle aimed at increasing the likelihood of conception should ideally be made at least three months before the intended time.

For the majority of pregnant women, a normal healthy baby will still be the result, even where there has been no attempt at a preconceptual program of optimum nutrition and lifestyle changes. The purpose of this section is for those women who are not yet pregnant, but who want to maximize their level of health in order to make the most of being pregnant and producing the healthiest possible baby.

Nutritional changes including adding fresh fruit and vegetables to the diet may improve health during the pregnancy and maximize the chance of producing a healthy baby.

Good levels of minerals and vitamins help to produce a healthy baby

Breast milk contains important antibodies

Do not use the contraceptive pill for three months before trying to conceive

Good body weight in the mother increases the chance of a healthy baby

A high intake of fresh fruit is a crucial part of a preconceptual nutrition program.

Food contaminated with pesticides might be a factor in birth defects.

PRECONCEPTUAL PROGRAM

To help prevent an increased risk of birth defects (congenital abnormalities), the following nutritional considerations should be taken into account:

◆ *protein/amino acid deficiency.*
◆ *essential fatty acid deficiency.*
◆ *excess refined carbohydrates.*
◆ *generalized vitamin and mineral deficiencies (low intake or poor absorption).*
◆ *low body weight.*
◆ *slimming diets.*
◆ *previous P.M.S. (as this confirms low nutritional status).*
◆ *previous taking of the contraceptive pill (which can encourage some deficiencies) – use other methods of birth control (the condom) for at least three months before attempting to conceive.*
◆ *alcohol (could produce babies with fetal alcohol syndrome).*
◆ *excess stimulants (tea and coffee).*
◆ *food additives.*
◆ *food allergy/intolerance – may need Hypoallergenic Diet prior to conception. Malabsorption of nutrients can compromise fetal development.*
◆ *heavy metal (lead, mercury, cadmium, etc.) and pesticide toxicity – may need Detoxification Diet but this should be undertaken well before getting pregnant.*

BABY CORN

DIET

In addition to following the New Pyramid diet:

● Maximize intake of immune-boosting fruit and vegetables, particularly those containing phytochemicals (this will increase alkalinity of the diet).

● Maximize intake of a good range of antioxidant fruit and vegetables.

● Maximize intake of freshly ground mixed seeds (sesame, sunflower, pumpkin, and linseed).

● Add carbohydrates like quinoa (good levels of amino acids), and wheatgerm/oatgerm to salads and soups.

● Eat at least some raw vegetables and sprouted seeds and pulses (legumes) daily.

● Balance animal protein (mainly oily fish and lean meat) with vegetable protein, such as soy, nuts, pulses (legumes), and seed vegetables such as scarlet runners.

● Minimize the intake of mucus-forming foods, such as dairy foods, meat, and eggs.

● Avoid alcohol, stimulants (tea, coffee, colas, sugar), refined carbohydrates, saturated and hydrogenated fats, trans-fatty acids, food additives (especially food dyes), monosodium glutamate, aspartame, processed food, pesticides (eat organic produce whenever possible), and common food allergens.

PUMPKIN SEEDS

RASPBERRIES

Suggested supplements

A high-quality multivitamin/multimineral formula with good levels of all vitamins (except vitamin A; beta–carotene can be substituted), folic acid in particular, and also with minerals especially zinc, magnesium, and iron; soy lecithin.

WARNING

Any woman planning a pregnancy, whether or not she has a previous child with a birth defect should always discuss diet and supplementation with her family physician before embarking on a self-help program.

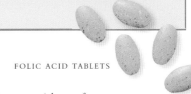

FOLIC ACID TABLETS

Folic acid is an essential part of preconceptual nutrition, as well as a diet high in fruit, vegetables, and seeds.

OPTIMUM NUTRITION DURING PREGNANCY

Optimum nutrition can greatly *improve your chances of having a healthy pregnancy, and a healthy baby. Since pregnancy is such a nutritionally demanding time for a woman, even the slightest deficiencies during pregnancy can have serious effects on the health of the baby. A healthy pregnancy will depend on a greater supply than normal of some essential nutrients to meet the needs of the mother and the growing fetus.*

As already mentioned, pregnancy is something that must be prepared for in advance. When the world was less polluted and food more wholesome, this was a consideration that was not required. However, things are now very different. Today, more than ever before, miscarriage is the greatest threat to any pregnancy, with perhaps one in ten pregnant women miscarrying, and maybe as many as one in two where previous miscarriage has occurred. Also, since early miscarriages often go unnoticed or unreported, this figure is likely to be a gross underestimate. Many experts believe that miscarriage is a fairly good indication that a woman (or the father of her child) has been exposed to "environmental hazards." The list of such "hazards" is endless, but includes such things as smoking, alcohol intake, heavy metal toxicity, environmental pollutants (including pesticides, exhaust gases, etc.), plastics, stress, and sub-optimum nutrition. All of these environmental hazards need to be avoided as far as possible, in addition to maximizing intake of antioxidant nutrients (by food and/or as part of a multi-supplement), especially selenium, which is at high levels in Brazil nuts.

Take Fetal Alcohol Syndrome (F.A.S.) as an example. Although in many cases miscarriage may be a natural way of terminating a scarcely viable pregnancy, many babies are born suffering from the

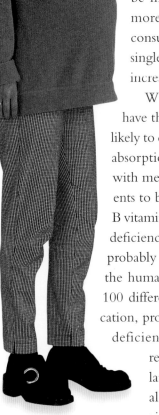

A good and regular intake of nutrients is vital throughout pregnancy.

effects of the mother's alcohol consumption. In 1985, the *British Medical Journal* reported that obvious F.A.S. occurred in ten out of 31 heavy-drinking mothers. This syndrome produces low-birthweight babies with mild facial deformity and poor mental development and behavioral problems. Many of these babies are hyperactive, jumpy, and have difficulty in sleeping. However, worse still, some research has indicated that a baby does not need to have the physical signs of this specific disorder to be mentally affected by alcohol. Furthermore, some studies have shown that the consumption by the mother of as little as a single alcoholic drink every other day can increase the risk of miscarriage.

Why do even small amounts of alcohol have this effect? One answer is that it is very likely to compromise nutritional status. It affects absorption of nutrients in the gut, interferes with metabolism, and causes other vital nutrients to be leached from the body tissues (e.g., B vitamins, especially B_6, iron, and zinc), causing deficiencies in these essential nutrients. Zinc is probably the most versatile of all minerals in the human body. It is a component in at least 100 different enzymes, involving D.N.A. replication, protein growth, and many others. Zinc deficiencies are common in children with retarded growth. There are striking similarities between the offspring born to alcoholic mothers and those born to zinc-deficient mothers. The good news is that if the diet is high in essential nutrients and a healthy lifestyle is followed,

FETAL DEVELOPMENT

For a baby to develop healthily in the womb, the mother should not only eat well, but avoid alcohol and other hazardous "environmental" factors.

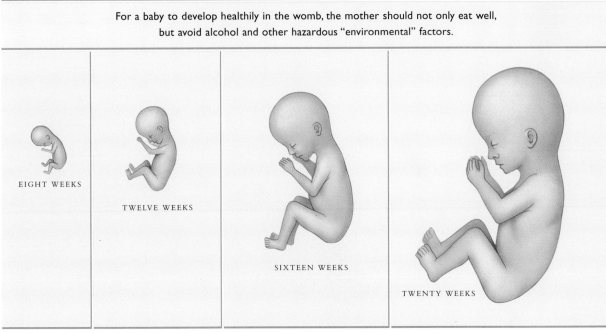

EIGHT WEEKS

TWELVE WEEKS

SIXTEEN WEEKS

TWENTY WEEKS

an occasional unit of alcohol is very unlikely to cause damage, particularly if only taken in the later stages of pregnancy.

On the whole, environmental hazards (including alcohol consumption) have their most far-reaching effects in the very early stages of pregnancy, when cell division is most prolific. This is, of course, a time when many women do not even know they are pregnant. Research work on animals has shown that alcohol can even damage sperm; therefore, alcohol really needs to be avoided right from the time a couple decide to have a family.

Even seemingly innocuous substances can have devastating effect. Very high levels of glucose in the diet are a common cause of blood sugar swings, but during pregnancy high glucose levels have a more profound effect, interfering drastically with normal metabolism, perhaps because of the production of A.G.E. proteins (*see* page 50), and have been indicated in birth defects. The same problems do not occur with fructose (fruit sugar) and lactose (milk sugar).

During the first three months of pregnancy all the organs of the baby are completely formed. This is the period when optimum nutrition is most important. Research has demonstrated that some vitamins and minerals exist in different ratios between mother and fetal blood

supply, indicating that some vitamins and minerals can be "pumped" via the placenta, while others only passively diffuse through. For some of these nutrients, the mother's blood supply offers the fetus only what can be spared. The mother may remain reasonably healthy, yet have very low levels of nutrients left over for the developing baby. It is even more important that good organ reserves have been built up by the mother preconceptually by following an optimum nutrition program, since these stores may dwindle quickly due to the common problem of "morning sickness." Around 75 percent of women may experience some degree of nausea during pregnancy. Some for a few days, some at only certain parts of the day, but for some it can last the whole pregnancy. If nausea and vomiting in pregnancy are excessive, consult your physician immediately.

Alcohol restricts the body's absorption of important nutrients, and it should be avoided in early pregnancy.

Nutritional Healing for Minor Problems in Pregnancy

Many of the following minor health problems can be prevented, or their symptoms alleviated, by optimum nutrition. Try to obtain the necessary nutrients from food (a good basic diet is the one given on page 206), and not from supplements, and in any case never self-prescribe supplements during pregnancy; consult with your physician beforehand.

MILD ANEMIA

Iron-deficiency anemia may be present in 20 percent of pregnant women in a mild form, since iron is required for the growth of the fetus. However, since menstruation is absent, normal monthly iron loss is prevented. Your general physician may prescribe iron supplements, if there is risk of anemia. However, it is as well to bear in mind that taking extra iron will depress zinc levels. Quite apart from the fact that many women suffer from constipation with iron supplementation, the fact that zinc absorption may be inhibited (especially as dietary zinc seems to be barely adequate, even quite low, in so many women) is of great concern; zinc is very important for the development of the fetus. It appears that zinc deficiency during the last two-thirds of pregnancy can alter the basic development of the immune system. Other research has indicated that babies and children with low zinc levels tend to be very much more hyperactive and suffer learning disabilities than those with normal zinc status.

Other nutrient deficiencies can also cause the symptoms of anemia. This list includes vitamin B_{12}, folic acid, manganese, and vitamin B_6. Insuring the diet contains extra wheatgerm, seeds (sesame, sunflower, pumpkin), and dark green vegetables will help provide these nutrients.

CONSTIPATION

For many women constipation is a real problem. This is not always the result of taking iron supplements, but may be the result of the fecal matter in the large intestine being more compressed because of the pressure from the developing baby. Do not be tempted to take laxatives, but instead drink plenty of water and other fluids; and eat fibrous fruit and vegetables, lentils, and beans containing soft fiber, cellulose, and pectin. Be careful with taking extra cereal bran, and avoid wheat bran, since this can make minerals and vitamins unavailable to the body.

LEG CRAMPS

Cramps are caused by muscles (usually the calf muscle) contracting strongly – in other words, going into "spasm." Deficiencies of calcium and/or magnesium may cause this to happen, because these minerals, together with potassium and sodium, provide the electrolyte balance needed for correct nerve and muscle function. Good dietary sources of these electrolytes are green leafy vegetables, nuts, and seeds (especially sesame seeds). Milk products are a good source of calcium, but nutritional therapists think there are two major problems with dairy foods. Firstly, although they are high in calcium, they are very low in magnesium. Secondly, dairy foods are particularly mucus-forming. For both of these reasons, nutritional therapists, unlike family physicians or dieticians, think the consumption of dairy foods should be kept at a low level during pregnancy.

> ### NOTE
>
> Iron is often prescribed for anemia in pregnancy, but extra iron can suppress zinc absorption, harming the fetus's immune system and possibly even leading to hyperactivity. The symptoms of anemia are not always caused by lack of iron.

Drink plenty of fluids rather than take laxatives to prevent constipation

Iron may be incorporated in the diet but lack of iron is not necessarily the cause of anemia

Many of the unwelcome side effects of pregnancy can be avoided or lessened by careful eating.

STRETCH MARKS

If the skin loses its natural elasticity accommodating the rapidly growing uterus, stretch marks may develop. These occur on the abdomen, thighs, breasts, and hips, and may be a sign of zinc deficiency. Vitamin C is needed to manufacture collagen in the skin, and vitamin E is involved in keeping skin supple. Zinc is essential for the activity of enzymes involved in cell division and growth and therefore vital for healthy growth of the developing baby. As with other essential nutrients, the requirement for zinc is greatly increased during pregnancy over and above normal levels, to insure proper development of fetal tissue. To supply zinc at an optimal level, natural body processes will extract this mineral from the mother's own resources in favor of the baby, even if this makes maternal tissues temporarily deficient. Good dietary sources of zinc are pumpkin seeds, fish, and shellfish. Vitamin C is found in fresh fruit and vegetables, and vitamin E in seed oils, cereals, seeds, and wheat or oatgerm.

A common cause of leg cramps in pregnancy is a deficiency of calcium or magnesium.

VARICOSE VEINS AND HEMORRHOIDS

These are caused because of a restriction in the flow of blood returning from the feet and legs to a large vein in the groin area. If this vein is compressed, as it might be by the baby, or by compacted fecal matter, the blood flow has to make use of smaller veins to complete the circulation of blood. These small veins become enlarged and sometimes lose their elasticity, at which point they are no longer able to maintain appropriate blood flow, and the blood "pools" and distends the vein. Therefore, the venous system needs to be kept in good shape. This can be achieved by eating a diet high in a wide variety of natural, unprocessed foods, supplying, in particular, the vitamin B-complex, vitamins C and E, and essential fatty acids. Vitamin B3 helps to dilate blood vessels; vitamin C (from fresh vegetables and fruit) helps to maintain the elasticity of collagen in the vessel walls; and vitamin E and the fatty acid E.P.A. (from oily fish) prevent the blood becoming viscous. Both conditions are made worse by constipation (*see* page 202).

KEEPING THE VEINS ELASTIC

Unlike most of the side effects of pregnancy, varicose veins will remain after the birth. However, veins can be kept free of the stiffening that makes them varicose with E.P.A. from oily fish, vitamin B3 from poultry, and vitamin C from fruit and vegetables. The vegetables, together with nuts and seeds, also help avoid cramps.

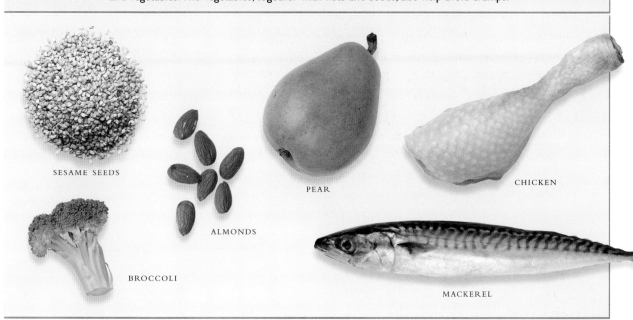

SESAME SEEDS

ALMONDS

PEAR

CHICKEN

BROCCOLI

MACKEREL

Nutritional Healing for Serious Problems in Pregnancy

In addition to the mild ailments of pregnancy, covered on pages 202-3, there are several that are much more serious and need careful management.

Bed rest is generally prescribed for any serious condition that occurs during pregnancy.

ECLAMPSIA AND PRE-ECLAMPSIA (TOXEMIA)

The first sign that eclampsia (a condition in which the mother may have convulsions) may be occurring is a rise in blood pressure. This is usually accompanied by swelling of the ankles, caused by fluid retention (edema), and protein appearing in the urine. This condition is known as pre-eclampsia. Eclampsia only occurs in pregnancy and is found in around five percent of women, commonly beginning during the last few weeks of pregnancy as the baby reaches its maximum size. Usually an optimum diet and bed rest are sufficient to keep the symptoms in check and after the birth the symptoms disappear. However, eclampsia can be very serious and the convulsions may endanger the life of mother and baby. To prevent this, prenatal check-ups are vital, since women suffering from this condition do not normally feel ill.

Incomplete formation of the placenta is one criterion related to eclampsia, which is thought to interfere with an appropriate immune function in the mother. It commonly occurs in first babies, as some degree of immune adaptation has taken place before a second pregnancy occurs.

Some research has also implicated high copper levels with pre-eclampsia, and this may be related to the usual drop in zinc in pregnancy. Additionally, there appears to be some evidence that low levels of vitamin B6 could predispose women to eclampsia. Calcium is useful for lowering blood pressure in nonpregnant adults, and when you realize that a pregnant woman is adding about 30 percent extra blood and nearly 50 percent extra fluid to her body, it makes perfect sense to insure good levels of calcium during pregnancy to protect against high blood pressure and toxemia. Also, low calcium intake during pregnancy results in the growing fetus "robbing" the mother's blood supply of calcium, which leads to a depletion in maternal bone stores and may cause osteoporosis later in life.

Magnesium, because of its close biochemical relationship with calcium, has also been shown to prevent pre-eclampsia. Gamma linolenic acid (G.L.A.), given as evening primrose oil, has been useful for helping to treat high blood pressure in pre-eclampsia.

Lastly, it has been found that those women having a high intake of zinc from their diet (and supplements) have fewer hypertensive problems of edema, high blood pressure, eclampsia, and toxemia. Obtaining sufficient calcium and magnesium along with vitamin B6, zinc, and essential fatty acids, during pregnancy and paying attention to any food allergies (especially to cow's milk) can be helpful in preventing toxemia (pre-eclampsia). Amino acids are crucial to proper fluid distribution in the body. Therefore, low protein intake may lead to edema and other hypertensive disorders of pregnancy, which may progress to pre-eclampsia and eclampsia: sufficient intake of protein is very important in pregnancy.

AFLATOXIN POISONING

Aflatoxin is a deadly substance produced by molds which live on improperly stored pulses (legumes) and grains. Peanuts and beans which have been stored in damp climates are particularly at risk of this contamination. Aflatoxins can cause liver damage in all adults, but in pregnant women they may cause mental retardation in the child. It is obvious, therefore, that these food items should be obtained from a reputable source with frequent turnover.

Peanuts can carry a mold that causes brain damage in the fetus.

LISTERIA POISONING

Listeria monocytogenes is a bacterium which can grow well in chilled food, especially "prepared" meals which are meant to be reheated in the microwave. It can grow, albeit slowly, at temperatures of 39°F (4°C), when other pathogens do not. It is also common in unpasteurized milk products (from contamination via cattle), soft cheeses, and pâtés. However, post-pasteurization contamination is also common, so pasteurized foods are not exempt.

Listeria is particularly dangerous in pregnancy since it can cross the placental barrier, or colonize the vagina. Babies who are infected can be stillborn, or may develop septicemia with meningitis and/or pneumonia, within 48 hours of delivery. Since this bacterium grows well at low temperatures, every effort should be made to insure refrigerators are working at the correct temperature (if temperatures rise above 39°F [4°C], listeria will start to grow quickly) and that they are kept clean to prevent cross-contamination. Because of listeria's fondness for microwave "prepared" meals (which you should not be eating anyway!), these must be cooked thoroughly, and must never be eaten after the "best before" date.

Soft and unpasteurized cheeses are particularly prone to listeria contamination.

Any pregnant woman would be well advised to avoid soft cheeses (especially deep-fried) and pâtés for the term of her pregnancy. Additionally, because of the "manure" connection, all vegetables, salads, and fruit, which are usually eaten raw, need to be washed thoroughly before consumption.

WARNING

Publicity over the dangers of listeria poisoning has focused on unpasteurized milk products, but the bacterium can be found in pasteurized soft cheeses and pâtés too. Raw vegetables, fruit and salads can also be contaminated.

PROTEIN DEFICIENCY

One of the most important risk factors in the health of a newborn baby is size. Birth weight is a good indicator of organ development and viability. A large number of newborn deaths occur in babies under 5½ pounds (2.5kg) at birth. A small baby may be underdeveloped. The lungs, kidneys, liver, immune system, and other vital functions are not ready to make that infant independent of its mother's womb. Of all the raw materials needed to build a healthy baby in the uterus, protein is the most critical, followed closely by energy foods.

Fetal development is the only period in a human being's life when new brain cells are being developed. A low-protein diet during this phase can stunt the number of brain cells and produce a smaller brain.

A smaller brain usually has a different behavioral response and is less tolerant of its environmental changes. Furthermore, a smaller brain may have a lower learning capacity and may cause the development of certain emotional problems which do not surface until later in life.

On the other hand, recent research on cardiovascular risk factors in children, undertaken in Britain, has found that factors in the childhood environment, especially those determining height, head size, and weight/height ratio, are more related to high blood pressure, than birth weight. The differences in risk factors were not accounted for by differences in birth weight, and this indicated that events occurring after birth, rather than before, are likely to be important in the development of cardiovascular risk.

Protein needs for a pregnant woman are around an extra 1 oz (about 25g) per day to her nonpregnant requirements. No absolute levels can be given owing to biochemical individuality, but making sure the diet includes adequate protein is very important, especially toward the later stages of pregnancy when fetal growth is rapid.

PREMATURE LABOR

Some women go into labor prematurely and have to be hospitalized and treated with drugs to stop the contractions of the womb. There is some evidence to suggest that taking calcium, magnesium, and evening primrose oil regularly, can be very helpful in avoiding prematurity.

Nutritional Considerations During Pregnancy

Upon conception, cells lining the uterus are stimulated to grow and divide rapidly. Similarly rapid cellular division occurs in the developing embryonic tissue. In between cell divisions, the cell accumulates nutrients, especially amino acids and zinc. Both of these nutrients are, therefore, in great demand. In fact, some estimates have indicated that the requirements for vitamin B-complex, vitamin C, calcium, zinc, and magnesium increase by 30 to 100 percent during pregnancy.

The intake of food as a whole, increases by around 15 to 20 percent. A point to realize is that although the new mother is supporting two people, "eating for two" does not literally mean consuming twice as much food. This is due to several reasons, the main ones being that, to start with, a fetus is not as big as an adult, and secondly, the mother's body absorbs more of the nutrients from the gut during pregnancy and, therefore, obtains and uses more of the calories and nutrients taken in; consequently fewer are excreted.

Having said all this, when you become pregnant, don't let choosing food and eating become a stressful activity. Some women become so worried about what to eat and what not to eat that they lose some of the enjoyment of being pregnant. Nutrition is very important during pregnancy, but so is relaxation and peace of mind.

In addition to the New Pyramid diet, the following are important:

- *Try to eat a little carbohydrate, or take a small glass of apple juice, or ginger tea before rising – to help blood sugar stabilize a little, and help prevent "morning sickness."*
- *Always eat breakfast – preferably a protein food such as yogurt.*
- *Eat five or six small meals a day and have some complex carbohydrate – choose from brown rice, buckwheat, barley, oats, fruit, pulses (legumes), or vegetables – along with a little protein – choose from fish, lean meat and poultry, egg, yogurt, tofu, nuts, cottage or soy cheese – at each meal.*

- *If you are advised by a nutritional therapist to minimize your intake of mucus-forming foods, such as meat, eggs, and dairy produce, you will need to take special care that you obtain adequate levels of calcium from other sources such as canned fish (mainly from their soft, edible bones), tofu, vegetables, seeds, nuts, and pulses (legumes).*
- *Maximize your intake of fresh fruit and vegetables in order to insure that your essential nutrient intake is kept high.*
- *Maximize your intake of freshly ground mixed seeds, sesame, sunflower, pumpkin, and linseed, for a good range of minerals, vitamins, and essential fatty acids.*
- *Add wheat- or oatgerm to salads and soups, for essential fatty acids, iron, folic acid, and B vitamins.*
- *Eat at least some raw vegetables and sprouted seeds or sprouted pulses (legumes) each day, for extra minerals, vitamins, and natural enzymes.*
- *Minimize your intake of refined carbohydrate, sweet fruit and dried fruit, to prevent blood-sugar swings. If you find you cannot do without sugar, use fructose for sweetening food instead of sugar.*
- *Drink plenty of bottled or filtered water between meals to help flush out toxins.*
- *Minimize intake of tea, coffee, colas, and salt – instead drink herbal and fruit teas, grain coffees or dandelion coffee, and diluted fruit juices; use more herbs instead of salt.*
- *Avoid alcohol, sugar, processed food, food additives (especially food dyes, monosodium glutamate, aspartame), environmental pollutants (eat organic products whenever possible), saturated and hydrogenated fat, soft cheeses (to prevent listeria infection), common food allergens (wheat in bread, cow's milk, citrus), and trans-fatty acids.*

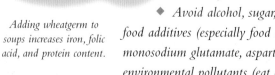

Adding wheatgerm to soups increases iron, folic acid, and protein content.

Suggested supplements

A high-quality multivitamin/multimineral complex containing all major nutrients but especially vitamins B6, B12, biotin, folic acid, vitamins C and E, calcium, magnesium, iron, and zinc; fish oils (not fish liver oils, but whole body fish oils) and evening primrose or starflower (borage) oil (make sure that any supplemented oils are described as pesticide-free). Avoid vitamin A.

NUTRITIONAL REQUIREMENTS DURING PREGNANCY

All nutrients are needed for a healthy pregnancy, just as they are at any time; the following are particularly important for the health of mother and baby.

NUTRIENT	REQUIRED FOR
Vitamin A	Fetal growth; visual development
Vitamin B6	Increased metabolism of protein
Vitamin B12	Red blood cell production; nervous system and brain
Folic Acid	Manufacture of D.N.A., and red blood cells; proper neural tube development
Biotin	Manufacture of fatty acids; insuring B12 and folic acid are used properly
Vitamin C	Collagen production; oxygen carriage; immune boosting
Vitamin E	Oxygen carriage; protection of R.N.A. and D.N.A.; wound healing
Iron	Red blood cells/oxygen carriage
Calcium	Fetal skeleton
Magnesium	Fetal skeleton; metabolism; muscle activity
Zinc	Enzyme reactions; growth; functioning of D.N.A. and R.N.A.; antagonist to heavy metals
E.P.A./D.H.A. in fish oils; G.L.A. in evening primrose oil	Prostaglandins and cell membranes; brain development; retina of the eye.

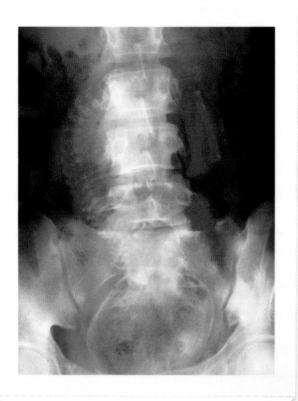

Colored X-ray of a healthy full-term fetus ready for birth with the head engaged.

BENEFITS OF GOOD NUTRITION FOR MOTHER AND BABY

- Reduces risk of certain major birth defects such as spina bifida and fetal alcohol syndrome.
- Prevents low birth-weight babies.
- Maximizes gestation period, to improve organ development and increase viability of the newborn infant.
- Reduces the frequency of miscarriages, premature deliveries, and other problems at delivery.
- Markedly lowers the incidence and severity of maternal health problems that are a risk to both mother and baby, such as hypertension (high blood pressure), edema, pre-eclampsia, and toxemia.
- Eliminates certain health problems in the mother, such as the risk of osteoporosis, infections, colds, varicose veins and hemorrhoids, gallstones, premature tooth loss, constipation, and leg cramps.
- Raises the physical, intellectual, and emotional health of most infants.

NOTE

There is controversy as to what constitutes a safe and sensible supplementation during pregnancy. There have been reports of isolated nutrients given in high doses causing congenital abnormalities, but a good-quality broad spectrum multiformula would not be dangerous. Always discuss your proposed supplement program with your physician beforehand.

OPTIMUM NUTRITION
AFTER THE BIRTH

T HE CONTINUATION OF AN *optimum nutrition diet is extremely important for the new mother. Nutritional therapists think that the distressing condition postnatal depression can be due to lack of several nutrients, especially vitamin B-complex, calcium, magnesium, and zinc. A good nutritional program such as the New Pyramid diet, or the more specific one for pregnancy (see page 206) is advised. The supplementation regime for pregnancy could be used in addition. There is, in part, a relationship between postnatal depression and thyroid disorders, so that a diet and supplementation program to nourish the thyroid glands might also be helpful.*

It is advisable for the mother to continue to follow a diet that is low in common allergens while she is breastfeeding. The reason for this is that even if she does not have an intolerance to any foodstuffs or any nutritional allergies herself, passing allergenic substances on to the delicate untrained system of the baby via the breast milk may encourage allergies and intolerances. (During pregnancy, such substances can be passed on through the placenta.) However, the risk is not as great as may be thought as breast milk contains an essential antibody which helps prevent the baby's immune system from reacting badly to foods. So long as breastfeeding continues for at least six months it will provide a good basis for preventing allergies, though not a guarantee against them.

Breastfeeding

It is very presumptuous of humans to assume that they can replace breast milk, which after all has been ideally formulated by nature, with "milks" of their own "scientific" design, as in the dried powdered varieties. No less of a problem is the use of milk of other animals – cow's milk is for calves, and, similarly, goat's milk is for kids, and sheep's milk for lambs. Giving any of these nonhuman milks to babies is likely to cause all manner of problems, from a range of nutritional imbalances to possible allergy. In fact, the closest milk to human milk is donkey milk! Some recent research has indicated that children who are breastfed up to a minimum of four months may have a reduced risk of high

Breast milk passes on to the baby an antibody that strengthens its immune system against contracting allergies

Even if the mother does not suffer from food intolerances they can still occur in the baby

Giving babies nonhuman milks can cause allergies or dietary imbalances

Food intolerances can be passed on through breast milk, although antibodies in the milk can protect against this occurring.

blood pressure, weight gain, and circulatory problems in adulthood. (However, there are many factors that relate to adult cardiovascular health.) Of course, if a woman is unable to breastfeed, then there is no other course of action but to use formula milks. However, if a mother can breastfeed her baby, she should be given every encouragement to do so.

Having said this, human milk is only going to be as good as the nutritional status of the mother, and if her diet has been anything less than optimum throughout her pregnancy, and even before, then there is a likelihood of her milk having sub-optimum levels of nutrients. Moreover, we are all exposed to environmental toxins, even those of us who eat organic food, and some of these toxins are passed into breast milk and then on to the infant, where, in susceptible babies, they may cause problems.

However, there is no reason why formula milks and nonhuman milks are any less contaminated than human breast milk; in fact, they are probably very much more so. Lead and other toxic metals, which can find their way into cow's milk, can have a disastrous effect on child development. In addition to being one of the causes of hyperactivity, lead toxicity in young children can cause retarded intelligence. The blood/brain barrier is not so well developed in young children and lead passes more easily from the blood, causing damage to the brain while it is still forming. Much of lead (and other metal) contamination comes from car exhaust fumes, or enters the body indirectly via contaminated foods.

Certain trace elements, amino acids, and essential fatty acids are present in human breast milk that are not available in the same form elsewhere. For example, breast milk contains, among many other nutrients, selenium and chromium. Neither of these minerals is usually present in formula milks. The mineral manganese in breast milk is in a much more absorbable form than in formula milk, vitamin E is higher in breast milk, and the vitamin D is more active in preventing rickets. Present, also, are some of the mother's antibodies which protect against certain infectious diseases during the first year of life. Breast milk tends to be deficient in zinc, but the good news is, that despite its lower levels, it is in a form that is much better absorbed than normal dietary zinc.

Eat as much organic produce as possible, so fewer toxins are passed into breast milk.

No matter what we are told by the scientists, biochemistry is still not sufficiently advanced to be able to identify every single item in breast milk, and it may well have other benefits not yet known about.

Sucking on a breast is much harder work than sucking on a teat of a bottle, and will encourage the development of much stronger jaw muscles, enabling the child to be much better at chewing good wholesome food later on. However, avoid breast/nipple creams based on peanut oil as it may cause nut allergies in children later on.

If you are unable to breastfeed your baby, choose the best formula milk you can find. Insure it does not contain added sugar or glucose. Compare the list of nutrient contents with other formula milks and choose the one with the highest amounts of nutrients. Especially important is the mineral zinc. It should also contain chromium, selenium, and manganese, though there are many formulas which don't contain these minerals.

USING FORMULA MILKS

If you have to use formula milks, insure they contain zinc, chromium, manganese, and selenium.

Formula milk may produce fewer allergies than fresh cow's milk, since allergenic components may have been altered.

PROBLEMS WITH BREASTFEEDING

The nutritional requirements of the mother are higher during breastfeeding than at other times, including during pregnancy. The nutrients that are required at higher levels are calcium, magnesium, iron, zinc, B vitamins, and folic acid. However, breast milk contains a vitamin K–inhibiting substance and to insure that the baby is obtaining sufficient vitamin K in his or her breast milk, the mother needs to eat sufficient cauliflower and cabbage, which are high in vitamin K. In the U.K. all babies are routinely given vitamin K at birth.

There is the possible problem of food allergy or intolerance developing as a result of the new infant reacting to allergens in the mother's milk. If defective genes are the cause of allergy and intolerance, then we might expect most allergies to begin early in life, as indeed they do. Symptoms cannot be produced the first time an individual is exposed to an allergen, since the immune system has to "prime" its recognition process; but, once this priming has occurred, a second exposure can stimulate antibody production. Despite this, a baby may react to a food allergen the first time he eats it because molecules of the food may have reached him by other means (e.g., in utero or through his mother's milk).

Some health problems in babies are a reaction to substances in their food.

A baby's immune system is not fully developed at birth. To protect it against infection in the first few months of life, the mother's milk contains antibodies to common micro-organisms, bacteria, and viruses. The baby's gut is "leaky" to allow these antibodies through into its bloodstream. Due to this necessary degree of permeability, far more undigested food molecules also get into the blood than in an older child or adult.

At the same time, the control reactions that regulate damaging immune reactions are not yet fully functioning. Any food that the baby eats or drinks during the first three months of life will be absorbed into the bloodstream in appreciable quantities. Some mechanisms, as yet poorly understood, prevent a baby from mounting a damaging reaction against its mother's breast milk proteins, although this can happen in extremely rare cases. Presumably this tolerance happens before birth while the baby is still in the womb. Because food molecules pass into breast milk from the mother's dietary intake, it is important for the mother to watch what she eats during the breastfeeding period. It would be beneficial if she could eat a basic but varied hypoallergenic diet.

Infantile colic is very often due to cow's milk intolerance. It is more common in bottle-fed babies, but breastfed babies are not immune. If a mother has taken cow's milk throughout pregnancy, and is still drinking cow's milk while breastfeeding, certain of the proteins derived from cow's milk will appear in her breast milk and will be taken into the gastrointestinal tract of the baby, where intolerance reactions may occur in a small number of susceptible babies.

The predominant organisms in the large intestine of breastfed infants are the bifidobacteria, which account for about 99 percent of the flora there. In formula-fed infants, the large intestinal flora resembles that of adolescents and adults, where, although the important bifidobacteria still make up the larger part, many more species are present. While these are not pathogenic bacteria, the reduced level

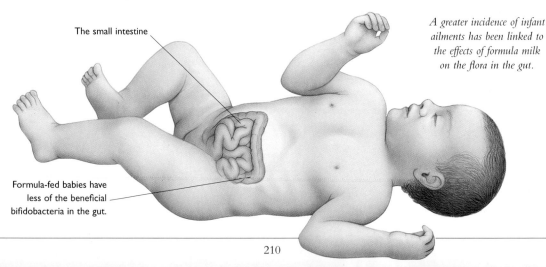

The small intestine

Formula-fed babies have less of the beneficial bifidobacteria in the gut.

A greater incidence of infant ailments has been linked to the effects of formula milk on the flora in the gut.

COW'S MILK

GOAT'S MILK

SOY MILK

A rotation system of formula milks (four days of cow's milk, four days of soy milk, and four days of goat's milk formula) may help your baby to avoid a milk allergy.

of bifidobacteria means that small influences, such as sudden changes in nutrition (e.g., at weaning), common infections, or vaccinations, may upset the microbial balance and bring on stomach aches, diarrhea, and other problems. Cultures of bifidobacterium, available in powder form specially formulated for infants, can be used to improve the levels of this bacterium in the infant's intestines, but you would be wise to discuss this with a nutritional therapist or your physician beforehand.

If a breastfed baby has eczema, skin problems, ear infections and blockage of the Eustachian tube, digestive problems, or problems sleeping, they are likely to be reacting to certain foods in the mother's diet. Cow's milk has already been mentioned as a potential "allergen" but others might be eggs, wheat, peanuts, some fish, some nuts, citrus, red wine, caffeine (in coffee, tea, colas, chocolate, etc.). The mother would be well advised to keep all major common food allergens out of her diet, and to note any consequent change in her infant's condition.

It is important that the mother's nutrition intake is not compromised in the process, and where a certain food, or group of foods, is removed from the diet, a good substitute should always be found. For example, if wheat is taken out, then rye, or other cereals can be used; soy or rice milk can be substituted in the mother's diet for cow's milk, or the mother may discover that although cow's milk produces digestive or skin reactions in her child, sheep's milk does not.

The direct genetic connection between mother's allergy picture and that of her offspring may not be so obviously derived as at first seems. For example,

identical twins (who have the same genetic makeup) can differ in terms of allergy. One twin may be affected, the other not. What does seem likely is that the *tendency* to allergy is inherited, and that early-life environmental factors, including nutrition, may push the system into allergic reaction. Early exposure to potential allergenic food is certainly a risk factor, especially for children of atopic parents (i.e., those showing classical allergic symptoms). The diet to follow then would be a hypoallergenic version of the New Pyramid program.

Nutritional therapists think that bottle-fed babies can escape the likelihood of intolerances if a rotation system is used for their formula milks. Four days of cow's milk formula, followed by four days of soy milk formula, and then four days of goat's milk formula, is a typical rotation. A rotation regime such as this is even more important if there is any family history of allergy.

Breast milk is prone to being low in vitamin K; mothers should eat cauliflower and cabbage to improve the content.

OPTIMUM NUTRITION FOR BABIES AND CHILDREN

B ECAUSE BABIES AND CHILDREN *are growing at a rapid rate, they are very susceptible to the effects of poor nutrition. Furthermore, young children have immune systems and detoxification mechanisms which are obviously immature, making them more susceptible to infectious agents, pollution, and toxins and additives in food. Being susceptible to infections is not always a bad thing, as it primes the immune system. But there is still the need for optimum intake of nutrients to allow a child to have a well-nourished immune system, so that when common childhood infections do strike (chickenpox, measles, German measles, etc.), the child will either suffer milder symptoms, and/or throw the infection off much more quickly.*

However, while it may be beneficial for children to be exposed to a certain level of infections, it is a different matter when considering pollutants and food allergens. Exposing very young children to such substances is not going to strengthen anything. So, what can be done?

Firstly, we can insure that a breastfed infant is receiving, as far as is possible, optimum, low-allergy, pollution-free nutrients in breast milk. This has to be done by paying attention to the mother's diet, as has been discussed on the previous pages. Secondly, for children at the weaning stage, we can insure that common allergenic foods, e.g., wheat, citrus fruit, are not given as "first foods."

Apples are a good source of soluble fiber for infants but they must be peeled and chopped into small pieces.

Good-quality prepared baby foods are now widely on sale, even organic ones.

Weaning

Babies' teeth usually start to erupt at around six months, so this is probably a good time to start weaning. Confirmation of "weaning time" might occur by baby needing many more milk feeds during the day or night. For example, going from a feed every four hours or so, to every two hours, indicates that a baby requires more nourishment. A general caution here, though, is that no baby should be given any "solid" food before the age of four months, since there is a very great likelihood of inducing food allergy before this time, due to immaturity of the digestive system. But certainly by about eight months, some food other than breast milk (or formula milk) ought to have been given regularly. For one thing,

Babies need to move to solid foods when they show signs of hunger more frequently

Care needs to be given to the baby's food when weaning starts in order to insure good nutrition and healthy habits.

the baby's iron stores will be getting low, and for another the risk of infection may increase if more complex foods are withheld, since good levels of all nutrients are needed for a well-functioning immune system.

Chewing on some solid food is a good way to encourage the teeth to come through properly. However, when looking at the types of food usually recommended for teething at this stage – "a crust of wholewheat bread," a teething cookie, or rusk – you find that most of them are wheat-based foods. A better idea would be to give them a crust of rye bread. Just as with healthy adults, healthy babies remain so by being given food that is fresh and unprocessed. Babies have no need of extra sugar, salt, or any other additives, and, indeed, if condiments are added to "give food more flavor," it might be the down-payment of problems later on, producing older children who are "faddy eaters." If parents eat a natural wholefood diet and the baby is encouraged to eat natural foods from the start, he/she will be more likely to fit in with the parents' meals as he gets older.

Soft fruits, such as banana, are nutritious weaning foods.

So many mothers these days seem to have to prepare one meal for themselves and their partners, and different meals for the children. This is very time consuming, and not the sort of example that should be encouraged to develop healthy lifestyles in our offspring. However, there will be times when meals need to be prepared hurriedly, or at different times from the parents, and then recourse may be made to good-quality baby foods. Prepared baby foods have improved enormously over the last ten years or so, as the message has been getting through. It is now very likely that you will be able to choose from a range of baby foods which do not contain any artificial additives, sugar, cow's milk, or wheat, and are made from good wholesome ingredients. Some are even organic ranges! As, on occasions we adults resort to something prepackaged, the important thing is to read the label carefully on all baby foods. If it contains cereal, it needs to be unrefined, and would be better if it were rice or oat cereal rather than wheat; plain white rice has a very low allergenicity and is highly digestible. Baby food should not contain added glucose, dextrose, sucrose, maltose, fructose, or modified starch, hydrolized protein, or any ingredient which sounds like a chemical.

Despite the fact that one of the aims of infant feeding is to help them to get to like the food you do, young children do not need the same amount of "fiber" as an adult. Even infants with large appetites will not have mastered chewing to such an extent that all fibrous foods will be broken down adequately. Soluble fibers found in apples, a little oatmeal, or rice pudding, will be more than sufficient to keep their bowels working properly. At the start of weaning, babies need food that is very easily digested and non-allergenic. Cooked, pureed vegetables and fruit are a good start. If your child can cope with a little raw apple, cucumber, or carrot, then let them (but supervise). If these raw foods are too difficult, then try a little banana, avocado, soft pear, or other such fruit. If you have a family history of allergy (eczema, asthma, hayfever, etc.), or if you suspect your child may react strongly to common allergenic foods, e.g., wheat, then leave these foods a while longer. Wheat should never be introduced before six months of age. Always leave the introduction of potential food allergens until as late as possible in the weaning period.

WEANING FOODS

"Ancestral foods" (fruit, vegetables, seeds, nuts, fish) can be introduced first, and as each group is taken without problems, move onto the next. Leave wheat, potatoes, milk (especially cow's), and citrus fruit until later.

Introduce new foods to your child gradually so that if any adverse reaction is experienced, it is easy to pinpoint the cause.

PUREES	FRESH FOODS
Carrots	Banana, avocado, soft pear
Cauliflower	Peeled apple, raw carrot, cucumber
Mixed vegetable – e.g., carrot/cauliflower/turnip	Creamed nuts – except peanuts, and seeds – except sesame. Insure no solid pieces remain for baby to choke on
Different vegetable mixes – e.g., carrot/cauliflower/celery/beans	Cooked (soft) lentils and haricot beans
Apple	Fish (well cooked insure no bones)/canned
Mixed fruit purees – e.g., apple and banana	Cooked white rice/cooked rice flakes
Different vegetable mixes, now including potato	Cooked ground lamb, chicken or turkey
Soy milk yogurt	Cooked oats, barley flakes, rye bread – introduced separately in case of a reaction
Cottage cheese	Other vegetables not yet used (introduce one at a time in case of reaction)
Goat's milk custards	Oranges
Sheep's milk products	Wheat flakes, whole wheat bread, wheat cereal
	Cow's milk, and milk products
	Eggs
	Other "high allergenic" foods and "nightshade" foods

As you proceed with weaning, continue to breast-feed or give formula milk and introduce one or two new foods into the child's diet every three or four days, starting with homemade cooked fruit purees. Make a note of any foods which may have caused a reaction in the child, such as a mild skin rash, drowsiness, runny nose, sneezing, or excessive thirst. If any of these reactions do occur, withdraw the suspect food until later on in the weaning process, when the digestive system is more mature, at which point you can try it again. Foods such as tomatoes, potatoes, and sweet peppers (which all belong to the same family as the deadly nightshade), together with citrus fruit, wheat, cow's milk products, and eggs (plus any foods to which either parent is known to have an intolerance), should be left out until the child is at least ten months old. Part of the problem with common allergens like wheat and cow's milk is that because the infant's intestine is much more permeable than the adult's, large protein fragments can be absorbed directly into the blood. If high-protein allergenic foods like milk, wheat, or eggs are introduced into the diet too early, they can set the stage for lifelong allergy. Breast milk seems to protect against this foreign protein absorption by sealing the intestinal mucosa and making it less permeable. In the case of wheat, the digestive enzymes necessary for proper starch digestion are not present until an infant is around four to six months old. Babies with the most colds and allergies have often been observed to eat the most starches.

It is important to supply the baby with some type of milk throughout the weaning process. Breast milk is best but, if this is not possible, nutritional therapists advise that you give the baby full cream sheep's milk, goat's milk or soy milk with added calcium until the age of at least 12 months. Take care that any children who are having goat's or sheep's milk, have the milk pasteurized, until the age of two. Other mothers will continue with formula milk through the weaning process.

The following simple rules apply throughout the weaning process:

- *Do not give a child any sugar – insulin swings can bring on irritability, crying spells, excessive thirst, and lead to a "sweet tooth."*
- *Encourage the fruit-eating habit – young children can get through three or four pieces a day.*
- *Encourage the drinking of water – plain (filtered) water should be the usual drink to quench a thirst, but diluted fruit juices can be given, too.*
- *Encourage chewing – most chewing is done by the molars (which babies haven't got) but many foods can be chewed by the gums to encourage strong tooth formation.*
- *Don't use "candy" as a treat – never give candy, cookies, chocolate, or cake as a reward or to cheer a child up – find something else (nonedible) to give them, or a big hug.*

- *Encourage eating a variety of foods – but remember that babies being weaned do not need the variety an adult needs.*
- *Encourage the habit of stopping eating when satiated – never tell young children they must clean up their plate, to please you or any other inducement to eat more than they need.*
- *Don't give infants foods you won't want them to eat when they're older – junk foods are very easy to eat; don't give them to your toddler, and expect them not to like them when they are a teenager.*
- *Set a good example – if the adults in the family eat good wholesome food, don't stuff themselves but appreciate an odd treat, it is likely your children will grow up to believe this is the norm.*

General rules on healthy eating do not apply so rigidly to the under-fives. Overzealous application of adult "low-fat, high-fiber" principles can result in underweight children. Where a child is given animal milk it should be full fat.

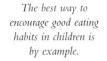

Do not give candies as a treat; this encourages bad nutritional habits.

The best way to encourage good eating habits in children is by example.

Teach your children to appreciate good wholesome food

Encourage children to chew food thoroughly

Offer healthy snacks, not junk food, as a treat

Supplements for Children

BABIES

Both breast-fed babies and those on formula milks may have their "diets" supplemented with vitamin drops, which are available from the baby clinic, the pharmacy, or health food stores. These drops usually contain reasonable levels of vitamins A, C, and D, and will satisfy basic vitamin needs. There are also available various "drops" and "tonics" suitable for babies from six months to three years of age which contain vitamins A and D, and several minerals (usually various salts) including iron, potassium, calcium, manganese, and copper, but to insure a child gets all the necessary nutrients (including minerals, vitamins, and essential fatty acids), a weaning program, started around six months of age, necessarily needs to include the foods as outlined for weaning.

YOUNG CHILDREN

When children have been used to fresh wholesome nourishment from birth, their diet will usually continue along the same lines, with occasional "hiccups" under peer pressure to eat junk food. If, however, you are a parent who came to nutritional healing a little after your babies became children, do not despair, simply encourage them, along with the rest of the family, to undertake the basics of the New Pyramid diet. Of particular importance is the type and level of fat eaten by growing children. No child should be eating great quantities of saturated or hydrogenated fat, or eating large amounts of sweet foods. Diets high in fat and sugar are just as bad for children as they are for adults. This is confirmed by results from a recent assessment of young children for cardiovascular fitness, which showed a great deterioration when compared to one or two decades ago. However, young children do need a good supply of essential fatty acids for brain development, immune function, and general health, and these can be supplied by fish and wholefoods (especially seeds).

For growing children, the nutrients especially important include: vitamin A (for membrane integrity – protecting against infection); vitamin B-complex (for energy production, growth, brain and nerve development); vitamin C (good development of skin, connective tissue, and brain); calcium and magnesium (for healthy bones and teeth); zinc (for R.N.A.

Insuring children establish a good cardiovascular system through diet is more important today, as in our modern lifestyle they tend to exercise less.

and D.N.A., and growth); fatty acids (proper cellular development, especially brain cells); and iron, chromium, selenium, and manganese.

The World Health Organization has found that around 85 percent of adult cancers are avoidable and, of these, around half are related to deficiencies of diet, some of which date back to childhood.

NUTRITIONAL SUPPLEMENTS AND INTELLIGENCE

There is also increasing evidence that poor diet not only affects children physically but also intellectually. A diet low in vitamins and minerals has been shown to affect behavior and concentration, as well as causing learning diffi- culties. Recent work carried out in the United States on nutrient levels in blood, indicates that adequate levels of vitamins A, B- complex, C, and E are important if children are to reach their highest potential nonverbal I.Q. (their ability to process information); vitamins B_1, B_3, B_6, and C, seem to be of particular significance to brain function. Iron and magnesium were found to be the most important minerals for boosting I.Q. levels. The most worrying data revealed that a high frequency of the children who were not receiving enough of the right nutrients for optimum brain function, were consuming an average Western diet. Some of the best sources of vitamins and minerals are green leafy vegetables, such as watercress and spinach, or herbs such as parsley. Unfortunately, these are the very foods that many children simply refuse to eat. If, therefore, you, as a parent, are concerned that your children are not getting suffi- cient vitamins and minerals, one solution is to give them a daily multivitamin and mineral supplement. However, parents need not rush out and buy mega- doses of vitamins and minerals for their offspring. The work undertaken so far indicates that those chil- dren whose blood showed borderline deficiencies improved by taking 50 percent of the U.S.A. recom- mended daily allowance (R.D.A.) dosage. Others taking megadoses did not show such great improve- ments over those who were taking around 100 percent of the U.S.A. R.D.A. (which is slightly higher than the U.K. R.D.A.). It is thought that the reason

Spinach, eaten raw, is an excellent source of vitamins and minerals.

for this is that high levels of certain nutrients impair the absorption of others. The experts now seem to agree that children with an insufficient intake of nutrients from their diet can significantly increase their nonverbal I.Q. potential by taking vitamin and mineral supplements.

Research history in the United Kingdom into the effect of vitamin and mineral supplements on children's I.Q. goes back to the late 1980s when clin- ical studies revealed that a proportion of the children taking supplements significantly increased their nonverbal I.Q. over those taking a placebo. A similar study was carried out in the United States at the same time. Soon after, however, additional studies discred- ited the theory that nutrition was important to intelligence. More than ten years on, the validity of the nega- tive studies is in question and the weight of positive evidence to support the theory seems conclusive.

SUPPLEMENTS AVAILABLE FOR GROWING CHILDREN

Supplements available for young children contain a variety of vitamins and minerals, and usually include vitamins B_6, folic acid, B_{12}, pantothenic acid, iron, zinc, and iodine, in addition to those nutrients found in "baby" drops. As with adults, supplements are not given instead of a wholesome diet, but in addition to it, as "insurance" against disease and ill-health. If you find you have a faddy child, giving them a supple- ment to tide them over would be one answer. Supplements for children are usually in liquid, powder, or chewable forms, for ease of swallowing. Make sure any you buy are not flavored with artifi- cial substances, or contain large amounts of sugar.

If you do decide to give your growing child a nutritional supplement, be very careful that you obtain a supplement correct for the age of your child, and do not be tempted to increase the dose if they decide on some days not to eat much. Children are more susceptible to vitamin toxicity than adults, so a great deal of care is needed. Once a child reaches the age of around 12 years, they can generally take multicomplexes at the dosage level of an adult, but it would always be wise to consult with a nutri- tionist or your physician first.

FOOD ALLERGIES AND HYPERACTIVITY IN CHILDREN

FOOD ALLERGIES CAN RESULT *in a vast range of different symptoms. The most common in children are asthma, eczema, behavioral problems, and hyperactivity (attention deficit disorder). With asthma and eczema, the cause of the allergies is often quite direct, with cow's milk products, eggs, wheat, or citrus being the more common ones. However, those symptoms which have some degree of emotional/intellectual involvement can be caused by food allergens which are much less easy to spot, and may be related to several food components, rather than one or two particular foods. For example, the association between food dyes and hyperactivity in young children is now very well documented. For these children a regime based on the Feingold Diet has had a tremendous amount of success. It is not all that easy to follow, particularly if your child is a "faddy" eater, but it is worth a try.*

Hyperactivity (sometimes called attention deficit disorder), minimal brain dysfunction, and behavioral problems can totally destroy family life. Parents often suffer incredible tension, profound helplessness, frustration, and guilt, as they attempt to deal with their own pent-up emotions, which arise in reaction to their child's behavior. For the unlucky families, hyperactivity in a child can transform parenthood from what was hoped would be a beautiful experience into an endless nightmare.

Conventional medicine uses a variety of drugs to sedate the child. Amphetamines, such as Ritalin, have also been used. The paradox is that this drug would normally intensify activity in someone without the disorder, but in the hyperactive child it encourages blood flow to the appropriate part of the brain, calming the child down. Some of these drugs may temporarily calm the symptoms, but do not heal the cause. The diet opposite uses the criteria of nutritional healing to get to the root of many of these symptoms.

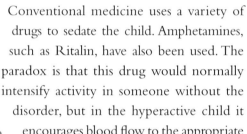

Inhalers help with the symptoms but do not cure the condition

In asthma the airways become constricted

Asthma can be caused by an allergy to a common food.

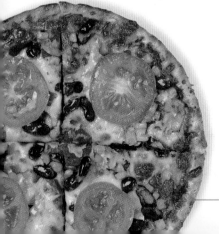

One of the most common childhood allergies is asthma, which can last throughout life.

HYPERACTIVITY AND BEHAVIORAL PROBLEMS

Hyperactivity, attention-deficit disorder, minimal brain dysfunction, and other behavioral problems often start in very young children and in any case before the age of seven years. They may continue in some form into adult life. Characteristics include restlessness, temper tantrums, self-inflicted damage, poor verbal communication, fearlessness, impulsiveness, egocentricity, short attention span, and marked distractibility. More boys than girls suffer and mostly they have golden blond hair. Many seem to have a high level of copper in their bodies, and this might be, in part, reflected in their hair color. High copper levels automatically raise the need for zinc. Zinc is vital for proper brain function, especially for the ability to absorb information. Zinc (together with vitamin C) is extremely useful in lowering levels of heavy metals such as lead in the body.

For these problems, the following nutritional considerations should be taken into account:

◆ *low intake of protein (a moderate protein diet has a calming effect, probably due to its effect on blood sugar).*
◆ *sugar.*
◆ *refined carbohydrates.*
◆ *low intake of zinc.*
◆ *food additives, flavorings, colors, preservatives, monosodium glutamate, aspartame.*
◆ *environmental pollutants.*
◆ *food allergy/intolerance.*
◆ *salicylate sensitivity.*
◆ *caffeine (colas, chocolate – also tea and coffee if used).*
◆ *heavy metal toxicity (causing lowered zinc levels etc.).*
◆ *generalized mineral and vitamin deficiencies (especially B3, B6, biotin, zinc, and magnesium – all needed to convert essential fatty acids to prostaglandins).*
◆ *hypoglycemia.*
◆ *low levels of essential fatty acids.*

Hyperactivity benefits from a diet which omits fruits containing salicylates.

DIET

In addition to following the New Pyramid diet:

- Maximize intake of vegetables and non-salicylate fruit e.g., bananas, mango, kiwi, pear, pineapple.
- Maximize intake of mixed seeds (pumpkin, sesame, sunflower, and ground linseed).
- Balance animal protein (oily fish, lean meat, free-range egg occasionally) with vegetable protein (tofu, soy yogurt, pulses [legumes], nuts, seed vegetables).
- Insure adequate fiber from brown rice, a small amount of oats and/or rye, fruit and vegetables (celluloses and pectins).

- Balance all meals with regard to protein and carbohydrate (equal balance – do not give either in excess). Avoid totally sugar, refined carbohydrates, all food colors, preservatives, flavorings, monosodium glutamate, aspartame, salt, yeast, common allergenic foods (wheat, cow's milk products, and salicylates), cola, and chocolate. As substitutes for some of these, a little fructose can be used, soy milk and rice milk instead of cow's milk, soy cheese, and sugar-free carob instead of chocolate.
- Convert as near as possible to a fully organic diet.

Suggested supplements:

A high-quality children's formula having good levels of vitamin B-complex (especially B1, B3, B6, and B12), vitamin C, vitamin E, calcium, magnesium, zinc, chromium, iron, iodine, and selenium; essential fatty acids – evening primrose oil (or starflower oil) and whole fish body oil (rather than fish liver oil); *Ginkgo biloba* (check this is a suitable level for children).

Foods containing natural salicylates

ALMONDS
APPLES
BLACKBERRIES
CHERRIES
CLOVES
CRANBERRIES
CUCUMBERS AND PICKLES
CURRANTS
GOOSEBERRIES
GRAPES/RAISINS
MINT AND MINT FLAVORS
NECTARINES
ORANGES/TANGERINES/
CLEMENTINES
PEACHES
PLUMS/PRUNES
RASPBERRIES
STRAWBERRIES
SWEET PEPPERS
TEA
TOMATOES
(AND TOMATO SAUCE)

Food colorings – many of which are linked with hyperactivity – should be avoided.

NUTRITIONAL CONSIDERATIONS DURING ADOLESCENCE

*D*ESPITE ALL PARENTS' ATTEMPTS *at providing good nutrition and being good examples themselves of both healthy lifestyle and impeccable nutrition, this is going to be the hardest time to insure your children are eating well. Peer pressure is very difficult for children to resist; they cannot be seen to be "health freaks" and stand out in a crowd. The wholesome foods you are sending them to school with will probably, on some occasions, end up in the trash, while they spend their hard-earned pocket money on chips and candy. There is not a lot you can do about this. Providing a nourishing evening meal (containing a good balance of high-quality protein and vegetables plus a little grain occasionally) when all the family sits down and eats together, insures at least some daily nutrient standards are being met. You may also get them to cooperate in taking a high-potency multiformula.*

Recent work in the U.S.A. on child vandals, and older offenders claims that a poor diet high in sugar (in particular), refined and processed foods and low in fresh wholefoods has a direct effect on the times an offender commits a crime. Some researchers also claim that juvenile delinquents, unresponsive to counseling, became more "counselable" when provided with essential fatty acid-rich oils. Other studies undertaken in jails claim that improving the quality of food, reducing sugar and wheat, and the addition of multicomplex supplements, has a great stabilizing effect on behavior. Improvements have been noted in some people with mental disorders such as schizophrenia when they have been placed on a whole-food diet and given specific supplements, often including zinc.

The additional problems of adolescence are usually focused around increased hormone production which may temporarily disrupt metabolism. This is also the age of "growth spurts." Adolescents need a high level of good-quality protein, complex carbohydrates (and if they refuse many of the vegetables you offer them, at least give them whole grains, pastas, rice, and bread) and adequate vitamins and minerals for their growth. One mineral commonly deficient in these years is zinc, especially if the young adult is not keen on seeds, shellfish, and vegetables. Often, low intakes of zinc, and other minerals, are said by some therapists to be associated both with "teenage spots" and more serious acne.

Much more worrying, however, is the idea among teenage girls that they are fat, no matter how slim they really are. Again we are back to peer pressure, but, more insidiously, we are confronted with the appearance of female models on the fashion runway, on television, in advertisements, and in magazines. This is a serious matter. Approximately one-third of anorexics die from their condition by starving themselves to death.

Although there is a nutritional component to diseases such as anorexia and bulimia, there is also psychological disturbance which may be triggered by nutrient deficiency and must be treated appropriately. Both anorexia nervosa and bulimia nervosa are primarily psychological disorders focusing on issues of

Good nutrition is especially important in adolescence, but harder to achieve.

"control." Both are also becoming much more common in young men.

Zinc deficiencies can play a key role in bizarre eating behavior, in particular the level of appetite. One of the functions of zinc is to help maintain a healthy appetite. Further to the findings that zinc supplementation has been effective in improving the appetite and attitude of anorexics, zinc has also been shown to improve the appetites of children who are "picky" eaters, and the elderly. Many of the symptoms of anorexia coincide with the symptoms of zinc deficiency, in particular the loss of sense of taste and smell, and loss of hair. It is interesting to note that taking of the contraceptive pill, even for short periods of time, encourages loss of zinc from the body.

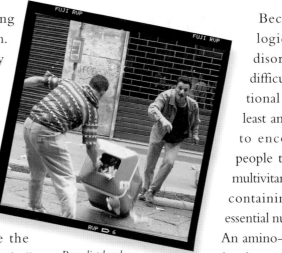

Poor diet has been found by research to be a factor in vandalism.

To go some way in solving the ever-growing problem of eating disorders in the young teenage population, a "preventive" strategy is likely to be a better approach than struggling with the psychological aspects of these conditions when they appear. Insuring children of prepubescent age eat well, and in particular regularly consume foods high in zinc, would be excellent grounding. It is likely that even "picky" eaters and those struggling with peer pressure, can be encouraged to a eat a handful of pumpkin seeds every day. Girls, especially, should be encouraged to have zinc-rich foods daily before the onset of puberty and beyond, so that in the event of the contraceptive pill being taken at a later stage, essential zinc status will not be compromised, and will remain adequate to fulfill bodily needs.

Bulimics have been found to have lower levels of circulating endorphins – the body's internally produced morphine-like "pleasure compounds." Binge-eating and an obsession with food may stem, at least initially, from a lack of pleasure. Copper deficiencies are also related to low endorphin levels in the brain, but since copper and zinc are antagonistic minerals, it has to be assumed here that low copper levels occur concurrently with low zinc levels.

Because of the psychological aspects of eating disorders, it is extremely difficult to suggest a nutritional regime. However, at least an attempt can be made to encourage these young people to take a good-quality multivitamin/multimineral daily, containing good levels of all essential nutrients, especially zinc. An amino-acid complement may also be very useful. However, because of the disturbed nature of their nutritional understanding, care must be taken to insure that overdosing does not occur. After successful psychological treatment, there may be a better case for arranging a healthy nutritional regime, based on the New Pyramid diet.

The look of models in the media is a powerful factor in the self-image of adolescent girls.

If adolescents refuse to eat properly, they might be persuaded to take supplements.

NUTRITIONAL CONSIDERATIONS DURING THE MENOPAUSE

MENOPAUSE WAS PROBABLY INTENDED *by nature to be a gradual process of reduced estrogen output by the ovaries with few, if any, side effects. In the normal, healthy, well-nourished, and active woman, during the menopause the pituitary sends signals to the other glands such as the adrenals, to increase their estrogen output. This back-up system helps to keep some estrogen in circulation and helps maintain a portion of the secondary sexual characteristics required to remain feminine. It is possibly due to adrenal gland exhaustion from poor diet, hypoglycemia, and stress that this back-up system starts to fail, leading to menopausal symptoms. These widely accepted symptoms of menopause include hot flashes, sweating, headaches, loss of libido, vaginal dryness, etc.*

Another, little mentioned, symptom is the emergence of food intolerances. This may be because of increased toxic load on the body. Lack of menstruation may prevent loss of toxins in menstrual blood, and thereby effectively reduces a woman's ability to eliminate them. Undertaking a detoxification diet (*see* Appendix Three, page 236) for a while may help eliminate some menopausal symptoms.

Commonly, though, the emergence of menopausal symptoms is related to change in hormonal status as a woman reaches the end of her childbearing years. Women who have been exposed to extra hormones in their mother's womb (from the mother having previously taken the contraceptive pill or fertility stimulants) may stop ovulating as early as their 20s,

and women who are zinc-deficient, smokers, or heavy drinkers may undergo an early menopause.

At the menopause, the eggs in a woman's ovaries are used up and fresh follicles can no longer be stimulated by her pituitary hormones. As a result her ovaries stop making estrogen and progesterone. The adrenal glands and fat (adipose) tissue continue, however, to make a small amount of estrogen. Some women simply stop bleeding. Others have severe hormone withdrawal symptoms, such as hot flashes with drenching night sweats. Hot flashes are thought by some people to be a reaction to a fall in estrogen levels, not a sign of estrogen deficiency. Also they are very similar in nature to some symptoms related to food intolerances. Nutritional therapists suggest that

Various side effects of the menopause, such as headaches, are widespread.

Sudden changes in mood can be very unsettling.

Hot flashes may be a reaction to the decline in levels of estrogen.

Some women who have not been prone to it before find they become easily upset.

hot flashes are the result of an allergic reaction and advise a hypoallergenic diet (*see* page 232). The more severe the intolerant reactions to foods (and chemicals, perfumes etc.), the greater the likelihood of essential nutrient deficiencies. Restoring the essential nutrient levels may decrease the number of reactive foods. Some nutritional therapists are against hormone replacement therapy (H.R.T.) because they believe that steroid and sex hormones raise copper and lower serum zinc levels, and also interfere with liver function, metabolism of food, and disrupt the balance of gut flora. This may mean that women who are given extra estrogen after the menopause are likely to have even more intense menopausal symptoms when they stop taking the extra hormones. There is anecdotal evidence for this.

NOTE

There are many extremely useful herbal concoctions which are said to be particularly nourishing to the glands involved. You will need to consult a herbalist or ask your health food store for a good-quality product.

Vitamin E supplements are said to be particularly useful for helping reduce hot flashes and cold sweats, and vitamin E oil can be applied externally for vaginal dryness.

MENOPAUSAL SYMPTOMS

The following nutritional considerations should be taken into account:

◆ *low intake of zinc and other important micronutrients (e.g., calcium, magnesium, vitamin B-complex, vitamin D, vitamin E, and E.F.A.s).*

◆ *toxicity – may need Detoxification Diet.*

◆ *food allergy/intolerance – may need Hypoallergenic Diet.*

◆ *refined carbohydrates and sugar (causing hypoglycemia).*

◆ *excess stimulants (tea, coffee, alcohol).*

◆ *poor intake of nutrients generally or poor absorption – may need Food Combining Diet.*

◆ *low stomach acid.*

Vitamin supplements can help with menopausal symptoms.

DIET

In addition to following the New Pyramid diet:

- Maximize intake of fresh vegetables and fruit (organic whenever possible).
- Maximize intake of freshly ground mixed seeds (sunflower, pumpkin, sesame, and linseed).
- Maximize intake of vegetable protein, especially tofu and other soy products (soy milk, soy yogurt, miso, tempeh), pulses (legumes), nuts, seeds, and seed vegetables (green beans, etc.).
- Add wheatgerm or oatgerm to your salads and soups for extra B vitamins and iron.
- Use cold-pressed olive oil on salads, for extra vitamin E.
- Use fructose to sweeten drinks and foods – go carefully though.
- Drink plenty of bottled or filtered water between meals.
- Eat at least some raw vegetables and sprouted seeds daily for natural plant enzymes.
- If indigestion is a problem – sip a little diluted freshly squeezed lemon juice with the main meal of the day.
- Minimize intake of animal protein – have a little oily fish, shellfish (for zinc), and lean meat.

- Minimize intake of grain carbohydrates (as high levels can lead to overweight), but have plenty of vegetable carbohydrates – pulses (legumes), fresh vegetables, and fruit.
- Minimize intake of stimulants such as tea and coffee and replace with fruit or herbal teas (Rooibosh or Luaka are more like ordinary tea) and grain coffees.
- Minimize intake of alcohol, as this can rob the body of important minerals.
- Avoid refined carbohydrates, sugar, processed food, saturated and hydrogenated fats, trans-fatty acids, food additives, environmental pollutants (eat organic whenever possible), and common food allergens.
- In addition to the symptoms listed to the left, some women start to suffer from an overgrowth of yeast as the hormone levels change. Avoiding yeast-containing, sweet food, refined carbohydrates, alcohol, and sweet fruit can help.

Suggested supplements

A high-potency multivitamin/multimineral complex containing good levels of vitamins A, B-complex (especially B_5 and B_6), C, and E, calcium, magnesium, zinc, iodine, and selenium; bioflavonoids (such as hesperidin); essential fatty acids (evening primrose oil and fish oils); royal jelly; kelp; Siberian ginseng; *Aloe vera* juice; lecithin; wild yam extract; Agnus castus; blackcurrant seed oil; Dong quai; gamma-oryzanol; digestive enzymes.

A probiotic supplement, such as *Lactobacillus acidophilus*, may be required for yeast overgrowth.

Hormone Replacement Therapy (H.R.T.)

Hormone replacement therapy is hormonal replacement to delay menopause. It involves the administration of estrogen and sometimes synthetic progesterone. Originally, H.R.T. consisted of an estrogen-only therapy, which undoubtedly reduced the risk of heart disease and decreased many of the unpleasant symptoms associated with menopause, but was shown in some studies to increase the risk of developing endometrial cancer (cancer of the uterine lining). To counteract the cancer-forming effect of estrogens, new combinations were introduced that included progesterone, which reduced the incidence of endometrial cancer, but lessened the protective advantage for heart disease and osteoporosis.

Progesterone is also linked to varicose veins, thrombosis, and several other conditions. However, many studies do indicate a real benefit from H.R.T. in terms of decreased menopausal symptoms. It is well known that estrogen decreases hot flashes and vaginal dryness, but unfortunately it can also cause side effects such as weight gain, bloating, moodiness, and irritability. It is also interesting to note that these side effects mimic the symptoms of P.M.S. which appear in women who are in estrogen dominance when progesterone falls rapidly (at a greater rate than estrogen) before menstruation.

This natural progesterone has been shown to decrease the risk of breast cancer and help reverse osteoporosis. Synthetic progesterone (progestin) has a molecular structure that is slightly different from natural progesterone, and this may be responsible for the side effects, mentioned above. H.R.T. is not as helpful in preventing osteoporosis as was first thought. It has been shown that only women who have been on H.R.T. for seven years or longer have a slower loss of bone density, and even those who have been on H.R.T. for more than ten years do not seem to be too well protected from fractures.

Dandelion and Milk thistle help the liver to detoxify artificial hormones.

Mostly, H.R.T. merely postpones symptoms of the menopause and, in addition, can mask real problems. It has been linked to cancers of the uterus and breast, cardiovascular disease, stroke, weight problems, and alterations in the balance of vitamins and minerals in the body. It has been demonstrated that H.R.T. increases the body's need for vitamin B-complex, especially B5, and vitamin E, and reduces zinc levels. Many general practitioners, quite rightly, do not believe that H.R.T. prevents vascular disease, as they have seen the identical hormones cause thrombosis, embolism, and high blood pressure. A great deal too many women on H.R.T. are developing breast and cervical cancers.

Remember, too, that taking large amounts of any hormones will put the liver under a great deal of stress as it tries to detoxify them. Liver-strengthening herbs like Milk thistle or dandelion may be appropriate, provided that you discuss this with your herbalist first.

Hormones can drive us wild with passion; they can also make us feel very uncomfortable. The dramatic fluctuations in estrogen around the time of the menopause may bring on depression, mood swings, anger, weepiness, and anxiety, and make you feel totally out of control. H.R.T. has not proved particularly helpful in stemming the tide of these emotional ups and downs, since it is adding to the intensity of the fluctuations. As a result of the current problems with H.R.T., many women are starting to question its use, as they are the contraceptive pill, and are asking for an alternative to synthetic hormones.

Much information now suggests that synthetic hormones do not act in the same way as the natural hormone does in the body, and current studies on natural hormones, such as the progesterone-like substance (diosgenin – a precursor to natural progesterone) extracted from wild yam, show they could counter menopausal symptoms, and reduce the risk of osteoporosis and heart disease. The adaptogenic herbs, such as Agnus castus and Dong quai, have been used for centuries to balance hormonal levels, prevent hot flashes, and relieve psychological symptoms. Vitamin E has multiple benefits including its ability to help prevent hot flashes, reduce the risk of heart disease, and protect the skin against aging. Evening primrose oil and fish oils complement vitamin E in providing additional protection against coronary disease and strokes, as well as improving skin conditions. After heart disease, avoiding osteoporosis is the biggest concern for women who have passed through the initial, uncomfortable symptoms of menopause. The demineralization of bones that causes fragility starts as early as the mid-20s, so a good diet is essential from a young age. Walking briskly for 20 minutes three times a week puts calcium back into bones.

Japanese women do not seem to suffer the same degree of menopausal debility that Western women do, and it is very likely that this is related to diet. To emulate the Eastern diet, reduce the amount of animal foods, except fish and shellfish, and processed foods, and place the emphasis on plenty of organic vegetables, fruit, and soy-based foods (tofu and miso), which contain natural hormone-like substances. Other foods containing phytoestrogens include fennel, celery, parsley, rhubarb, hops, linseed oil (flax seed oil), nuts, and seeds. The estrogen-like substances found in plants, have not been associated with the side effects

of H.R.T. However, women with endometriosis must not take hormones, including phytoestrogens, and women with poor liver function do not experience relief of symptoms. Carrying out a detoxification program (*see* Appendix Three) before using plant estrogens is likely to have a greater effect.

There is a good case for using minimal, safer levels of H.R.T. for women who have undergone a surgical menopause at an early age. However, many of the symptoms of menopause are closely linked with the symptoms of general nutrient deficiencies, food intolerances, toxicity, and stress, so optimum nutrition has a powerful impact on health at this time.

Japanese women generally suffer less from the effects of the menopause than Westerners.

The lower incidence of unpleasant side effects of the menopause among Japanese women is probably due to the nature of their diet.

Soy-based foods contain hormone-like substances

Much more fish is eaten in Japan than meat

PART SIX

APPENDICES
AND USEFUL
INFORMATION

FOOD COMBINING

FOR COMPLETE AND EFFICIENT DIGESTION

T HE FOLLOWING WILL SHOW *you how to combine fresh, vital foods to promote optimum digestion, remove intolerances, energize the system, and strengthen your entire body. Try it out for three or four weeks, then, if you feel things are better, try the digestion questionnaire again to see how you score.*

FOOD GROUPS

Proteins	Cheese, coconut, eggs, fish, poultry, meat, milk, nuts (raw), nut butters, olives, seeds (sunflower, linseeds [flax seed] pumpkin, sesame) seed butters, soy beans, tofu, yogurt.
	FISH
	CHEESE
Carbohydrates	Acorn squash, banana squash, beans, bread, cereals/grains (wheat, oats, rice, rye, millet), pasta, split peas, "seed" vegetables (runner beans), potatoes.
	BREAD
	BEANS
Fats Neutral Foods	Avocado, butter, butter substitutes, nuts (raw).
	AVOCADO
	NUTS
Oils Neutral Foods	Corn, nut, olive, sesame, sunflower, soy.
	OLIVE OIL
Vegetables Non-starchy	Asparagus, beet greens, broccoli, Brussels sprouts, cabbage, celery, chicory, cucumber, eggplant, endive, green beans, kale, lettuce, parsley, spinach (always eat raw), summer squash, sweet peppers, tomatoes, turnips, watercress, zucchini.
	EGGPLANT
	RED CABBAGE
Vegetables Mildly Starchy	Artichokes, beets, carrots, cauliflower, corn, peas.
	CAULIFLOWER
	CARROTS
Vegetables which can be irritants	Garlic, leeks, onions, radishes, scallions, shallots. (Note: These should be used sparingly.)
	SCALLIONS

COMBINATIONS

EXCELLENT COMBINATIONS	GOOD COMBINATIONS	POOR COMBINATIONS
Proteins + non-starchy vegetables. Carbohydrates + non-starchy vegetables.	Proteins + mildly starchy vegetables. Carbohydrates + mildly starchy vegetables. Fats/oils + non-starchy vegetables. Fats/oils + carbohydrates.	Proteins + carbohydrates. Proteins + fats/oils.

FRUIT

Acid Fruit	Blackberries, grapefruit, kumquats, lemons, limes, oranges, pineapple, plums (sour), pomegranates, raspberries, sour apples, strawberries, tangerines.	STRAWBERRIES ORANGE PLUM
Sub-acid Fruit	Apples, apricots, blueberries, cherries, fresh figs, grapes (not muscat), kiwi fruit, mangoes, nectarines, papaws, peaches, pears, plums (sweet).	KIWI FRUIT BLUEBERRIES APRICOT
Sweet Fruit	Bananas, dates, dried fruit, grapes (muscat), persimmons, raisins.	BANANAS
Melon	Galia melon, cantaloupe, casaba, cranshaw, honeydew, musk, Persian, watermelon.	MELON

Each day aim to have:

- One fruit meal. Best time to have this is breakfast. Do not mix acid/sub-acid and sweet fruit. Acid and sub-acid fruit can be eaten also at the start of any meal, but not afterward.

- One protein meal. Best time to have this is lunch. Vary your choice of protein daily, and eat with salads and vegetables. Keep dairy foods to a minimum.

- One carbohydrate meal. Best time to have this is dinner/supper. Vary your choice of carbohydrate daily and eat with salads and vegetables. Fats and oils are also good combinations with carbohydrate.

Alcohol should be kept to a minimum. Beers, lagers, and ales are best drunk with carbohydrate meals, while wines are best consumed along with protein. In either case you can have only a very small amount (a bottle of beer or lager, or one small glass of wine) with the meal.

Note:

- Sweet fruit should be eaten after other fruit; they combine poorly with sub-acid fruit and melon.

- Melon is best eaten alone, but can also be mixed with acid or sub-acid fruit.

- Do not eat fruit with any other food.

HELPFUL INFORMATION

Food combining has usually been promoted for digestive problems and, in some cases, weight loss. It is used here primarily as an aid to increasing the rate and extent to which foods are digested and absorbed. It is not intended as a long-term diet, but only until digestion has improved.

☞ There are three basic types of food – concentrated foods (proteins and carbohydrates), high water content foods (vegetables and especially fruit), and fats. In some books and recipes, vegetables and fats/oils and the seeds they come from are known as neutral foods. The concentrated foods are generally those which are acid-forming within the body, whereas those which are alkaline-forming (i.e., the ones most Western diets are lacking) are most of the vegetables, fruit, nuts, and the grain millet.

☞ Proteins are the most complex (concentrated) food and require the most time and energy to digest and assimilate, and therefore need the greatest time lapse before any other food is eaten. A general rule of thumb is to leave around four to five hours' gap.

☞ Fruit is the least complex (high water content) food and takes the least amount of time and energy to digest and assimilate. It can be eaten right before but not after any other food. After a meal you must wait at least two hours before eating more fruit. Sweet fruit should not be eaten right before a meal. All fruit except bananas, dried fruit, and avocados pass directly through the stomach to be digested in the intestines.

☞ In the past, food scientists and nutritionists have classified all sugar-containing foods as carbohydrates. Therefore, fruit is usually classified as carbohydrate, but its makeup is so entirely different from other carbohydrates that it must be thought of as a separate group of foods in the context of food-combining. The classification of fruit as a carbohydrate and the consumption of fruit along with proteins and carbohydrates has probably led to more digestive difficulties than any other dietary habit.

☞ In the digestive system, the breakdown process of proteins, carbohydrates, and fruit requires entirely different conditions of acidity-alkalinity. Therefore, to insure the most efficient digestion of these three food groups, they should not be eaten simultaneously. For example, if protein and carbohydrate, such as meat and potatoes, are eaten at the same time, the different digestive juices needed for each food will neutralize each other's actions. The protein will putrefy and the carbohydrate will ferment. Similarly if a carbohydrate is eaten with a fruit, such as oats and banana, the carbohydrate and fruit will both ferment. The result is gas and flatulence, in both cases!

☞ Proteins should be eaten with steamed vegetables and/or salads for optimum digestion.

☞ Carbohydrates should be eaten with steamed vegetables and/or salads, together with some fat or oil for optimum digestion.

☞ If fruit is eaten alone on an empty stomach it will have the effect of cleansing the digestive tract, leaving it more capable of absorbing nutrients.

☞ Although seeds, such as sunflower, sesame, linseed (flax seed), and pumpkin, are classed here as protein foods, some food-combining books class them as neutral, and in such cases you can happily use seeds with protein or carbohydrate dishes.

Bananas and avocados are the only fresh fruits that are digested in the stomach as well as the intestines.

SOME PROBLEM FOODS

Despite the fact that healthy eating encourages a proper balance of carbohydrates, proteins, and fats, it is likely that some natural foods could cause problems if eaten in large quantities or if treated in such a way that some undesirable characteristics of the foods come to the fore.

☞ When spinach is cooked, the oxalic acid forms into crystals and the spinach's beneficial properties are lost. Always eat spinach raw.

☞ Fresh tomatoes are an acid food, but in the digestive tract they are extremely alkaline, helping neutralize acid build-up in the body. However, when tomatoes are cooked they become highly acid-forming within the body and it would be healthier to consume them with an alkalizing food, such as a green salad. So, when making your pasta sauce, make sure you serve it with a very large green salad.

☞ Dairy products are highly mucus-forming and difficult to digest, and, therefore, should only make up a small percentage of your protein meals. They do not combine well with anything really. When they are eaten, it would be best to have them with a large green salad. For example, feta cheese cubes with a mixed vegetable salad.

☞ Fluids, even water, should not be consumed along with, or straight after, a meal because they dilute the digestive juices, and may even wash them through the system before they have had time to digest much food. When this happens, it forces the body to secrete more digestive juices and hence causes unnecessary usage of energy.

Spinach should always be eaten raw as cooking it destroys its beneficial qualities by crystalizing the oxalic acid.

By adhering to the helpful information of proper food-combining, the digestive system will work better and energy will be conserved. This extra energy can be used by the body to cleanse the system of accumulated toxic waste, and encourage weight loss and improve health.

Nutritional therapists believe that improper food-combining is one of the main reasons why so many people are unhealthy and have an excess weight problem. The theory is that the energy necessary to break down and eliminate the excesses in the diet is being used instead by the digestive system. There is, then, simply not enough energy at the body's disposal to carry out the functions of digestion and eliminate unwanted food break-down products at the same time. Food-combining removes this burden on the digestive process.

With particular regard to weight loss, the critical point to remember is that when you are on a healthy diet your body will automatically return to your most optimum body weight and will stay there.

If this system is new to you, it can look extremely daunting, but if you have found from the questionnaire that your digestion is under par, and/or you seem to have some food intolerances, then a few weeks on this diet might be all you need to set you on the way to improved health and weight loss. Try it and you will be surprised at how easy it all becomes. Once you get into it you'll wonder why you ever thought you couldn't go a week without pizza, or pie, meat and potatoes. You need not upset the family meals either (although a few weeks on your food-combining diet can only do them good) since your typical meat, potatoes, and vegetable meals can still be served; you just have to decide whether you miss out the meat or the potatoes!

THE HYPOALLERGENIC DIET

IF YOU THINK THAT *you may have intolerances to foods, then try the following suggestions for a minimum of two weeks. This length of time is usually long enough to rid the body of any of the effects of foods that might be irritating your system. After two weeks, retest yourself with the Food Allergy and Intolerance questionnaire.*

FOODS OMITTED FROM THE DIET

The Hypoallergenic Diet aims to omit all of the common allergenic foods and all those to which intolerance is common. These foods include all of the following:

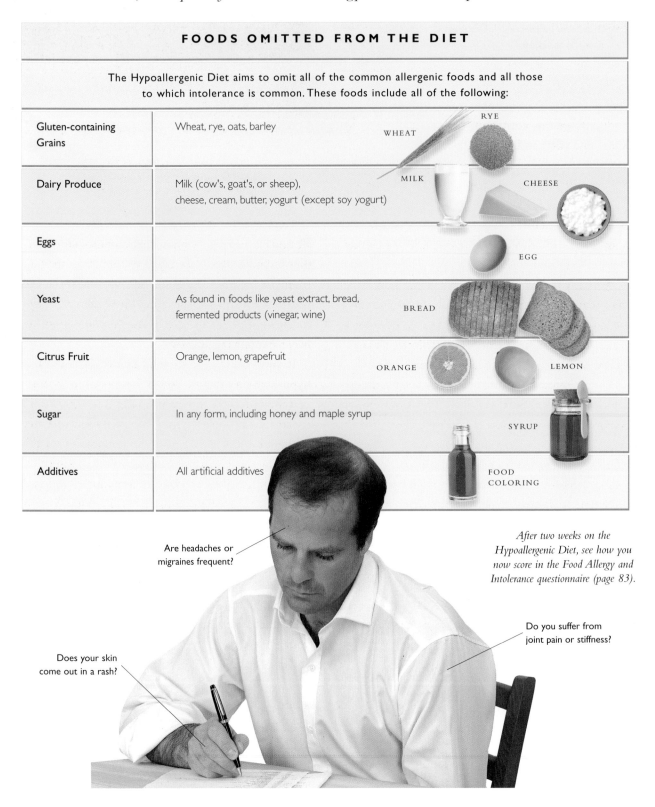

Gluten-containing Grains	Wheat, rye, oats, barley
Dairy Produce	Milk (cow's, goat's, or sheep), cheese, cream, butter, yogurt (except soy yogurt)
Eggs	
Yeast	As found in foods like yeast extract, bread, fermented products (vinegar, wine)
Citrus Fruit	Orange, lemon, grapefruit
Sugar	In any form, including honey and maple syrup
Additives	All artificial additives

Are headaches or migraines frequent?

After two weeks on the Hypoallergenic Diet, see how you now score in the Food Allergy and Intolerance questionnaire (page 83).

Do you suffer from joint pain or stiffness?

Does your skin come out in a rash?

If there are any other specific foods to which you know you already have an allergy or intolerance, e.g., Brazil nuts, beans, then these must be omitted as well.

After approximately two weeks on the hypoallergenic diet, start to reintroduce the food groups which have been omitted if your symptoms have gone. However, you must start by introducing only one group at a time (see the table opposite; additives should never be reintroduced if at all possible). Which group you introduce first will depend on those foods you have most missed or those which you feel will improve the variety in your diet.

Also, when reintroducing a food group back into your general diet, choose one item at a time. For example, when reintroducing gluten-containing grains, start with, say, oats, and have some of these twice a day for three days. If no symptoms return, then you can fairly safely reintroduce oats back into your diet at a low level. Then go on to the next grain you want to have. If you have no intention of returning a certain food to your diet, e.g., barley, then you need not test this food.

Where you have combination foods like bread (wheat and yeast), then these should ideally be eaten separately. You can carry this out effectively by testing yourself on yeast-free bread, or pasta, or wheat cereal before testing the yeast-containing varieties.

The pulse test is a simple test for food reactions based on the fact that, mostly, foods that cause an allergic reaction also cause the pulse to rise suddenly. It involves the taking of your resting pulse (while sitting still); consuming the suspect food and retesting the pulse 10 minutes or so later. Any major increase in pulse rate, not due to an increase in activity, may relate to a reaction from the food.

Liver congestion and toxemia may also be a factor in food intolerance. If this is coupled with digestive enzyme deficiency and leaky gut, the allergic/intolerance reaction will be enhanced. Undigested or partially digested foods can sometimes stimulate an increase in histamine, which may be initiating an

When reintroducing gluten-containing grains back into your diet, start with one grain only, such as oats, for a few days.

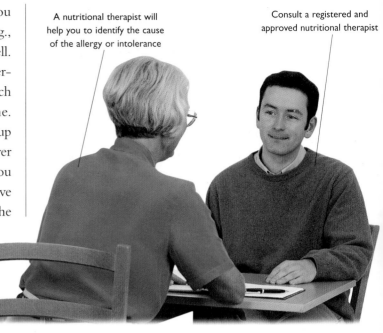

A nutritional therapist will help you to identify the cause of the allergy or intolerance

Consult a registered and approved nutritional therapist

If you see no improvement in your condition after two weeks, consult your physician, and if he or she cannot help, then go to a nutritional therapist.

allergic reaction by the cells. The liver normally detoxifies histamine, but a damaged or toxic liver may do so inefficiently causing histamine to build up in the system. Unfortunately, antihistamines, used as allergy medication, are likely to add a further burden to the liver's detoxifying capacity.

If you find that at the end of the 14 days on a hypoallergenic regime you still have some of what you thought were intolerance symptoms, you could try continuing with the basic hypoallergenic diet but, at the same time, use one or a combination of the following supplements: digestive enzymes (to improve general digestive capacity), hydrochloric acid and pepsin (to digest proteins fully), L-glutamine or glucosamine (to encourage healing of leaky gut), Milk thistle herb (to aid liver function), and/or a probiotic supplement together with fructo-oligosaccharides (to encourage appropriate microbial balance to aid digestion). However, you might feel at this point that you would be better having a word with your physician.

If he or she feels there is nothing seriously wrong, you might decide on a thorough investigation by a nutritional therapist. If this is the case, then apply to a national nutritional therapy organization such as the S.P.N.T. in the U.K. for a list of registered and approved therapists in your area (*see* Useful Addresses on pages 248-249).

RECIPES FOR THE HYPOALLERGENIC DIET

The following are tried and tested recipes which use a wide variety of foods while omitting all common allergens. If, however, you know or suspect you are allergic or intolerant to any of them, omit them from the diet. It is important to use fresh foods, and, wherever possible, ones from an organic source as sometimes it is pesticides or pollutants in the food that are triggering the reaction.

BREAKFAST IDEAS

☞ Rice cakes spread with unhydrogenated, dairy-free polyunsaturated margarine and sugar-free jam.

☞ Millet flakes with golden raisins (sultanas) soaked overnight in apple juice.

☞ Millet flakes with chopped nuts and/or bananas.

☞ Millet flakes with ground mixed seeds (sesame, sunflower, pumpkin, linseed) and dried apricots.

☞ Fruit salad, seeds, and soy yogurt.

Rice cakes spread with a sugar-free jam make a nutritious hypoallergenic breakfast.

☞ Kallo puffed rice with soy or rice milk, mixed seeds, and golden raisins (sultanas) or apricots.

☞ Porridge made with millet flakes and brown rice flakes (instead of oats) with soy milk or rice milk, or soy cream.

☞ Avocado, strawberries, or banana liquidized with soy or rice milk, with cooked millet added for extra protein.

☞ Buckwheat pancakes (made with buckwheat flour and water) and sugar-free jam, with a little soy cream.

LUNCH IDEAS

☞ Kidney bean/butter bean/ haricot bean (cooked or sugar-free canned) mixed salad with grated carrot, sweet green pepper, celery, tomatoes, cucumber, radishes, brown rice, in any combination. For salad dressing, mix extra virgin olive oil or cold-pressed sunflower or sesame or walnut oil with crushed garlic. For extra flavor, add some herbs and/or mustard. For a creamy dressing, mix tofu with a little oil (as before), mustard and/or herbs.

A lunch of different beans and mixed salad.

☞ Homemade vegetable soup. Be imaginative, include any vegetable with several pulses (legumes), e.g., lentils, beans, or grains, e.g., rice, millet.

☞ Baked potato with beans or with a little thick soup/stew poured on top, or with salad and one of the dressings.

☞ Fish and vegetables, either braised or salad.

☞ Lamb chops (broiled and all fat removed) and salad or steamed vegetables.

☞ If you decide to eat fruit as part of your lunch, always eat the fruit first, about 10 minutes before your main course.

This diet is based on information originally written by
S.P.N.T. – The Society for Promotion of Nutritional Therapy and is reproduced here with their permission.

DINNER/SUPPER IDEAS

- Stir-fried (braised) mixed vegetables e.g., zucchini, cauliflower, broccoli (calabrese), carrots, parsnips, green beans, celery, snow peas, etc. all cut into small pieces, and added to chopped onion and garlic which has been partly cooked in 1 Tbsp (15ml) of olive oil, in a heavy-bottomed pan. After all the vegetables have been stir-fried for a few minutes, add 2 to 3 Tbsp (30 to 45ml) water, vegetable stock, or fruit juice (not citrus) and a few herbs. Cover and simmer for about 20 minutes. Serve with potatoes, brown rice, and/or millet or buckwheat.

- A similar stir-fry to that above, but add a few red kidney beans or other beans toward the end of the simmering stage, and heat through thoroughly.

- Kedgeree, using poached haddock, stir-fried onion, and other vegetables mixed together with preboiled brown rice.

- Organic chicken roasted with garlic. Remove all chicken skin. Serve with salad or braised/steamed vegetables.

- Rabbit (or game) and vegetable casserole. Dice the rabbit and mix with stir-fried onion, garlic, and a mixture of vegetables. Add a yeast-free vegetable bouillon cube, and sufficient homemade vegetable stock. Cook slowly in a slow oven until the rabbit is tender.

Stir-fried mixed vegetables with brown rice and baked potato omit common allergens.

- Thick vegetable soup/stew. Start by lightly frying in olive oil a large chopped onion and some garlic. Add chopped potato, leeks, parsnips, turnip, green cabbage, etc. Flavor with herbs or an organic yeast-free vegetable bouillon cube, or some sesame paste (tahini). Add some rehydrated seaweed for extra minerals. Cook over a low heat for about 30 minutes, then extract a mug-full of the mixture and blend before returning it to the stew. Add a little arrowroot, corn starch, or soy milk for a creamier soup.

- Ratatouille. Use canned red kidney beans, or black-eyed peas (or dried beans soaked overnight and pre-cooked), and mix together with a partly stir-fried onion and some garlic in a large heavy bottomed pan or wok. Add zucchini, canned tomatoes (sugar-free), herbs, and black pepper, and cook a while longer. Serve with brown rice and/or millet, potatoes, quinoa, or buckwheat.

DESSERTS

- Always try to leave 20 to 30 minutes between your main course and your dessert.

- Brown rice pudding and apricots, prunes or golden raisins (sultanas). Use brown rice flakes and cook in about twice their volume of milk for about 20 minutes. Stir in the fruit.

- Fresh fruit and soy yogurt. Make sure you have a good range of interesting fruit, e.g., fresh figs, sharon fruit, papaw (papaya), kiwi fruit, mango, etc., dried fruit, soaked, and with a little apple juice.

- Seed/nut/fruit cream. Liquidize unroasted cashew nuts and sunflower seeds with banana and 2/3 cup (150ml) water. Sprinkle with ground nuts/seeds and decorate with kiwi fruit.

SNACKS AND DRINKS

- Fruit, raw carrots and celery stalks, fresh nuts (e.g., almonds, Brazils, hazelnuts, walnuts, fresh coconut), good-quality tortilla chips, low-fat and low-salt chips (no other additives), dried fruit (nonsulfured), rice cakes and sugar-free jelly, mixed seeds (sunflower, pumpkin, and sesame).

- Herb tea, fruit tea, rooibosh (red bush) tea with rice milk, wheat and yeast-free bouillon cubes in hot water, dandelion coffee (lactose-free), pure fruit juice mixed with mineral water, elderflower cordial, and filtered or bottled water.

Pieces of coconut or other nuts make a healthy snack.

APPENDIX THREE

THE DETOXIFICATION DIET

A FULL DETOXIFICATION DIET *can last from three days to 13 days, though you can continue longer under medical supervision if necessary. Remember that anyone who has an eating disorder, a serious mental problem, or is pregnant, breastfeeding, or currently taking prescription medication, should not attempt a detoxification diet without speaking first to their physician.*

Instead of going on the full diet, you can, as suggested in the section on Toxin Levels (*see* page 84), detox one day a week, or do a "split" detox, where you eat fruit only during the morning until lunchtime, every day. The Detoxification Diet is a diet very low in fat, oil, and gluten with very few concentrated protein foods, e.g., fish. There is also no caffeine (coffee, tea, cola), alcohol or artificial substances. It is high in a variety of natural fibers, high in nutrients (especially vitamins A, as beta-carotene, and C, and powerful nutrient antioxidants such as zinc and selenium), high in phytochemicals, all of which will help to neutralize toxins and revitalize the body.

Kiwi fruit – a rich source of vitamin C.

If you are short of time, you can make large batches of boiled brown rice, soups, and stews and freeze them in smaller portions, or make large bowls of salad to keep in the refrigerator to dip into.

What you must do is insure you have the greatest variety of fruit, vegetables, non-gluten grains (brown rice, millet, buckwheat), pulses (legumes) (beans, peas and lentils), fresh unsalted, unroasted nuts (walnuts, pecans, almonds, Brazils, hazelnuts, cashews), and fresh seeds (sunflower, pumpkin, sesame, linseed) as you possibly can. The fruit and vegetables listed here are the best detoxifiers. Make sure that wherever possible you purchase organic produce.

FRUIT AND VEGETABLES FOR STAGE ONE DETOXIFICATION

Certain fruit and vegetables are particularly good for stage one of detoxification. The range of fruit and vegetable detoxifiers is wide, so no one need become bored.

FRUIT

☞ Apples help to stabilize blood-sugar levels, lower blood pressure, and dampen appetite, and the pectin in them helps to lower cholesterol.

☞ Avocado should be used sparingly, but has an excellent combination of essential fatty acids.

☞ Bananas should be used sparingly, but they are an excellent source of potassium and tryptophan, which helps you sleep, and they are high in natural sugar, which helps satisfy a sweet tooth.

☞ Grapes are rich in potassium, which is especially useful for people with heart conditions. Grapes also help stop the formation of mucus in the gut and are good cleansers for the skin, liver, intestines, and kidneys.

☞ Kiwi fruit is an excellent source of the antioxidant vitamin C, and is, therefore, very useful in mopping up toxic free radicals.

☞ Mango is a rich source of an enzyme called papain which helps to break down excess protein. It is also a good cleanser for the system and is thought to lift depression.

☞ Peaches are a good source of three antioxidants: beta-carotene, selenium, and vitamin C.

☞ Pears are packed with carbohydrates and, therefore, a good source of energy and fiber. They are also a good source of folic acid and vitamin C.

☞ Strawberries are an excellent source of vitamin C.

Peaches contain useful antioxidants that help to destroy toxic free radicals.

VEGETABLES

Beet is a great detoxifier. It contains minerals that sweep through the kidneys and liver. The juice has a strong flavor so that it is best to mix beet juice with carrot juice.

Broccoli is a nutrient-packed vegetable rich in chlorophyll (natural green coloring), and is thought to give some protection against most cancers, particularly those of the esophagus, stomach, colon, lungs, larynx, prostate, mouth, and pharynx.

Cabbage, both red and white, is bursting with health-giving benefits. It helps lower the risk of colon cancer, helps prevent and heal ulcers, helps stimulate the immune system, and helps kill bacteria and viruses. It is also good at cleaning mucous membranes in the intestines.

Carrots are a good digestive aid, skin and eye cleanser. They are also one of the richest sources of the antioxidant beta-carotene. They are excellent at helping to block virulent cancers of the lung and pancreas. One carrot a day appears to cut the risk of lung cancer by 50 percent, even among ex-smokers. Carrots, because of their pectin, also help to lower blood cholesterol and prevent constipation.

Cauliflower is a close cousin to the cabbage and broccoli, and similarly helps to reduce the risk of colon and stomach cancers.

Celery has alkaline properties which make it an excellent detoxifier, clearing out waste from the tissues. It is also high in potassium, which helps to maintain the balance of body fluids and minerals needed for the nervous and circulatory systems.

LEEK

Chicory/endive is a good source of folate (folic acid) and vitamin C.

Cress is an excellent source of the antioxidant vitamin C, iron, and calcium. It stimulates the metabolism, aids digestion, and helps the elimination of phlegm and mucus.

Lettuce contains vitamins A, C, folic acid, and the minerals calcium and iron. It also helps with intestinal and liver function, and helps you sleep.

Onions/garlic/leeks are good for the circulatory system and the heart. They increase levels of the beneficial cholesterol, help thin the blood, help reduce clotting, help lower total cholesterol, help regulate blood-sugar, are antibacterial, and ease bronchial conditions.

Potatoes are very useful for their starch content, though use sparingly because of their high glycemic index. Excellent source of potassium and vitamin C.

Sweet peppers are excellent as a source of vitamin C and fiber.

BROWN RICE

The organic fruit, vegetables, and grains in the Dextoxification Diet will help neutralize toxins and energize the body.

Select your fruit and vegetables from these lists and, wherever possible, obtain them from organic growers. If this is not possible, make sure you wash their skins thoroughly in filtered water to which you have added 1 Tbsp (15ml) organic cider vinegar (this will help neutralize many pesticide residues which are mainly of an alkaline nature).

GRAINS (CEREALS)
FOR STAGE TWO DETOXIFICATION

Buckwheat is not a grain at all but is the seed from a plant related to rhubarb. It is useful because of its carbohydrate and fiber content, and its lack of gluten.

Millet is used alongside short-grain brown rice, because like rice it is gluten-free and, additionally, it is the only alkaline-forming grain. Useful, therefore, for both stage one and stage two detoxification.

Short-grain brown rice is one of the best types of grain for attracting and retaining toxins within the intestines, to remove them from the body. It is also an excellent source of the vitamin B-complex.

All of the above can be prepared in bulk and then frozen in smaller portions. Add 1 cup (225ml) of grain to 2 cups (450ml) of filtered water and heat to boiling. Cover with a tight saucepan lid and leave to stand until all water is absorbed.

RECIPES FOR THE DETOXIFICATION DIET

The following recipes use a variety of foods to encourage liver activity and accelerate the release of stored and circulating toxins. Of particular importance are beets, which encourage liver drainage, and cruciferous vegetables (broccoli, cauliflower, Brussels sprouts, cabbage, and so on), which aid cytochrome activity and increase sulfur-containing compounds for stage two detoxification.

BREAKFAST IDEAS

☞ Organic puffed rice or crumbled rice cakes and organic soy milk or rice milk.

☞ Fresh fruit salad; choose any fruit from the list but vary the ingredients.

☞ Stewed apple chunks and raisins or golden raisins (sultanas).

☞ Porridge made with rice flakes, millet flakes, and filtered water.

Fresh fruit salad may be included in a detoxification diet.

☞ Rice cakes spread with tahini (sesame spread) and/or sugar-free jam.

☞ Avocado and banana milkshake (made with soy milk or rice milk and liquidized).

☞ Stewed prunes.

☞ Rice flake and millet flake muesli with dried apricots, soaked overnight in apple juice.

LUNCH IDEAS

☞ Cooked brown rice and millet with stir-fried (in a little extra virgin olive oil) vegetables, and a few nuts and/or seeds (choose from walnuts, Brazils, almonds, sesame seeds, sunflower seeds, pumpkin seeds, celery seeds).

☞ Lentil and onion soup, seasoned with an organic vegetable bouillon cube or some brown rice miso paste.

☞ New potato salad with chopped scallion and mint.

☞ Butter bean, potato, and onion soup.

☞ Baked potato with baked beans (use canned organic baked beans from a health food store) and a large mixed salad.

☞ Homemade coleslaw (shredded white cabbage, grated carrot, diced onion and apple, with a little tofu and garlic dressing).

☞ Canned mackerel/sardine/ salmon and a large mixed salad.

☞ Three-bean salad, using cooked/canned red kidney beans and butter beans, and freshly cooked green beans.

☞ Split pea, lentil, and vegetable soup (use a good variety of root, stem and leaf vegetables).

☞ Walnut, celery, and apple salad.

☞ Large mixed salad with beets and cruciferous vegetables, with seeds and hummus.

Organic baked beans, here with a mixed salad and a baked potato, can be found in health food stores.

DINNER/SUPPER IDEAS

🖙 Vegetable lasagne with millet. Stir-fry, in a little extra-virgin olive oil, chopped sweet green pepper, finely chopped carrot, celery, and garlic, a few sliced mushrooms for texture, and add a pinch of mixed herbs, a large can of additive-free chopped tomatoes and around ³/₄ cup (100g) brown, washed and cooked lentils. Add a dash of tamari sauce. Let simmer until most of the juice has been absorbed. Partially cook some potato, then slice. Layer this with the mixture in a dish, making three pairs of layers and finishing with the vegetable mixture. Cover the dish and bake for an hour. Sprinkle with finely chopped walnuts and serve with boiled millet or buckwheat.

🖙 Broiled fish (salmon, cod, haddock, or halibut) with fresh steamed vegetables and mixed salad.

🖙 Thick vegetable (large variety) stew; add rice and/or pulses (legumes). Include chopped garlic and a few herbs.

🖙 Vegetable risotto with garbanzo beans, onion, garlic, mixed chopped vegetables (lots of color), and a dash of tamari sauce.

🖙 Stir-fried (in a little extra virgin olive oil) vegetables with buckwheat and a green side salad.

Broiled salmon with fresh steamed vegetables and a green side salad help release toxins.

DESSERTS AND DRINKS

Leave 30 minutes or so after main course

🖙 Fresh fruit.

🖙 Stewed prunes.

🖙 Tropical fruit salad (mango, papaw [papaya], kiwi etc.).

🖙 Fresh strawberries and kiwi fruit with soy cream.

🖙 Soaked Hunza apricots and creamed (liquidized) cashew nuts.

🖙 Soy fruit yogurt.

🖙 Handful of seeds and/or nuts.

🖙 To help remove toxins from the system drink around eight glasses of filtered or spring water daily. In addition, you can have herb or fruit teas or tisanes, or lactose-free dandelion coffee. To further encourage detoxification, try potassium broth (see recipe below), which will help to alkalize the system very quickly to counter-balance the effects of an acid toxic system. Consume it while still hot to counteract the coldness of the salad and raw vegetables.

POTASSIUM BROTH

INGREDIENTS

2 large potatoes, scrubbed but unpeeled

8 ounces (225g) carrots, scrubbed but unpeeled

8 ounces (225g) beets

8 ounces (225g) celery (with leaves)

8 ounces (225g) beet tops, turnip tops, or parsley

4 ounces (100g) cabbage

METHOD

Put all the washed vegetables in a saucepan and add 8 cups (2 liters) filtered water. Bring to a boil and cook for 30 minutes. Leave to stand; when coolish, strain off the broth and drink during the day.

The cooked vegetables can be eaten with rice and millet later.

APPENDIX FOUR

THE CYCLICAL DIET

T HE MORE COMMON *bodily changes that women who are menstruating normally find over the month involve: mood, skin and hair texture/oiliness, physical energy level, emotions, appetite, and food cravings. It would be advisable to remain with the following eating program until you have lost the desired amount of weight and/or your monthly change of symptoms is less severe.*

The Cyclical Diet is divided into three separate phases – one, two, and three – each with a different dietary balance and energy level to match your changing body chemistry during a complete menstrual cycle. The essence of this is that you start the diet during your period and then follow each phase of the diet, one after the other, according to the phase of your cycle, until your next period when you repeat the sequence. The New Pyramid program is one of the options (*see* pages 36–41).

KEEPING A SYMPTOMS DIARY

If you found from the questionnaire on cyclical appetite changes (page 137) that your monthly rhythms are causing your dieting downfall, then the first step is to see just when your "changes" occur. Before attempting to moderate your monthly intake of food along these lines, you would need to keep a "symptoms" diary for a month or two, so that you can pinpoint fairly accurately at what point you need to decrease/increase the amount of food to accommodate your change in appetite. Make a record of your symptoms along the lines recorded here:

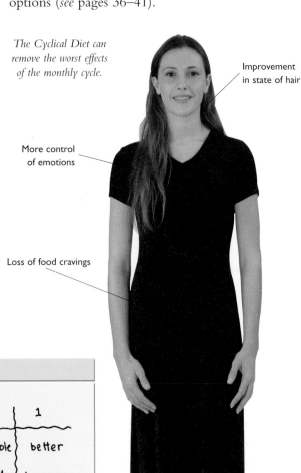

The Cyclical Diet can remove the worst effects of the monthly cycle.

Improvement in state of hair

More control of emotions

Loss of food cravings

SYMPTOMS DIARY

DAY OF CYCLE	1	7	14	21	28	1
MOOD	OK	OK	OK	irritable	v.irritable	better
SKIN/HAIR	good	good	good	slightly greasy	greasy + spots	improving
ENERGY	fine	fine	fine	tired	slightly better	fine
EMOTIONS	OK	OK	OK	OK	tearful depressed	happier
APPETITE	normal	normal	growing	v.large	large	normal
FOOD CRAVINGS	none	none	none	chocs pastry	chocs pastry	none

PHASE ONE

The first 14 days or so of the cycle, starting on day one of your period. This is the most food-energy-reduced phase. Low in grains (i.e., very little in the way of breakfast cereals, porridge, bread, pasta, rice) and natural sugars (i.e., sweet fruit like bananas and dried fruit). High in fiber-rich vegetable carbohydrates (such as runner beans, lentils, beans), green and orange vegetables, and fresh low-sugar fruit (apples, citrus fruit, strawberries). Balance this carbohydrate well with good-quality proteins: oily fish, poultry, pulses (legumes), cottage cheese, tofu, and a few seeds (but no nuts, yet).

If you undergo a moderate to high exercise program, you can have more food than if you did no exercise. Be led by your true hunger.

Eat low-sugar fruit

Eat good quality protein

During phase one, keep high-energy foods to a minimum.

PHASE TWO

Introduce bread

More protein allowed

Mood changes take place in phase two.

The phase when your mood or other obvious changes (whichever apply most to you) take place. For most women this will be about 10 to 14 days before your period is due.

The diet is as above, but allows some extra starchy treats; for example, you may have a little pasta, bread, or rice, and balance this extra carbohydrate with a little more protein. You may also now add a few nuts and more seeds to the high-quality protein in phase one. Be led by your true hunger, and choose something that is very healthy for your extra starchy snack. Save it for the time of day when you feel that you will need it most.

PHASE THREE

The last week or few days of your cycle is when your mood is lowest and cravings are at their worst. In this phase the diet allows, in addition to your main meals, three healthy snacks or treats, including a little bit of chocolate, if you are able to have just one little bit without going mad. For your healthy snacks choose soy fruit yogurt, low-sugar cereal bars, breakfast cereals, seeds, or nuts. The food energy content during this phase is relatively generous, so that you will need to keep this phase as short as possible.

We need not go into detailed recipes for this diet, simply follow the general guidelines of the New Pyramid program and the recipes in Appendix Five.

Choose healthy food for snacks

A little chocolate is permissible

Cravings are typical of phase three.

APPENDIX FIVE

RECIPES FOR THE NEW PYRAMID DIET

T HE ESSENCE OF *the New Pyramid Diet is balanced eating. You can achieve this without having to endure a boring diet of only a few approved dishes, and the following recipes are only suggestions intended to establish the principles. All are for one person unless otherwise stated.*

BREAKFASTS

1 *To make kedgeree, first bring to the boil 3 cups (700ml) of filtered water, add 1¼ cups (225g) long-grain brown rice.*

2 *Boil the rice for about 25 minutes, with a lid on the pan. Meanwhile steam 12 ounces (325 g) of color-free smoked haddock.*

3 *Flake the haddock and combine with the rice. Stir in 1 sliced hard-boiled egg. Garnish with parsley and paprika. (Serves four.)*

Kedgeree, a dish of fish, rice, and egg, makes a protein-rich breakfast.

Although there are several recipes here that contain cereals (including bread), remember that having large amounts of cereals (even whole grain cereals) can cause large blood-sugar swings. Therefore, it is advisable to have no more than two "cereal" breakfasts a week. In addition to the recipes below, other suggestions are kipper and fresh tomatoes; and fresh sliced apple and cottage cheese.

Pear and Nut Yogurt

Take ½ cup (125g) good-quality live yogurt (sheep, goat or soy, or make your own) add a chopped pear and a handful of cashews or other nuts and 1 Tbsp (15ml) wheatgerm or oatgerm and ground linseeds.

Porridge

• Take 1¼ cups (300ml) water and ⅔ cup (150ml) rice milk, soy milk, or oat milk (or organic cow's milk) and pour into a saucepan; sprinkle in ¼ cup (25g) organic porridge oats and bring to a boil.
• Boil for 5 minutes, stirring all the time. Serve with another ⅔ cup (150ml) milk and stir in 1 tsp (5ml) Manuka (or other good quality) honey.
• For extra nutrients, add a handful of mixed seeds and oatgerm.

Banana and Coconut Yogurt

• As a variation to Pear and Nut Yogurt, to your ½ cup (125g) live yogurt add a chopped banana, 1 Tbsp (15ml) of toasted coconut, or fresh coconut chips and one or two chopped dates and/or figs.

Fruit Cocktail

• Choose fruit in season (apple and pear, orange and banana, orange and peach, strawberry, raspberry and red/ blackcurrant mix, etc.).
• Put 4 ounces (100g) fruit in a blender with 1½ Tbsp (20ml) shredded coconut, ¼ tsp (1.25ml) vanilla extract, and a dash of soy cream.
• Liquidize and serve.

Fruit Milkshake

• As a variation on the above, to 2 ounces (50g) fruit add 1 Tbsp (15ml) ground almonds, 1 Tbsp (15ml) shredded coconut and liquidize.
• Add ⅔ cup (150ml) rice or oat milk and liquidize again.

Eggs on Toast

• Poach or scramble an organic/free-range egg (with a little butter and oat milk); serve on 2 slices of toasted rye bread.

Puffed Rice

• Take 1 cup (75g) organic puffed rice, and add soy cream, chopped fresh dried fruit, almonds and Brazil nuts.
• Drizzle with a little Manuka honey.

Apple Granola *(muesli)*

• Buy a good-quality, sugar-free muesli from your local health food store or make your own from brown rice flakes, millet flakes, oat flakes, barley flakes, sunflower/ sesame/pumpkin seeds, dried fruit, and nuts.
• Soak ⅓ cup (50g) muesli overnight in ⅔ cup (150ml) filtered water.
• Add sufficient rice milk, soy milk, or oat milk and one grated apple.
Note: The grains included in this granola are moderate to low glycemic index.

LUNCHES

Corn and Butterbean Soup makes a warming, nutritious lunch.

1 *To make Corn and Butter-bean Soup, chop 1 large onion and 3 stalks of celery, crush 1 clove of garlic, and sauté them in a little olive oil or organic butter.*

2 *Add 1¹/₄ cups (325g) frozen corn, ²/₃ cup (100g) cooked butter beans, and a little dried thyme and black pepper.*

3 *Add 1¹/₄ cups (300ml) organic cow's milk and 1¹/₄ cups (300ml) homemade vegetable stock. Simmer for 10 minutes. (Serves four.)*

Remember to have pasta, bread, potato, and rice dishes not more than two or three times a week.

Three Bean Salad
• Take ²/₃ cup (100g) of cooked mixed beans (haricot, red kidney, flageolet, black-eyed, butter bean, or cut green beans), and some defrosted corn.
• Add some walnuts, chopped parsley, fennel, and scallions and stir in 1 Tbsp (15ml) French dressing or hummus.

Thick Vegetable Soup
(4 servings)
• Sauté 1 chopped medium-sized onion and 2 cloves of garlic in 1 Tbsp (15ml) olive oil.
• Add a 14-ounce (400-g) can tomatoes (sugar-free if possible) and 1½ pounds (650g) chopped, seasonal vegetables (potatoes, turnips, celery, leeks, carrots, broccoli, sweet peppers, cabbage), and enough homemade vegetable stock (or water with an organic vegetable bouillon cube) to cover the vegetables.
• Add some pot barley, lentils, or a little brown rice or small amount of soup pasta. Simmer until cooked.
• Add more liquid if necessary.

Baked Potato, Baked Beans and Salad
• Oven-bake 1 medium scrubbed potato.
• Serve with ½ large can of organic sugar-free baked beans and a large mixed salad.
• A little crushed garlic or hummus can be added for extra flavor.

Lentil Soup *(4 servings)*
• Simmer 1¹/₄ cups (225g) washed brown or green lentils (or a mixture) in 3 cups (700ml) filtered water (or homemade vegetable stock) until tender in a covered pan.
• Add a 14-ounce (400-g) can of tomatoes, some dried oregano, 2 crushed cloves of garlic, and freshly ground black pepper to taste. Simmer for 5 minutes more.

Coleslaw *(4 servings)*
• Finely chop 1 pound (450g) mixture of red, white and green cabbage, and mix with 2 cups (225g) grated carrots.
• Add 1 diced medium onion.
• Mix with ²/₃ cup (100g) raisins and 2 Tbsp (30ml) plain yogurt plus a little good-quality low-fat mayonnaise.
• Serve with celery, carrot sticks, and cucumber sticks; a green salad and some fish, shellfish, or cottage cheese.

Avocado and Alfalfa Sandwich
• Spread 4 small slices of rye bread with hummus and pile on slices of a fresh avocado.
• Place a handful of alfalfa sprouts on the top and 1 sliced tomato.
• For a change, the avocado can be replaced with cottage or goat cheese, or the cheese can be in addition to the avocado.

Tuna and Green Bean Salad
• Drain a small can of tuna and combine with 1 chopped apple, 2 chopped stalks of celery, a handful of sliced crisp lettuce leaves, a handful of beansprouts and 2 Tbsp (30ml) natural sheep/goat yogurt plus a little good quality low-fat mayonnaise and black pepper to taste.
• Mix together with (or serve on top of) 4 ounces (100g) cooked sliced scarlet runner beans, French beans, or flat beans.

Greek Salad
• Mix together as many salad and chopped root and stem vegetables as you have available and add to this ¹/₂ cup (50g) cubed feta cheese (ewe's cheese).
• Add 1 to 2 black olives if required.

Tomato "Pasta" *(4 servings)*
• Mix together 8 ounces (225g) cooked vegetable pasta (from summer squash, or vegetable marrow) and a jar of good-quality tomato pasta sauce.
• Mix in some grated parmesan cheese and sprinkle some more on the surface.
• Bake in a medium oven for 20 minutes. Serve with mixed green salad.

Brown Rice Salad
• Mix ¹/₄ cup (50g) of cooked brown rice with 1 chopped tomato, grated raw beet, sliced spring onion, chopped peppers, diced carrot and alfalfa sprouts.
• Mix in 2 Tbsp (30ml) hummus.

Baked Beans on Toast
• Toast 2 small slices Russian rye bread, spread with a little nut or seed butter or hummus and pour on ½ can organic baked beans.
• Serve with sliced fresh tomato.

MAIN MEALS

1 *To make Almond Couscous sauté 1 large onion and 1 clove of garlic in 1 Tbsp (15ml) of virgin olive oil.*

2 *Add 8 ounces (225g) sliced zucchini, 8 ounces (225g) sliced mushrooms, 2 ounces (50g) raisins, 2 ounces (50g) chopped almonds, 1 chopped red pepper, 2 sliced medium carrots and a 14-ounce (400-g) can of sugar-free tomatoes (or fresh skinned ones). Cook the mixture for a further 3 minutes, as you would a stir-fry.*

3 *Cover with just sufficient home-made vegetable stock. Simmer for about 15 minutes. Meanwhile pour boiling water over 8 ounces (225g) couscous, stir in a dissolved organic vegetable stock cube, and leave to stand for 15 minutes. Serve cooked vegetables on a bed of couscous.*

Almond Couscous includes a wide range of nutritious vegetables.

Remember to have pasta, potato, and rice not more than three times a week.

Garbanzo Bean Goulash
(4 servings)
• Sauté 1 chopped onion, 1 chopped clove of garlic, diced sweet red pepper, and 2 sliced celery stalks in olive oil.
• Place in a casserole.
• Add 2 scrubbed, unpeeled and diced potatoes, 4 ounces (100g) diced parsnips, 14-ounce (400-g) can sugar-free tomatoes, 14oz (400g) can garbanzo beans (or freshly cooked garbanzo beans), and 1 tsp (15ml) of paprika.
• Bake in a medium oven for 45 minutes or until cooked.

Chicken Salad
• Serve a piece of cooked free-range chicken breast with a large mixed salad and steamed (starchy) vegetables.
• Use hummus instead of salad oil, or use a homemade mixture of virgin olive oil, crushed garlic, and whole grain mustard.
• For a change, have the same salad and vegetables with a broiled lamb chop, turkey, or venison, etc.

Lentil Curry *(4 servings)*
• Sauté 1 medium chopped onion in virgin olive oil.
• Add 1¼ cups (225g) red lentils, 1 to 2 tsp (5–10ml) curry powder (or your own mixture of Indian spices), 2½ cups (600ml) filtered water, 1 tsp (5ml) brown rice miso paste, and 1 Tbsp (15ml) tomato paste.
• Bring to a boil in a saucepan and simmer until lentils are soft and nearly all the liquid is absorbed.
• Put into dish and garnish with 2 sliced hard-boiled eggs.
• Serve with a mixed green salad or steamed broccoli.

Mackerel Crumble *(4 servings)*
• Bake, bone, and flake the mackerel.
• Sauté 2 large onions and 2 cloves of garlic in some virgin olive oil.
• Add 3 large sliced zucchini to the onions and a 14-ounce (400-g) can sugar-free tomatoes.
• Mix in the flaked mackerel and put into a baking dish.
• Sprinkle with rolled oats and grated cheese. Bake in a medium oven until cooked.

Burgers *(4 servings)*
• Sauté 1 medium onion in 1 Tbsp (15ml) virgin olive oil, remove from the pan into a bowl, and add 1 cup (100g) chopped mixed nuts, ½ cup (50g) chopped mixed seeds, ½ cup (50g) finely chopped peanuts, 1 Tbsp (15ml) good-quality peanut butter and 1¼ cups (125g) buckwheat flour with a little chopped parsley.
• Shape into burgers (add a little filtered water to bind) and place on a nonstick baking sheet.
• Bake in a medium oven for 30 minutes, turn them over, and bake for 15 minutes.
• Serve in whole wheat buns, or bagels, with homemade chutney and a large mixed salad including lettuce, spinach, alfalfa sprouts, tomato, beet, celery, carrot, snow peas, and scallions.

Mushroom Pilaff *(4 servings)*
• Heat 1 Tbsp (12g) butter and 1 Tbsp (15ml) virgin olive oil in a heavy bottomed pan and fry 8 ounces (225g) brown rice/millet/lentil mixture until it is pale brown.
• Add 1 chopped onion and cook for 5 minutes more.

• Add 2½ cups (600ml) hot water or hot home-made vegetable stock, ⅓ cup (50g) raisins, and 2½ cups (225g) sliced mushrooms. Cover and simmer until liquid is absorbed and the rice is just tender.
• Stir in 1 tsp (5ml) brown rice miso paste and 1 tsp (5ml) finely chopped root ginger.
• Cook 1½ cups (225g) frozen peas (or fresh peas if they are in season), drain them, and add to the rice mixture.
• Serve garnished with parsley.

Vegetable Lasagne *(4 servings)*
• Sauté 1 chopped onion and 2 cloves of garlic with 2 stalks of sliced celery, 2 medium diced carrots, 1 chopped leek, 4 ounces (100g) sweet green and red pepper, and 6 ounces (175g) broccoli spears.
• Place the mixture in a bowl and mix with either tomato pasta sauce or cheese sauce.
• Layer the mixture with cooked mixed lentils and sprinkle with grated hard goat cheese (goat cheddar).
• Bake in a medium oven until browned.

DESSERTS

1 To make a fruit pie which will serve four, first stew about 1½ pounds (650g) in total of rhubarb and apple. Add ⅓ cup (50g) golden raisins (sultanas) toward the end of the stewing process.

2 Mix in a little sweet spice, such as ginger, and place the mixture in an ovenproof dish. Set aside while you make the topping.

3 Take 12 ounces (325g) Quark, low-fat curd cheese, fromage frais, low-fat sour cream or cream and mix with ⅔ cup (150ml) rice milk. Add 1 Tbsp (15ml) honey. Cover the stewed fruit with the cream mixture and sprinkle with mixed nuts. Grill lightly.

Many combinations of fruit can be used for this recipe, according to your taste.

As an alternative to these desserts, try any of the yogurt breakfasts as desserts.

Stuffed Apple
- Take a large cooking apple and remove the core.
- Place in an ovenproof dish and stuff the center with golden raisins (sultanas) or chopped figs, and chopped nuts.
- Sprinkle with cinnamon, a little nutmeg and honey.
- Pour filtered water into the dish to a depth of about ½ inch (1.5cm).
- Bake in a medium oven for about 1 hour.
- Serve with soy cream or frozen yogurt.

Fresh Fruit Salad
- Take any fruit in season.
- Wash and chop the fruit, and pour over some freshly squeezed orange juice.
- Sprinkle with some shredded coconut and a few mixed seeds.

Apricots and Cream (4 servings)
- Soak 8 ounces (225g) Hunza apricots in boiling filtered water or overnight in cold filtered water.
- When soft, remove the pits; the centers of the apricots can be filled with shelled nuts if desired.

- Grind 1¼ cups (175g) cashew nuts in a blender until creamy, and serve on top of the apricots.

Rice Pudding (4 servings)
- Take ¾ cup (100g) part-boiled short-grain brown rice and mix with 3¾ cups (900ml) skimmed organic cow's or soy milk, ⅓ cup (50g) raisins or golden raisins (sultanas), and 1 tsp (5ml) honey and the zest of an organic (or nonwaxed) lemon in an ovenproof dish.
- Stir well until the honey has mixed in completely.
- Bake in a slow oven for 1½ hours.

Sorbet
- Use any home-grown or organic fruit; berries and chopped larger fruit.
- Keep in freezer.
- Defrost for about 5 minutes at room temperature, then liquidize the fruit in a blender or food processor.

Raw fresh fruit and vegetables make a healthy snack.

SNACKS AND DRINKS

With all the food to get through at your three meals (or five meals of smaller size, if you are a "grazer") it is unlikely that you will require any other type of snack than fruit and/or raw carrot, celery, or cucumber sticks.

If, however, you do have a hunger attack, have a handful of mixed unground seeds or a few nuts. Savor them and chew them really well.

CELERY

Herb teas, water, milk-free coffee substitutes, e.g., barley or dandelion coffee, and water, can be taken as often as required. Diluted fruit juices or vegetable juices (1:1 juice to filtered or bottled water), or any herbal/fruit juice drink are best limited to three per day, since the natural sugars within these drinks may affect blood-sugar levels adversely.

Alcohol and "treat" drinks, e.g., a good-quality cup of Indian/Chinese tea, or a cappuccino, should be limited to one per day at the start of the program, because of their very direct effect as stimulants.

STRAWBERRIES

MEDICINE CHEST

NUTRIENTS AND ESSENTIAL OILS USED FOR MINOR PROBLEMS

The "treatments" are taken internally, unless otherwise stated.

HELPFUL FOR	HERB/PLANT EXTRACT	HELPFUL FOR	HERB/PLANT EXTRACT
Antifungal (General)	Garlic; tea tree oil applied directly to skin.	Headlice	A few drops of geranium, lavender, rosemary oils added to a carrier oil (e.g., almond oil) and massaged into scalp; larkspur rinsed through hair.
Antiseptic (General)	Garlic; tea tree oil applied directly to skin.		
Athlete's Foot	Tea tree oil or live plain yogurt – both applied directly to skin.	Insect Bites (General)	Tea tree oil rubbed on to affected area.
Bee Stings	Remove sting, treat area with a little bicarbonate of soda in water.	Insecticide (General)	Lavender oil sprinkled on bedding or clothing.
Burns (Minor)	*Aloe vera* gel or vitamin E oil – both applied directly to skin.	Leg Cramps	Calcium and magnesium supplement; vitamin E.
Catarrh/Sinusitis (Nasal)	Garlic; watercress; radish; vitamin A, beta-carotene.	Low Energy	Vitamin B-complex.
Chilblains	Vitamin B-complex; vitamin E; tea tree oil or vitamin C cream applied directly to skin.	Mouth Ulcers/ Sore Tongue	Vitamin B-complex; iron (if anemic); Manuka honey.
		Pimples	Tea tree oil rubbed on to affected area.
Colds and Flu	Garlic; Manuka honey and hot freshly squeezed lemon; Echinacea; Astralagus; elderberry juice; vitamin C; vitamin A; zinc; cat's claw tea.	Pulled/Sore Muscles	Tea tree oil rubbed on to painful area.
		Ringworm	Tea tree oil rubbed on to area.
Cold Sores	Beta-carotene; vitamin C; amino acid L-lysine; tea tree oil applied directly to skin.	Skin-burrowing Bugs	Garlic, crushed juniper berries; Chickweed cream, applied to area.
Conjunctivitis/ Sore Eyes/ Infected Eyes	Bathe eyes in saline (salt and cooled boiled water), or milk, or cold tea.	Sore Throats	Zinc and vitamin C lozenges; high-potency garlic supplement; tea tree oil gargle (not if asthmatic).
		Stomach Cramps	Cinnamon tea (dried cinnamon in boiled cooled water).
Constipation	Psyllium husks; whole linseeds with full glass of water; oat bran; fresh raw vegetables; *Lactobacillus acidophilus*.	Stomach Upsets /Mild Food Poisoning	High-potency garlic supplement; *Lactobacillus acidophilus/bifidus* supplement; ginger tea; black tea.
Coughs	Garlic; Manuka honey; tea tree oil inhaled (a few drops in boiling water in a bowl, don't use if asthmatic).	Sunburn	Live plain yogurt, *Aloe vera* gel, or vitamin E oil (from a capsule), all applied directly to skin.
Cuts and Grazes	Tea tree oil applied to the cut/graze; use sugar on a bleeding lip.	Threadworms	Crushed garlic and molasses taken by the spoonful; pomegranates, pumpkin seeds;
Cystitis	Cranberry juice; garlic.		
Diarrhea	Dry, white, unbuttered toast; plain white boiled rice; cooled boiled water.	Thrush (Vaginal)	Garlic; high-potency garlic extract; grapefruit seed extract; live yogurt; *Lactobacillus acidophilus*; live yogurt and/or tea tree oil applied to affected area; also tea tree oil pessaries.
Earache	A drop of warm olive oil plus tea tree oil dropped into ear.		
Gritty Eyes	Vitamin B-complex; vitamin A.	Travel Sickness	Crystalized ginger chewed slowly.
Hangover	Vitamin C; essential fatty acids; water.	Verrucae	Tea tree oil applied on a dressing.
Headaches	Magnesium; calcium; chromium; iron (only if anemic); feverfew; inhaled marjoram oil.	Warts	Tea tree oil applied on a dressing.
		Wasp Stings	Vinegar applied to inflamed area.

GARLIC
CAPSULES

GINGER

GLOSSARY

Amino acid – Building blocks of protein, eight of which are essential for growth and body maintenance. They have to be supplied in the diet because the body cannot make them.

Antioxidant – A substance that delays or prevents oxidation, a normal part of the respiration process (energy production in the cells) which produces potentially harmful free radicals.

Carcinogens – Substances that initiate or promote the development of cancer.

D.H.A. – Docosahexanenoic acid. A polyunsaturated fatty acid belonging to the Omega-3 family of fatty acids.

D.N.A. – Deoxyribonucleic acid. The genetic material found in the nucleus (center) of cells and consisting of coiled strands of 46 chromosomes in 23 pairs.

Dysbiosis – Imbalances between the helpful and the unhelpful bacteria.

E.A.R. – Estimated Average Requirement. Because we are all different, standards have been set for average needs, recognizing that some people need more and some less.

E.F.A.s – Essential fatty acids. They are needed from the diet because they cannot be made in the body. (There are two main types of fatty acid: saturated and unsaturated, the latter subdivided into polyunsaturated and mono-unsaturated.) There are two families of essential fatty acids: the Omega-6 family derived from linoleic acid that is found in vegetable oils such as sunflower, and the Omega-3 family derived from linolenic acid

that is found in some vegetable oils such as soybean and rapeseed, and in oily fish, linseeds (flax seed), pumpkin seeds, and walnuts.

E.H.A. – Eicosapentaenoic acid. A polyunsaturated fatty acid from the Omega-3 family of fatty acids.

Free radical – A highly reactive molecule made inside the body. Free radical molecules are one electron short (electrons are usually paired), so they grab an electron from another molecule, disturbing the chemical balance by making this molecule one electron short, thus setting up a chain reaction. Free radicals are produced constantly in the body as a part of normal functions. They need to be dealt with immediately because they can damage D.N.A., resulting in premature aging.

Heterogeneity – Diversity. Biochemical heterogeneity – completely different biochemical types.

Homeostasis – The body's ability to keep its systems in balance.

L.R.N.I. – Lower Reference Nutrient Intake. The amount needed by those with low needs. If people habitually eat less than the L.R.N.I., they are likely to be deficient in nutrients.

Metabolic rate – Speed at which the following series of chemical changes in the living body occur.

Metabolism – Chemical changes in the body that maintain life by building up and breaking down materials.

Mineral – Inorganic substance needed for normal function of the body (e.g., calcium). Trace elements are minerals required in minute amounts (e.g., zinc).

Nutrients – Vitamins, minerals, amino acids, and E.F.A.s.

Optimum nutrition – The vitamin and mineral intake that is needed to fulfill a person's full health potential.

Oxidation – The process in which oxygen is combined with other substances. When another molecule is oxidized, it may go on to produce free radicals. Oxidation therefore increases the demand for antioxidant nutrients.

Oxidative damage – A condition in which free radicals are formed in excess of the body's ability to remove them, resulting in damage to body cells and to tissues.

Phytochemicals – Biologically active compounds found in food.

Prostaglandins – Hormone-like chemicals.

R.N.I. – Reference Nutrient Intake. For protein, or a vitamin or mineral. Amount of the nutrient that is enough, or more than enough for about 97 percent of people in a group. If average intake of a group is at R.N.I. then the risk of deficiency is small.

Symptomatology – The study of symptoms, the branch of pathology which treats symptoms of disease.

Synergistic effect – Combined effect which is greater than the effect of a substance on its own.

Vitamin – Organic substance needed in small amounts by the body for growth and normal body chemistry. It is essential to eat vitamins in food because the body cannot make them (except for vitamin D, made by the action of sunlight on the skin, and vitamins B12 and K, made by intestinal bacteria).

USEFUL ADDRESSES

AUSTRALIA

Australian College of Nutritional & Environmental Medicine
13 Hilton Street
Beaumaris
Victoria 3193
Australia
Tel: 9589 6088
For a referral service for all conventionally trained physicians and specialists who are interested in a wider and more natural approach to illness.

Australian Natural Therapists Association
Taren Point
P.O. Box 2517
Sydney 2232
Australia

CANADA

Canadian College of Naturopathic Medicine
60 Berl Avenue
Etobicoke, Ontario
Canada M8Y 3C7

National Institute of Nutrition
2565 Carling Avenue, Suite 400
Ottawa, Ontario
Canada K1Z 8RI
Tel: (613) 235 3355

Society for Orthomolecular Medicine
16 Florence Avenue
Toronto
Canada M2N 1E9
Tel: (416) 733 2117

NEW ZEALAND

Association of Natural Therapies
81 Forest Hill Road
Milford
Auckland
New Zealand

New Zealand Natural Health Practitioners Accreditation Board
P.O. Box 37-491
Auckland
New Zealand

Society of Naturopaths
Box 19183
Auckland 7
New Zealand

U.K.

**B.A.N.T.
(British Association of Nutritional Therapists)**
P.O. Box 17436
London
SE13 7WT
U.K.

The Breakspear Hospital
Belswains Lane
Hemel Hempstead
Herts HP3 9HP
U.K.
Tel: (01442) 261333
International environmental medicine treatment unit, for laboratory diagnosis of chemical poisoning and environmental illness, and medically supervised nutritional detoxification programs.

Bristol Cancer Help Center
Grove House
Cornwallis Grove
Clifton
Bristol BS8 4PG
U.K.
Tel: (0117) 9809505
A residential and day center for cancer patients who wish to learn about holistic approaches to cancer care.

British Society for Allergy and Environmental Medicine
P.O. Box 28
Totton
Southampton
Hants
SO40 2ZA
U.K.
Tel: (01703) 812124
A society of physicians who recognize the broad principles of nutritional therapy and treat patients accordingly.

Eating Disorders Association
1st Floor
Wensum House
103 Prince of Wales Road
Norwich NR1 1DW
U.K.
Tel: (01603) 621414
Provides help and guidance for those with eating disorders.

The Hyperactive Children's Support Group
71 Whyke lane
Chichester
West Sussex
PO19 2LD
U.K.
For information on helping children with Hyperactivity, A.D.D.H., Autism etc.

Institute for Optimum Nutrition (I.O.N.)
Blades Court
Deodar Road
London SW15 2NU
U.K.
Tel: (0181) 877 9993

Community Health Foundation
188 Old Street
London EC1V 9FR
U.K.
Tel: (0171) 251 4076
International center for training in oriental nutritional therapy (macrobiotics).

National Institute of Medical Herbalists
56 Longbrook Street
Exeter
Devon
EX4 6AH
U.K.
Tel: (01392) 426022
Send large S.A.E. and two stamps to the above address.

The Society for Promotion of Nutritional Therapy (S.P.N.T.),
P.O. Box 47
Heathfield
East Sussex
TN21 8ZX
U.K.
Tel: (01825) 872921. E-mail and Internet:
100045.255@compuserve.com.
800 practitioners. For information, membership of the society, and a list of your nearest practitioners, send an S.A.E. plus £1 (U.S.$3) to the above address.

The Soil Association
Bristol House
40–56 Victoria Street
Bristol
BS1 6BY
U.K.
Tel: (0117) 9290661
Send large S.A.E. for information on organic growers in your area.

U.S.A.

American Academy of Environmental Medicine
4510 W. 89th Street
Prairie Village
KS 66207
U.S.A.
Tel: (913) 341 3625
Register of practitioners of environmental medicine.

American College of Advancement in Medicine
PO Box 3427
Laguna Hills
CA 92654
U.S.A.
Tel: (714) 583 7666

American Dietetic Association
216 W. Jackson Blvd.,
Suite 800
Chicago
IL 60606
U.S.A.
Tel: (312) 899 0040
National nutrition organization.

American Environmental Health Foundation
8345 Walnut Hill Lane
Suite 200
Dallas
TX 75231-4262
U.S.A.
Tel: (214) 368 4132
Organization for the recognition and appropriate treatment of environmental illness. Books and publications available.

American Preventive Medical Association
275 Millway
P.O. Box 732
Barnstable
MA 02630
U.S.A.
Tel: (508) 362 4343
Register of practitioners sympathetic to a natural approach to medicine.

Citizens for Health
P.O. Box 1195
Tacoma
WA 98401
U.S.A.
Tel: (206) 922 2457
Campaigning for consumer rights in natural medicine.

The Feingold Association
56 Winston Drive
Smithtown
NY 11787
Tel: (516) 543 4658
Send an S.A.S.E. for their brochure.

Linus Pauling Institute
440 Page Mill Road
Palo Alto
CA 94306-2031
U.S.A.
Tel: (415) 327 4064
Center for research into vitamin C.

BIBLIOGRAPHY
AND FURTHER READING

PART ONE

Dietary Reference Values for Food Energy and Nutrients for the United Kingdom,
HMSO, 1991.

The Food System – A Guide,
Geoff Tansey and Tony Worsley,
Earth Scan, 1995.

The New Nutrition,
Dr. Michael Colgan,
Apple Publishing, 1995.

Nutrition and Evolution,
Michael Crawford and David Marsh,
Airlift, 1995.

Toxemia: The Basic Cause of Disease,
John H. Tilden M.D.,
Natural Hygiene Press, 1982.

PART TWO

Acid & Alkaline,
Herman Aihara, George Ohsawa
Macrobiotic Foundation, 1986.

The Antioxidants,
Richard A. Passwater Ph.D.,
Keats Publishing, 1985.

Aspartame (NutraSweet): Is It Safe?
H. J. Roberts M.D., Charles Press, 1990.

Encyclopaedia of Nutritional Supplements,
Michael T. Murray, Prima, 1996.

Essential Nutrients in Supplements,
European Health Products Manufacturers' Association, 1995.

Excitotoxins: The Taste that Kills,
Russell L. Blaylock M.D.,
Health Press, 1994.

Fats that Heal, Fats that Kill,
Udo Erasmus, Alive Books, 1993.

Food and Healing,
Annemarie Colbin,
Ballantine Books, 1986.

Food Science, Nutrition and Health,
Brian A. Fox and Allan G. Cameron,
E. Arnold, 1995.

Foods to Heal,
Barry Fox, St Martin's, 1996.

Fundamentals of Food Chemistry,
W. Heimann,
John Wylie and Sons, 1982.

Healing Nutrients,
Patrick Quillin, Penguin, 1989.

The Healing Nutrients Within,
Dr. Eric Braverman and Dr. Carl Pfeiffer,
Airlift, 1997.

Health Essentials: Vitamin Guide,
Hasnain Walji,
Element Books, 1992.

The Natural Health Guide to Antioxidants: Using Vitamins and Other Supplements to Fight Disease, Boost Immunity, and Maintain Optimal Health,
Nancy Pauline Bruning,
Bantam Books, 1994.

Natural Life Extension,
Leon Chaitow, Thorsons, 1992.

The Natural Lunch Box,
Judy Brown,
The Book Publishing Press, 1996.

Nutritional Medicine,
Dr. Stephen Davies and Dr. Alan Stewart,
Pan Books, 1987.

In a Nutshell: Vitamins and Minerals,
Karen Sullivan,
Element Books, 1997.

The Optimum Health Guide,
Eileen Fletcher,
Hodder & Stoughton, 1993.

Optimum Nutrition,
Patrick Holford, I.O.N. Press, 1992.

Raw Energy Recipes,
Leslie and Susannah Kenton, Century, 1985.

The Super Supplements Bible,
Dr. Michael E Rosenbaum and Dominick Bosco,
Thorsons, 1988.

The 20-Day Rejuvenation Diet Program,
Jeffrey Bland Ph.D. with Sara Benum M.A.,
Keats Publishing, 1997.

Your Body's Many Cries for Water,
F. Batmanghelidj M.D.,
Global Health Solutions, 1995.

PART THREE

Allergies Make You Fat,
Alan Hunter, Ashgrove Press, 1995.

Allergy and Intolerance,
G. Lewith, J. Kenyon and D. Dowson,
Merlin Press, 1992.

The Biogenic Diet,
Leslie Kenton, Arrow Books, 1987.

Chemical Sensitivity,
Sherry A. Rogers M.D.,
Keats Publishing, 1995.

The Complete Book of Food Combining,
Jan and Inge Dries,
Element Books, 1997.

The Dries Cancer Diet,
Jan Dries,
Element Books, 1997.

Easing Anxiety and Stress Naturally,
Susan M. Lark M.D.,
Keats Publishing, 1996.

The Elimination Diet Cookbook,
Jill Carter and Alison Edwards,
Element Books, 1997.

Enter The Zone,
Barry Sears Ph.D., Regan Books, 1995.

F-Plus Diet,
Audrey Eyton, Penguin, 1984.

Fit for Life,
Harvey and Marilyn Diamond,
Warner Books, 1987.

The Food-combining Diet: Lose Weight the Hay Way,
Kathryn Marsden, Thorsons, 1993.

How to Improve your Digestion and Absorption,
Christopher Scarfe, I.O.N. Press, 1989.

How to Protect Yourself from Pollution,
Patrick Holford and Dr. Philip Barlow.,
I.O.N. Press, 1990.

Lean Revolution: Eat more to shed fat the energy way,
Leslie Kenton, Ebury Press, 1994.

Low Blood Sugar (Hypoglycemia),
Martin L. Budd, Thorsons, 1987.

Melatonin and the Biological Clock,
Alan E. Lewis and Dallas Clouatre Ph.D.,
Keats Publishing, 1996.

Natural Alternatives to Antibiotics,
Ray C. Wunderlich M.D.,
Keats Publishing, 1995.

Nutritional Biochemistry and Metabolism,
Maria Linder,
Appleton and Lange, 1991.

The Nutron Diet,
Dr. P. Kingsley and Ian Stoakes,
Penguin, 1994.

Optimum Sports Nutrition,
Dr. Michael Colgan,
Advanced Research Press, 1993.

The People's Guide to Deadly Drug Interactions,
Joe and Teresa Graedon,
St. Martin's Press, 1995.

Prescription for change: Health and the Environment,
Friends of the Earth, 1995.

The Principles of Nutritional Therapy,
Linda Lazarides, Thorsons, 1996.

Probiotics,
Leon Chaitow N.D. D.O. and Natasha Trenev, Thorsons, 1990.

The Rotation Diet,
Martin Katahn, Bantam Books, 1987.

The Rotation Diet Cookbook,
Jill Carter and Alison Edwards,
Element Books, 1997.

Super Fast Foods,
Michael Van Straten and Barbara Griggs,
Dorling Kindersley, 1994.

The Super Foods Diet Book,
Michael Van Straten and Barbara Griggs,
Dorling Kindersley, 1992.

Thyroid Problems,
Patsy Westcott, Thorsons, 1995.

Wheat, Milk and Egg-Free Cooking,
Rita Greer, Thorsons, 1989.

The Wright Diet,
Celia Wright, Grafton Books, 1989.

PART FOUR

A Cancer Therapy,
Max Gerson M.D., Gerson Institute, 1986.

Encyclopaedia of Natural Medicine,
Michael Murray and Joseph Pizzorno,
Macdonald & Co., 1992.

Ginkgo Biloba,
Christopher Hobbs, Botanica Press, 1991.

The Healing Power of Amino Acids,
Leon Chaitow N.D. D.O.,
Thorsons, 1989.

Healing through Nutrition,
Dr. Melvyn R. Werbach,
Harper Collins, 1995.

The Health Benefits of Soy,
Jack Challem and Victoria Dolby,
Keats Publishing, 1996.

Maximum Immunity,
Michael A. Weiner Ph.D.
Gateway Books, 1986.

Natural Prescriptions: Dr Giller's Natural Treatments and Vitamin Therapies for More Than 100 Common Ailments,
Kathy Matthews and Robert M. Giller
Ballantine Books, 1995.

The New Holistic Herbal,
David Hoffman. Element Books, 1992.

Nutrition and Cancer,
Sandra Goodman Ph.D.,
Green Library Publications, 1995.

Nutritional Influences on Illness,
Melvyn Werbach M.D.,
Third Line Press, 1996.

Overcoming Candida: The Ultimate Cookery Guide,
Xandria Williams,
Element Books, 1998.

Prescription for Nutritional Healing,
James F. Balch M.D. and Phyllis A. Balch,
Avery Publishing Group Inc., 1990.

PART FIVE

Anorexia and Bulimia,
Alexander Schauss Ph.D. and Carolyn Costin M.A. M.F.C.C.,
Keats Publishing, 1997.

Balancing Hormones Naturally,
Kate Neil, I.O.N. Press, 1994.

Beat Candida Cookbook,
Erica White, White Publishing, 1997.

Boost Your Child's Brain Power,
Gwilym Roberts, Thorsons, 1988.

Diet, Crime and Delinquency,
Alexander Schauss, Parker House, 1981.

Food Children Enjoy,
Petta Jane Gulliver,
Cornish Connection, 1992.

How to Feed Your Family for £4 a Day,
Bernadine Lawrence, Thorsons, 1989.

The Hyperactive Child,
Belinda Barnes and Irene Colquhoun,
Thorsons, 1986.

Natural Treatment of Fibroid Tumours and Endometriosis,
Susan M. Lark M.D.,
Keats Publishing, 1996.

Natural Progesterone,
John R. Lee, B.L.L. Publishing, 1993.

Overcoming Dyslexia,
Dr. Beve Hornsby, Martin Dunitz, 1985.

Sexual Chemistry,
Dr. Ellen Grant,
Mandarin Paperbacks, 1994.

Wholefood for the Whole Family,
Sue Scott, Elliot Right Way Books, 1986.

Zinc and Other Micro-Nutrients,
Dr. Carl C. Pfeiffer, Keats Publishing, 1978.

If you have difficulty in tracing any of the above literature, write to I.O.N., or S.P.N.T. (*see* page 248), in the United Kingdom.

INDEX